D0203646

Living with Defined Contribution Pensions

Pension Research Council Publications

A complete listing of PRC publications appears at the back of this volume.

Living with Defined Contribution Pensions

Remaking Responsibility for Retirement

Edited by
Olivia S. Mitchell and Sylvester J. Schieber

Published by
The Pension Research Council
The Wharton School of the University of Pennsylvania
and
University of Pennsylvania Press
Philadelphia

Printed in the United States of America on acid-free paper

10 9 8 7 6 5 4 3 2 1

Published by
University of Pennsylvania Press
Philadelphia, Pennsylvania 19104-4011

Library of Congress Cataloging-in-Publication Data

Living with defined contribution pensions : remaking responsibility for retirement / edited by Olivia S. Mitchell and Sylvester J. Schieber.
p. cm.
"Pension Research Council publications."
Includes bibliographical references and index.
ISBN 0-8122-3439-1 (cloth : alk. paper)
1. Defined contribution plans—United States. 2. Old age pensions—United States—Finance. 3. Pension trusts—United States—Finance. I. Mitchell, Olivia S. II. Schieber, Sylvester J.
HD7105.45.U6L58 1998
331.25'2'0973—dc21 98-13584
CIP

Contents

Preface

Olivia S. Mitchell

The Pension Research Council has previously explored a number of promising and sometimes worrisome developments in the pension field, always seeking better ways to design and deliver retirement income security. In building this volume around defined contribution pension plans, we seek to add insight to discussions regarding the strengths and weaknesses of these rapidly growing and very popular plans in the pension arena.

Readers seeking either blanket approval or denunciation of participant-directed pension savings account will find neither in this book. Rather, we have gathered some of the world's most eminent pension experts and collected their well-reasoned views on what defined contribution plans do well, and what they do poorly. Their conclusions are based on solid research evidence and new data, as well as on many years of practical experience in the pension field. While the analysis is aimed at the interested layperson, it is important to note that the experts represented herein include people who matter in the pension field—plan sponsors, economists and lawyers, actuaries and benefit plan consultants, and policymakers.

As always, the Advisory Board of the Pension Research Council was instrumental in focusing our attention on this important topic. Several Council Board members played key roles in bringing this volume to fruition, particularly Sylvester Schieber, who coedited the book with diligence, good humor, and substantive insight. We are grateful to Ray Schmitt and Anna Rappaport, who read and commented on portions of the research, and to Juan Tang, who helped with the important production phase. The Council also acknowledges valuable financial support for the research received from the U.S. Department of Labor, the Population Aging Research Center at the University of Pennsylvania, and The Wharton School. Our Institutional Members are always invaluable in affording ongoing financial support for the work of the Council and in participating in our research process actively. We thank all of these for their support while noting that all views expressed herein are those of the authors and not of the Pension Research Council at the Wharton School.

Chapter 1
Defined Contribution Pensions: New Opportunities, New Risks

Olivia S. Mitchell and Sylvester J. Schieber

Each month the U.S. financial press reports vast sums of money rushing into defined contribution (DC) pensions. Pensions known as 401(k) plans lead the pack: soon the nation's 401(k) pension system will amount to more than $1.5 trillion in assets and will include almost 30 million private sector employees (EBPR 1996). Recent legislation has extended the availability of DC plans to the public sector as well, virtually guaranteeing rapid growth of this pension type for decades to come.

This tremendous appeal of defined contribution plans in the United States is attributable to several factors. For some groups, mainly small and medium-sized employers, there has been a shift away from defined benefit (DB) to DC pensions, a pattern evident in the left panel of Figure 1. After the passage of the Employee Retirement Income Security Act (ERISA) in 1974, the number of DB plans with fewer than 100 participants grew until the early 1980s, then leveled off for a few years, and declined steadily after 1987. The number of DB plans sponsored by larger employers, on the other hand, remained relatively constant over this same period. The right panel of Figure 1 shows that the prevalence of DC plans in larger firms grew significantly over the period, from slightly under 9,000 plans in 1975, to over 39,000 plans almost twenty years later. But the growth by firm size was uneven: while larger companies were adding 30,000 defined contribution plans, small employers were adding nearly 400,000 new plans.

Data on numbers of workers participating in DC plans corroborate these trends. Figure 2 shows the number of participants in private DB and DC plans segmented by plan size. The left panel of that figure reveals that participation in DB plans with under 100 participants has been relatively flat since just after the passage of ERISA: DB participation grew from 1.6

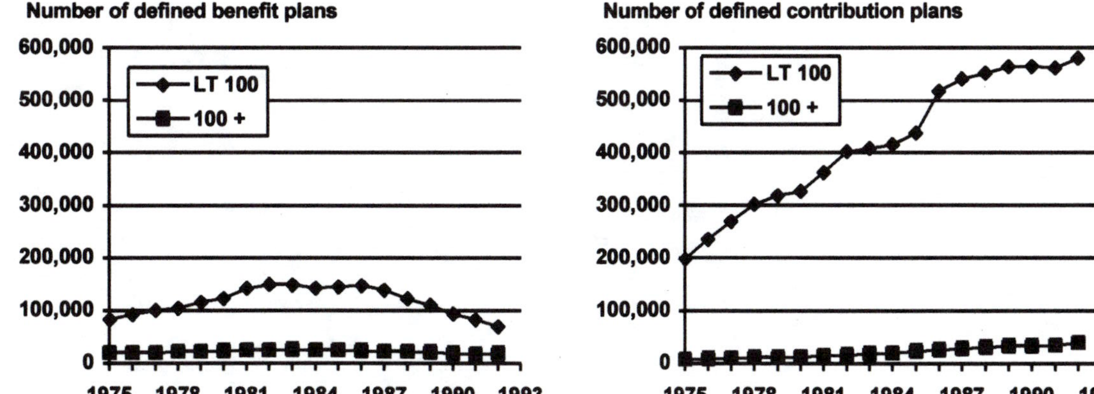

Figure 1. Trend in number of private defined benefit and defined contribution plans, 1975–93. Source: USDOL (1996): 60–61.

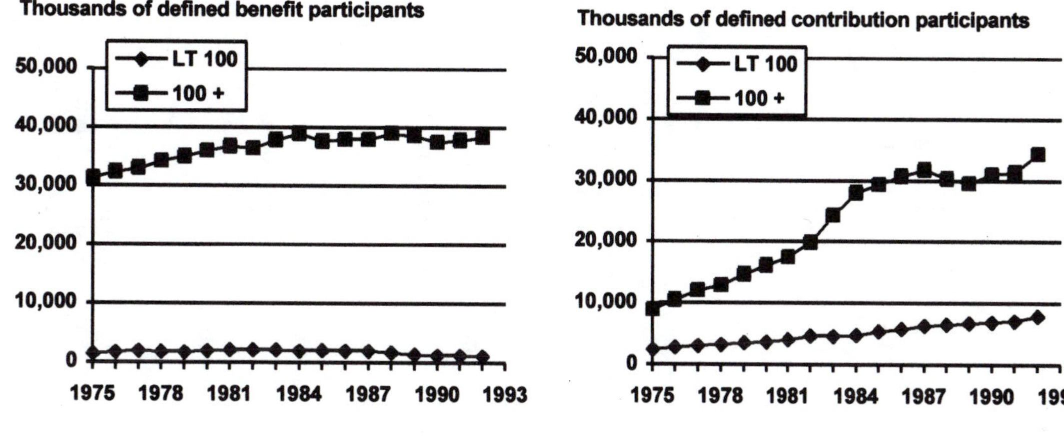

Figure 2. Trend in number of participants in private defined benefit and defined contribution plans, 1975–93. Source: USDOL (1996): 63–64.

million participants in 1975 to 2.2 million participants in 1982, but then declined to 1.1 million participants by a decade later—below coverage levels twenty years previously. Participation in larger DB plans grew significantly during the first decade after the passage of ERISA, but has remained relatively constant since then. By contrast, the right panel of Figure 2 depicts more positive trends for DC plans. Among both larger and smaller plans, the last 15 to 20 years have seen significant growth in the numbers of DC-covered participants. Among smaller employers, a DC plan is often the only retirement accumulation vehicle offered. Among larger employers, DC plans are often supplemental in nature, augmenting the benefits being provided through traditional DB arrangements.

What are the challenges and opportunities that this DC pension revolution offers? In this volume we take stock of theoretical and empirical benefits and costs that arise in the DC arena, and we outline some new concerns as well. This discussion is of critical importance to a wide range of audiences including potential savers as well as those interested in helping them save—employers and money managers, policymakers concerned with the health of national retirement income systems, regulators charged with fashioning a healthy financial system, and members of the next generation of taxpayers, who are vulnerable to bear the burden of any shortfalls incurred in retirement savings.

Reasons for Defined Contribution Retirement Plan Growth

There are several reasons that defined contribution plans have grown so quickly in the United States and around the world. Probably most importantly, both plan sponsors and plan participants perceive the DC plan as "flexible." Employees with a DC plan generally contribute a fraction of their pay; this fraction is often self-determined and sometimes has an employer match (the match typically depending on the employee's contribution level). Employees also usually have some say over how these contributions are to be invested during the accumulation phase.

This flexibility is well illustrated by recent U.S. Department of Labor data on medium and large private sector firms. As Table 1 shows, the modal number of investment options permitted in a defined contribution plan is about four, with a quarter of plan participants eligible for five or more. In defined benefit plans, by contrast, the plan participant is promised a retirement benefit payout, but has no control over his or her plan investments during the worklife. For example, about half of all DC plan participants can take employer pension contributions when they leave their firms, and employees remaining on the job are often able to borrow against their account balances (Table 2). Also the accounts may

TABLE 1 Savings and Thrift Plans: Trends in Investment Choices for Full-Time Participants

	Employee contributions (%)		*Employer contributions (%)*	
	1991	*1993*	*1991*	*1993*
Employees permitted to choose investments	62	86	91	58
Number of choices				
2	10	12	14	7
3	20	21	29	13
4	16	30	26	17
5		15		13
6	14	3	18	3
7+		6		5
Not determinable	3	7	5	7
Types of investments allowed				
Common stock fund	56	68	79	49
Company stock	22	43	46	49
Long term interest bearing securities	29	42	40	28
Diversified stock & bond fund	17	42	24	33
Government securities	21	23	30	14
Guaranteed investment contracts	43	43	65	30
Money market funds	27	26	35	20
Certificates of deposit	1	1	2	1
Other	4	6	4	1
Not determinable	3	3	4	3

Source: USDOL (1991–93).
Note: Data exclude supplemental pension plans. Sums may not equal totals because of rounding.

be withdrawn (albeit with a tax penalty) in the event of a hardship, often defined as the purchase of a house, high healthcare bills, or college expenses. Loans for workers who are currently employed at the pension-sponsoring firm are virtually unheard of in traditional DB pension plans.

Flexibility at retirement also is appealing to many DC plan participants. One issue is that participants can decide how much to take in a lump sum versus how much to annuitize. Almost all participants in pension plans surveyed are able to take some or all of their funds in a lump sum (Table 3); half may access their money in installments if desired; and fewer than one-third of DC plan participants may convert their pension funds to lifetime annuities. This wide range of options contrasts with the typical pattern in DB plans, where benefits commonly must be paid in the form of a life annuity.

Recent research on the largest pension plan covering university re-

TABLE 2 Trends in Provisions for Withdrawal of Employer Contributions Prior to Retirement, Disability, or Termination of Employment: Savings and Thrift Plans

	Full-time participants (%)						
Type of formula	*1985*	*1986*	*1988*†	*1988*	*1989*	*1991*	*1993*
No withdrawals permitted	20	18	29	28	29	50	51
Withdrawals permitted	80	82	71	72	71	50	47
For any reason	61	56	42	41	37	24	29
No penalty	30	19	15	14	17	16	NA
Some penalty	30	37	26	25	18	8	NA
For hardship reasons*	19	26	29	30	34	26	18
No penalty	14	21	21	22	27	17	NA
Some penalty	3	5	6	7	7	7	NA

Source: USDOL (1985–93) and unpublished data from the BLS for 1988† figures. The EBS sampling frame changed in 1988 to include smaller firms and more industries than before, so data for 1988 on are not precisely comparable with previous years' tabulations.

*Commonly expressed hardship reasons include purchase or repair of primary residence, death or illness in the family, education of an immediate family member, or sudden uninsured loss.

†In a few cases the Bureau of Labor Statistics tabulated 1988 results using a sampling frame similar to that employed in previous years. For comparability purposes these figures have been presented, where available, under columns headed "1988," whereas tabulations from 1988 on employ the new, larger survey sampling frame.

Note: Data exclude supplemental pension plans. Sums may not equal totals because of rounding. NA means data not available.

TABLE 3 Trends in Method of Distribution of Account at Retirement: Savings and Thrift Plans

	Full-time participants (%)					
*Type of distribution**	*1985*	*1986*	*1988*	*1989*	*1991*	*1993*
Cash distribution	99	99	97	97	99	99
Lifetime annuity	29	25	25	28	30	30
Installments	59	52	49	52	52	48
Lump sum	99	98	95	96	99	98
Stock distribution	—	1	1	1	NA	NA

Source: USDOL (1985–93). The EBS sampling frame changed in 1988 to include smaller firms and more industries than before, so data for 1988 on are not precisely comparable with previous years' tabulations.

*Many plans offer more than one form of cash distribution, so sums of individual items exceed total.

Note: Data exclude supplemental pension plans. Sums may not equal totals because of rounding. NA means data not available, and " — " means less than 0.5 percent.

TABLE 4 Trends in Employer Contributions in Savings and Thrift Plans

	Full-time participants (%)					
Employer matching contributions*	*1985*	*1986*	*1988*	*1989*	*1991*	*1993*
Fraction of salary						
≤ 5%	12	28	35	36	39	40
6%	52	54	47	47	43	46
≥ 7%	14	11	11	12	11	15
Specified dollar amount/other	9	7	5	4	3	—

Source: USDOL (1985–93). The EBS sampling frame changed in 1988 to include smaller firms and more industries than before, so data for 1988 on are not precisely comparable with previous years' tabulations.
*Employees may contribute a percentage of salary up to a maximum; ceilings on employer matching contributions are generally lower.
Note: Data exclude supplemental pension plans. Sums may not equal totals because of rounding. "—" means less than 0.5 percent.

search and teaching faculty (the TIAA-CREF plan) suggests that patterns of retirement payouts are changing in important ways over time, with rising demand for 10- and 20-year certain payout periods (Hammond, this volume). In general, then, employees with DC plans find appealing the degree of leeway they have over the amount of money paid in, the investment options during the build-up phase, and the way the funds may be paid out.

A different appeal of DC plans is the fact that employers are able to target their matching contributions to reward specific behaviors and specific types of employees. A typical DC pension design has the employer depositing up to 5 percent of an employee's pay into the DC pension if that worker contributes the maximum allowed (Table 4). However, if an employee chooses not to contribute, or contributes less than the maximum allowed, the company will generally contribute less as well. The same pattern is evident with company contributions to profit-sharing plans, where payments are increasingly determined by participants' contributions, rather than by pay levels (Table 5). This approach is probably designed to allow the employer to effectively pay more to those workers willing to save more—a practice explained by Richard Ippolito (this volume) as making sense when saving behavior signals greater productivity potential. Having the match feature in the pension plan allows more productive employees to be rewarded accordingly.

Economists generally agree that employers' costs associated with the sponsorship of retirement plans are part of the total cost of labor. That is, an employer must pay the worker his or her marginal value to the firm, whether in the form of cash or deferred compensation. Richard Ippolito

TABLE 5 Trends in Provision of Deferred Profit Sharing Plans

Type of formula	*Full-time participants (%)* 1986	1988	1989	1991	1993
Employer contributions					
Based on stated formula	59	55	60	52	40
Fixed % of profits	NA	16	10	10	9
Variable % of profits	NA	12	18	24	32
Other formulas	NA	27	33	17	
No formula	41	45	40	48	60
Allocation of profits to employees					
Equally to all	1	1	1	2	7
Based on earnings	61	74	64	52	52
Based on earnings and service	10	12	9	13	11
Based on participants' contributions	—	—	—	12	19
Other	8	13	26	21	11
Loans from employees' accounts					
Permitted	25	32	19	27	23
Not permitted	75	68	81	73	77

Source: USDOL (1985–93). The EBS sampling frame changed in 1988 to include smaller firms and more industries than before, so data for 1988 on are not precisely comparable with previous years' tabulations.
Note: Data exclude supplemental pension plans. Sums may not equal totals because of rounding. "—" means less than 0.5 percent.

argues that this translates into differential economic rewards for different workers when the company offers a defined contribution pension plan with matching options. In particular, some workers, particularly the very present-oriented (or "high discounters" in Ippolito's terminology), do not participate in a voluntary contributory defined contribution plan even though they forgo the value of the tax benefit or employer match accorded such contributions. This is sensible when the company feels that the high discounter may not be workers that such firms wish to compensate highly in the first place—perhaps because they exhibit behaviors associated with relatively low marginal productivity or perhaps because they impose relatively high maintenance costs on the company.[1]

One of the issues that Ippolito leaves unexplored is whether or not high discounters could, under some circumstances, be converted into low discounters. Other writers in this volume show that improvements in financial education could go a long way to encouraging greater saving on the part of workers (Bernheim, this volume). Likewise, increased employer matching of employee contributions in 401(k) plans and more intense communications programs can increase levels of participation in voluntary contributory programs (Clark and Schieber, this volume). This research, then, suggests that some workers are high discounters simply because they are ignorant of the long-term costs that short-term consumption decisions may imply. Of course other younger, lower-wage workers may lack the wherewithal to save, which remains a challenge for the economy as a whole.

An additional explanation for DC plans' popularity is that they are often perceived as less expensive than the defined benefit alternative. Data from the U.S. Department of Labor show that joint employer/employee contribution rates in DC plans are widely variable, ranging in practice from 1 to 16 percent of pay (Table 5). Obviously it is possible to design DB plans that would mimic these cost ranges, so it is not necessarily the case that DC plans are less expensive to operate. On the other hand, administrative costs associated with DC plans are generally lower than those of DB plans, making a given dollar of contribution go farther toward retirement payments. For instance, in 1996, annual administrative expenses in 1996 were $287 per participant in small DC plans while similar-sized DB costs exceeded $600 per participant (Hustead, this volume). For a large DC pension plan, administrative costs were approximately $49, and for DB plans they were $68 per year in 1996. (These cost data exclude investment management fees, but include mandatory government insurance premiums for the defined benefit pension plans.) Edwin Hustead's analysis in this volume shows that the cost of administering defined benefit plans rose steadily during the 1980s, both in absolute terms and in relation to the cost of administering a defined contribution plan as a result of various legislative and regulatory measures adopted during that time. These increases in per capita administration costs were much more significant for smaller defined benefit plans than for larger ones. In addition to increasing administrative costs, the value of the tax advantages accorded the sponsors of many small defined benefit plans were substantially eroded during the 1980s. For many smaller defined benefit plans, the economic value of continuing them was simply not worth the cost of so doing.

As a factor explaining their rising popularity over time, proponents of DC plans have often pointed out that these plans are less risky than the DB plan alternative. For instance, in the United States, DC plan assets are owned by plan participants and held in trust, leaving little potential for loss in the event of corporate sponsor bankruptcy. By contrast, a defined benefit plan could find itself with assets inadequate to meet promised obligations, the condition known as underfunding. In the United States, at least, DB plan underfunding risk is partially covered by a government insurance group, the Pension Benefit Guaranty Corporation, though at a nontrivial premium cost noted above. In other countries, underfunding risk is handled in different ways (Bodie, Mitchell, and Turner, 1997) and in any event this risk arises only in the DB pension plan scenario, not in the DC environment.

Do Defined Contribution Plans Offer Reasons for Concern?

Having explained why DC plans are growing in popularity, we should also note concerns about this trend. One factor is that defined contribution pension plans tend to place a great deal of responsibility on participants' shoulders, more so than in the case of DB pensions. For example, employees offered a DC plan sometimes do not avail themselves of the chance to save in a tax-qualified account (Hinz and Turner, this volume). In addition, people who save more in their DC account may offset these funds with less saving outside their pension account. Nevertheless, empirical studies using nationally representative cross-section data from the United States are hard-pressed to detect a large and statistically significant result confirming this hypothesis (Gale and Milano, this volume).

Failure to participate in a tax-qualified pension plan may be a rational economic decision for workers who are particularly income-constrained. On the other hand, for many, nonparticipation may be due to myopia or lack of information. Data from several large firms show that the amount and quality of pension information provided to participants by the employer has a powerful effect on pension participation rates, in many cases even more potent than additional employer funds spent in matching employee contributions (Clark and Schieber, this volume). Clearly there is more to be learned about how to interest workers covered by a pension to actually participate in the plan.

Even when employees do join their company's plan, they are often poorly informed about investment options, a condition that may lead them to make seemingly unwise or irrational portfolio choice decisions. Surveys of average Americans document workers' substantial ignorance about key aspects of financial markets, raising profound questions about how ready workers are to make DC investment choices with lifelong consequences (Bernheim, this volume). One instance where questions are raised is when workers are found to be investing in substantial quantities of employer stock, perhaps under an incentive plan offered by the corporate sponsor. This investment pattern is not, per se, problematic though it suggests that employees may not fully understand the benefits of portfolio diversification. Another study, by Andrea Kusko et al. (this volume), reveals remarkable worker insensitivity to dramatic changes in employer contributions.

A related issue salient in many plan sponsors' minds of late is that of potential liability if employee investments in a DC plan fail to perform well. This concern has recently resurfaced when a guaranteed investment contract (GIC) was offered as one of several investment options to participants in a large employer's 401(k) pension plan. After the insurance company issuing the GIC filed for bankruptcy, pension plan participants sued the large employer, charging it with having selected an investment option that lost money (Ortelere, this volume). This case and others have prompted the U.S. Department of Labor to issue guidelines regarding pension investments that employers hope will clarify their responsibility toward participants in company-sponsored DC pension plans.

As a result of these issues, pension education is becoming increasingly important to sponsors of DC plans. Participants vary according to the types of information they need and can process regarding investment risk, return, and related issues. Examining alternative approaches to pension education reveals that the way pension information is presented can have a large impact on pension plan members' investment behavior. For example, 401(k) plan participants tend to hold much of their money in bonds, but appear to move funds to equities after learning more about the relative risk and return of alternative portfolios (Vanderhei and Bajtelsmidt, 1997). A related concern is whether unsophisticated investors are likely to overreact when the market falls, manipulating their pension funds to inadvertently lock in short-term losses when a better strategy would be to invest for the long term. Available evidence suggests that mutual fund investors have been rather unresponsive to large downward movements experienced in the market to date, and since many 401(k) pension plans are invested in mutual funds, it seems likely that this pattern will also carry over to the DC environment (Rea and Marcis, this volume).

Several implications flow from increased understanding of how plan participants make decisions about their pensions. One is that industry is growing more aware of how to communicate with employees effectively about their pensions. More forward-looking and technologically advanced firms are exploring the multi-media route, using the Internet and financial-planning software libraries. Other firms use videos and glossy materials, along with around-the-clock toll-free telephone service to answer participant questions and permit changes in investment decisions. As a result, many plan sponsors find their role changing over time as plan participants interact directly with the customer service representative at the pension investment house, rather than channeling pension questions through their corporation's benefits manager (Hurt, this volume). And benefits consulting firms as well as third-party plan administrators are facing new challenges related to delivering better benefits service at the retail level.

The Road Ahead

The rapid growth of defined contribution pension plans in the United States and around the world offers new opportunities and also new risks. As we show in this volume, DC plans serve both participating employees and sponsoring employers. In the process, they are working to educate a new generation of pension savers. This transition process is far from foolproof, however, and diligent oversight is needed to protect retirement assets from unwise investment behavior, premature cash outs, and excessive administrative expenses. This volume illustrates how exciting research advances can be used to inform improved decision making about pension design, particularly for defined contribution plans, in the future.

Note

1. Such a worker also would undervalue the possibility of defined benefit pension at some distant future time, and hence would be unlikely to stay with an employer that is reducing current cash wages for the traditional pension offering.

References

Bernheim, B. Douglas. "Financial Illiteracy, Education, and Retirement Saving." This volume.
Bodie, Zvi, Olivia S. Mitchell, and John A. Turner. *Securing Employer-Based Pensions: An International Perspective.* Philadelphia: Pension Research Council and University of Pennsylvania Press, 1997.
Clark, Robert L. and Sylvester J. Schieber. "Factors Affecting Participation Rates and Contribution Levels in 401(k) Plans." This volume.
Employee Benefit Plan Review (EBPR). "401(k) Assets Climb." July 1996: 60.
Gale, William G. and Joseph M. Milano. "Implications of the Shift to Defined Contribution Plans for Retirement Wealth Accumulation." This volume.
Hinz, Richard P. and John A. Turner. "Pension Coverage Initiatives: Why Don't Workers Participate?" This volume.
Hurt, Ronald D. "The Changing Paradigm of 401(k) Plan Servicing." This volume.
Hustead, Edwin C. "Trends in Retirement Income Plan Administrative Expenses." This volume.
Ippolito, Richard A. "Disparate Savings Propensities and National Retirement Policy." This volume.
Kusko, Andrea L., James M. Poterba, and David W. Wilcox. "Employee Decisions with Respect to 401(k) Plans." This volume.
Ortelere, Brian T. "Emerging Problems of Fiduciary Liability." This volume.
Rea, John D. and Richard G. Marcis. "Responses of Mutual Fund Investors to Adverse Market Disruptions." This volume.
U.S. Department of Labor (USDOL), Bureau of Labor Statistics. *Employee Benefits in Medium and Large Firms.* Washington, D.C.: USGPO, 1985–93.
U.S. Department of Labor (USDOL), Pension and Welfare Benefits Administra-

tion. *Abstract of 1992 Form 5500 Annual Reports. Private Pension Plan Bulletin* No. 5, Washington, D.C.: USGPO, 1996: 60–61.

Vanderhei, Jack and Vickie Bajtelsmidt. "Risk Aversion and Retirement Income Adequacy." In Michael S. Gordon, Olivia S. Mitchell, Marc M. Twinney, eds., *Positioning Pensions for the Twenty-First Century.* Philadelphia: Pension Research Council and University of Pennsylvania Press, 1997: 46–66.

Part I
The New Responsibility of Defined Contribution Plans

Chapter 2
Pension Coverage Initiatives: Why Don't Workers Participate?

Richard P. Hinz and John A. Turner

As the baby boom generation approaches retirement (the oldest will receive their first Social Security checks in a decade), concern is being raised that baby boomers are saving inadequately. Optimistic assessments conclude that, at best, baby boomers are saving at the same rates as their parents at an equivalent point in life.[1]

The private pension system provides a possible solution to the savings problem. The system has already made a huge contribution to the increasing affluence of the elderly, with income from employer-sponsored pensions increasing from 14 percent of the income for the elderly (age 65 and older) in 1958 to 19 percent in 1992, and the proportion reporting some type of benefit increasing from 14 percent in 1962 to 47 percent in 1992 (Chen 1992; Grad 1992). Whether additional retirement savings provided through the private pension system is a reasonable hope is a matter of considerable conjecture.

The Supply of Private Pension Coverage

Despite its widely acclaimed success, the private pension system has its own problems. Following the creation of substantial tax incentives in the early part of the century and the emergence of organized labor as a powerful advocate, the proportion of the workforce covered by employer-sponsored pensions grew rapidly, increasing from 15 percent at the outset of World War II to 45 percent of all private wage and salary workers in 1975, the year after comprehensive federal legislation, the Employment Retirement Income Security Act (ERISA), was enacted. However, despite the efforts of three Republican and two Democratic administrations, twelve Congresses, three major recessions, the longest postwar expan-

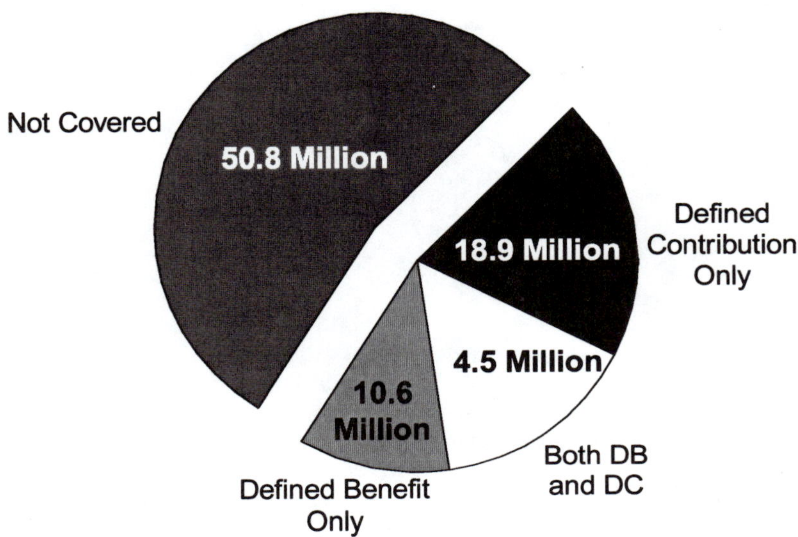

Figure 1. Private sector wage and salary workers by pension status, 1993. Source: USDOL (1994) and authors' computations using April 1993 CPS and Form 5500 filings.

sion, and the most enduring bull market in history, there it has remained. The result is the distribution of pension coverage shown in Figure 1. Among the roughly 96 million private wage and salary earners compromising the current workforce, nearly 51 million are not accruing benefits on their current job.

The stability of the pension coverage rate, varying by no more than a percentage point or two for more than twenty years, is remarkable. This is especially so in light of the fundamental changes in the size and composition of the workforce that have accompanied the aging of the baby boomers, the entry of women into the labor force, and the economic uncertainties that last year made workplace security an issue in presidential election politics. It is also remarkable given the major changes in the provision of pensions, with the decline in the percentage of the workforce covered by a traditional defined benefit plan and the rapid growth of 401(k) plans.

While inadequate to describe the complexity of the forces at play in this stable (or stagnant) level of pension coverage, "standard economic theory" has effectively defined the available "policy levers" to address the perceived problem. It has essentially viewed the problem as a problem of supply.

The standard assumption seems to be that there is an adequate level of demand for pension coverage by most workers. This inevitably results in a perspective that coverage expansions originate on the supply side, leading to a menu of alternatives that has become nearly exclusively oriented to facilitating the ability of employers to sponsor plans. This tendency is in no way reduced by the constant reminders from well-organized and funded employer groups (interestingly enough almost exclusively comprised of those already sponsoring plans) about costs, regulatory burdens, and their alleged effects on otherwise philanthropic tendencies toward workers.

While simple in construct and thereby efficient in communication, these implicit assumptions warrant scrutiny. The passage of ERISA would appear to provide a considerable price shock on the supply side. Yet the coverage rate remained unchanged.

Since then an alphabet soup of TEFRAs, DEFRAs, TRAs, and REAs has emanated from Congress.[2] While many of the legislative provisions were motivated more by revenue raising than by an interest in pension coverage, many had the effect of imposing significant new costs on plan sponsors by either accelerating funding requirements or limiting the scope of tax subsidies.

While the increase in employer costs has surely affected the reduction in the number of small firms sponsoring defined benefit plans, the overall coverage rate remains essentially unaltered. The periodic Employee Benefit Supplements to the Current Population Survey (CPS) yield a coverage rate for full-time private wage and salary workers that has remained at around 50 percent from 1972 to 1993.

At the broadest level, the available data on pension coverage provide what appears to be compelling confirmation of the supply side presumption. As Figure 2 shows, according to the April 1993 CPS supplement, slightly more than 59 percent of the private wage and salary workforce are employed in firms that offer pension coverage. One in five of those not covered is ineligible for the plan provided by his or her current employer. On the other hand, nine of ten workers in firms offering coverage report that they participate in the plan, resulting in a coverage rate of about 45 percent of workers.

Looking at the factors associated with the employers of the covered workers lends further credence to the second tenet of the conventional wisdom, that the supply problem is one of small firms and is a result of cost differences. Figure 3 shows what has perhaps become the most com-

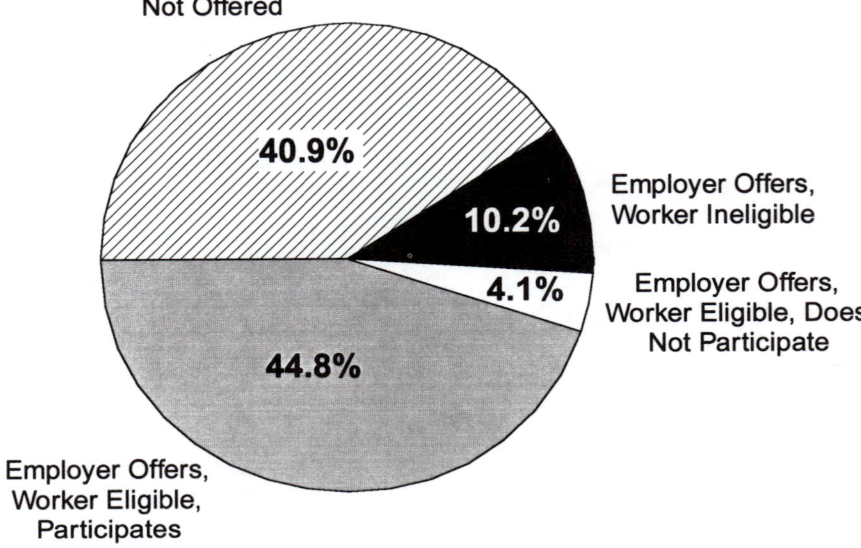

Figure 2. Pension plan sponsorship/participation categories, 1993. Source: USDOL (1994) and authors' computations using April 1993 CPS Employee Benefits Supplement.

monly cited statistic in the coverage debate, the relationship between firm size and pension coverage. This shows that for the smallest firms, those with fewer than 10 workers, the pension coverage rate is only about one-seventh that of the larger firms. The simplest way in which this relationship is usually described is to note that, while more than 70 percent of the workers in firms with more than 100 workers are earning pension benefits, the rate is less than 25 percent for employers with fewer than 100 employees (the most commonly used definition of small business).

The source of this outcome is easy to identify in examining by firm size intervals the proportion of workers whose employers do not offer a pension plan. While 86 percent of those working in firms that employ 10 or fewer workers do not work for an employer that offers a plan, only 11 percent of workers in firms with more than 1,000 employees face a similar limitation in access to the system.

A look at the relationship of administrative costs and size seems to readily indicate the cause for this inequity. Analysis by Hustead (this volume) of administrative expenses provides an estimate of the cost per participant. The per capita administrative costs for the smallest firms are

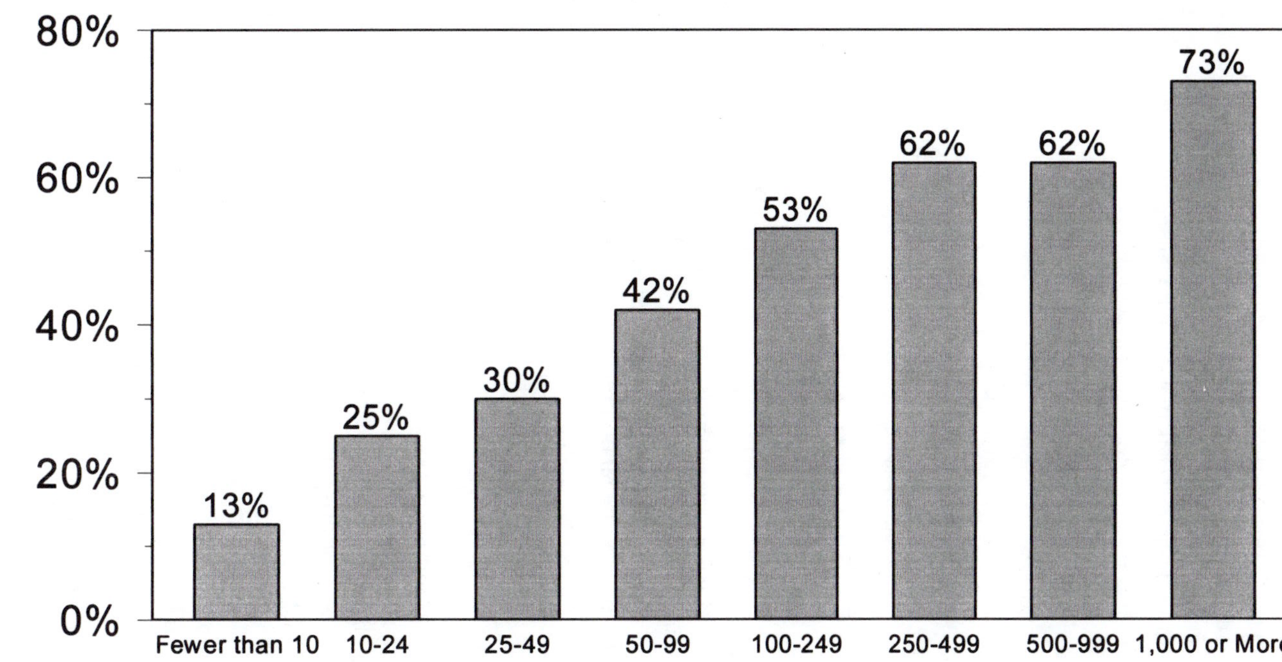

Figure 3. Pension coverage rates by firm size, 1993 (full-time private wage and salary workers). Source: USDOL (1994) and authors' computations using April 1993 CPS.

nearly eight times as great as those of the largest firms for defined contribution plans.

This analysis, both simple in construct as well as conveniently confirming policymakers' intuitive notions and the complaints of their most vocal critics, generally ends the diagnosis and dictates the prescriptions. Not surprisingly, on the rare occasions when coverage expansion rather than revenue enhancement has been a paramount concern, legislative initiatives have been guided by the desire to "level the playing field" for small firms.

The Demand for Pension Coverage

However seductive in simplicity is the administrative cost explanation, a closer look at the data belies the notion that the origins of the pension coverage problem are so easily discerned. Stephen Long and Susan Marquis, using 1988 CPS data, provide a framework so straightforward in illuminating the limitations of the supply side analysis in the context of employer-sponsored health benefits that it merits replication with the 1993 CPS for pension coverage (Long and Marquis 1994).

Workers in firms that do not offer pension benefits share some notable characteristics. They are far more likely to be low-wage workers. More than two-thirds of workers earning less than $10,000 per year are employed at firms with no pension plan. Similarly, they tend to be workers with short tenure. While 59 percent of workers with less than one year on the job are working in firms without a plan, fewer than one-quarter of workers with more than ten years of service have no access to the pension system through their own employer.

There is a considerable degree of interaction between earnings, tenure, and firm size. Small firms tend to be less profitable and employ more mobile and younger workers. They also tend to employ more part-time workers. Age, tenure, and earnings are factors that define the demand for pension benefits. Benefits from defined benefit plans are of less value for younger and shorter-tenure workers because of the lower probabilities that they will vest and because of the back loading of benefit accrual. Earnings provide a good proxy for the extent of the tax subsidy, an equally if not more powerful determinant of demand for deferred compensation.

An array of these variables permits inferences about whether the coverage issue is simply one of the distribution of opportunity or whether there is an equally powerful element of demand at play, in which workers with some group of attributes may be seeking employment at firms not providing coverage, preferring instead cash wages.

Figure 4 shows worker tenure in relation to the pension participation

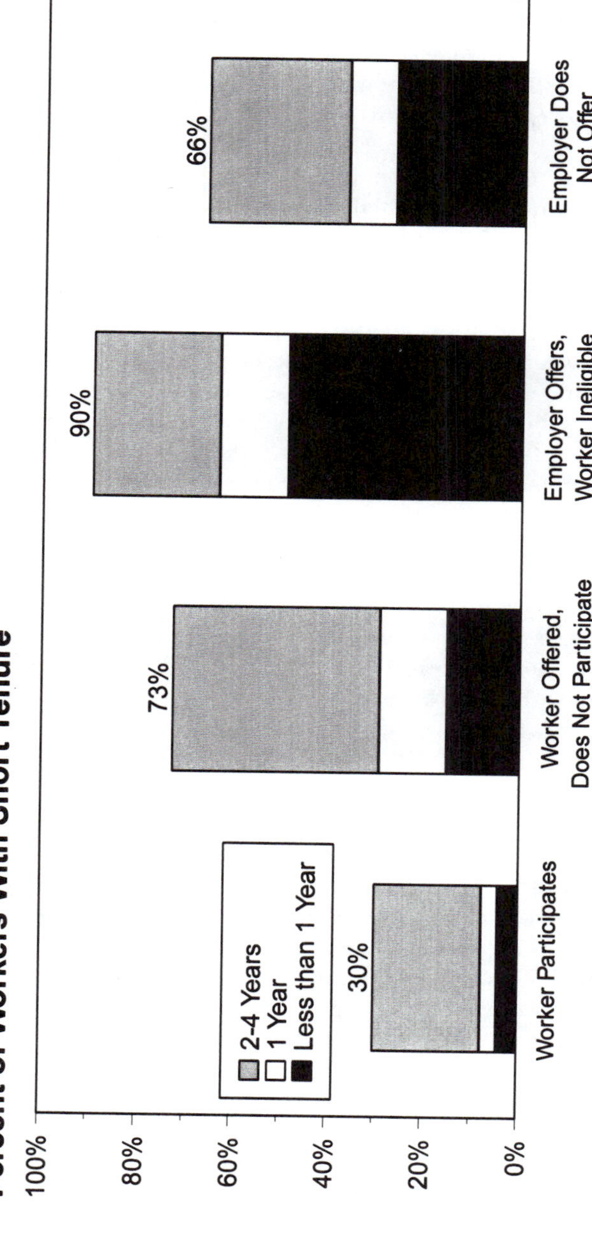

Figure 4. Sponsorship/participation categories by tenure, 1993. Source: USDOL (1994) and authors' computations using April 1993 CPS Employee Benefits Supplement.

status of workers in April 1993. The first column indicates the percentage of workers whose employer offers a plan and who participate in it; the second shows the percentage of workers who turn down an offer to participate; the third, those who are ineligible; and the fourth column, the proportion of those whose employer does not offer a pension plan. Viewing the coverage from this perspective leads to two general conclusions. The first supports the conventional wisdom. There are evidently a number of workers who are substantially "frozen out" of pension coverage due to the terms of eligibility imposed by their employer. More broadly, however, workers at firms that do not offer pension coverage share many of the attributes of those who decline to be covered even when offered the opportunity. This raises some question about whether workers would elect coverage even if their employer could be induced to sponsor a plan.

As the foregoing discussion illustrates, pension coverage is determined by a complex interaction of factors both on the supply and demand side, with workers and firms sorting so that workers with low demand for pension coverage tend to work in firms where the cost of providing pension coverage is relatively high. Small employers appear to be significantly disadvantaged in their ability to offer coverage due to the economics of scale. These same firms have a concentration of workers with attributes that suggest a low demand for compensation in the form of retirement benefits. We need look no further than the response to offers of 401(k) participation to confirm the latter. In 1993, only 65 percent of workers in firms with a 401(k) offering reported coverage. This is largely driven by low-wage and younger workers' turndowns.

Uncovered Workers

The low coverage of employees at small firms may be due in part to characteristics of those employees, such as low wages, that cause them to have low demand. Because of their low wages, many employees working for small employers may prefer wages to benefits.

To illuminate that issue, we examine characteristics of workers who are offered pension coverage by their employer but turn it down. This situation arises in 401(k) plans where employee contributions are required for employee participation. Some workers turn down participation in 401(k) plans but participate in a defined benefit plan offered by their employer. Because those workers are covered, while our focus is on workers not covered, we do not consider them.

Workers in firms that offer 401(k) plans that turn down participation and do not participate in another plan offered by their employer ("401(k) turndowns") tend to be younger than participants, to be female, and to have lower education, earnings, and tenure (Table 1). In

TABLE 1 Characteristics of 401(k) Plan Participants Compared with Other Workers (all private wage and salary workers age 16 or older)

	Characteristic 401(k) turndowns	*All pension nonparticipants*	*401(k) participants*	*All private sector pension participants*
Median age	31	33	39	40
Median job tenure	3	2	7	8
Median annual earnings ($)	18,200	13,700	31,400	27,300
Percent female	51	49	40	41
Percent that work full-time, full-year	84	65	93	92
Percent employed in firms with 1,000+ workers	54	22	60	56

Source: Authors' computations using the April 1993 CPS; N=19,380.

those respects, the turndowns are more similar to other nonparticipants than to 401(k) participants.

While pension nonparticipants and 401(k) turndowns are more similar to each other than to participants, pension nonparticipants have lower tenure and earnings than the 401(k) turndowns, and are less likely to work full time, full year, less likely to work in a firm with 1,000 or more employees, and less likely to have graduated from college. Because nonparticipants are less likely that 401(k) turndowns to have these characteristics associated with coverage, many nonparticipants would probably turn down coverage if their employer were to offer it.

While in most respects 401(k) turndowns resemble other pension nonparticipants, they are more similar to 401(k) participants in two respects: they are more likely to work in large firms and are more likely to work full time, full year. Firm size is an important determinant of which firms offer pension plans. Full-time, full-year status is an important determinant of eligibility in firms that offer pensions.

Among 401(k) turndowns and nonparticipants, particularly striking is the low tenure of both groups. The median job tenure of turndowns is three years, compared to two years for all pension nonparticipants and eight years for pension participants.

We further examine the low coverage rate of low-tenure workers. For each year increase in job tenure at low levels, the percentage of the labor force covered by a pension plan of any type, or by a 401(k) plan, increases (Table 2). The pension coverage rate rises from 9 percent for workers with less than one year of tenure to 52 percent for workers with 5 years.

These statistics illustrate the correlation between high turnover jobs

TABLE 2 Pension Coverage Status of Short-Tenure Workers (% of all private wage and salary workers age 16 or older, except as indicated)

	Job tenure (%)					
Pension status	*<1*	*1*	*2*	*3*	*4*	*5*
Covered	9	20	7	40	49	52
401(K) covered	5	10	15	21	28	27
Offered 401(k) but not participating*	73 (13)	59 (14)	44 (12)	39 (13)	30 (12)	26 (10)
Employer does not offer†	63	53	52	42	38	39

Source: Authors' computations using the April 1993 CPS; N = 11,497.
*Percentage of all workers in parentheses.
†Includes "don't know."

TABLE 3 401(k) Contributions for Low- and Middle-Income Workers Contributing to 401(k) Plans, 1993

Annual earnings	*Mean contributions ($)*
Under $10,000	503
$10,000–14,999	782
$15,000–19,999	1,000
$20,000–24,999	1,418
$25,000–29,999	1,746
$30,000–34,999	2,198
$35,000–39,999	2,784
$40,000–49,999	3,242

Source: Authors' computations using the April 1993 CPS; N = 16,120.
Note: These figures represent employee contributions only.

and lack of pension coverage. This correlation indicates that defined benefit plans would not appeal to many workers lacking pension coverage because they have high job turnover and would suffer portability losses in a defined benefit plan. Thus, policies to expand coverage may be more successful if they focus on defined contribution rather than defined benefit plans.

The percentage of workers offered a 401(k) plan that chooses not to participate decreases sharply with tenure, from 73 percent with less than one year tenure to 26 percent with 5 years tenure.

Andrea Kusko, James Poterba, and David Wilcox (this volume) provide further evidence concerning 401(k) turndown and eventual job tenure. Using data from a single large firm, they find that the participation rate among new hires was lower than among other workers: only about 50 percent participated, versus 80 percent overall. The participation rate among new hires in 1989 who left the firm in 1990 was only 6.5 percent.

In sum, the typical characteristics of workers turning down 401(k) participation suggest that public policies designed to affect the supply side of pension coverage (i.e., employer's costs) may have limited effect. Even when employers offer pension coverage, workers with low tenure and other characteristics typical of nonparticipants frequently choose not to participate.

When low- and middle-income workers do participate in 401(k) plans, their contributions are generally low (Table 3). Low- and middle-income workers generally contribute far below the maximum they are allowed to contribute.

A Predicted Probability Analysis of Nonparticipants

To extend the analysis of nonparticipants, we estimate a logistic regression on pension coverage. Our concern is whether noncovered workers would choose to be covered by a pension plan if their employer offered one. To investigate this, we estimate a standard regression on the probability of participating in a pension plan. Because we are focusing on worker demand for coverage, we used as explanatory variables gender, age, race, education, work status (full versus part time), earnings, and tenure. We then calculated individual prediction probabilities for all observations that appeared in the regressions, and we sorted them from low to high probability separately for covered and noncovered workers.

There is little overlap between covered workers and noncovered workers in terms of the predicted probability of coverage. Among noncovered workers, those at the top quartile in probability of coverage have a 46 percent probability of being covered. By comparison, among covered workers, those at the bottom quartile have a 48 percent probability of being covered (Tables 4, 5).

From the predicted probabilities of coverage for noncovered workers, it appears reasonably likely that 10 percent of noncovered workers would participate if offered a pension. The top 10 percent of noncovered workers have a predicted probability of coverage of at least 67 percent.

Conversely, discrimination rules may be expanding coverage among workers who have a low probability of being covered but who work for large firms. Among workers whose personal characteristics place them in the bottom quartile of predicted probabilities of coverage but who are covered, 50 percent work for firms with 1,000 or more employees.

Examining further the role of firm size in explaining low-probability coverage and low-probability lack of coverage, covered workers in the

TABLE 4 Predicted Probability That Workers Would Participate in a Pension if It Were Offered, 1993

Percentile	*Covered workers*	*Noncovered workers*
10	.326	.038
25	.484	.106
50	.696	.251
75	.840	.461
90	.924	.672

Source: Authors' computations using the April 1993 CPS.

TABLE 5 Percentage of Workers by Quartile of Predicted Probability of Coverage, Coverage Status, and Firm Size, 1993

	First quartile (%)		*Fourth quartile (%)*	
Firm size	*Yes*	*No*	*Yes*	*No*
Fewer than 25	13.2	42.3	5.9	43.6
25–249	24.5	24.2	16.4	31.7
250–999	11.9	7.1	12.8	7.4
1,000+	50.3	26.5	64.9	17.3

Source: Authors' computations using the April 1993 CPS.

lowest earning quartile are more than twice as likely to work for a firm with more than 1,000 employees that are noncovered workers in the highest earnings quartile (Table 6). In most other respects, noncovered workers in the highest earnings quartile have characteristics that make them more likely to be covered than do covered workers in the lowest earnings quartile. These statistics suggest that some high-income workers would be covered by a pension if they worked for an employer that offered one, but are not because they are working for a smaller employer that does not offer a plan.

All these statistics ultimately leave those charged with formulating policies for addressing what the Committee for Economic Development (1995) recently proclaimed to be a "looming crisis" with four essential insights. First, the conventional view of coverage gaps as a supply problem originating in small firms explains part of what is happening. Second, there is also a demand side problem. Third, there is a mismatch of some workers with high-demand characteristics in low-supply firms. The fourth point is the most vexing to the economists' attempts to explain labor market and savings behavior. There are apparently many workers whose behavior does not comport with rational optimizing models. Some workers rationally do not seek coverage because social security benefits pro-

TABLE 6 Characteristics of Workers in the Highest Earnings Quartile Who Do Not Have Pension Coverage and Workers in the Lowest Quartile Who Do

Characteristic	*Highest earnings quartile—nonparticipants*	*Lowest earnings quartile—participants*
Median age	37	37
Median job tenure	3	5
Median annual earnings ($)	39,520	9,880
Percent female	27	72
Percent who are full-time full-year workers	95	49
Percent employed in firms with 1,000+ workers	20	55
Percent college graduates	43	9

Source: Authors' computations using the April 1993 CPS; N = 1,889.

vide a high replacement rate for low-income workers, because pension saving is illiquid and thus cannot be used as precautionary saving, or because the life cycle model suggests that young workers will have low savings. Pension coverage, however, is essentially a highly regimented form of savings, and there is evidently a substantial part of the population whose behavior may be predicted more on some deeper psychological imperative than the current economic model incorporates.

What Is Wrong with the Traditional Economic Model?

The traditional economic model of pension coverage is based on the supply and demand for pension coverage. The demand for pension coverage is determined by workers' demand for retirement savings, which is determined by the life cycle model of retirement savings.

The supply-demand model is usually extended to recognize that coverage at a firm is not entirely an individual decision but is determined by the collective demand of workers at the particular firm. Individual workers who wish pension coverage may not be covered because they work for a firm where other workers have a low demand for coverage. Nondiscrimination rules require that most workers at a firm be covered if any are covered. That point is seen when examining characteristics of workers in the highest earning quartile without coverage and workers in the lowest earnings quartile with coverage (Table 6).

The traditional supply-demand model for expanding pension coverage focuses on changes in prices. Policies based on this model focus largely on the supply side—on reducing the cost of providing benefits.

If households act as the life cycle theory of saving predicts, absent the distorting effect of other government programs, public policy initiatives to encourage pension coverage would be unnecessary. Households would save adequately for retirement, and there would be no need for public policy to encourage retirement saving. However, transfer programs conditioned on lack of savings, such as college scholarship programs, discourage families from saving.

Further, while the life cycle model may predict the behavior of sophisticated workers who save adequately for retirement based on its principles, the life cycle model is unlikely to predict retirement savings for many workers as Thaler (1994) argues. Figuring out how much to save and the optimal savings path to take are difficult problems. With risk aversion by households causing them to weight undersaving more heavily than oversaving in utility calculations, it is not evident, however, that the difficulty of determining the optimal amount to save leads to undersaving. The preference of present over future consumption may cause households to err on the side of undersaving when they are uncertain as to how much to save.

Also, given that people only save for retirement once, the opportunities for learning by doing and correcting mistakes in subsequent repetitions are minimal. This problem is mitigated to the extent that people can adjust their hours worked, their savings rate, and their retirement date as they approach retirement and are better able to judge the amount of savings they need. However, many workers find that their labor market opportunities become more limited as they approach retirement, which decreases their flexibility in making adjustments.

The only plausible ways in which people might approximate an optimal savings plan are by learning from others (role models or experts) or by using good rules of thumb. Learning from the experience of others is difficult because changes in social security and private pension benefits make the experience of current retirees of limited value for current workers. Simple rules of thumb do not exist because the amount saved to meet a target income replacement rate depends on the age at which the savings program starts and the expected return and risk of the investment portfolio.

A further problem with the life cycle theory stems from the human failing of lack of self-control. Even if an individual could calculate the optimal amount to save in order to maximize lifetime utility, he or she might not resist the temptation of current consumption versus consumption 30 or more years hence. Rational discounting of future consumption by the probability of being alive at a distant future date also reduces the incentive to save. Insufficient self-control, however, may prevent households from saving through pension plans when theory predicts they would.

It is psychologically easier to save in some situations than others. In the past, when defined benefit plans were more prevalent, workers did not face a decision as to whether or how much to save through their pension plan. Given that they worked for an employer offering a pension plan, coverage and saving were automatic. Currently, with 401(k) plans, more burden is placed on the worker to determine how much retirement saving is needed.

Ippolito (this volume) provides an alternative explanation for why workers do not participate in pension plans. He argues that some workers have high discount rates. For them, the life cycle model does not work because they heavily discount future periods. It seems that some workers heavily discount the future because they place a low utility on future events.

Reasons Workers Do Not Participate in Pension Plans

Critics of the life cycle model suggest that some workers do not participate in pension plans because of psychological factors. Economic studies indicate characteristics of workers who choose not to participate when offered a pension plan, but do not tell us specifically the reasons why they choose not to participate. A survey of federal government workers covered by the Thrift Savings Plan in 1990 provides evidence on that issue. It asked why workers choose not to contribute the plan (Table 7). In terms of standard price theory, it is difficult to understand why workers who expect to vest and who would receive dollar-for-dollar matching contributions would not contribute. The matching contribution guarantees a high rate of return on their contribution. The most common response, given by more than a fourth of men (29 percent) not contributing and more than a third of women (34 percent), was that they could not afford to contribute. While for some that response may reflect a liquidity constraint, for others it may reflect a lack of self-control in saving for retirement.

Factors other than income clearly are among the determinants of the response that a workers is unable to contribute. Eighty-one percent of the workers in the lowest income quartile do not give that response, while 7 percent of the workers in the highest quartile responded that they cannot afford to contribute (Table 8).

A number of the reasons given in the survey for not participating do not fit into the economic framework of financial reasons for nonparticipation. Nearly one in six men and women (16 percent) did not contribute because they did not understand the Thrift Savings Plan, and nearly as many (12 percent of men and 15 percent of women) did not invest because they did not have enough information. A tenth (10 per-

TABLE 7 Reasons for Not Contributing to the Federal Thrift Savings Plan (percent of sample not contributing)

Reasons for not contributing	*Men*	*Women*
Can't spare the money	28.7	34.2
Prefer other investments	24.2	19.7
Too close to retirement	16.7	13.1
Don't understand the Thrift Savings Plan	15.7	16.0
Don't want money tied up	14.2	14.2
Don't have enough information	12.0	14.5
No confidence in the plan	10.3	5.8
Haven't considered the Thrift Savings Plan	10.1	9.6
Never got around to it	7.3	13.7
May not stay in federal government	3.9	3.8

Source: Authors' computations from 1990 Federal Retirement Thrift Investment Board data; N = 1,042.
Note: Respondents could check all applicable reasons.

TABLE 8 Workers Responding They Cannot Afford to Contribute to the Thrift Savings Plan, by Income Quartile

Quartile	*Male*	*Female*	*All*
(1) $25,000 or less	17.1	21.0	19.4
(2) $25,000–$35,000	11.4	13.4	12.2
(3) $35,001–$55,000	12.6	4.8	10.0
(4) More than $55,000	3.8	10.1	6.5
All	11.9	14.7	13.1

Source: Authors' computations from 1990 Federal Retirement Thrift Investment Board data.

cent) of both men and women not contributing did not contribute because they had not considered contributing to the plan. More than one-eighth of the women (14 percent) but fewer men (7 percent) did not invest because they had not bothered to do it. Thus, lack of knowledge and inertia are important reasons why workers did not contribute.

A recent study provides further evidence that the complexity of the problem of determining how much retirement income is necessary for maintaining one's standard of living in retirement may cause some people to save inadequate amounts. A Putnam Investments survey found that almost two thirds of Americans said they were "not worried" about having enough money to live on during retirement, despite not knowing how much retirement income they will need (Putnam Investments 1995). Supporting the evidence as to lack of knowledge about the amount of saving necessary for retirement, a survey by the Employee Benefit Research Institute (EBRI) found that 70 percent of survey respondents did not know how much they needed to save for retirement (Yakaboski 1995). These reasons suggest that better participant education by plan sponsors may increase pension coverage (Bernheim, this volume).

What Can Public Policy Do?

Legislative initiatives in recent years have reflected a growing (although rarely explicit) recognition of both supply and demand elements of pension coverage. By 1990, legislation designed to expand pension coverage had been sponsored by members of Congress from both parties, including such luminaries as Senator Lloyd Bentson, then chairing the Senate Finance Committee, and Representative Dan Rostenkowski, presiding over the House Ways and Means Committee. Their efforts originated with the concept of "pension simplification," whose lineage was readily traceable to the so-called "tax simplification" efforts of the mid 1980s. These multipronged initiatives ultimately culminated in the passage of H.R. 11, the Revenue Act of 1992, shortly before the presidential election.

That bill directly addressed two of the limitations to coverage outlined above. It sought to expand the sponsorship of defined contribution plans by easing perceived limitations for small employers. And by providing simplified rules for nondiscrimination testing, it tried to address the problem of the high-demand worker in a firm with workers with a lower propensity to participate in a pension plan.

These objectives were approached in two ways. The bill would have expanded the availability of Salary Reduction Simplified Employee Plans (SARSEPs, or essentially employer-organized IRAs with higher contribution limits) by permitting firms with up to 100 employees to sponsor the plans. It would also have relaxed the nondiscrimination rules by allowing contributions to these plans even if fewer than 50 percent of the sponsor's employees elected to contribute. It also would have provided two alternative ways of satisfying the 401(k) nondiscrimination rules: by permitting sponsors (1) to match 100 percent of the first 3 percent of elective deferrals and 50 percent of employee contributions up to the first 5 percent of salary, or (2) to provide an employer contribution of 3 percent for each non-highly compensated participant.

Returning from Houston following his defeat by Bill Clinton, however, President George Bush vetoed the bill on the basis of the tax increases it also contained.

In June 1995, the Clinton administration announced its version of pension simplification. That bill, however, met the same fate as its predecessor, its demise resulting from the fact that it was included in a legislative package emerging from the new Republican majority's grand plans to balance the budget by extracting unprecedented changes in the structure and spending on entitlement programs, most notably Medicare. Much like President Bush before him, while apparently continuing to support the objectives of the pension simplification measures, President Clinton vetoed the bill in late 1995.

The first two rounds of legislative failures, with similar bills passed by Congresses dominated by both parties and vetoed by both a Republican and Democratic president, demonstrated the capacity for consensus on the issues, if not a practical resolution.

Despite this history, or more likely because of the continued popularity of the approach, in early 1996 President Clinton announced an expanded version of the earlier pension proposals, and in August 1996, he signed the Small Business Job Protection Act. This act established a new type of pension plan, the Savings Incentive Match Plan for Employees—or SIMPLE. Employers with 100 or fewer employees earning $5,000 or more in the previous year are eligible to establish this type of plan. A SIMPLE pension is a salary reduction plan that allows employees to contribute up to $6,000 of pretax pay per year (the amount to be indexed for inflation in $500 increments). The employer must either (1) make a 100 percent matching contribution, not to exceed 3 percent of compensation, or (2) make a 2 percent nonelective contribution to all eligible employees with $5,000 or more in compensation the preceding year. For the nonelective contribution, there is a compensation ceiling of $150,000. All contributions vest immediately. This plan is intended to reduce the administrative and financial burden on small employers associated with establishing and maintaining a pension plan.

Policy Impact

CPS data can be used to assess the likely increase in coverage that would result from various policies. Policies that take a supply side approach attempt to encourage small firms with relatively high costs to act more like large firms with relatively low costs. An estimate of the maximum effect of such policies, including the maximum effect of the SIMPLE plan, can be obtained by assuming that workers in small firms are actually in large firms. We recalculated the predicted probability of coverage for small firm workers assuming they were employed in large firms, of more than 1,000 workers. The predicted probability calculations were done by removing the effects of variables whose estimated coefficients were statistically insignificant at the 5 percent level. The predicted probability of participation for small firms (fewer than 100 workers) more than doubles from 0.22 to 0.53. When this increase in probability is applied to the 1993 CPS weighted population of nonparticipating workers in small firms, an increase in coverage of 9.7 million workers is predicted. Because this estimate uses 1993 worker counts, it underestimates the likely effect of a policy change occurring in a later year.

The second type of policy considered focuses on reducing or eliminating the requirements of nondiscrimination in small firms so that high-demand workers in those firms could obtain coverage. The effect of such a policy can be estimated by calculating the number of workers in small firms who are not covered, but have a high predicted probability of coverage. There are 6.2 million workers in firms of 249 workers or fewer who are not covered with a predicted probability of coverage of 74 percent or higher.

Third, there is the large group of workers in both small and large firms who are predicted to be covered but are not. We estimate that there are 7.7 million workers in firms of all sizes with a predicted probability of coverage of 80 percent or higher, who are not currently covered. This figure provides an upper bound estimate on the number of workers who are predicted to be covered on the basis of economic and demographic variables but who are not covered, perhaps because of psychological reasons or because of economic reasons not currently recognized in empirical models. Combining that figure with the figure for workers in small firms who are not covered but probably would be if they were in large firms involves some double counting, but provides an upper bound estimate of 17.4 million additional workers who might be covered by pension coverage initiatives.

Conclusion

More than 50 million Americans do not participate in a pension plan at their current job. This is the result of a complex array of factors that include lack of opportunity to participate in such plans, a low level of demand for compensation in the form of pension benefits by many workers, and limitations related to the composition of workers within many firms. Recent years have seen a fairly narrow range of legislative initiatives directed toward enhancing coverage, although these have increasingly recognized the demand side of the coverage equation.

At best, we can expect legislative changes to extend coverage to a quarter to a third of currently uncovered workers, with actual results likely to be considerably lower. The apparent dynamics of pension coverage indicate that achieving greater results is likely to require efforts to address the psychological elements that limit workers' capacity or motivation for saving to as great an extent as they are directed to by economic considerations. In this respect, we have, as Winston Churchill said, reached "not the beginning of the end, but rather the end of the beginning" in our efforts to achieve universal coverage.

The authors gratefully acknowledge the assistance and comments of Daniel Beller, Susan Benner, David McCarthy, Phyllis Fernandez, and William Ross. The paper represents the views of the authors and does not represent the position of the U.S. Department of Labor or of the International Labor Office.

Notes

1. The issues related to the debate over the savings of the baby boom generation are surveyed in Hinz and Turner (1994).
2. Tax Equity and Fiscal Responsibility Act of 1982, Deficit Reduction Act of 1984, Tax Reform Act of 1986, and Retirement Equity Act of 1984.

References

Bernheim, B. Douglas. "Financial Illiteracy, Education, and Retirement Savings." This volume.

Chen, Yung-Ping. "The Role of Private Pensions in the Income of Older Americans." In John A. Turner and Daniel J. Beller, eds., *Trends in Pensions 1992.* U.S. Department of Labor. Washington, D.C.: USGPO, 1992: 343–417.

Committee for Economic Development. *Who Will Pay for Your Retirement? The Looming Crisis.* New York: Committee for Economic Development, 1995.

Hinz, Richard P. and John A. Turner. "Baby Boomers in Retirement." *Contingencies* (March/April 1994): 20–23.

Hustead, Edwin C. "Trends in Retirement Income Plan Administrative Expenses." This volume.

Korczyk, Sophie M. "Pension Coverage Gaps in Firms with Coverage." Report to the U.S. Department of Labor, Pension and Welfare Benefits Administration, 1994.

Kusko, Andrea L., James M. Poterba, and David W. Wilcox. "Employee Decisions with Respect to 401(k) Plans." This volume.

Long, Stephen H. and M. Susan Marquis. "Gaps in Employment-Based Health Insurance: Lack of Supply or Lack of Demand." In U.S. Department of Labor, Pension and Welfare Benefits Administration, *Health Benefits and the Workforce.* Washington, DC: USGPO, 1994.

Putnam Investments. " '. . . Like There's No Tomorrow': Examining Americans' Attitudes About Retirement and Saving." Boston: Putnam Investments, 1995.

Thaler, Richard H. "Psychology and Savings Policies." *American Economic Review* 84 (May 1994): 186–92.

U.S. Department of Labor, Pension and Welfare Benefits Administration. *Pension and Health Benefits of American Workers: New Findings from the April 1993 Current Population Survey.* Washington, DC: USGPO, 1994.

U.S. Small Business Administration. *The Annual Report on Small Business and Competition.* Washington, D.C.: USGPO, 1993.

Yakoboski, Paul. "Are Workers Kidding Themselves? Results of the 1995 Retirement Confidence Survey." *EBRI Issue Brief* No. 168. Washington, D.C.: Employee Benefit Research Institute, 1995: 1–3.

Chapter 3
Financial Illiteracy, Education, and Retirement Saving

B. Douglas Bernheim

Most Americans save too little to maintain their standards of living after retirement. In the past, the typical worker has reached retirement with total savings insufficient to sustain his or her preretirement living standards (Diamond 1977; Hammermesh 1984).[1] Since social security benefits provide rather modest earnings replacement, and since defined benefit plans supplement this income for a shrinking minority of American workers, retirement income security has become increasingly dependent on the adequacy of personal saving. Yet recent research on the adequacy of saving has found that, through the combination of defined contribution plans and nonpension saving, the typical baby boom household is saving at slightly more than one-third the rate required to finance a standard of living during retirement comparable to the standard of living that it enjoys before retirement (Bernheim 1993, 1994a, 1995a; Arthur D. Little, Inc. 1993).[2] Even workers with defined benefit plans fall short of the mark.[3] It is important to emphasize that this calculation does not represent a "worst case" scenario. On the contrary, it is based on many optimistic assumptions concerning longevity, future rates of taxation, and anticipated social security benefits.[4] Even a moderate increase in future taxes would reduce relative saving adequacy below 30 percent, and a moderate reduction in social security benefits would depress it even further, to less than 20 percent. If social security benefits were eliminated, baby boomers would be saving only about one-tenth of what is required to avoid a precipitous decline in standard of living after retirement.

The increasing popularity of 401(k) accentuates these concerns, because it leaves critical decisions concerning participation, contributions, and investments in the hands of employees. Many employees choose to contribute little, or nothing at all, while others invest heavily in safe, low-return, fixed income funds. As a result, fewer than one-third of pension plan sponsors believe that their employees will accumulate adequate plan balances.[5]

Why do Americans make such poor financial decisions? One possibility is that they lack the training, skill, and/or guidance to recognize financial vulnerabilities and to formulate prudent plans. If so, then education policy may prove to be a powerful tool for stimulating rates of saving—particularly as 401(k) plans continue to grow. This possibility led the Department of Labor in 1995 to launch a "national pension education program aimed at drawing the attention of American workers to the importance of taking personal responsibility for their retirement security" (Berg 1995). The desire to shape behavior through education is also presumably behind the recent explosion of retirement education in the workplace. As of 1994, 88 percent of large employers offered some form of financial education, more than two-thirds of which added these programs after 1990.[6]

In this chapter, I examine a series of questions central to the issues discussed above. First, is low saving associated with a failure to appreciate financial vulnerabilities? Second, even if individuals were aware of their vulnerabilities, would they typically possess the decision-making skills required to formulate sensible retirement plans? Third, when the requisite decision-making skills are absent, do individuals obtain authoritative advice and guidance? Finally, if low saving and poor investment choices are attributable in part to the absence of knowledge, skill, and guidance, is it possible to address these problems effectively through programs of retirement education, particularly in the workplace?

In answering these questions, I review existing evidence and, where appropriate, offer pertinent new evidence. Many of my conclusions are pessimistic: the typical household decision-maker underappreciates financial vulnerabilities, is ill equipped to formulate sensible retirement plans, and does not make significant use of authoritative guidance. However, I ultimately find considerable cause for optimism in the emerging body of evidence on the effects of employer-based retirement education.

Do Households Appreciate Their Financial Vulnerabilities?

The extent to which households perceive their financial vulnerabilities, and the relation between these perceptions and accumulated wealth, is revealed through an analysis of annual household survey data gathered by Merrill Lynch, Inc. The first of these surveys was administered in two "waves" during the fall of 1993 to a random, nationally representative sample of individuals between the ages of 29 and 47 (the "baby boom" cohort). Both waves contain a detailed battery of questions concerning household assets, earnings, income, pension coverage, employment status, and demographic information. The first wave, which surveyed 1,209 households, also contains various self-assessments of current financial status and of future financial needs, intended saving, and actual saving. Additionally, it measures beliefs and expectations concerning Social Security, including current and future benefit levels, and other information on attitudes and expectations concerning unfunded government obligations. The second wave, which surveyed 806 households, assesses economic literacy, financial knowledge, developmental experiences that may be relevant to financial behavior, and sources of financial information and advice.[7]

The 1993 survey instrument contains several questions designed to elicit self-evaluations of financial status. These questions include the following:

> Would you describe the state of your own personal finances these days as very shaky, fairly shaky, fairly secure, or very secure?
>
> Overall, how well prepared do you think you are financially for your eventual retirement? (very well prepared, somewhat prepared, somewhat unprepared, very unprepared, or not prepared at all)
>
> Do you expect to have a standard of living that is much worse, somewhat worse, somewhat better, much better, or have the same standard of living after you retire as you do today?

Overall, the answers to these questions indicate a fairly high degree of optimism about personal finances: 68 percent of respondents described their personal finances as fairly secure or very secure, 58 percent believed that they are very well prepared or somewhat prepared for retirement, while only 19 percent described themselves as very unprepared or not at all prepared. Virtually identical fractions of the population (31 percent) expected better and worse standards of living in retirement.

Provided that we have some objective measure of financial vulnerabilities, the answers to questions about personal financial status can be used to evaluate the extent to which individuals recognize these vulnerabilities. One possible measure of financial vulnerabilities is the ratio of wealth to earnings.[8] A lower value of the wealth-to-earnings ratio does not, however, necessarily indicate greater vulnerability. A particular value of this ratio may indicate vulnerability for households with certain characteristics, while indicating relative security for households with other characteristics.

I therefore separate the population into four "adjusted-wealth" quartiles (Bernheim 1995b). Intuitively, this approach amounts to dividing

TABLE 1 Perceptions of Financial Security versus Household Financial Preparation

	Index of financial preparedness (quartiles) (%)			
	1	*2*	*3*	*4*
State of personal finances				
Secure/fairly secure	53.9	71.0	66.4	78.3
Shaky/very shaky	46.1	28.6	33.7	21.7
State of preparation for retirement				
Very well/somewhat	44.6	55.2	62.0	68.2
Very unprepared/not at all	29.9	9.5	13.0	14.3
Standard of living during retirement				
Better/much better	29.9	28.6	29.8	36.4
Worse/much worse	37.3	32.9	31.7	23.0

Source: Bernheim (1995b). The sample is taken from the 1993 Merrill Lynch household survey.
Note: The "index of financial preparedness" is based on the ratio of wealth to earnings, adjusting for other household characteristics. Households falling into the first quartile have the lowest level of financial preparedness (relative to similar households), while households falling into the fourth quartile have the highest level of financial preparedness.

the population into numerous subgroups based on age, earnings, gender, marital status, education, pension coverage, and number of children and then further subdividing each of the groups into quartiles based on wealth-to-earnings ratios. The first, or lowest, adjusted-wealth quartile corresponds to those individuals in the lowest wealth-to-earnings quartile within each population subgroup. Those individuals in the lowest adjusted-wealth quartile thus have very low levels of wealth compared to other individuals with identical characteristics. The other three adjusted-wealth quartiles are defined similarly.[9]

A household's adjusted-wealth quartile is a good measure of its financial vulnerability, relative to that of similar households. If individuals understand their financial vulnerabilities, then those in higher adjusted-wealth quartiles should regard themselves as more secure than those in lower adjusted-wealth quartiles.

Table 1 examines this possibility, reporting answers to survey questions concerning household financial status, separately for each adjusted-wealth quartile. The table exhibits a moderately strong relation between actual and perceived financial vulnerability. The fraction of the population that regards its personal finances as secure or fairly secure rises significantly between the first and second adjusted-wealth quartiles, as well as between the third and fourth quartiles. Oddly, this fraction declines slightly between the second and third quartiles. The fraction of the population describing itself as very well or somewhat prepared for retirement rises monotonically with the household's adjusted-wealth quartile. The respondent's expected relative standard of living in retirement shows the weakest relationship to adjusted wealth. The fraction of the population expecting a better standard of living in retirement is highest in the top adjusted-wealth quartile, but varies little across the first three quartiles. On the other hand, the fraction of the population expecting a worse standard of living in retirement falls significantly between the first and second quartiles, and again between the third and fourth quartiles. (There is also a slight decline between the second and third quartiles.)

Although these results indicate some awareness of relative financial vulnerabilities, they also exhibit an unrealistic degree of optimism. Within the lowest adjusted-wealth quartile—a group that is poorly prepared by any objective measure of adequacy—more than half of the respondents (54%) regard their personal finances as secure or fairly secure, 45 percent believe that they are very well or somewhat prepared for retirement, and only 37 percent expect to achieve a lower standard of living after retirement.

To put these findings somewhat differently, among the least well-prepared segment of the population, nearly two-thirds believe that their standard of living during retirement will be as high or higher than it is today. This is particularly surprising in light of the fact that most of these individuals acknowledge that they save significantly less than they should and express little or no confidence in Social Security (Bernheim 1995b). Thus, for a substantial fraction of the population, the failure to save adequately may result in a failure to appreciate financial vulnerabilities adequately, coupled with possible self-deception.

Do Households Have Adequate Decision-Making Skills?

The existing literature contains a fair number of studies that shed considerable light on the general public's level of financial sophistication. Sophistication, or the lack thereof, is reflected in both knowledge and choices.

Collectively, existing studies paint a rather bleak picture of Americans' economic and financial literacy.[10] For example, only 20 percent of adults can determine correct change using prices from a menu, and many have trouble determining whether a mortgage at 8.6 percent is better than a mortgage at 8¾ percent.

The sophistication of choices has also been the subject of extensive study. Numerous authors have observed that decision making under uncertainty gives rise to a variety of behavioral anomalies (Kahneman,

Slovic, and Tversky 1982). A large number of papers provide formal tests of rational intertemporal choice, with many authors concluding that the life cycle model does not accurately describe behavior (Shefrin and Thaler 1983, 1988; Levin 1992; Kotlikoff, Johnson, and Samuelson 1987). Numerous authors have also identified particularly naive or unsophisticated patterns of financial behavior. Examples include: a widespread failure to take advantage of clear arbitrage opportunities (Warshawsky 1987); the common practice of waiting until the end of a tax year to contribute to an IRA (Feenberg and Skinner 1989); the use of rough rule-of-thumb saving targets (Bernheim 1994b); the frequency of identifiable errors in personal financial management, including insufficient diversification and excessive conservatism in selecting investments (O'Neill 1990, 1993); limited familiarity with all but the simplest investment instruments (O'Neill 1993); the use of costly methods of borrowing (Hira 1993); the frequency with which personal bankruptcy results from poor credit management (Hira 1993); the prevalence of "compulsive spending addictions" (Faber and O'Guinn 1989); and the high frequency with which individuals fall prey to financial scams (Alliance Against Fraud in Telemarketing 1992).

In summary, the existing literature demonstrates that most Americans know little about managing personal finances and their choices reflect this ignorance. While these findings are useful and important, they leave many central questions unanswered. In particular, it is important to know whether identifiable population subgroups are particularly at risk of making uninformed or otherwise unsophisticated decisions, and whether this lack of information and sophistication relates systematically to behavior.

In this section, I address these issues using information collected in the 1993 Merrill Lynch household survey. The survey instrument contained eleven questions designed to assess the respondent's knowledge of economic matters. These questions are reproduced in the appendix. I have divided the questions into two subcategories: those that concern financial issues, and those that concern macroeconomic issues. These permit us to examine (1) overall performance on these test questions, (2) variation in relative knowledge over identifiable population subgroups, (3) individuals' awareness of their own sophistication, and (4) preliminary findings concerning the relation between knowledge and behavior.

An Analysis of Absolute Performance

The sample of respondents surveyed generally performed poorly on economic and financial test questions. This is consistent with the evidence reviewed at the outset of this section. Even allowing for an appropriate margin of error on certain questions (such as the Dow Jones average), more than 80 percent of the sample answered at least five of the eleven questions incorrectly.

It is possible to characterize the nature of financial illiteracy more precisely. Nearly two-thirds of the sample would not hazard a guess as to the level of the Dow Jones average, despite the fact that this number is reported on the front page of virtually every business section in every daily newspaper, as well as on virtually every national television and radio news program. The median answer for those professing knowledge was 3,400—more than 300 points below the true range of the average during the week of the survey.

More than 90 percent of the sample answered the questions concerning unemployment and inflation, but they overestimated both statistics. The median response concerning unemployment was 8 percent, compared to 6.7 percent nationally at the time of the survey, and roughly one-third named a figure of 10 percent or higher. Similarly, the median response concerning inflation was 4 percent, compared to a rate of 2.8 percent at the time of the survey.

Respondents severely underestimated the size of the federal debt, with one-third of the sample reporting a number below $1 trillion. Among those answering this question, the median response was $3 trillion, whereas the correct answer was nearly $4.4 trillion. This discrepancy may be partially attributable to confusion about the differences between the debt and the deficit, as well as to inadvertent errors in orders of magnitude (i.e., saying "billions" rather than "trillions"). The survey separately asked for the federal debt per household. In theory, this number is far more relevant to the typical taxpayer than the total federal debt, since it measures the amount of liabilities that the government has incurred on his or her behalf. It is therefore striking—but perhaps not too surprising—that respondents were far more ignorant of the federal debt per household. Whereas 17 percent professed ignorance of the federal debt, more than one-third, or nearly twice as many, would not hazard a guess as to the federal debt per household. Those answering the question on debt per household severely underestimated this liability. The median answer was $18,000, compared with an actual liability of $45,700.

As noted in other studies, individuals tend to underestimate the power of compound interest. Nearly one-third of the sample indicated that $1,000, left in the bank for 30 years at 8 percent interest, would earn less than $5,000, whereas the correct answer is more than $10,000. Many respondents also poorly understand common financial instruments. Roughly 42 percent could not identify the proper explanation for the difference in average returns between mutual funds and federally insured CDs.

Respondents did perform relatively well on a small number of questions. The median response concerning the national minimum wage was \$4.35—only \$0.10 high—and 34 percent of the sample said \$4.25. Most respondents also provided reasonably accurate answers to the question about conventional mortgage rates, with homeowners performing noticeably better than renters.

An Analysis of Relative Performance

Despite these rather stark findings, it is difficult to obtain a meaningful absolute measure of financial literacy, since any such measure is necessarily predicated on subjective judgments concerning the set of things that a well-informed household ought to know. Test questions, such as those contained in the Merrill Lynch survey, are best suited for evaluating the relative sophistication of different population subgroups. For this purpose, I depart from the standard practice of coding responses as simply "right" or "wrong." These binary measures are necessarily arbitrary; for example, how close to the actual Dow Jones average would an answer need to be to be scored as correct? Instead, I assign a "relative knowledge score" to each question. This score is defined as the fraction of the population who gave answers that were further in absolute value than the respondent's answer from the true answer.[11] This procedure has the additional benefit of normalizing the score on each question to reflect difficulty, so that no question (or group of questions) dominates the variation in total scores.

Average scores for different population subgroups appear in Table 2. To interpret differences in test scores between subgroups, it is helpful to keep in mind the following information. Scores range between 25.8 and 96.5, with 25 percent of the population scoring between 25.8 and 54.2, 25 percent between 54.2 and 64.2, 25 percent between 64.2 and 73.5, and 25 percent above 73.5. Thus, toward the central portion of the population distribution, a 10 point increase in an individual's score would move him or her past roughly one-quarter of the population.

Surprisingly, test scores do not rise or fall systematically with age. This may reflect the effects of various offsetting factors. For example, individuals both acquire new knowledge and forget old knowledge as they age. It is also important to keep in mind that all respondents were surveyed at roughly the same point in time. As a result, I cannot separately identify the effects of age and birth year. Younger cohorts may have received more—or less—financial training than older cohorts.

Several other clear patterns emerge from an examination of Table 2. Males score higher than females, and whites score higher than blacks. Due to the size of the sample, it was impossible to draw reliable inferences

TABLE 2 Average Normalized Scores from a Test of Economic and Financial Knowledge

Population subgroup	*Overall score*	*Financial score*	*Macroeconomic score*
Age			
29–34	63.5	70.1	55.7
35–40	63.1	69.8	55.0
41–47	64.2	70.6	56.6
Gender			
Male	68.5	74.0	62.0
Female	58.9	66.5	49.8
Race			
White	64.3	71.0	56.3
Black	55.9	62.0	48.6
Education			
College degree	68.3	74.8	60.4
No college degree	60.6	67.2	52.8
Earnings			
First quartile	59.4	65.8	51.8
Second quartile	64.1	69.9	57.2
Third quartile	65.5	72.4	57.1
Fourth quartile	67.3	74.2	59.0

Source: Author's calculations. Sample taken from the 1993 Merrill Lynch household survey.
Note: Test scores are normalized to lie on a scale of 0 to 100, based on relative performance.

for any other ethnic subgroup; indeed, even the sample of black respondents is relatively small, and a corresponding measure of caution is therefore warranted when evaluating differences between blacks and whites. Average scores rise with both education and income, although perhaps not by as much as one might expect.

Similar patterns are observed for overall scores, financial scores, and macroeconomic scores. This reflects the fact that financial and macroeconomic scores are very highly correlated (the correlation coefficient is quite large—0.51—and highly statistically significant). This is reassuring, since it suggests that the questions are consistently measuring underlying characteristics.

One must exercise considerable caution when interpreting any of the patterns described above. For example, since earnings, education, gender, and race are all correlated, it is impossible to discern from any given comparison whether one is observing the incremental effect of changing the characteristic in question. Proper interpretation of the data requires

TABLE 3 Regression Analysis of Normalized Scores from a Test of Economic and Financial Knowledge

Explanatory variable	*Dependent variable*		
	Overall score	*Financial score*	*Macroeconomic score*
Age/10^4	0.464	−2.27	3.74
	(8.44)	(8.90)	(11.4)
Gender	0.0800	0.0580	0.106
	(0.0094)*	(0.0099)*	(0.013)*
Black	−0.0561	−0.0576	−0.0544
	(0.0232)†	(0.0245)†	(0.0315)
Earnings/10^7	1.39	3.19	−0.775
	(0.89)	(0.91)*	(1.17)
Employment status	0.0278	0.0261	0.0298
	(0.0139)†	(0.0147)	(0.0188)
High school only	0.0290	0.0409	0.0146
	(0.0289)	(0.0302)	(0.0388)
High school plus	0.0746	0.0848	0.0624
(no college degree)	(0.0283)*	(0.0299)*	(0.0383)
College degree	0.111	0.122	0.0977
	(0.028)*	(0.030)*	(0.0384)*
Constant	0.494	0.562	0.414
	(0.043)*	(0.046)*	(0.059)*

Source: Author's calculations. Sample taken from the 1993 Merrill Lynch household survey.
*Denotes statistical significance at 1% level.
†Denotes statistical significance at 5% level.
Note: For the purpose of this table, the dependent variables (test scores) are normalized to a scale of 0 to 1, rather than 0 to 100 (as for Table 2). Estimates are based on ordinary least squares regression. Standard errors are in parentheses.

the estimation of equations that explain test scores as a function of many demographic and economic factors.

Regression results are presented in Table 3. With respect to overall test scores, virtually all the patterns noted in Table 2 hold up. There is no systematic relation between test performance and age. Differences based on gender and race are statistically significant, even holding other variables (such as education and earnings) constant. More educated individuals generally obtain higher scores, and these differences are also statistically significant. Higher earnings are also associated with higher test scores, even controlling for education (as well as the other explanatory variables), but this effect is not statistically significant at conventional levels. In Table 3, I have also controlled for employment status, on the theory that gainfully employed individuals may be more knowledgeable about economic matters. Indeed, the estimates bear this out.

Further insight is obtained by examining results for financial knowledge and macroeconomic knowledge separately. These results are nearly identical, with one important exception: financial scores rise with earnings, and this increase is statistically significant, whereas earnings have essentially no effect on macroeconomic scores. Although macroeconomic scores are correlated with earnings (Table 2), this correlation disappears once one controls for education, gender, race, and employment status. This finding is intuitive. Individuals with higher earnings almost certainly have greater incentives to acquire *financial* knowledge. For example, those who are able to purchase homes are more likely to follow movements in mortgage rates, and those who own stock are certainly more likely to follow the Dow Jones average. Thus, it is not surprising that I find a very strong positive relation between earnings and financial test scores, even when I control for education and other factors. However, those with greater resources do not necessarily have greater incentives to acquire macroeconomic information. Indeed, those with fewer resources are more vulnerable to unemployment and may therefore may pay more attention to employment statistics. Likewise, they may be more concerned about the minimum wage, and at least as worried about inflation. Thus, it is not surprising that, once one controls for education and other factors, there is essentially no relation between earnings and macroeconomic test scores. This observation features prominently in the analysis below.

An Analysis of Self-Assessed Financial Knowledge

The 1993 Merrill Lynch household survey also contained an additional question designed to elicit a self-assessment of financial literacy. Specifically, respondents were asked:

> Do you consider yourself very financially knowledgeable, somewhat financially knowledgeable, only a little financially knowledgeable, or not at all financially knowledgeable?

Answers to this question reflect a blend of actual knowledge and self-confidence. It is therefore of interest to evaluate the accuracy of self-assessments by comparing them with test scores, and to examine systematic differences in self-assessments across population subgroups.

Table 4 provides average test scores (overall, financial, and macroeconomic) broken down by self-assessments of financial knowledge. This table reveals a strong correlation between self-assessments and test scores. Nevertheless, this correlation is, perhaps, less pronounced than one might imagine. The average overall score among those pronouncing themselves "very financially knowledgeable" was 67.1, corresponding to the 57th percentile, whereas the average overall score among those describing themselves as "not at all financially knowledgeable" was 58.9, corresponding to the 38th percentile. It is noteworthy that those who are,

TABLE 4 Mean Normalized Scores from a Test of Economic and Financial Knowledge versus Self-Assessed Financial Knowledge

	Mean normalized score		
Self-assessed knowledge	*Overall score*	*Financial score*	*Macroeconomic score*
Very financially knowledgeable	67.1	73.5	59.4
Somewhat financially knowledgeable	64.2	70.8	56.3
Only a little financially knowledgeable	59.7	65.9	52.3
Not at all financially knowledgeable	58.9	68.2	47.7

Source: Author's calculations. Sample taken from the 1993 Merrill Lynch household survey.
Note: Test scores are normalized to lie on a scale of 0 to 100, based on relative performance.

by their own account, "not at all financially knowledgeable" actually obtained a higher average financial score than those who called themselves "only a little financially knowledgeable." In contrast, the average macroeconomic score rises monotonically with self-assessed knowledge. This observation raises the possibility that self-assessments of *financial* knowledge might actually reflect *macroeconomic* knowledge more closely than financial knowledge. I return to this issue below.

Table 5 provides summary statistics for self-assessed knowledge for various population subgroups. For each subgroup, I report the fraction of respondents describing themselves as either "very financially knowledgeable" or "somewhat financially knowledgeable." Most of the patterns here are similar to those noted for test scores (Table 2). There is no apparent relation between age and self-assessed financial knowledge; the youngest and oldest baby boomers consider themselves equally well informed on financial matters. Males generally believe themselves to be more financially knowledgeable than females, and self-assessed financial knowledge rises with education and earnings. There are, however, some notable differences between the patterns exhibited in Tables 2 and 5. The quantitative impact of gender, education, and earnings are very similar in Table 2 (test scores). For example, average overall scores for males and females differ by 9.6 points, scores for those with and without college degrees differ by 7.7 points, and scores for those in the top and bottom earnings quartiles differ by 7.9 points. In contrast, the relation between self-assessed knowledge and earnings is much more pronounced than the relation between self-assessed knowledge and education, which is in turn more pronounced than the relation between self-assessed knowledge and gender. Specifically, the difference between the summary statistics reported for those in the top and bottom earnings quartiles in Table 3 is 0.201, compared to a difference of only 0.109 for those with and with-

TABLE 5 Demographic Patterns in Self-Assessed Financial Knowledge

Population subgroup	*Percent considering themselves either somewhat or very financially knowledgeable*
Age	
29–34	80.2
35–40	78.6
41–47	80.1
Gender	
Male	83.6
Female	75.8
Race	
White	80.2
Black	78.8
Education	
College degree	86.3
No college degree	75.4
Earnings	
First quartile	70.1
Second quartile	75.7
Third quartile	79.8
Fourth quartile	90.2

Source: Author's calculations. Sample taken from the 1993 Merrill Lynch Household Survey.

out college degrees, and a difference of 0.078 between men and women. In addition, there is practically no difference in self-assessed financial knowledge between whites and blacks, despite the differences in test scores noted in Table 2.

Of course, these preliminary observations are based on simple correlations. Estimates of probit specifications explaining high self-reported financial knowledge are presented in Table 6. The central patterns observed in Table 5 are unchanged: men have higher self-assessed knowledge than women; self-assessed knowledge is essentially unrelated to race, but rises with education. Notably, self-assessed knowledge is strongly related to earnings. Recall that, once other variables are controlled for, financial test scores are strongly related to earnings, while macroeconomic test scores are not. In this important respect, self-assessed financial knowledge behaves more like financial test scores than like macroeconomic test scores.

A comparison of the results in Tables 3 and 6 reveals that our explanatory variables affect test scores differently than they affect self-assessed

TABLE 6 Probit Regression Analysis, Explaining High Self-Assessed Financial Knowledge

Explanatory variable	*Coefficient*
Age/10^4	0.482
	(1.04)
Gender	0.293
	(0.116)*
Black	0.0913
	(0.280)
Earnings/10^7	66.6
	(21.0)†
Employment status	0.0968
	(0.160)
High school only	1.06
	(0.309)†
High school plus	1.16
(no college degree)	(0.305)†
College degree	1.34
	(0.309)
Constant	−1.07
	(0.505)*

Source: Author's calculations. Sample taken from the 1993 Merrill Lynch Household Survey.
Note: Estimates are based on a probit regression, which explains the probability that self-assessed financial knowledge is high. The dependent variable is set equal to 1 when self-assessed financial knowledge is high, and zero otherwise. Standard errors are in parentheses.
*Denotes statistical significance at 5% level.
†Denotes statistical significance at 1% level.

knowledge. Under the obviously debatable assumption that test scores accurately measure economic and financial knowledge,[12] this suggests that certain population subgroups may systematically overestimate or underestimate their financial sophistication. Young baby boomers are no more likely to be excessively or insufficiently confident than older baby boomers. The most obvious candidates for overconfidence include those with high earnings, those with high school diplomas, the nonworking, and blacks (alternatively, low earners, those not finishing high school, workers, and whites may be underconfident). College-educated individuals and women may also, on average, be overconfident in their financial sophistication.

The Relation Between Saving and Financial Knowledge.

Thus far, I have argued that many individuals are relatively ignorant of economic and financial matters, that they underappreciate their finan-

TABLE 7 Knowledge and Retirement Savings

	Stock of retirement savings as % of annual earnings	
	Median	*Mean*
Test score quartile		
4	37.6	87.3
3	28.3	69.7
2	22.2	52.8
1	14.9	42.1
Self-assessed financial knowledge		
Very	41.3	126
Somewhat	26.4	62.4
Only a little bit	13.5	33.2
Not at all	0.0	31.6

Source: Author's calculations. Sample taken from the 1993 Merrill Lynch Household Survey.

cial vulnerabilities, and that they save too little. It is natural to conjecture that these phenomena are related. If so, then there is reason to hope that behavior is responsive to education. I discuss direct evidence on the relation between education and behavior below. Here, I consider an intermediate question: does greater financial knowledge tend to promote more adequate saving?

There is, without any question, a powerful quantitative relation between economic knowledge and personal saving. As shown in Table 7, the median ratio of retirement savings to earnings for those receiving the highest test scores (those in the fourth quartile) was roughly two-and-a-half times as large as the median ratio of retirement savings to earnings for those receiving the lowest test scores (those in the first quartile). Similarly, the typical individual who describes him/herself as "very financially knowledgeable" has accumulated more than three times as much as the typical individual who describes him/herself as "only a little financially knowledgeable." Moreover, among those who consider themselves "not at all financially knowledgeable," the median individual has accumulated nothing for retirement. Similar patterns are observed for sample means.

These results do not, however, establish that individuals save more in response to the acquisition of economic knowledge. They are equally consistent with the possibility that individuals acquire economic knowledge after accumulating significant wealth, in order to manage their resources with greater competence. As observed above, people may pay little attention to mortgage rates until they have accumulated sufficient resources to purchase a house, and they may begin to follow the Dow Jones average only after making significant investments in the stock market. Consequently, the direction of causality in Table 7 is far from clear, and requires further analysis.

Although the accumulation of wealth provides one possible motivation for the acquisition of financial knowledge, the level of knowledge presumably varies significantly across the population for other reasons as well. If one can identify a portion of the variation in financial literacy that does not result from differences in wealth, then it should be possible to distinguish between the hypothesis that knowledge causes the accumulation of wealth, and the hypothesis that wealth causes the acquisition of knowledge. This is done through the use of an instrumental variable. In this context, an instrumental variable must be correlated with financial literacy, but must not itself be affected by wealth.

Above, I also noted that, although financial test scores are strongly related to earnings, macroeconomic test scores are not. This result is intuitive, since those with greater resources do not necessarily have a greater incentive to acquire macroeconomic knowledge. Nevertheless, the correlation between financial knowledge and macroeconomic knowledge is extremely high. Thus, an individual's macroeconomic test score is a plausible instrument for his or her financial test score.

Table 8 contains the results of two regressions that explain a measure of retirement wealth as a function of demographics, economic characteristics, and financial knowledge.[13] In the first of these, the potential endogeneity of the respondent's financial test score is ignored. As expected, there is a strong positive relation between wealth and the test score, even when one controls for a range of other household characteristics; however, this finding is consistent with the hypothesis that wealth causes the acquisition of financial knowledge. In the second regression, I treat the endogeneity of the financial test score by reestimating the specification using two-stage least squares, where macroeconomic test score serves as the instrument. Note that the estimated effect of education is actually stronger in the second (instrumented) equation than in the first. Thus, a strong relation between wealth and financial knowledge persists even when the causal effects of wealth on the acquisition of knowledge are removed.

The relative sizes of the coefficients on the financial test score variable may at first seem surprising. Even if knowledge does affect saving, one might expect to observe a weaker relation between wealth and knowledge after using an instrumental variable to remove some of the factors that cause these variables to be related. However, one must also recall that the respondent's financial test score measures actual financial knowledge with error. For standard econometric reasons, this measurement

TABLE 8 Regression Analysis Explaining a Measure of Accumulated Retirement Wealth

Explanatory variable	*Ordinary least squares estimates*	*Two-stage least squares estimates*
Financial test score	4.26	7.26
	(1.35)*	(2.94)†
Married	0.266	0.130
	(0.565)	(0.579)
Single male	0.005	−0.143
	(0.657)	(0.672)
Black	0.109	0.270
	(0.881)	(0.896)
Respondent's age	0.040	0.0412
	(0.028)	(0.0282)
Number of children	−0.206	−0.219
	(0.140)	(0.141)
Household earnings x 10^6	3.23	2.45
	(3.18)	(3.27)
High school only	1.34	1.20
	(1.00)	(1.01)
High school plus	1.53	1.24
	(0.99)	(1.02)
College degree	2.82	2.37
	(1.00)*	(1.08)†
Constant	−9.69	−11.4
	(1.73)*	(2.28)*

Source: Author's calculations. Sample taken from the 1993 Merrill Lynch Household Survey.
Notes: The dependent variable is ln[(RS + 1)/(EARN + 1)], where ln is the natural log, RS is the stock of retirement savings, and EARN is total annual household earnings. I take logs in recognition of the fact that the distribution of wealth is extremely skewed, in order to reduce the influence of outliers. I add 1 to the numerator and denominator to assure that the argument is strictly positive. Standard errors are in parentheses.
Statistical significance: * = 1% level, † = 5% level.

error biases the coefficient of financial knowledge toward zero. The use of an instrument treats both the endogeneity problem and the measurement error problem. Since these effects work in opposite directions, the coefficient of financial test score could, in theory, either rise or fall; in practice, it rises.

While these finding are consistent with the hypothesis that greater financial knowledge stimulates saving, my analysis has not proven causality. Even if there is no direct causal relation (in either direction) between macroeconomic knowledge and wealth, it is possible that these two variables are both systematically related to some unobserved third factor (e.g., the respondent's innate interest in economic issues). For this reason, it is particularly important to examine the effects of education directly.

Do Households Obtain Authoritative Advice and Guidance?

The fact that households are ill equipped to formulate complex, long-term financial plans does not necessarily imply that they will make poor decisions. In principle, individuals can seek advice and guidance from a variety of qualified sources, including professional financial planners. In practice, the market for professional guidance is highly imperfect (see Bernheim 1994b for a discussion of the reasons). Consequently, there is no reason to assume that the mere availability of qualified assistance translates into high-quality decision making. In this section, I examine empirical evidence concerning the extent to which households rely on different forms of guidance.

Table 9 summarizes data from the 1993 Merrill Lynch household survey concerning the relative importance of the five most common sources of financial information and advice (parents and other relatives, friends, personal judgment, financial professionals, and print media).[14] As in previous sections, the data are disaggregated by age, gender, race, education, and earnings. A number of interesting patterns are readily apparent. Younger baby boomers tend to rely more on parents and relatives and less on their personal judgment. The use of financial professionals appears to peak between ages 35 and 40. For women, parents and relatives are by far the dominant source of financial information and advice. In contrast, for men, parents and relatives rank third behind personal judgment, but these differences may not be representative given the small size of the black subsample. Surprisingly, college-educated individuals are, if anything, slightly less likely to rely on their own personal judgment. Parents and relatives are also less important as sources of financial information and advice for those with college degrees. College education and earnings are both correlated with greater reliance on financial professionals and print media. Those with higher earnings also tend to seek less information and advice from friends. Although those in the lowest earnings quartile rely to a much greater extent on personal judgment, and to a lesser extent on parents and relatives, earnings bear little systematic relation to the use of these sources beyond the lowest quartile.

Given the general state of financial literacy, it is worrisome that so many individuals rely primarily on their own judgment. In the majority of cases, reliance on parents, relatives, and friends amounts to the blind leading the blind. It is therefore noteworthy that somewhere in the neighborhood of 60 percent of virtually every population subgroup relies primarily on parents, relatives, friends, and personal judgment. The fraction relying on financial professionals and print media does not exceed 40 per-

TABLE 9 Primary Sources of Financial Information and Advice

Population subgroup	*Parents/ relatives* (%)	*Friends* (%)	*Personal judgment* (%)	*Financial professional* (%)	*Print media* (%)
Age					
29–34	34.9	7.8	22.6	9.1	17.7
35–40	27.1	6.3	25.6	16.5	17.3
41–47	23.0	8.0	29.3	11.1	20.2
Gender					
Male	21.5	7.2	29.9	11.5	23.8
Female	34.6	7.7	22.2	13.1	13.3
Race					
White	28.0	7.6	24.9	13.3	20.0
Black	36.4	0.0	36.4	3.0	15.2
Education					
College degree	23.6	9.3	24.0	15.3	23.3
No college degree	31.1	6.2	27.3	10.4	15.3
Earnings					
First quartile	24.7	10.9	32.2	9.2	10.3
Second quartile	29.5	11.0	18.5	12.1	19.1
Third quartile	27.2	5.8	26.6	11.6	21.4
Fourth quartile	29.5	4.6	23.1	15.6	24.3

Source: Author's calculations. Sample taken from the 1993 Merrill Lynch Household Survey.

cent for any population subgroup. Thus, it seems likely that most individuals lack an authoritative, reliable source of information and advice.

The Effects of Retirement Education in the Workplace

At this point, it is useful to summarize a number of key findings. Most Americans are not making adequate financial preparations for their futures. As a result, financial vulnerabilities are widespread. Poor financial planning tends to be associated with a failure to appreciate these vulnerabilities. Households generally exhibit an excessive degree of optimism concerning their financial status. This perceptual failure may reflect a more general problem of financial illiteracy. Although those with high earnings and college degrees tend to obtain higher scores for financial literacy, their scores still indicate substantial deficiencies. Finally, most households do not compensate for the lack of financial decision-making skills by seeking and obtaining assistance from qualified authorities.

In the past few years, numerous companies—particularly those that sponsor participant-directed plans—have moved to bridge the financial literacy gap by offering retirement education programs. In light of the evidence developed in the preceding sections, it is conceivable that these programs could have a significant impact on behavior. In this section, I review some of the existing evidence on this topic, and provide some new evidence.

Previous Studies

Much of the evidence on the effects of retirement education in the workplace is derived from qualitative surveys and case studies. According to Milne et al. (1995), 92 percent of 401(k) participants say that they read materials provided by their employers; of those, 44 percent say that they allocate their funds differently, and 33 percent say that they contribute more to their plans. Employers who enhanced their educational efforts also tend to report increases in participation (A. Foster Higgins & Co., Inc. 1994), and case studies frequently cite dramatic changes in behavior (Milne et al. 1995; Borleis and Wedell 1994).

Two recent studies provide formal econometric evidence on the effects of employer-based retirement education. One analysis, by Bernheim and Garrett (1996), is based on a fall 1994 Merrill Lynch household survey of roughly 2,000 individuals between the ages of 30 and 48. The authors examine the relations between various measures of saving and two key educational variables. The first measures whether the respondent's employer offers some sort of retirement education program, while the second indicates whether the respondent actually makes use of the program.

Conceptually, it may seem more appropriate to control for participation in educational programs, rather than the mere availability of such programs. The authors are concerned, however, about the possible effects of endogeneity. They provide various kinds of evidence in support of the proposition that education tends to be adopted as a remedial measure, and therefore is negatively correlated with factors that predispose respondents to save more. This means that cross-sectional relations between saving and the availability of education are probably conservative, in the sense that they understate the causal effect of education. It is conceivable, however, that the usage of education, conditional on availability, is positively correlated with the inclination to save. This could produce a spurious positive correlation between saving and educational usage.

Bernheim and Garrett's measures of employer-based retirement education are obviously coarse. Unfortunately, the 1994 Merrill Lynch household survey did not gather detailed descriptions of program structure and content. One must therefore view their study as an investigation of

TABLE 10 The Effects of Retirement Education in the Workplace: Results Based on a Survey of Households

	Availability of education, incremental effect	*Usage of education, incremental effect*
Total saving rate (%)		
First quartile	1.29*	1.83*
Median	1.65*	2.18*
Third quartile	0.82	1.04
Retirement saving rate (%)		
First quartile	0.60†	1.50*
Median	0.92*	1.83*
Third quartile	0.94	1.62*
Respondent's 401(k)		
Participation rate (%)	11.8*	19.5*
Balances, first quartile	1,113†	2,161*
Balances, median	2,508‡	2,826*
Balances, third quartile	6,084†	2,714
Spouse's 401(k)		
Participation rate (%)	9.5†	8.0†
Balances, first quartile	1,022‡	1,069*
Balances, median	420	1,205
Balances, third quartile	466	436

Source: Bernheim and Garrett (1996). Sample taken from the 1994 Merrill Lynch Household Survey.
Notes: Effects on saving rates and participation rates are measured in percentage points. Statistical significance: * = 99% level, † = 95% level, ‡ = 90% level.

the average effects of educational activities: it probably understates the effects of the best programs.

Key findings from Bernheim-Garrett are summarized in Table 10. Several robust patterns emerge. One is that the availability of education has a powerful effect on the typical respondent, raising the median total saving rate by 1.65 percent of income. This reflects a 28 percent increase over the median saving rate among those who do not have access to retirement education in the workplace (6 percent of income). Similarly, the median retirement saving rate rises by 0.92 percent of income, which is a 31 percent increase over the median retirement saving rate among those without access to employer-based retirement education (3 percent of income). Finally, median 401(k) balances increase by just over $2,500, which represents a 50 percent increase over median 401(k) balances among those without access to retirement education ($5,000). These effects represent large proportional changes, relative to those for whom education is unavailable.

Another conclusion is that the estimated effects for usage of education are generally greater than those for availability. This stands to reason. However, it is worth reiterating that one should exercise caution when interpreting the results for usage. Perhaps the strongest results (both in terms of proportional effect and in terms of statistical significance) are obtained for those who are least inclined to save (i.e., at the first saving quartile of the population distribution). In contrast, little or no effect is usually detected among those who are most inclined to save (i.e., those at the third quartile). This is exactly what one expects to find. If education nudges each household toward an appropriate mode of behavior, its impact on low and average savers should bear little resemblance to its impact on high savers; even the sign of the effect could be different. One exception is the substantial positive effect of educational availability on respondents' 401(k) balances among high savers ($6,084). It is particularly interesting that a stronger result is obtained for availability than for usage ($2,714). There is, however, a natural explanation. High savers may be constrained by plan limits on 401(k) contributions that are necessitated by nondiscrimination requirements. If education induces other employees to contribute more, then the respondent can contribute more as well, irrespective of whether he or she makes use of the education. Under this hypothesis, the primary factor determining the effect of education on 401(k) contributions at the third quartile would be availability, rather than usage, exactly as the results indicate.

Additional results illustrate that education has a particularly powerful effect on rates of participation in 401(k) plans. This is consistent with other findings indicating that education is most effective at modifying the behavior of those who are least inclined to save. Finally, the availability (and usage) of education at the respondent's workplace appears to have positive spillovers on choices made in the context of a spouse's 401(k) plan. The effects are, however, smaller than for respondents, and only statistically significant among those least inclined to save (i.e., at the first quartile, and for participation rates).

A second study, by Bayer, Bernheim, and Scholz (1996), analyzes employer surveys fielded by KPMG Peat Marwick in 1993 and 1994. KPMG Peat Marwick annually surveys roughly 1,000 plan sponsors, approximately half of which have 401(k) plans. There is an effort to survey the same firms in consecutive years, so it is possible to use the surveys as a short panel. The analysis of employer survey data is complementary to Bernheim and Garrett's (1996) use of household survey data. With employer survey data, one cannot investigate the effects of education on

TABLE 11 The Effects of Frequent Retirement Seminars in the Workplace: Results Based on a Survey of Employers

Incremental impact of frequent seminars on:	*Non-highly compensated*	*Highly compensated*	*All employees*
Participation rates (%)			
No fixed effects	11.5*	6.4†	8.2*
Fixed effects	12.1‡	6.6	7.7‡
Contribution rates (%)			
No fixed effects	0.8*	0.3	0.7*
Fixed effects	1.1†	−0.1	0.4

Source: Bayer, Bernheim, and Scholz (1996). Sample taken from the KPMG Peat Marwick employer survey.
Note: The coefficients in this table measure the incremental effects of offering frequent retirement seminars in the workplace. Statistical significance: * = 99% level, † = 95% level, ‡ = 90% level.

saving outside of pension plans. However, offsetting this disadvantage, one has access to more detailed data on the nature of education in the workplace, and more accurate data on choices (participation and contributions).

One of the key findings in Bayer-Bernheim-Scholz is that firms tend to establish or enhance educational offerings when participation rates are low among non-highly compensated workers. This finding supports the hypothesis that education is generally remedial, in the sense that it is intended to address inadequate retirement saving. As a consequence, cross-sectional relations between plan activity and education will tend to understate the effects of education.

The KPMG Peat Marwick survey provides information on the type of education offered, as well as the frequency. Types of programs are divided into print media (newsletters, plan descriptions, etc.) and seminars. There is no indication in the data that either participation or contributions are affected by programs that rely on print media. However, there is strong evidence that seminars—particularly frequent ones—are effective.

Some of the central findings of Bayer-Bernheim-Scholz are summarized in Table 11. All results are based on the pooled 1993 and 1994 samples. In addition to educational seminars, each regression controls for other educational initiatives (through newsletters and summary plan descriptions), matching rates, loan provisions, the number of investment options offered, the existence of other pension plans, the number of employees at the firm, the fraction of employees covered by the 401(k), and year.

As indicated, some regressions control for firm-specific fixed effects, while others do not.[15] Since employees' predispositions to save may differ systematically across firms, and since (as discussed above) these predispositions may be related to the employer's decision to offer retirement education, the inclusion of firm-specific fixed effects is potentially important. However, since the 1993 and 1994 samples are not identical, the inclusion of fixed effects significantly reduces sample size. Regressions without fixed effects are based on between 658 and 1,027 observations, while regressions with fixed effects are based on between 147 and 291 observations. Estimates with fixed effects therefore tend to be less precise. The inclusion of fixed effects may also increase the noise-to-signal ratio for the educational variable (measured changes may not be actual changes), which creates a bias that results in an understatement of the educational effect.

The coefficients reported in Table 11 measure the effects of instituting a program with frequent retirement seminars at a firm with no previous educational initiatives. An examination of these coefficients leads to two central conclusions. First, retirement seminars have substantial effects on overall rates of participation and contributions. Second, these effects appear to be concentrated among non-highly compensated employees. Although seminars may also affect the decisions of highly compensated employees, the evidence for this proposition is weak. The inclusion of fixed effects does not materially alter this qualitative picture, though (as expected) it does reduce the precision of the estimates.

Based on these estimates, one infers that the establishment of frequent seminars raises rates of participation for non-highly compensated employees by roughly 12 percentage points. To put this figure in perspective, consider the fact that the average participation rate among non-highly compensated employees is 59 percent for this sample. The contribution rate among non-highly compensated employees rises by roughly one percentage point (0.8 points without fixed effects, 1.1 points with fixed effects), which is large relative to an average contribution rate of 3 percent (for the non-highly compensated) in the sample. While participation rates for highly compensated employees rise by about 6 percentage points (versus an average of about 80 percent for the sample), there is little indication that education significantly affects the contribution rate of this group. For the reasons discussed above, these findings should be regarded as conservative.

Some New Evidence

More recently, I had an opportunity to design and administer a short survey to plan sponsors who attended a Merrill Lynch conference on

401(k)s. Surveys were mailed to the participants in advance of the conference so that respondents would have access to relevant company records. Approximately 200 employers were represented at the conference, of which roughly 20 percent (40 companies) completed surveys. While there is precedent in the academic literature for using small employer surveys to examine aspects of 401(k) plans (Papke, Petersen, and Poterba 1993), it is certainly natural to wonder whether the current survey is representative. It is possible to get some sense for this issue by comparing responses to those obtained from broader surveys.

Reported rates of participation in 401(k) plans averaged 71 percent, ranging from a low of 20 percent to a high of 98 percent; 89 percent match employee contributions, and 84 percent permit loans against plan balances. Of those providing education (78% of the total), 97 percent cover principles of asset allocation, 83 percent discuss retirement income needs, and 79 percent cover retirement income sources. All these numbers are similar to figures obtained from larger surveys that are regarded as representative.

Among respondents offering education, newsletters (69%) and other written materials (86%) were the most common forms of employee communications. However, more than half (55%) used seminars, 38% provided one-on-one counseling, 21 percent offered interactive software, and 16 percent sponsored participatory workshops. The most important reasons given for offering education, both among those with programs and among those thinking about establishing programs, were that "employees were not thinking enough about retirement" and to "increase participation generally." This reinforces the finding that education is remedial (and hence that cross-sectional relations between participation and education understate the effects of education).

Table 12 reports three regressions based on this 1995 survey. The first relates 401(k) participation rates to the availability of education, the availability of an employer match, the ability to take loans against plan balances, and the vintage of the 401(k) program (i.e., the number of years the program has been in effect). Despite the small size of the sample, the estimated effects of education and matching provisions are large and highly significant. Controlling for other factors, participation is, on average, 18.5 percentage points higher in firms that offer education. The estimated effects of matching and loan provisions are consistent with results based on the much larger KPMG Peat Marwick surveys. The regression also indicates that participation rates tend to be higher for older programs.

As discussed above, the survey also contained information on the type of education offered. Unfortunately, the sample size is too small to identify statistically significant differences between the effectiveness of differ-

TABLE 12 The Effects of Retirement Education in the Workplace: New Regression Analysis

Explanatory variable	Dependent variable		
	Participation rate (%)	*Participation rate (%)*	*Change in participation rate*
Education	18.5 (7.6)*	13.2 (8.2)‡	12.0 (4.8)*
High frequency	—	11.9 (7.6)‡	—
Match	23.6 (9.81)*	22.5 (9.6)*	5.0 (4.4)
Loan	−4.44 (9.15)	−9.1 (9.4)	−9.5 (4.5)*
Vintage	0.62 (0.35)†	0.46 (0.35)	—

Source: Author's calculations. Sample taken from the Merrill Lynch 401(k) Plan Sponsor Survey.
Note: The dependent variable is rate of participation. Effects are measured in percentage points. Statistical significance: * = 95% level, † = 90% level, ‡ = 85% level.

ent approaches. The one exception to this concerns the frequency of education interventions. Nearly one-third of respondents (32%) provide education monthly or quarterly, while 46 percent provide it at lower frequencies. The second regression in Table 12 adds a variable that indicates "high frequency" educational offerings, meaning programs with monthly or quarterly activities. The coefficients of "education" and "high frequency" are not estimated with a great deal of precision, owing to the small sample size. However, these estimates do provide some support for the view that frequency is a key determinant of impact. While the provision of low-frequency education raises participation rates on average by 13 percentage points, high-frequency education increases this rate on average by 25 points. This qualitative pattern is consistent with results based on the KPMG Peat Marwick survey.

The final regression in Table 12 is based on retrospective questions, which ask whether there have been any changes in educational offerings, matching rates, or loan provisions during the preceding five years. These variables are coded as +1 if the firm has become more aggressive or generous with respect to the activity in question, −1 if it has become less aggressive or generous, and 0 if there has been no change. Firms also reported their participation rates from five years before the survey was taken; using this response in combination with the current participation rate, I constructed the change in participation over a five-year period. This final regression is of considerable interest, since it removes one important source of potential bias by controlling for firm fixed effects. In some ways, it is superior to the panel estimates based on the KPMG sample, in that it covers a longer time frame and in that differencing may not have as large an effect on the noise-to-signal ratios for the independent variables (since the questions on current and past plan provisions are answered by the same individual).

The results demonstrate that changes in education are strongly related to changes in participation. This finding is broadly consistent with the result obtained from cross-sectional estimates. Notably, the coefficient of education proves far more robust to differencing than the coefficients of matching provisions or loans. Once again, this result is qualitatively similar to that obtained with the KPMG Peat Marwick sample.[16]

Conclusion

This chapter reviews existing evidence and presents new evidence concerning the financial status of American workers. This evidence depicts a crisis in financial planning. Most Americans are not making prudent financial decisions. To a large extent, they are unaware of their financial vulnerabilities, and they lack the knowledge, sophistication, and/or authoritative guidance required to set them on the right track. The evidence suggests that improvements in economic and financial education and training could go a long way toward encouraging greater saving.

Appendix: Economic and Financial Test Questions

Financial knowledge

What is the current Dow Jones Industrial average?

For people who pay federal income taxes, what is the lowest income tax bracket?

What is the 30 year conventional mortgage rate right now?

If you deposited $1,000 and earned 8%, compounded annually, over thirty years, at the end of this period would you have earned more or less than $5,000?

Why do mutual funds typically have higher rates of return than federally insured bank CDS? (Options: (1) It's the law; (2) Mutual funds are bigger; (3) Mutual funds are riskier; (4) Inflation)

Which investment situation would you prefer: a chance to earn 8% when inflation is at 6%, or a chance to earn 5% when inflation is at 1%?

Macroeconomic knowledge

What is the current national unemployment rate?

What is the national minimum wage?

What is the annual rate of inflation?

What is the size of the total federal debt?

What is the size of the total federal debt per household?

I am indebted to Laurence Kotlikoff, Brett Hammond, Steven Ross, and Olivia Mitchell for valuable comments and suggestions. Financial support from National Science Foundation (Grant Number SBR-9409043 and Grant Number SBR95-11321), Merrill Lynch, and an anonymous private foundation is gratefully acknowledged. I would also like to thank Merrill Lynch, Inc. for collecting much of the data required to conduct this study.

Notes

1. Although Kotlikoff, Spivak, and Summers (1982) dispute this finding, they attribute the adequacy of retirement preparation to an enormous unanticipated increase in Social Security benefits, rather than to adequate saving.

2. Even if baby boomers are unable to maintain their preretirement standards of living after retirement, they may still fare well in comparison to retirees of previous generations. According to a study conducted by the Congressional Budget Office (1993), baby boomers have significantly higher real incomes and greater accumulated wealth than their parents did at comparable ages. Kingson (1992), Easterlin, Schaeffer, and Macunovich (1993), Cantor and Yuengert (1994), and Yakoboski and Silverman (1994) have reached similar conclusions. While these findings appear to suggest that baby boomers are on track to match or exceed their parents' standard of living during retirement, caution is warranted for a number of reasons; see Bernheim (1994c).

3. See Bernheim (1993, 1994a, 1994b). Arthur D. Little, Inc. (1993) concurs that even those with pension plans typically will have only 50–60 percent of what they need to retire comfortably.

4. A study by Auerbach and Kotlikoff (1994) demonstrates that deep cuts in Social Security, or steep increases in taxes, will be required to achieve long-run fiscal balance between revenues and expenditures. Bernheim (1994a, 1995a) analyzes the importance of these policy scenarios for the adequacy of saving by baby boomers.

5. Shultz (1996). The article references a recently released survey of 520 plan sponsors, conducted by RogersCasy, a pension-consulting firm.

6. *Pensions and Investments* (1995).

7. See Bernheim (1995b) and Bernheim and Garrett (1996) for discussions of the accuracy and representativeness of the data contained in the Merrill Lynch household surveys.

8. The measure of wealth used in this analysis is total nonhousing wealth, including financial assets, real property, and business interests, net of debt. For married couples, I use the combined earnings of both spouses.

9. Formally, this is accomplished by estimating three quantile regressions (median, first quartile, and third quartile), explaining the wealth-to-earnings ratio as a function of household characteristics. Households are then placed into adjusted-wealth quartiles based on the relation between their actual wealth-to-earnings ratios and the fitted ratios from the quantile regressions.

10. See for example Walstad and Soper (1988), Walstad and Larsen (1992), Jordon (1993), the Consumer Federation of America and the American Express Company (1991), and Crenshaw (1993).

11. Suppose, for example, that we ask three individuals, A, B, and C, the same question. Suppose that the true answer is "5," that A answers "6," B answers "8," and C answers "0." Then A would receive a score of 100, B would receive a score of 67, and C would receive a score of 33.

12. The test of economic knowledge contained in the Merrill Lynch survey is obviously imperfect. Some discrepancies between self-assessed knowledge and test scores may be attributable to subtle biases. In particular, cultural bias may account for the disparate effects of race in Tables 3 and 6. Consider, for example, the question on the national unemployment rate. It is well known that survey respondents often reinterpret questions, providing answers that are more relevant to their own circumstances. Blacks might well report an unemployment figure that is accurate for blacks, but not for the general population. A closer inspection of answers to this particular question reveals that, although the median rate of unemployment reported by blacks and whites is identical (8 percent), a far larger fraction of blacks report rates in excess of 15 percent. Thus, it appears that a sizable minority of black respondents may be interpreting the question differently than intended, and providing an answer that is both more relevant, and more accurate, for their circumstances.

13. The dependent variable is $\ln[(RS+1)/(EARN+1)]$, where ln is the natural log, RS is retirement savings, and EARN is total household earnings. I take logs in recognition of the fact that the distribution of wealth is extremely skewed, in order to reduce the influence of outliers. I add 1 to the numerator and denominator to assure that the argument is strictly positive.

14. One notable omission from this list is information disseminated by government agencies (e.g., the Social Security Administration). As sources of information and advice on financial planning, government sources ranked behind "prayer," which was volunteered by a surprising number of respondents.

15. When firm-specific fixed effects are omitted, we correct the estimated standard errors by allowing for a correlation between observations on the same firm.

16. The estimated effects of education are generally larger for the Merrill Lynch employer survey sample than for the KPMG Peat Marwick sample. It is certainly possible that firms in attendance at the Merrill Lynch conference tended to have more aggressive education programs than the typical firm. It is also possible that the conference sample measures vendor-specific effects. In either case, the results suggest that the impact of the best educational programs may be significantly larger than that of the average program, as inferred from the broader KPMG Peat Marwick sample.

References

A. Foster Higgins & Co., Inc. "Survey of Employee Savings Plans, 1994, Report 2: Plan Participation and Discrimination Testing." Princeton, N.J.: A. Foster Higgins & Co., 1994.

Alliance Against Fraud in Telemarketing. "Top Emerging Scams of 1992." Washington, D.C.: Alliance Against Fraud in Telemarketing, Winter 1992.

Arthur D. Little, Inc. "America's Retirement Crisis: The Search for Solutions." Final Report to Oppenheimer Management Corporation, June 1993.

Auerbach, Alan J. and Laurence J. Kotlikoff. "The United States' Fiscal and Saving Crises and Their Implications for the Baby Boom Generation." Merrill Lynch, Pierce, Fenner & Smith, Inc., February 1994.

Bayer, Patrick J., B. Douglas Bernheim, and J. Karl Scholz. "The Effects of Financial Education in the Workplace: Evidence from a Survey of Employers." Stanford, Calif.: Dept of Economics, Stanford University, mimeo, 1996.

Berg, Olena. "DOL to Launch Savings and Pension Education Campaign." *EBRI Notes,* June 1995: 2.

Bernheim, B. Douglas. "Is the Baby Boom Generation Preparing Adequately for Retirement? Summary Report." New York: Merrill Lynch, Pierce, Fenner & Smith, Inc., January 1993.

———. "The Merrill Lynch Baby Boom Retirement Index." New York: Merrill Lynch, Pierce, Fenner & Smith, Inc., July 1994. 1994a.

———. "Personal Saving, Information, and Economic Literacy: New Directions for Public Policy." In Charles E. Walker, Mark Bloomfield and Margo Thorning, eds. *Tax Policy for Economic Growth in the 1990s,* Washington, D.C.: American Council for Capital Formation, 1994: 53–78. 1994b.

———. "The Adequacy of Saving for Retirement: Are the Baby Boomers on Track?" In Dallas Salisbury and Nora S. Jones, eds., *Retirement in the 21st Century: Ready or Not?* Washington, D.C.: Employee Benefit Research Institute, 1994: 73–82. 1994c.

———. "The Merrill Lynch Baby Boom Retirement Index: Update '95." Merrill Lynch, Pierce, Fenner & Smith, Inc., mimeo, 1995. 1995a.

———. "Do Households Appreciate Their Financial Vulnerabilities? An Analysis of Actions, Perceptions, and Public Policy." In *Tax Policy and Economic Growth in the 1990s,* Washington, D.C.: American Council for Capital Formation, 1995: 3–30. 1995b.

Bernheim, B. Douglas and Daniel M. Garrett. "The Determinants and Consequences of Financial Education in the Workplace: Evidence from a Survey of Households." Stanford, Calif. Department of Economics: Stanford University, mimeo, 1996.

Borleis, Melvin W. and Kimberly K. Wedell. "How to Spark Employee Interest with Employer Matching Contributions." *Profit Sharing,* January 1994: 7–16.

Cantor, Richard and Andrew Yuengert. "The Baby Boom Generation and Aggregate Savings." New York: Federal Reserve Bank of New York, mimeo, 1994.

Congressional Budget Office (CBO). "Baby Boomers in Retirement: An Early Perspective." ACBO Study, Washington, D.C., September 1993.

Consumer Federation of America and the American Express Company. "High School Competency Test Report of Findings." Working Paper, Washington, D.C., 1991.

Crenshaw, Albert B. "For Too Many, Managing Money Isn't Child's Play." *Washington Post,* October 3, 1993: B1–B3.

Diamond, Peter A. "A Framework for Social Security Analysis." *Journal of Public Economics* 8, 3 (December 1977): 275–98.

Easterlin, Richard A., Christine M. Schaeffer, and Diane J. Macunovich. "Will the Baby Boomers Be Less Well Off Than Their Parents? Income, Wealth, and Family Circumstances over the Life Cycle." Los Angeles: University of Southern California, mimeo, 1993.

Faber, R. and T. O'Guinn. "Compulsive Consumption and Credit Abuse." *Journal of Consumer Policy* 11 (1989): 97–109.

Feenberg, Daniel and Jonathan Skinner. "Sources of IRA Saving." *Tax Policy and the Economy* (1989): 25–46. V3

Hamermesh, Daniel S. "Consumption During Retirement: The Missing Link in the Life Cycle." *Review of Economics and Statistics* 66, 1 (February 1984): 1–7.

Milne, Deborah, Jack Vanderhei and Paul Yakoboski. "Can We Save Enough to Retire? Participant Education in Defined Contribution Plans." *EBRI Issue Brief* No. 160: Washington, D.C.: Employee Benefits Research Institute, April 1995: 3–23.

Hira, Tahira K. "Financial Management Knowledge and Practices: Implications for Financial Health." Iowa State University, mimeo, 1993.

Jordan, Mary. "90 Million Lack Simple Literacy." *Washington Post,* September 9, 1993: A1, A5.

Kahneman, Daniel, Paul Slovic, and Amos Tversky. *Judgment Under Uncertainty: Heuristics and Biases.* Cambridge: Cambridge University Press, 1982.

Kingson, Eric. "The Diversity of the Baby Boom Generation: Implications for Their Retirement Years." American Association of Retired Persons, Monograph, Washington, D.C., April 1992.

Kotlikoff, Laurence, Steven Johnson, and William Samuelson. "Can People Compute? An Experimental Test of the Life Cycle Consumption Model." NBER Working Paper No. 2183, 1987.

Kotlikoff, Laurence, Avia Spivak, and Laurence Summers. "The Adequacy of Savings." *American Economic Review* 72, 5 (December 1982): 1056–69.

Levin, Laurence. "Are Assets Fungible? Testing Alternative Theories of Life-Cycle Savings." Santa Clara, Calif.: Santa Clara University, mimeo, 1992.

O'Neill, Barbara. *How Real People Handle Their Money: 35 Financial Planning Case Studies.* New Brunswick, N.J.: Rutgers Cooperative Extension Publications, 1990.

——. "Assessing America's Financial IQ: Realities, Consequences, and Potential for Change." Rutgers Cooperative Extension, mimeo, 1993.

Papke, Leslie E., Mitchell Petersen, and James M. Poterba. "Did 401(k) Plans Replace Other Employer Provided Pensions?" NBER Working Paper No. 4501, October 1993.

Pensions and Investments. "Employees Getting More: Investment Education, Planning Help on the Increase." January 23, 1995: 74.

Schultz, Ellen E. "Executives See Trouble in Employee's Nest Eggs." *Wall Street Journal,* March 27, 1996: C1.

Shefrin, Hersh and Richard Thaler. "Life Cycle vs. Self-Control Theories of Saving: A Look at the Evidence." Unpublished mimeo, 1983.

——. "The Behavioral Life-Cycle Hypothesis." *Economic Inquiry* 26 (1988): 609–43.

Walstad, William B. and Max Larsen. "A National Survey of American Economic Literacy." National Council on Economics Education, Monograph, Washington, D.C., July 1992.

Walstad, William B. and John C. Soper. "A Report Card on the Economic Literacy of U.S. High School Students." *American Economic Review* 78, 2 (May 1988): 251–56.

Warshawsky, Mark. "Sensitivity to Market Incentives: The Case of Policy Loans." *Review of Economics and Statistics* 69, 2 (May 1987): 286–95.

Yakoboski, Paul and Celia Silverman. "Baby Boomers in Retirement: What Are Their Prospects?" *EBRI Special Report and Issue Brief* No. 151. Washington, D.C.: Employee Benefits Research Institute, July 1994.

Chapter 4
Factors Affecting Participation Rates and Contribution Levels in 401(k) Plans

Robert L. Clark and Sylvester J. Schieber

In recent years there has been a growing dependence on section 401(k) plans that require voluntary employee contributions as a primary source of retirement plan funding. Table 1 shows the growth in the role of 401(k) plans in the private, employer-sponsored retirement system between 1984 and 1992. In 1984, 2.9 percent of all private plans and 4.0 percent of all private defined contribution plans had a 401(k) feature. By 1992, 19.7 percent of all plans and 22.5 percent of the defined contribution plans included a 401(k) feature. In 1984, 12.4 percent of all plan participants and 24.6 percent of all defined contribution participants were in a 401(k) plan. By 1992 this had grown to 34.9 and 57.6 percent respectively. Over the period, the percentage of assets in 401(k) plans grew from 8.8 to 26.4 percent of all plan assets and from 35.7 to 45.8 of defined contribution plan assets. Contributions to 401(k) plans grew from 18.0 to 50.0 percent of all contributions to private plans and from 37.5 to 68.7 percent of contributions to private defined contribution plans.

By most measures, it appears that 401(k) plans are becoming the predominant form of retirement saving through employer-sponsored plans as we come to the close of the twentieth century. This development has not met with universal endorsement. Some critics of 401(k) plans suggest that "do-it-yourself" retirement plans leave many with inadequate retirement accumulations. They argue that workers may start to save too late in life and end up accumulating less than they need for retirement; they may select overly conservative investment options that provide inadequate returns; or they may simply save too little over their working lives.

TABLE 1 Relative Sizes of 401(k) Plans in Comparison to All Private Tax-Qualified Plans and All Private Defined Contribution Plans for Selected Years (%)

	Plans		*Participants*		*Assets*		*Contributions*	
Year	*All plans*	*DC plans*	*All plans*	*DC plans*	*All plans*	*DC plans*	*All plans*	*DC plans*
1984	2.9	4.0	12.4	24.6	8.8	35.7	18.0	37.5
1985	4.7	6.5	16.6	31.1	11.5	36.9	25.6	45.7
1986	5.2	6.9	18.3	33.4	13.2	39.6	31.9	50.1
1987	6.1	7.9	20.7	37.6	15.4	40.9	36.0	53.3
1988	9.3	11.7	24.5	44.6	18.4	41.3	43.2	60.7
1989	11.4	13.9	28.3	51.0	21.3	41.8	47.1	63.0
1990	13.7	16.3	31.6	55.1	23.0	41.7	49.6	64.7
1991	15.9	18.6	31.1	53.5	22.7	42.5	46.4	63.6
1992	19.7	22.5	34.9	57.6	26.4	45.8	50.0	68.7

Source: USDOL (1996).

In addition, critics claim that the accessibility to 401(k) savings prior to retirement means that many workers will end up at retirement with little or nothing left in their old-age nest egg (Ferguson and Blackwell, 1995). Others argue that people fail to participate in 401(k) plans because they do not appreciate their economic vulnerabilities or the favorable saving opportunities that voluntary retirement plans offer them (Bernheim, 1994, 1995). While mandating contributions and locking them into 401(k) plans might be perceived as a good way to enhance the retirement security of current workers, one estimate suggests that a mandatory 3 percent contribution rate would only raise aggregate pension benefits for workers participating in employer programs less than 2 percent (Samwick and Skinner, 1997).

The growing reliance on voluntary contributory retirement plans increases the importance of participation in these plans. In this study, we examine the factors associated with variations in participation rates and workers' contribution levels in a number of 401(k) plans based on personal data records of workers eligible to participate in these plans. The analysis is restricted to a set of employers that offer 401(k) plans. In that regard, it does not consider the potential biases in saving behavior of workers who seek out and tend to stay with employers offering such plans (Ippolito, 1993). We provide a brief review of other studies that have evaluated participation in 401(k) plans. Next, we describe the data set used for the analysis and summarize the general nature of the plans offered and the participation in them, followed by statistical analyses of participation in and contribution rates to the plans under study.

Previous Research

Relatively few empirical studies have examined the probability that individual workers will contribute to a 401(k) plan and each of these studies has important data limitations. Here we briefly review five articles that have examined 401(k) participation rates and/or the annual contribution into these plans, and draw some preliminary findings and identify major shortcomings in the data employed in these earlier studies. Detailed analysis of 401(k) contributions requires information on individual workers and plan characteristics. These data need to be from a set of representative firms in order to capture variation in match rates and other plan parameters. To date, no study has had access to data of this quality. Thus, one must be cautious in interpreting the results from prior studies concerning the participation in 401(k) plans.

Andrews (1992) presents data showing the growth of 401(k) coverage during the 1980s using the Form 5500 data. Her analysis included firms where the 401(k) plan was either the primary or secondary pension plan. Andrews then used the May 1988 Current Population Survey (CPS) to examine the determinants of participation in 401(k) plans. She estimated the probability that a worker would be participating in a 401(k) plan and found that the likelihood of being in a plan rose with increases in age, earnings, family income, and tenure. In addition, Andrews estimated that employer contributions increased the probability that a worker would participate in the 401(k) plan but that individuals with other pension coverage were less likely to participate. An important limitation to the CPS data is the lack of data on plan characteristics such as the employer match rate.

Andrews also estimated the amount of annual contributions conditional on 401(k) participation. Key findings were that older persons had higher contribution rates, as did workers with larger family income; however, increases in annual earnings did not raise 401(k) contribution rates. Individuals enrolled in plans with employer matches tended to contribute less to the 401(k) plans.

The Employee Benefit Research Institute study (EBRI 1994) compares information from the CPS from May 1988 with April 1993. Between these surveys, the proportion of workers employed by firms offering 401(k) plans increased from 26.9 percent to 36.8 percent. During this period, the participation rate for all workers increased from 15.3 to 23.8 percent. The fraction of those eligible to participate in a 401(k) plan rose from 57.0 to 64.6 percent. The report presents sponsorship and participation rates by age, earnings, sex, and hours worked. Comparisons indicated that the participation rate in plans with an employer match was slightly higher (78 percent) than participation rate in plans without an employer match (72 percent).

Further cross-tabulations indicate a nonlinear age relationship, with participation rates rising with age until around 50 and then declining. In addition, the participation rate is shown to increase with higher levels of annual earnings. EBRI also reports a nonlinear relationship between earnings and the proportion of salary contributed to the 401(k) plan with the annual contribution rate rising with earnings up to $20,000 and then declining before increasing again for persons with earnings in excess of $30,000. The contribution rate is lower for participants in plans with employer matches compared to plans without an employer contribution.

Papke (1995) uses Form 5500 data for 1986 and 1987 to estimate participation and contribution rates. A significant shortcoming of this analysis is the lack of marginal employer match rates. Papke calculates an average match rate using aggregate employer and employee contribution rates for each plan. The participation ratio for each plan is determined by the ratio of active plan participants to the number of employees eligible to participate. Participants include all persons with positive account balances. She then estimates a plan participation rate using plan average data as a function of firm size, the presence of another pension, and a series of dichotomous variables indicating the level of the employer match. Thus, this study is unable to capture the effects of any worker characteristics such as age and earnings.

Papke's primary finding is that increases in the match rate are associated with increases in the plan participation rate; however, these marginal effects are rather small. For example, a 20 percent employer match increases the plan participation rate compared to a plan with no employer contributions by 6.6 percentage points and a 50 percent match raises the participation by 10.2 percentage points compared to a plan with no employer match. A dollar for dollar match increases the participation rate by 17.4 percentage points over a zero match. In addition, she finds that the participation rate rises slightly (1.2 percentage points) when the company does not have another pension plan and that increases in firm size decrease participation in the 401(k) plan. There is no change in the participation model between 1986 and 1987.

Papke estimates a fixed effects model to control for unobservable factors that are affecting the participation rate such as the fact that some firms attract workers who are more likely to be savers. The estimated effects for the match rates in the fixed effects model are much smaller and are statistically insignificant. Papke concludes "that match rates do not affect the level of participation once plan unobservables are controlled for." She speculates that the efforts of benefit staff and the quality of their communications may be one of the unobservables affecting participation rates.

Papke also examines annual employee contributions using the same model. She finds that contributions are higher in plans with employer matches up to 80 percent compared to a plan with no match; however, the marginal effect of increasing the match rate above 10 percent are small, generally insignificant, and often negative. Plans with matches in excess of 80 percent have lower employee contributions compared to plans without any employer match.

Kusko, Poterba, and Wilcox (this volume) estimate employee contributions to a 401(k) plan sponsored by a single medium-sized manufacturing firm between 1988 and 1991. The employer match rates varied substantially during this period from 25 percent of the first 6 percent of eligible compensation in one year to over 100 percent in another before the match was entirely eliminated in the final year. The data represent information on 12,000 salaried and nonunion hourly employees. Annual participation rates varied from 78 to 84 percent with only those actually making contributions in a given year being counted as participants.

The large changes in the match rate from one year to the next resulted in only small changes in the annual participation rate while changes in the match rate had a small but noticeable effect on the contribution rates of participants. The authors report large bunching of participants at the maximum plan contribution limit of 10 percent of compensation, the maximum employee contributions that receive an employer match (6 percent of compensation), and the IRS contribution limits of $7,000. They report that three-quarters of all employees are at one of the kinks or constraints and that participants rarely change their contribution levels to reflect changes in the plan structure.

Bernheim and Garrett (1995) evaluate the effects of employer-based education programs on participation in retirement plans. This analysis is based on a survey of household finances done during the fall of 1994. The survey covered a nationally representative sample of people between the ages of 30 and 48. It gathered standard economic and demographic data on the respondents plus levels of knowledge on financial matters, sources of information on such matters, and information on financial education or information provided in the workplace. The data used in the analysis did not include information on matching of worker contributions to 401(k) or similar plans covering workers. The authors developed two measures of educational information for the participants in the survey. The first was a binary variable indicating whether the employer offered informative materials and programs to assist in retirement planning. The second was a binary variable indicating whether the employee used such materials.

Burnheim and Garrett estimated that participation rates were 19.5 percentage points higher for workers who used educational materials than for those who did not receive or use such materials. They found that participation was lower for workers eligible for another pension plan, higher for workers with higher wages, and not significantly different on the basis of worker's age or education. The authors also estimated that the effects of education were large and highly significant on contribution levels to the plans. Finally, they found that there were spillover effects from communications programs positively affecting workers' spouses' participation in their own 401(k) plans, but found the effect on spouses' accumulated balances to be insignificant.

Although research examining participation in and contributions to 401(k) plans is very limited, several consistent findings have emerged. These previous studies suggest that the probability of participation is a positive but nonlinear function of age and annual earnings, that higher employer match rates raise the likelihood of participation, that the presence of other company pensions reduces the proportion of workers participating in 401(k) plans, and that a lower percentage of workers in large firms opt to participate in 401(k) plans. Annual contributions as a percent of salary rise with age of the worker while higher employee matching rates seem to reduce annual contributions. These findings suggest an empirical model for estimating the determinants of 401(k) participation and contributions. Each of these hypotheses will be tested using a relatively large number of workers employed during 1994 in a number of firms from which we could get administrative record data.

New Empirical Evidence

The data used in the present analysis were collected by Watson Wyatt from employer administrative records at the end of 1994. The 401(k) plans included in the data set represent 19 firms ranging in size from 700 to 10,000 employees from a variety of industries, have a wide range of match rates, and include some firms with relatively generous defined benefit plans in addition to the 401(k) plan as well as firms whose only retirement plan is the 401(k) plan. These 19 firms were not randomly selected, but were rather a set of firms where we could accumulate the necessary data to develop the analysis. While these firms are not statistically representative of the universe of firms sponsoring 401(k) plans, we have no reason to believe that the firms, their 401(k) plan, or the workers eligible to participate in them have characteristics that would specifically bias our results.

The analysis of participation in a range of 401(k) plans presented below allows us to explore some of the hypotheses elaborated above in somewhat more detail. We have the benefit of having administrative records on employee wage levels, contribution and match rates, and other variables that workers sometimes have difficulty recalling in survey settings. We can also control for the existence of a defined benefit plan, and further can estimate the overall generosity of such plans. Like many other studies in this area, we lack information on the nonpension assets owned by workers covered under the plans being studied or by other persons in their immediate families.

The general characteristics of the plans are summarized in Table 2, which describes plan incentives that might influence participation rates and contribution levels and shows 401(k) coverage and participation rates in each of the plans studied. The second column of the table shows the employer matching pattern in the various plans. All of the plans included in this study match some level of employee contributions. While the majority of plans have a constant matching rate, there are a number that have variable rates. Plans O, Q, and R are somewhat different than normal in that they provide for some matching, but limit it in a relatively unique fashion. Plan O restricts matching to workers with pay levels below $50,000 and matches contributions on up to 4 percent of the first $30,000 of pay. Plan Q matches only 25 percent of the first $400 per year that the worker contributes to the plan but contributes $0.12 for each hour worked under the plan. Plan R matches 25 percent of contributions up to the first $3,000 per year contributed to the plan without regard to pay level. The third column in the table shows the maximum percentage of pay on which contributions are matched by the plan sponsor. For all but three of the plans, the sponsor matches contributions on amounts up to 2 to 6 percent of pay, with the modal rate being 6 percent.

The fourth column in the table shows the relative generosity of the defined benefit plan offered by the sponsor of the 401(k) plan under study. This measure was derived by calculating a projected defined benefit pension at age 65 and the potential replacement of projected earnings for the year prior to retirement under that plan for workers eligible to participate in that firm's 401(k) plan. Job tenure and age was used to project each worker's ultimate years of coverage under the defined benefit plan, assuming the worker stayed until age 65. Covered pay under the plan was projected by incrementing current pay by 5 percent per year from 1994 until the year the worker would attain age 65. The average defined benefit level presented in the table is stated as a percent of final salary for the average worker.

The reason for including the generosity of the defined benefit plan in the analysis relates to the nature of the employer-sponsored retirement plans as target savings vehicles that allow workers to accumulate sufficient wealth to maintain preretirement standards of living after they retire. If

TABLE 2 Matching Provisions of 401(k) Plans, Generosity of Defined Benefit Plans, Workers Covered in the 401(k) Plans, and Participation Rates for Individual Plans

Plan	*Employer matching rates and patterns*	*Maximum percent of pay matched*	*Average defined benefit replacement rate at 65*	*Number of employees*	*Participation rate*
A	50%	6%	33.4	1,853	78.7
B	100% of 2% of pay, 75% of next 1% of pay, 50% of next 1% of pay	4%	45.6	1,627	62.8
C	100%	3%	27.8	3,458	76.84
D	50%	6%	18.9	1,422	91.8
E	25%	6%	21.5	864	81.9
F	60%	4%	26.1	1,372	93.1
G	25%	4%	0.0	1,660	90.7
H	100% of 1% of pay, 25% of next 3% of pay	4%	25.9	5,746	97.7
I	100%	3%	20.7	9,637	61.5
J	25%	6%	27.9	1,342	65.4
K	100%	3%	41.1	9,598	88.9
L	50%	2%	0.0	2,388	53.2
M	50%	6%	32.2	1,891	98.8
N	50%	6%	38.7	10,585	47.4
O	25% for workers with pay up to $50,000 on pay up to $30,000 per year	4%	22.4	2,035	58.7
P	75%	6%	*	774	91.5
Q	$0.12 per hour, 25% up to first $400 or employee contributions		*	750	56.8
R	25% on first $3,000 of employee contributions		0.0	966	71.2
S	100%	6%	*	2,951	91.4

Source: Authors' computations using Watson Wyatt Worldwide data.
*Signifies company had no defined benefit plan.

TABLE 3 Average Contributions to 401(k) Plans by Age of Worker for Workers Aged 21 to 64 with Annual Wages $5,000 or Above and One or More Years Tenure

Contribution quintile	*Average contribution by age of participant ($)*					
	20–29	*30–39*	*40–49*	*50–59*	*60+*	*All ages ($)*
1st 20%	177	348	427	458	379	338
2nd 20%	440	816	1,049	1,136	955	825
3rd 20%	708	1,348	1,777	1,970	1,717	1,436
4th 20%	1,137	2,178	2,844	3,378	3,061	2,418
5th 20%	2,609	4,918	6,178	6,983	6,542	5,592
Total participants	6,081	16,254	13,809	7,338	1,263	44,745
Mean contribution	1,014	1,921	2,455	2,785	2,533	2,122
No. at limit*	1	94	255	206	33	589
% at limit	0.02	0.58	1.85	2.81	2.61	1.32

Source: Authors' computations using Watson Wyatt Worldwide data.
*In 1994, federal tax law limited a worker's pretax contributions to a 401(k) plan to $9,240 of earnings.

employer-sponsored retirement plans do work as target savings vehicles, the more generous a worker's defined benefit plan, the less he or she would have to save under the 401(k) plan to accumulate sufficient wealth to meet the retirement savings target.

The last two columns in Table 2 show the number of employees eligible to participate in each of the 401(k) plans under study, and the plan's participation rate during 1994. In order to be considered a plan participant, a worker had to have contributed to the plan during 1994. Participation rates ranged from a low 47.4 percent to a high of 98.8 percent; the overall participation rate across the whole set of plans during 1994 was 73.5 percent.

Average contribution rates by plan participants distributed by age appear in Table 3. The table excludes nonparticipants. The number of participants shown at the bottom of the table as being at their maximum dollar contribution limit imposed by the IRS reflects the number in each age group that contributed the statutory maximum of $9,240 to their 401(k) during 1994. We find it surprising that so relatively few workers contributed at this level—fewer than 3 percent even for the older age groups. Generally, contribution levels confirm our expectations that older workers would contribute at higher levels than younger ones. The one exception is that average contributions at each quintile level for workers over age 60 are lower than for workers in their fifties at the same quintile level. Workers age 60 and over have somewhat lower wage levels than workers aged 50 to 59. As a result the lower dollar contributions actually represent higher contribution rate, as we show later (see Table 6).

TABLE 4 Average Contributions to 401(k) Plans by Workers Aged 21 to 64 with Annual Wages $5,000 or Above and One or More Years Tenure

Contribution quintile	*Average contribution by annual salary of participant (thousands of $)*					*All salary levels ($)*
	0–25	*25–50*	*50–75*	*75–100*	*100+*	
1st 20%	172	544	1,200	1,922	2,865	338
2nd 20%	404	1,103	2,001	3,007	5,200	825
3rd 20%	635	1,621	2,843	4,251	7,521	1,436
4th 20%	949	2,410	4,311	6,377	9,078	2,418
5th 20%	1,832	4,811	7,520	8,738	9,240	5,592
Total participants	14,680	19,832	7,683	1,641	909	44,745
Mean contribution	798	2,098	3,575	4,861	6,785	2,122
No. at limit	0	0	217	117	255	589
% at limit	0.0	0.0	2.8	7.1	28.1	1.3

Source: Authors' computations using Watson Wyatt Worldwide data.

TABLE 5 Participation Rates in 401(k) Plans by Workers' Ages for Workers Aged 21 to 64 with Annual Wages $5,000 or Above and One or More Years Tenure

Plan	*Plan participation rate*	*Participation rate by age of workers*				
		20–29	*30–39*	*40–49*	*50–59*	*60+*
A	78.7	60.8	77.9	85.1	85.1	87.5
B	62.8	40.0	57.7	63.9	75.5	73.4
C	76.8	75.9	83.9	75.3	70.7	70.4
D	91.6	81.9	91.3	94.7	98.3	89.9
E	81.9	47.3	83.5	84.4	86.8	81.8
F	93.1	83.0	92.8	94.4	95.1	91.7
G	90.7	86.6	91.8	91.7	91.0	85.4
H	97.7	98.4	97.9	97.1	97.5	96.8
I	61.5	49.7	70.4	68.8	75.3	83.0
J	65.4	55.8	60.7	69.0	73.0	80.9
K	88.9	72.5	88.0	89.5	92.9	91.2
L	53.2	40.0	56.8	59.3	52.7	46.2
M	98.8	98.4	99.2	97.8	99.4	100.0
N	47.4	36.6	43.7	49.2	58.6	61.4
O	58.7	50.5	58.3	62.9	58.5	53.5
P	91.5	85.7	90.8	90.1	93.2	100.0
Q	56.8	51.3	53.0	59.1	62.7	64.3
R	71.2	52.1	72.3	76.5	76.1	88.9
S	91.4	75.2	90.1	94.0	96.4	97.7
All plans	73.5	62.3	73.4	75.1	81.1	80.5

Source: Authors' computations using Watson Wyatt Worldwide data.

TABLE 6 Average Contribution to 401(k) Plans as a Percentage of Pay by Age of Workers Aged 21 to 64 with Annual Wages $5,000 or Above and One or More Years Tenure

Plan	*Average contribution amount*	*Average contribution rate*	*Average % of pay contributed by age of workers*				
			20–29	*30–39*	*40–49*	*50–59*	*60+*
A	$2,121	5.7	4.3	5.4	5.8	7.0	6.9
B	1,456	4.3	2.6	3.4	4.1	5.2	6.6
C	2,771	8.1	6.9	8.0	7.8	8.7	9.8
D	1,613	6.1	4.9	5.8	6.1	7.3	7.5
E	3,114	6.4	4.6	5.5	6.5	8.4	8.2
F	3,029	5.8	4.1	5.2	5.9	6.8	6.2
G	2,034	5.3	4.4	5.0	5.8	6.4	7.8
H	1,177	4.7	3.8	4.4	4.9	6.1	6.8
I	880	3.5	3.0	3.7	3.8	4.2	4.6
J	3,271	6.3	5.4	5.9	6.3	7.4	7.2
K	3,470	6.9	6.0	6.4	6.7	8.2	8.7
L	1,229	3.7	3.2	3.7	3.9	3.8	4.2
M	2,091	7.2	6.2	6.7	7.4	8.5	9.3
N	1,498	2.9	2.7	2.8	3.0	3.3	3.3
O	924	2.7	2.5	2.3	2.6	3.3	4.3
P	1,668	6.4	6.0	6.0	6.1	7.2	7.6
Q	1,079	4.9	3.4	4.5	4.3	6.4	8.2
R	4,379	6.8	5.9	6.6	7.0	9.1	7.9
S	3,236	6.3	5.0	5.9	6.5	7.1	7.3
All plans	2,122	5.3	4.0	5.0	5.4	6.7	7.1

Source: Authors' computations using Watson Wyatt Worldwide data.

The quintile distribution of contributions by 401(k) participants on the basis of salary level during 1994 appears in Table 4. In this case the distributions show a consistent pattern of increasing at each successively higher salary level. For workers whose annual pay fell below $50,000 in 1994, none were at the 401(k) contribution limit for the year. Even among those whose annual salaries were $100,000 or more for the year, only 28 percent contributed at the maximum dollar rate. It is possible that many workers at this level are constrained by the actual deferral percentage (ADP) limits in their plans. These ADP limits, set by law, often constrain contributions for highly compensated employees (HCEs) well below the dollar maximums established by law. In at least one case, we know the plan sponsor has established a nonqualified plan that substitutes for participation in the 401(k) plan for employees whose pay exceeds $100,000 per year.

Participation rates in the individual plans by the age of covered worker are presented in Table 5. In general, participation rates rise with a

TABLE 7 Participation Rates in 401(k) Plans by Workers' Salary Levels for Workers Aged 21 to 64 with Annual Wages $5,000 or Above and One or More Years Tenure

Plan	*Plan participation rate*	*Participation rate by workers' annual salary level (in thousands of $)*				
		0–25	*25–50*	*50–75*	*75–100*	*100+*
A	78.7	62.4	89.2	93.1	97.4	97.4
B	62.8	48.1	78.2	85.2	92.3	100.0
C	76.8	63.7	84.8	89.0	94.0	60.0
D	91.6	88.8	97.7	100.0	100.0	93.8
E	81.9	50.0	83.6	91.3	93.5	89.5
F	93.1	91.3	92.7	93.8	100.0	96.8
G	90.7	88.3	90.4	96.2	100.0	100.0
H	97.7	98.0	97.0	98.8	100.0	100.0
I	61.5	56.0	83.8	94.9	49.4	6.8
J	65.4	30.3	70.3	79.8	90.5	91.8
K	88.9	69.1	86.4	94.0	97.3	97.5
L	53.2	36.8	76.7	87.7	84.9	100.0
M	98.8	98.2	99.3	100.0	100.0	100.0
N	47.4	33.6	38.4	67.4	82.5	88.4
O	58.7	45.7	66.4	62.2	55.6	61.5
P	91.5	90.5	92.6	NA	NA	NA
Q	56.8	55.7	59.4	NA	NA	NA
R	71.2	34.5	60.9	80.7	78.0	83.3
S	91.4	80.5	90.7	94.4	94.2	96.7
All plans	73.5	66.3	74.2	84.9	88.7	80.4

Source: Authors' computations using Watson Wyatt Worldwide data.

worker's age. On average, workers in their fifties and sixties have participation rates that are about 20 percentage points higher than those in their twenties. Participation rises the most as workers move from their twenties to thirties, increasing 11.2 percentage points. There is considerable variation in participation patterns among the plans, however. In some cases, high participation rates are achieved even among workers in their twenties. In Plan C, for example, participation for workers in their twenties actually exceeds the rates for workers in their fifties and sixties.

Average contribution amounts and rates for participants in each of the plans are reported in Table 6. Average contributions to the 401(k) plans vary from a low of $880 per year to a high of about $4,380 per year. In virtually every case, there is a steady increase in the average contribution rate at successively higher ages up through workers in their fifties, and, in most cases, workers in their sixties participating in a plan contribute at higher rates than those in their fifties.

TABLE 8 Average Contribution to 401(k) Plans as a Percentage of Pay by Pay Level for Workers Aged 21 to 64 with Annual Wages $5,000 or Above and One or More Years Tenure

Plan	*Average contribution amount*	*Average contribution rate*	*Average % of pay contributed by age of workers' salary levels (in thousands of $)*				
			0–25	*25–50*	*50–75*	*75–100*	*100+*
A	$2,120	5.7	5.0	6.1	6.5	4.9	4.6
B	1,456	4.3	4.0	4.5	4.5	4.7	4.9
C	2,771	8.1	6.8	8.7	9.3	8.0	5.5
D	1,613	6.1	5.7	6.6	7.1	7.5	5.8
E	3,114	6.4	5.3	6.2	7.0	6.7	6.2
F	3,029	5.8	5.6	6.3	6.6	6.7	5.0
G	2,034	5.3	4.4	5.5	6.6	6.1	6.4
H	1,177	4.7	4.3	5.3	5.8	3.8	3.7
I	880	3.5	3.3	4.0	4.4	4.9	4.6
J	3,271	6.3	5.7	5.9	6.8	7.3	6.6
K	3,470	6.9	5.2	6.8	7.4	6.7	6.3
L	1,229	3.7	3.6	3.7	4.7	3.6	4.1
M	2,091	7.2	7.4	6.9	7.9	7.9	5.6
N	1,498	2.9	2.5	2.8	3.2	3.4	2.7
O	925	2.7	2.8	2.6	3.4	2.5	2.8
P	1,668	6.4	6.4	6.5	NA	NA	NA
Q	1,079	4.9	4.9	4.6	NA	NA	NA
R	4,379	6.8	6.4	7.6	7.5	6.6	4.4
S	3,236	6.3	6.2	6.6	6.1	6.2	5.7
All plans	2,122	5.3	4.5	5.6	6.0	5.8	5.0

Source: Authors' computations using Watson Wyatt Worldwide data.

Participation rates by annual pay, provided in Table 7, show that workers at successively higher pay levels generally have higher participation rates, although the rates in a number of the plans drop at earnings levels of $75,000 per year or higher. Undoubtedly the ADP limit considerations come into play in a number of cases. Plan I, for example, has a non-qualified benefit for highly compensated workers that reduces participation by those in the upper end of the wage distribution in the 401(k) plan.

Contributions as a fraction of pay appear in Table 8. Though contribution rates rise with pay levels, this tendency is attenuated for employees earning over $100,000 during 1994. Here the percent of pay contributed to the 401(k) plan was less than for workers at the $50,000 to $75,000 level. Also, in more than half the cases the contribution rates for workers earning between $75,000 and $100,000 fell below the contribution rate for workers at the $50,000 to $75,000 level of earnings.

A Multivariate Model of Participation in and Contributions to 401(k) Plans

To test the observed relationships between worker and plan characteristics and participation in 401(k) plans more formally, we estimate (1) the probability that individual workers participate in a 401(k) plan and (2) the size of workers' annual contributions as a percent of annual earnings, given that a worker chooses to participate in a plan.

Deciding to Participate in a 401(k) Plan

We model the probability that an individual worker will participate in a 401(k) plan as a function of the worker's age, his or her annual earnings, the value of any other company-provided pension, and other personal characteristics such as other family wealth, retirement plans, marginal income tax bracket, etc.[1] Considerable information suggests that retirement savings increase with age; however, this tends to be a nonlinear relationship and savings may actually decline as the actual date of retirement approaches. The value of tax deferred savings is greater for persons with higher earnings and, as a result, high-wage workers will be more likely to participate in 401(k) plans. In addition, higher-income workers may need to save more to attain the level of desired retirement income due to the progressive nature of the social security benefit formula. Of course, workers with higher income may have more discretionary income out of which to save. For these reasons, workers with higher earnings are expected to be more likely to participate in 401(k) plans. If workers have a target for retirement income, the existence of other pension benefits would be expected to reduce the probability of participation in the 401(k) plan.

In addition to these worker variables, several employer and plan characteristics are expected to influence the 401(k) participation decision. These include the rate at which the company matches the first dollar of individual contributions, the extent of communications concerning the 401(k) plan, and the size of the company. Higher match rates are expected to entice a larger percentage of workers to participate in the 401(k) plan by increasing the value of each dollar contributed to the plan. In developing the model of participation and contribution rates, we had no plans that did not match participant contributions to their 401(k) plans at some level. Better communications by the company will improve the worker's understanding of the program and should lead to increased participation.

Participation in a 401(k) plan is estimated using a multivariate logit model; the results are shown in Table 9.[2] The values reported in the table

TABLE 9 Logit Estimation of 401(k) Participation Rates

Variable	*Estimation with 17 companies* Logit estimate	t-value of the parameter*	*Estimation with 15 companies* Logit estimate	t-value of the parameter*
CONSTANT	−29.194	−13.19	−28.754	−12.74
AGE	2.071	11.81	2.637	11.27
WAGE	0.657	38.52	0.813	43.21
AGE^2	−9.690	−11.23	−9.494	−10.77
$WAGE^2$	−4.419	−23.89	−5.350	−26.89
AGE^3	15.026	10.71	14.779	10.31
$WAGE^3$	8.796	15.76	10.631	17.67
AGE^4	−8.492	−10.22	−8.396	−9.89
$WAGE^4$	−5.375	−11.62	−6.519	−13.03
REPRATE			−0.028	−20.17
MATCH2	0.928	21.08	1.611	29.88
MATCH3	2.143	50.48	2.691	55.47
SIZE	−1.917	−67.40	−2.029	−67.36
COM1	0.388	12.25	0.864	20.77
COM2	0.740	21.28	1.204	28.38
Likelihood ratio chi-square		10,924.98		10,678.38
Observations		59,203		55,478
Percent correctly predicted		77.6		77.0
Madalla's pseudo R-square		0.1685		0.1751
McFadden's pseudo R-square		0.1601		0.1637

The regression results presented here are based on 55,000 to 60,000 worker observations, but the workers are grouped in a relatively small number of plans. Regression models using such data can result in "group effects" that result in a downward bias in the estimation of standard errors of estimated coefficients. To investigate the group effects in our model, we estimated a random-coefficient logit model (see Jain et al., 1994). The results of this estimation (available from the authors on request) show that although most t-ratios from the random-coefficient logit model are smaller than those reported here, all the parameter estimates still have the same signs and all are still statistically significant at the 5 percent level. The relative magnitudes of the parameter estimates also remain the same as those reported here. These results lead us to conclude that even though the group effects exist in our model, the results and related conclusions reported in the paper are still valid. To simplify our analysis and explanations, the results from the ordinary logit model are all that are presented here.

approximately represent the change in the probability of participation due to a one-unit change in the continuous explanatory variables such as age or the change in the dichotomous variables from a value of zero to one with other explanatory variables held constant at their mean values.[3] Levels of significance for the estimated parameters are reported in the table. (The logit coefficients from which these marginal effects are derived are available from the authors upon request.) The values reported in the second column are based on employment records from 17 companies while the results in the fourth column include only 15 companies.

The difference is due to the elimination of two companies for whom we were unable to calculate replacement rates from other company-provided pensions. Thus, the results reported in the second column are from a logit equation that did not include the replacement rate variable while the results presented in the fourth column are from a similar equation that does include the replacement rate variable. Since the results are fairly consistent between the two equations, only the estimates reported in the fourth column are discussed.

Earlier, we showed that there was not much variation in the match rate of employee contributions across the plans in this data set. As a result, match rates were grouped into three categories: 25 percent, 50 to 75 percent, and 100 percent. The estimates in column 4 of Table 9 indicate that relative to being in a plan with a 25 percent match rate, a worker covered by a plan with a 50 to 75 percent match rate is 28 percentage points more likely to participate in the 401(k) plan. Workers in plans with a 100 percent match rate are 47 percentage points more likely to make an annual contribution to the plan than those in a plan with only a 25 percent match rate. These results are statistically significant and imply that increased match rates increase the participation rate in a 401(k) plan. These findings are in general agreement with early studies that showed employer matches increasing the level of participation; however, the estimated magnitude of the increases in the probability of participation associated with higher match rates found here is considerably larger than that found in earlier studies.[4] Since all the plans in our sample provided some employer match, we were unable to test the effect of some match versus no employer match on the probability of participation.

The larger estimated effect of increases in the match rate on the probability of participation in the 401(k) plan found in this analysis may be due, in part, to the inclusion of the value of the current coverage in an employer-provided defined benefit plan. This variable has been omitted in previous studies. If the generosity of the defined benefit plan that has a negative effect on participation is positively correlated with the match rate on the 401(k) plan, excluding this variable from the estimation equation will result in biased estimates of the effect of match rates on the probability of participation in the 401(k) plan. Thus, the lower estimates found in earlier studies may be due to their omission of other company-provided pension benefits.

Workers are more likely to enroll in plans when they understand and feel comfortable about the investment opportunities. A key to the participation decision is the amount and quality of information provided by the plan sponsor. We attempt to measure this activity by considering three levels of plan communications. The first level of communication consists of only distributing plan enrollment forms and required periodic statements of account balances. All plans in the sample provided this level of communication. The second level of employer communication (COM1) provides workers with generic newsletters related to participation in 401(k) plans. These statements are generally prepared by consulting firms and investment managers, and they discuss current financial market trends, personal investment strategies, and the national economic environment. The third level of communications (COM2) involves sending workers communication materials specifically tailored to the individual company's 401(k) plan. These materials generally give more detailed information about the specific plans covering the workers receiving the materials and may even suggest appropriate savings levels in the 401(k) plan, given Social Security and other pension coverage offered by the firm.

Companies can provide COM1, COM2, or both types of information to their employees. Approximately 60 percent of the workers in the Watson Wyatt data are enrolled in plans that provide the generic information, and approximately 60 percent are in plans that provide individually tailored information. About 20 percent are enrolled in plans where both types of communication are used. The logit analysis estimates these two communications strategies as having independent effects on participation.[5]

The estimated effects indicate that increasing the quality of communications significantly increases participation rates. If a company provides generic materials in addition to the required forms and statements, the probability of a worker's participating in the 401(k) plan increases by 15 percentage points. Further use of specifically prepared information tailored for a company's own plan increases the probability of participation relative to only having the required information by 21 percentage points. The estimated effects of communication efforts indicate that a firm using both generic and specifically tailored information can increase participation rates by 36 percentage points while holding the match rate constant.

This finding suggests that firms with relatively low participation rates may use increased education to attempt to raise participation rates. Thus, firms with low past participation rates may be found to have high and increasing levels of education. While this may suggest that the educational activities of the firm are made simultaneous with the participation decisions of its workers, the process is more likely to be recursive. Increased education in time t follows low participation in time $t-1$. If this model correctly captures the participation effect on education, education in time t is exogenous to the participation decision in time t and our participation equation is correctly specified. Thus, workers make current participation decisions based on education programs that were put in place by the firm at an earlier date.

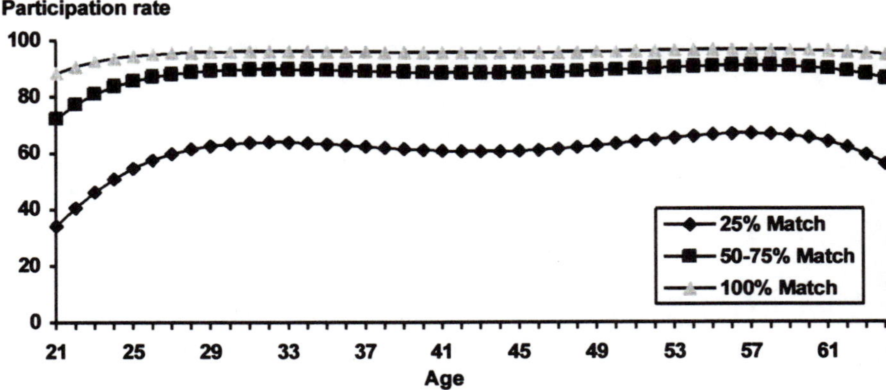

Figure 1. Probability of participating in a 401(k) plan by age under alternative matching assumptions (COM1 = 1, COM2 = 0, WAGE = $35,000, SIZE = 0, REPRATE = 20%). Source: Authors' computations using Watson Wyatt Worldwide data.

Increases in the replacement rate (REPRATE) expected from other employer-provided pension plans significantly reduces the probability of participation in the 401(k) plan, but the estimated effect is very small, as Table 9 shows. The logit estimates indicate that a 10 percentage point increase in the replacement rate would decrease the probability of participation in the 401(k) plan by 0.48 percentage points. Workers employed in smaller firms are more likely to participate in the 401(k) plan than are comparable workers in large firms.

Prior research, discussed earlier, suggested that age and wage have nonlinear effects on the probability of participation in a 401(k) plan. To allow for these effects, we include four moments for both age and annual earnings in the logit equation. The nonlinear relationships between age and participation and wage and participation can not be easily read from the parameter estimates shown in Table 9. In order to describe the full effects of advancing age and increases in annual earnings, we have derived age/wage profiles that are shown in Figures 1 to 6. These profiles also enable us to better illustrate the relative effects of alternative match rates and communication strategies on the probability of participation in the plan. All profiles in the figures are drawn assuming a replacement rate from other pension plans of 20 percent (REPRATE = 20.0) and the company is among the smaller firms in our sample (SIZE=0). In the age profiles, annual earnings are set equal to $35,000, and in the earnings profiles, age is assumed to be 40. Finally, each figure either holds the

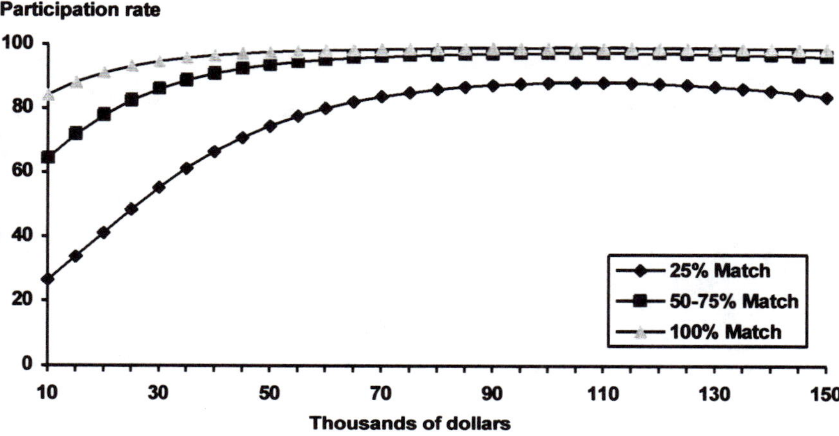

Figure 2. Probability of participating in a 401(k) plan by wage under alternative matching assumptions (COM1 =1, COM2 = 0, AGE = 40, SIZE = 0, REPRATE = 20%). Source: Authors' computations using Watson Wyatt Worldwide data.

communication strategy or the match rate constant while the other is allowed to vary. With the exception of Figure 5, all figures with a constant match rate are based on a match rate of 25 percent and the figures with a constant communication strategy assume that the firm provides generic but not specific plan and investment information.

Figure 1 illustrates how the probability of participation changes with advancing age for three different match rates. Holding the match rate constant, the age profiles indicate that the probability of participation increases fairly rapidly for workers during their twenties and then remains relatively stable from age 30 to age 58. The participation probability then declines for the oldest workers. For example, the predicted probability of participation for workers aged 21 in a plan with a match rate of 25 percent is just below 40 percent. By age 30, the likelihood of participating in the plan has risen to over 60 percent. The predicted probability declines with age for older workers, falling back to approximately 50 percent for workers aged 65. Figure 1 also illustrates the impact of increasing the match rate on the probability of participation at each age. Raising the match rate from 25 percent to 50 to 75 percent increases the participation probability of workers in their early twenties from around 40 percent to approximately 70 percent. The effects of higher match rates is less for older workers.

Figure 2 presents the relationship between the participation proba-

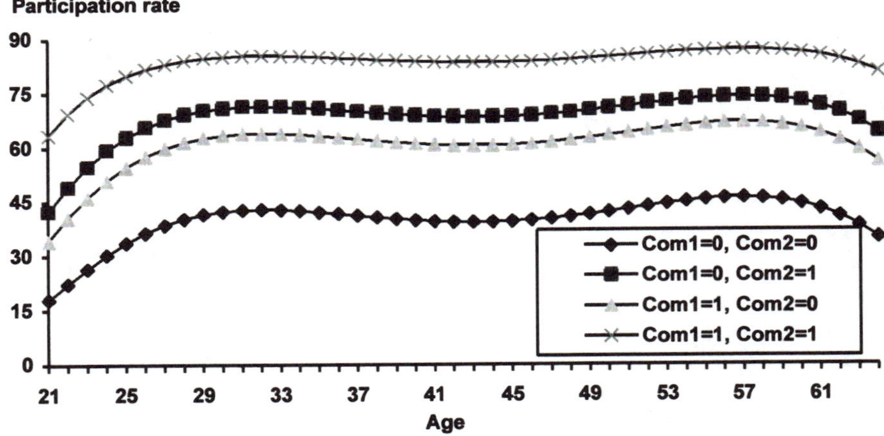

Figure 3. Probability of participating in a 401(k) plan by age under alternative communications programs (MATCH = 25%, WAGE = $35,000, SIZE = 0, REP-RATE = 20%). Source: Authors' computations using Watson Wyatt Worldwide data.

bility and annual earnings. Holding the match rate constant, the likelihood of participating in a 401(k) plan increases sharply as earnings rise from $10,000 to $50,000. For a plan with a 25 percent match rate, the participation probability for a worker with earnings of less than $20,000 is around 30 percent. The likelihood of participation increases to 70 percent for workers with earnings of $50,000. The probability of participating in a plan then remains fairly stable with a slight decline in the likelihood of being in the plan for persons with very high earnings. Once again, the figure shows how increases in the match rate raise the probability of participation in the plan.

Figures 3, 4, and 5 show similar age and wage relationships holding constant the match rate while allowing for alternative communication strategies. In each case, the age and wage profiles are shifted up as the firm provides more and higher-quality information concerning the 401(k) plan. These profiles clearly illustrate the substantial impact that information programs can have on worker decisions to contribute funds to a 401(k) plan.

The significance of communication programs is further highlighted in Figure 6. This figure shows a wage participation profile while allowing both the match rate and the communications strategy to vary. The lowest profile is based on a match rate of 25 percent and assumes that the

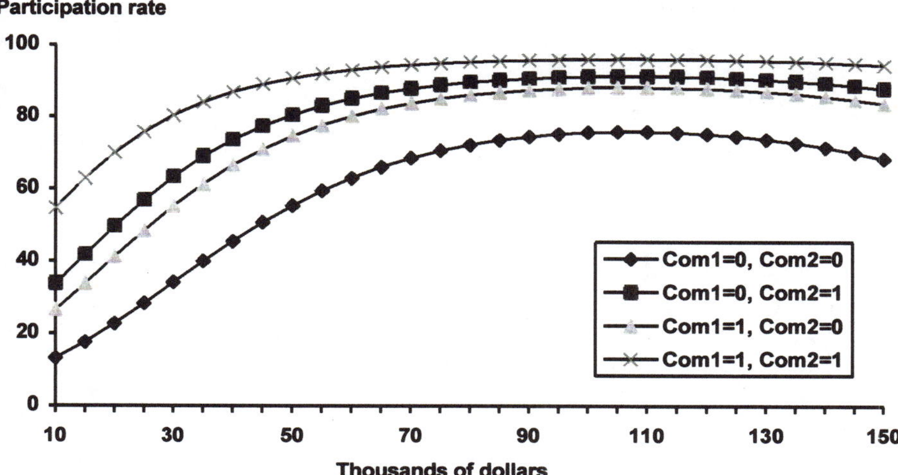

Figure 4. Probability of participating in a 401(k) plan by wage under alternative communications programs (MATCH = 25%, AGE = 40, SIZE = 0, REPRATE = 20%). Source: Authors' computations using Watson Wyatt Worldwide data.

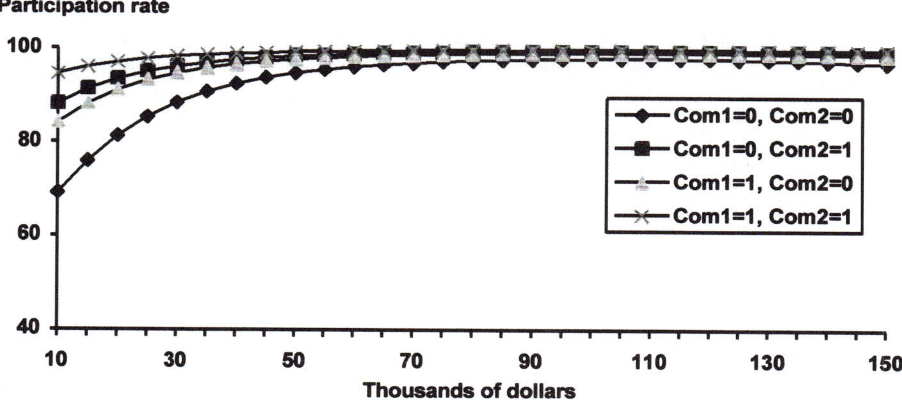

Figure 5. Probability of participating in a 401(k) plan by wage under alternative communications programs (MATCH = 100%, AGE = 40, SIZE = 0, REPRATE = 20%). Source: Authors' computations using Watson Wyatt Worldwide data.

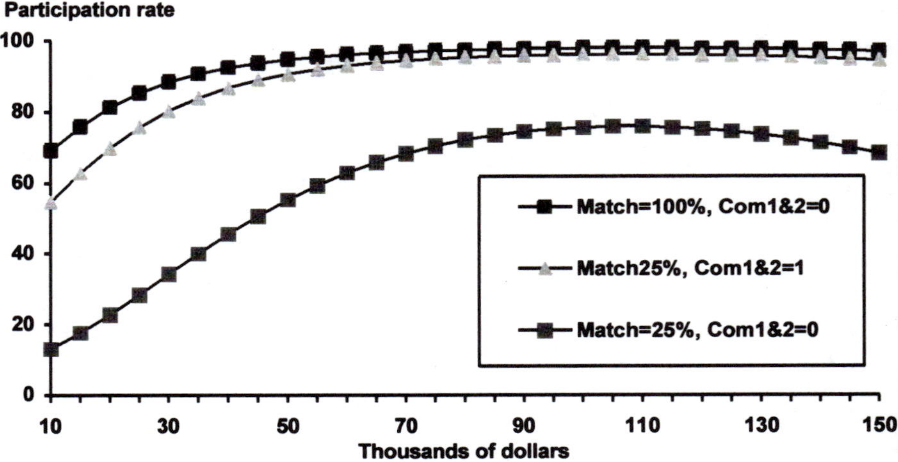

Figure 6. Probability of participating in a 401(k) plan by wage under alternative communications and matching programs (AGE = 40, SIZE = 0, REPRATE = 20%). Source: Authors' computations using Watson Wyatt Worldwide data.

firm only provides the required communications concerning the plan (COM1=0 and COM2=0). Participation probabilities can then be compared for two scenarios: (1) the match rate is increased to 100 percent, holding the communication strategy constant (the top profile) and (2) both generic and plan-specific information is provided and the match rate remains at 25 percent (the middle profile). As shown in the figure, improving communications concerning the plan has nearly as significant effect on the probability of participation as does increasing the match rate from 25 to 100 percent.

To illustrate this point, compare the participation probabilities for a worker earning $30,000 under each of the three assumptions. The probability that a worker in a plan with a 25 percent match and only required communications will participate in the 401(k) plan is slightly over 34 percent. Increasing the match rate to 100 percent without improving plan communications results in an increase in the probability of participation to just over 88 percent. In contrast, if the match rate is held constant at 25 percent but the firm provides both generic and specific information, the likelihood that the worker will participate in the plan increases to slightly more than 80 percent.

This is an extremely important finding. It indicates that firms struggling to meet discrimination rules can increase participation rates by doing a better job of informing their workers about the 401(k) plan and its investment options. The figure indicates that the magnitude of this effect is much large for workers with lower annual earnings and, therefore, firms providing high-quality plan information will have an easier time meeting discrimination requirements. In general, this option of improved communications will be much less expensive to the company than increasing the match rate.

Annual Contribution Rates

Conditional on participation in a 401(k) plan, workers must decide on their annual contribution. Table 10 presents the results of ordinary least squares (OLS) estimates of workers' annual contributions as a percent of annual earnings for each of the 401(k) plan participants in all 17 companies, and also separately for the 15 companies with for which we derived defined benefit replacement rates. The two specifications are so similar that we again focus on the plans with projected defined benefit replacement rates for workers at age 65. Once again, most of the variables are statistically significant and the direction of influence is consistent with the earlier results on participation.

The results show that increasing age and wage levels have a strong positive and statistically significant effect on workers' contribution rates under the plans. The generosity of the expected benefit from the defined benefit pension plan has a very small negative but statistically insignificant effect on workers' contributions to the plans. The size variable, once again, has a negative and significant effect on workers' contributions, just as it did on the probability of participation in the 401(k) offerings.

The estimates indicate that higher match rates produce significant increases in workers' annual contribution rates. Having a match of between 50 and 75 percent raises the annual contribution rate by 0.8 percentage points compared to the contributions of workers in plans with a 25 percent match. Workers in plans with a 100 percent match have annual contribution rates that are 2.0 percentage points higher than the rate for participants in plans with only a 25 percent match. Figure 7 shows the estimated contribution rates across the age spectrum under the three alternative matching rates in the plans under study. The positive relation between age and contribution rate mentioned earlier is clearly reflected in the graph. Given the linear nature of the model, the effects of match rates are constant across the age spectrum.

Figure 8 shows the estimated contribution rates across the wage spectrum at the three match levels used in the analysis. Workers' contribution rates rise gradually until the annual wage level reaches $70,000 to $80,000 and then begin to decline. The decline at the higher wage levels is un-

TABLE 10 Ordinary Least Squares Estimation of 401(k) Contribution Rates

	Estimation with 17 companies			*Estimation with 15 companies*		
Variable (1)	*Estimated coefficient* (2)	*t-value* (3)	*Standardized estimate* (4)	*Estimated coefficient* (5)	*t-value* (6)	*Standardized estimate* (7)
CONSTANT	−33.60	−8.38	—	−33.76	−8.03	—
AGE	3.43	8.46	8.96	3.41	8.00	8.74
WAGE	0.72	23.99	0.49	0.96	28.92	0.64
AGE²	−12.38	−8.28	−27.36	−12.33	−7.83	−26.60
WAGE²	−7.13	−19.51	−1.09	−8.76	−22.68	−1.36
AGE³	19.46	8.15	28.71	19.36	7.70	27.80
WAGE³	18.85	15.08	1.48	22.46	17.23	1.81
AGE⁴	−11.04	−7.93	−10.11	−10.95	−7.45	−9.73
WAGE⁴	−13.97	−12.97	0.80	−16.38	−14.66	−0.96
REPRATE				−0.00	−0.34	−0.00
MATCH2	0.61	8.62	0.07	0.79	9.19	0.09
MATCH3	1.55	24.60	0.20	2.00	26.68	0.26
SIZE	−1.40	−33.93	−0.19	−1.79	−38.82	−0.24
COM1	0.38	7.73	0.05	0.05	0.78	0.01
COM2	1.91	36.59	0.25	1.97	31.99	0.26
Valid cases		41,701			38,354	
R-squared		0.14			0.15	
Rbar-squared		0.14			0.15	
F		508.98			480.80	
Std error of estimate		3.41			3.44	
Durbin-Watson		1.76			1.78	

doubtedly related to the combined effects of IRS maximum dollar limits on pretax contributions to 401(k) plans and to the limits imposed by the ADP tests on these plans. At the upper wage levels reflected in the figure, some workers would have reached the dollar limits with contributions of 7 percent of pay. Workers whose wage levels were above $65,000 in 1994 would have been in the highly compensated employee category and would have been subject to the ADP limits imposed on plans. While the figure suggests that the ADP tests appear not to have been a problem in general, they likely result in limitations in individual plans.

Estimated contribution rates to the plans by participants at various wage levels under the four alternative levels of communication are shown in Figure 9. Introduction of specifically tailored plan information results in a considerable increase in the annual contribution rate of two percentage points. The use of generic information does not alter annual contributions of participants at all. Each of the lines in Figure 9 actually reflects the outcomes under two different communications scenarios. The bot-

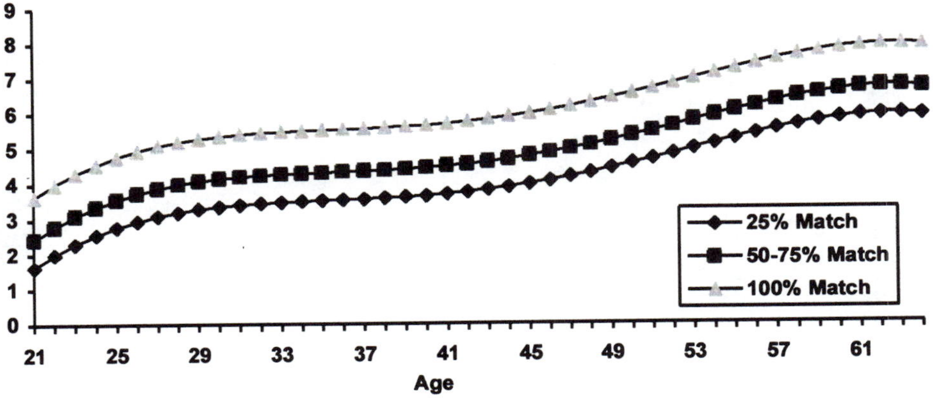

Figure 7. Estimated employee contribution rates to 401(k) plans by age of participant under alternative matching assumptions (COM1 = 0, COM2 = 0, WAGE = $35,000, SIZE = 0, REPRATE = 20%). Source: Authors' computations using Watson Wyatt Worldwide data.

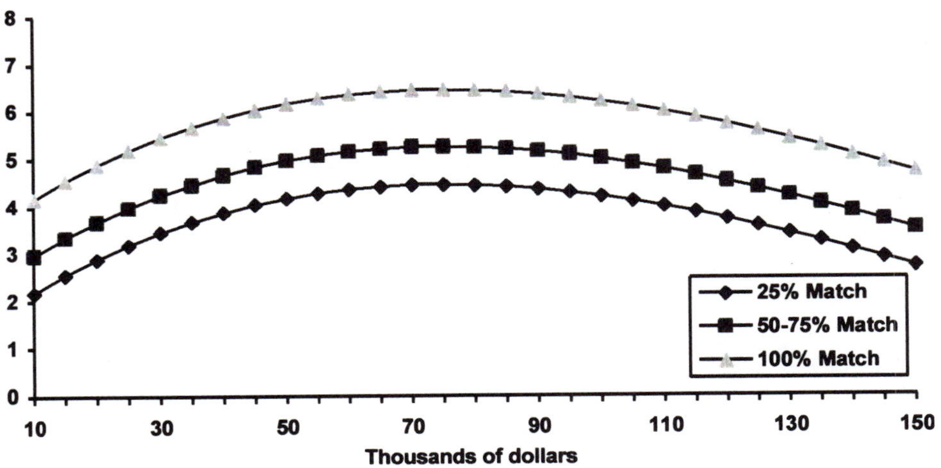

Figure 8. Estimated employee contribution rates to 401(k) plans by participant's wage level under alternative matching assumptions (COM1 = 0, COM2 = 0, AGE = 40, SIZE = 0, REPRATE = 20%). Source: Authors' computations using Watson Wyatt Worldwide data.

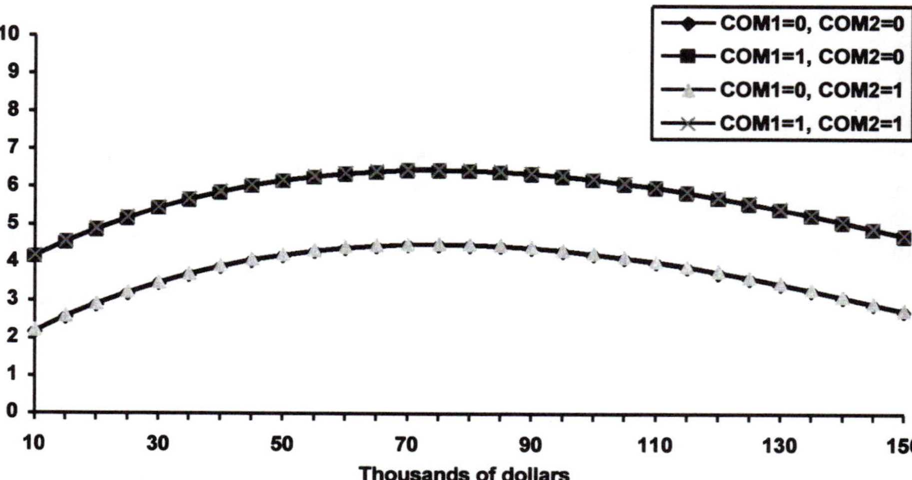

Figure 9. Estimated employee contribution rates to 401(k) plans by participant's wage level under alternative communications programs (MATCH = 25%, AGE = 40, REPRATE = 20%). Source: Authors' computations using Watson Wyatt Worldwide data.

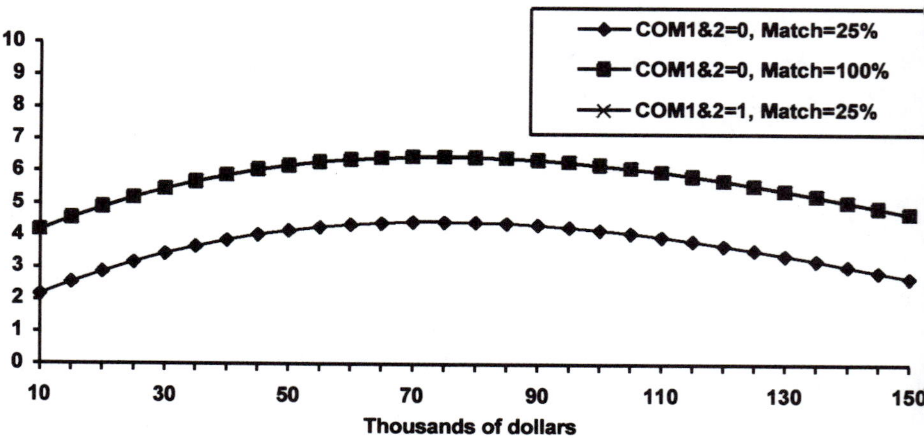

Figure 10. Estimated employee contribution rates to 401(k) plans by participant's wage level under alternative communications and matching programs (WAGE = $35,000, SIZE = 0, REPRATE = 20%). Source: Authors' computations using Watson Wyatt Worldwide data.

tom line includes the case where only enrollment materials or enrollment materials plus generic communications materials are distributed to participants. The top line includes the cases where individually tailored communications materials are distributed either with or without generic communications.

Once again, it is clear that there is some tradeoff between higher matching of employee contributions to 401(k) plans and more intensive communications of the programs as alternative means of improving the participation in these plans. Figure 10 shows the estimated employee contribution rates in these plans at various wage levels under three alternative scenarios. The bottom line in the figure reflects the estimate under the scenario where the employer provides a 25 percent match of employee contributions and provides no communications materials beyond the basic materials needed to enroll in the plan and move one's money around. The top line in the figure represents the estimated participation rates in the other two scenarios. One scenario would have the sponsor increase the match rate in the plan from 25 percent to 100 percent. The other scenario would have the sponsor maintain the contribution rate at 25 percent but implement a communications program that was tailored to its own workforce and retirement plans. The outcome under these two scenarios is identical for all practical purposes.

Conclusions

This analysis examines the factors affecting both participation and contribution rates in 401(k) plans using a limited cross-section of companies. Our results generally find that plan characteristics and communications have a somewhat larger effect on both participation and contribution levels than prior studies have indicated. The results of the current analysis suggest that further work should be done to expand the range of plans to include a set of plans that provide no match on employee contributions. Also the important effects of alternative communications programs on participation in these plans suggests that more detailed classification of the communications materials for future analyses would be worthwhile. The data also suggest virtually no pension offset; that is, 401(k) participation and contribution rates are only negligibly affected by corporate defined benefit generosity.

The authors wish to acknowledge the contributions of WeiKe Hai and Gordon Goodfellow of Watson Wyatt Worldwide for preparing the data and developing the statistical analyses that are included in this chapter. The opinions stated in this chapter are the authors', as is the responsibility for any errors in the analyses.

Notes

1. The Watson Wyatt data set is based on company employment records and contains only those items routinely collected by employers. For this study, we were able to determine the workers' current age, their annual earnings for 1994, and the expected value of future benefits from other pensions offered by the company. While other factors may be influence participation in a 401(k) plan, these variables represent some of the most important factors that workers consider when deciding whether to make a 401(k) contribution.

2. In developing the estimates, we dropped the two plans Q and R, where matching was on the basis of participant dollar contributions to the plan.

3. The participation profiles discussed below illustrate how the estimated effects of alternative match rates and communications strategies vary with different values of the other variables such as worker's age and annual wage.

4. For example, Papke (1993) reports an increase in plan participation rates of 17.4 percent associated with going from a zero match rate to a dollar-for-dollar match.

5. The authors are currently investigating the potential interactive effects associated with using both of these types of communications at the same time.

References

Andrews, Emily. "The Growth and Distribution of 401(k) Plans." In John A. Turner and Daniel J. Beller, eds., *Trends in Pensions 1992.* Washington, D.C.: USGPO, 1992.

Bernheim, B. Douglas. "Personal Saving, Information, and Economic Literacy: New Directions for Public Policy." In Charles E. Walker, Mark Bloomfeld, and Margo Thorning, eds., *Tax Policy for Economic Growth in the 1990s.* Washington, D.C.: American Council for Capital Formation, 1994: 53–78.

——. "Do Households Appreciate Their Financial Vulnerabilities? An Analysis of Actions, Perceptions, and Public Policy." In *Tax Policy and Economic Growth.* Washington, D.C.: American Council for Capital Formation, 1995: 1–30.

Bernheim, B. Douglas and Daniel M. Garrett. "The Determinants and Consequences of financial Education in the Workplace: Evidence from a Survey of Households." Paper developed under grants from the Smith-Richardson Foundation and the National Science Foundation, August 1995.

Employee Benefit Research Institute (EBRI). "Salary Reduction Plans and Individual Saving for Retirement." *Issue Brief* No. 155. Washington, D.C.: EBRI, November 1994.

Ferguson, Karen and Kate Blackwell. *Pensions in Crisis.* New York: Arcade Publishing, 1995: 173–78.

Ippolito, Richard A. "Discount Rates Imperfect Information and 401(k) Pensions." Mimeo; Washington, D.C.: Pension Benefit Guaranty Corporation, November 1993.

Jain, Dipak C., Naufel J. Vilcassim, and Pradeep K. Chintagunta. "A Random-Coefficients Logit Brand-Choice Model Applied to Panel Data." *Journal of Business and Economic Statistics* 12, 3 (July 1994): 317–28.

Kusko, Andrea L., James M. Poterba, and David W. Wilcox. "Employee Decisions with Respect to 401(k) Plans." This volume.

Papke, Leslie. "Did 401(k) Plans Replace Other Employer Provided Pensions?" NBER Working Paper No. 4501, 1995.

U.S. Department of Labor (USDOL), Pension and Welfare Benefits Administration. *Abstract of 1992 Form 5500 Annual Reports. Private Pension Plan Bulletin,* No. 5. Washington, D.C.: USGPO, Winter 1996: 59–81.

Samwick, Andrew and Jonathan Skinner. "Abandoning the Nest Egg? 401(k) Plans and Inadequate Pension Saving." In Sylvester J. Schieber and John Shoven, eds., *The Economics of U.S. Retirement Policy: Current Status and Future Directions,* Cambridge, Mass.: MIT Press, 1997.

Chapter 5

Employee Decisions with Respect to 401(k) Plans

Andrea L. Kusko, James M. Poterba, and David W. Wilcox

In the last decade, 401(k) plans have grown rapidly. These plans, also known as cash and deferred compensation accounts, permit individuals to defer taxes on current earnings and to earn pretax returns on their retirement savings. Most employers who offer 401(k)s also match at least part of their employees' contributions to these plans. In 1993, the most recent year for which data from Form 5500 has been tabulated, contributions to 401(k) plans totalled $69.3 billion, substantially greater than the $52.1 billion that employers contributed to defined benefit pension plans. The number of active participants in 401(k) plans grew from 7.5 million in 1984 to 23.1 million in 1993 (USDOL, 1996).

In spite of the popularity of 401(k) plans, there is no consensus on how plan characteristics, such as the employer match rate or the IRS- and employer-imposed limits on worker contributions, affect 401(k) contributor behavior. These issues are central to understanding the rapid growth of these plans, to assessing the impact of potential legislative changes on participation in these plans, and to evaluating the impact of employer-initiated campaigns to affect employee participation (see Hinz and Turner, this volume). Two studies that explore the relationship between 401(k) plan characteristics and contribution decisions are Andrews (1992) and Papke (1995). The former constructs a proxy for the employer match rate based on a question on the May 1988 Current Population Survey (CPS) about whether the employer as well as the employee contributes to the 401(k) plan, and then uses this variable to estimate 401(k) contribution equations. Andrews' results suggest that employee participation rates are higher when the employer offers a matching contribution, but that contribution rates conditional on participation are lower. One less than fully satisfactory aspect of the CPS data is that they include neither the *rate* at which employers match employee contributions nor the fraction of employees for whom the employer match applies at the margin. The latter deficiency is potentially important because many employers match contributions only up to a fixed fraction of the employee's salary.

Papke (1995) estimates contribution equations using a data set based on the Forms 5500 that pension plans file with the Internal Revenue Service. She studies the relationship between the average contribution per plan member and the ratio of employer to employee contributions, the average employer match rate. She finds a positive association between average match rates and employee contributions at low match rates, but a negative relationship at match rates above 50 percent. These correlations might not represent the true behavioral response of contributions to changes in the match rate, however, if average and marginal match rates are different. For example, it could be that employers with more generous match rates set a lower cap on the fraction of employee compensation that they will match. In this case, cross-sectional comparisons of 401(k) plans could spuriously show a negative correlation between the match rate and the amount contributed to the plan.[1]

More generally, self-selection makes it difficult to evaluate cross-sectional evidence on the correlation between contribution rates and plan characteristics. If some firms institute high match rates or offer to match a high percentage of salary in order to attract workers who are interested in saving and therefore value these benefits, then the observed correlation between these plan features and contribution rates may simply reflect the nature of equilibrium matching between workers and firms, not the effect of match rates on contribution decisions. Ippolito (1993) argues that precisely such self-selection explains the rapid increase in the popularity of 401(k)s. He postulates that workers who value retirement saving are on average better workers than their "short-horizon" counterparts, and that by offering a 401(k) plan, an employer can attract and retain high-quality workers. Poterba, Venti, and Wise (1996) present some evidence, based on comparisons between 401(k) eligibles and not-eligibles in the mid-1980s, suggesting that such selection effects are not empirically important. The importance of selection effects nevertheless remains an unresolved issue.

Papke (1995) is the only researcher who has considered self-selection effects in an empirical analysis of contribution decisions. In an extension of the results described above, she relates *changes* in average contributions at a set of plans to *changes* in match rates at the same plans, and thus controls for time-invariant employee characteristics and plan-specific effects. The resulting estimates, while less precise than her findings in the cross-section, continue to suggest a positive, then negative, association between match rates and contributions as the match rate increases.[2]

The present chapter differs from other recent studies of 401(k) contributors in that it exploits panel data on the 401(k)-related decisions of individuals at a single medium-sized manufacturing firm.[3] Our goal is to investigate the determinants of 401(k) participation and contribution rates and the dynamics of 401(k) contributor behavior. Employee records are an excellent data source for investigating some issues relating to 401(k) plans and a very poor data source for others. On the one hand, our use of these data insulates us from the problems of plan-specific effects and selection bias noted above. Moreover, these data provide very detailed information on the patterns of 401(k) contributions across age and income classes within the firm, and on how individual employees change their participation and contribution status when the plan's structure changes. Clark and Schieber (this volume) and Goodfellow and Schieber (1996) examine similar data sets for a larger set of firms.

The disadvantage of firm-level data, however, is that they provide only an incomplete profile of the household setting in which individuals make decisions about retirement saving. These data do not give us any information on household income received from sources other than the firm from which the data have been collected. Retirement plan data also lack information on household assets or liabilities other than those held in the plan, and thus provide a more limited sketch of the household balance sheet than some household surveys.

This chapter is divided into five sections. The first summarizes the basic structure of the 401(k) plan at the firm we analyze and presents summary statistics on participation and contribution rates. The next section examines the importance of contribution limits, both those imposed by the 401(k) plan itself and those imposed by the IRS, in influencing contributor behavior. We then present simple tabulations showing the correlation between employee age, income, and contribution rates. We compare these with the results in other studies that could not control for plan characteristics. The next section sketches the dynamics of participation and demonstrates that there is substantial inertia in 401(k) contributor behavior. Most employees who contribute in one year also contribute in the next year, and they typically contribute the same share of salary in both years, even though the match rate at the firm varied substantially between years. There is a brief conclusion.

An Overview of the 401(k) Plan at Firm X

Our data set contains information on employee contributions to a 401(k) plan at a medium-sized manufacturing firm, which we shall refer to as "Firm X," in four consecutive years. In three of the four years for which we have data, the plan offered an employer match on contributions up to the first 6 percent of eligible compensation, defined as regular base compensation including some commissions but excluding bonuses and overtime. Employees were allowed to defer up to 10 percent of eligible compensation, but contributions in excess of 6 percent were not matched.

One of the unusual features of the 401(k) plan at Firm X is substantial volatility in the employer match rate. During the first three years of our sample, the match rate was linked to Firm X's earnings per share in the previous calendar year, and the firm's earnings performance during this period resulted in large changes in the match rate. Between April 1, 1987 and March 31, 1988, the match rate was 25 percent. It increased to 65 percent on April 1, 1988, and then to 150 percent on April 1, 1989, before declining to 139 percent on April 1, 1990. In the fourth year of our sample, Firm X changed the formula determining the match rate. Starting April 1, 1991, the new formula resulted in a match rate of zero. Such large swings in the match rate are unusual; Papke, Petersen, and Poterba (1996) find that match rates typically exhibit strong persistence. Changes in the match rate at Firm X were announced a few months before they went into effect, thus allowing eligible employees ample time to adjust their participation and contribution status.

There were no other major changes in Firm X's 401(k) plan during this time period. Employees could direct their contributions into a Standard and Poor (S&P) stock fund, a guaranteed income fund (GIC) with a predetermined rate of return, or a company stock fund. Employer contributions were all placed in an employee stock ownership plan (ESOP), and thus were invested in company stock.

Until April 1989, the firm also sponsored a "thrift plan" to which employees could contribute using after-tax income. There was no employer match for this plan, but taxes on the capital income from plan assets were deferred until the contributions were withdrawn. When both plans were in effect, contributions were capped at 10 percent of salary for each plan individually and 15 percent of salary for the two plans combined.[4] Firm X also provided a defined benefit retirement plan with benefits determined by average pay over the last five years of employment.

Our data set consists of annual observations on roughly 12,000 salaried and nonunion hourly employees at Firm X for the years 1988 through 1991. Unionized hourly employees are not included in the dataset because they participated in a separate deferred compensation plan. The data base was provided to us by Buck Consultants, a major benefits consulting firm. Of the workers eligible to participate in this plan in 1989, 8 percent were younger than 25 years of age, 58 percent were between 25

TABLE 1 Participation and Contribution Rates for the 401(k) Plan at Firm X

	1988	*1989*	*1990*	*1991*
Calculated from dollars contributed during the year (%)				
Participation rate	82.4	82.3	83.4	78.0
Contribution rate of participants				
Mean	5.8	6.0	6.4	5.8
Median	6.0	6.0	6.0	6.0
Fraction of employees contributing <6 percent	52.0	50.3	44.0	51.8
Calculated from end-of-year contribution designations (%)				
Participation rate	84.0	83.8	82.6	82.3
Contribution rate of participants				
Mean	6.0	6.3	6.3	6.0
Median	6.0	6.0	6.0	6.0
Fraction of employees contributing <6 percent	48.3	37.7	39.2	42.1
Employer match rate				
Annual average	55.0	129.0	142.0	34.7
Year-end	65.0	150.0	139.0	0.0

Source: Authors' calculations using data provided by Buck Consultants.
Note: Employees with unused corporate match contributions are defined as those making actual contributions of less than 5½ percent of salary (top panel) or those with year-end designations of less than 6 percent (bottom panel).

and 45, 32 percent were between 45 and 65, and 2 percent were over 65. Forty-seven percent earned less than $25,000, 23 percent earned between $25,000 and $40,000, and the remaining 30 percent earned more than $40,000. About 75 percent of the eligible employees were men.

Table 1 presents summary statistics on contributor behavior during the years 1988–91.[5] The overall participation rate, whether measured for the 401(k) alone (as reported in the table) or for the 401(k) and thrift plans combined, was between 78 and 84 percent in all four years. These participation rates are higher than those reported in most surveys of 401(k) plans. For example, Poterba, Venti, and Wise (1994) report that data from the Survey of Income and Program Participation (SIPP) suggest that, in 1991, only 71 percent of workers eligible to participate in 401(k) plans did so. The difference is even more striking because household survey responses are biased toward *overstating* the 401(k) contribution rate in any year. Our analysis counts only those employees making contributions to the plan in a given year as participants in that year. In some surveys, individuals may be counted as participants if they have nonzero balances in their 401(k) accounts, regardless of whether they actually contribute in a given year.

Despite the very substantial changes in Firm X's employer match rates over our sample period, the overall participation rate in the 401(k) plan varies little from year to year. One way to summarize this information is to divide the change in the participation rate between two years, measured for example using end-of-year contribution designations, by the change in the end-of-year employer match rate. This calculation yields "derivative effects" of match rates on participation that are approximately zero and vary in sign from year to year. The participation rate declined between 1988 and 1989, when the match rate increased from 65 percent to 150 percent. When the employer match was eliminated in 1991, the contribution rate as calculated from dollars contributed during the year declined by less than six percentage points; according to the data on end-of-year designations, the contribution rate hardly changed at all. These patterns raise questions about whether employer matching is a key factor in explaining the rapid expansion of 401(k) plans.[6]

One potential explanation of the small responsiveness of participation to the match rate at Firm X is that the employees are accustomed to big swings in the employer match rate, make decisions for the "long haul," and do not make annual adjustments to the share of salary that they contribute to the plan. Shefrin and Thaler (1988) and Thaler (1994) suggest that 401(k) participants may view contributions to the 401(k) plan as separate from other current income flows. Another potential explanation for this insensitivity is that saving through 401(k) accounts is more attractive than saving through other channels without favorable tax treatment, so those who are saving continue to contribute to these accounts even when the match rate is zero. The force of this argument is somewhat diminished, however, by the observation noted below that fewer than 20 percent of all participants contributed the full 10 percent of salary allowable under the plan.

Changes in the match rate exhibit a more pronounced relationship with the contribution rates of active participants. Between 1988 and 1990, the mean contribution rate rose by between one-half and one-quarter percentage point, depending on which measure of the contribution rate one uses. In 1991, when the employer match was eliminated, the increase in the mean contribution rate over the preceding three years was reversed. The median 401(k) contribution rate for participants held steady at 6 percent of compensation, the maximum amount eligible for the employer match, in all four years.[7]

Another key indicator of contributor behavior is the fraction of employees who failed to exhaust the employer match, either by not contributing at all or by contributing less than 6 percent of their salary. These employees passed up the opportunity to earn extraordinarily high returns on additional savings. For example, in 1989 these employees could have earned an immediate return of 150 percent in addition to the usual benefits of tax-free accumulation in the 401(k) plan. The fraction of employees in this category fell by about one-fifth between 1988 and 1990, the second year of the extraordinarily high match. Nonetheless, even in 1990, roughly 40 percent of employees failed to exhaust the employer match.

The failure of employees to exhaust the employer match requires some explanation. One possibility is that the participants who contributed less than the match limit were liquidity constrained. Given the very high return on matched 401(k) contributions, however, at least some individuals close to retirement could profitably have borrowed even at credit card interest rates and used the proceeds to increase their 401(k) contributions.

Even if liquidity constraints should not have been a relevant consideration for older workers, they may have been perceived as such by younger workers because employees could not withdraw plan assets before age 59½ unless they terminated employment with the firm. Firm X did not allow "hardship" withdrawals from the 401(k) plan, but plan participants were allowed to borrow against their plan assets.[8] Relatively few 401(k) participants at Firm X took advantage of the loan provisions. In 1988, for example, just over 5 percent of plan members had outstanding loan balances. This suggests that once assets are placed in a 401(k) account, contributors are unlikely to draw them down, at least so long as they remain with the current employer. This pattern supports the notion that contributions to 401(k) plans are likely to remain invested for long periods and therefore to have a substantial impact on household net worth at retirement.

The Importance of Contribution Limits

Firm X's 401(k) plan is an attractive saving vehicle, with an after-tax rate of return that exceeds that on traditional taxable saving instruments. Precise delineation of the opportunity set confronted by eligible employees is complicated, however, because the marginal incentive to save depends on various plan-specific and IRS-imposed rules and on the individual's contribution level.

At Firm X, an individual's contribution is limited to the smaller of 10 percent of compensation, a plan-imposed limit, or $7,000 (1987 dollars), an IRS-imposed limit. Contributions of up to 6 percent of salary are matched by the employer, while contributions of more than 6 percent are not matched. Employees at Firm X who earned more than $116,667 (1987 dollars) would have reached the IRS-imposed limit on dollars contributed ($7,000) before exhausting the employer match. Both matched and unmatched contributions are combined in the individual's account,

TABLE 2 Distribution of Employees and Contributions by Contribution Rate, 1990

Contribution rate (% of salary)	*End-of-year contribution election (%)*		*Contributions during the year (%)*	
	Employees	*Contributions*	*Employees*	*Contributions*
0	17.4	2.1	16.6	0.0
1–5	21.8	9.1	31.6	17.0
6	37.4	38.5	17.0	22.6
7–9	3.3	5.4	19.4	22.6
10	18.9	39.4	14.5	32.8
IRS maximum	0.9	4.5	1.0	5.0
$ contribution	0.2	0.9	n.a.	n.a.

Source: Authors' calculations using data provided by Buck Consultants.
Note: Contributions for 1990 totaled $16.7 million, with 10,840 contributing employees. The last row shows employees who chose to specify contributions as dollar amounts (other than the IRS maximum).

and the balance accumulates at the pretax rate of return.[9] For the typical employee, these rules induce two kinks in the budget set: one when the employer match is exhausted at 6 percent of compensation, and one when the plan's contribution limit is reached at 10 percent of compensation.

Table 2 presents evidence on the importance of the various contribution constraints at Firm X. As in Table 1, we present results based on two different measures of contribution status: the contribution rate recorded at the end of the year and the effective annual contribution rate, calculated by dividing dollars contributed during the year by base pay earned during the year. By either method, the kinks and corners in the budget set appear to have played an extremely important part in determining contributor behavior.

Measured by end-of-year contribution elections, three-quarters of all employees were at one of the kinks or corners, contributing either nothing, 6, or 10 percent of pretax base pay, or the maximum dollar amount allowed by the IRS. Moreover, these employees accounted for more than four-fifths of all dollars contributed. Nearly 40 percent of all contributions came from employees contributing 6 percent of their salary; another 40 percent came from those contributing 10 percent; and another 5 percent came from those contributing the maximum dollar amount allowed by the IRS. The clustering of contributions at these points is important because changes in the employer match rate may have little or no effect on these contributions. Conversely, changes in other plan parameters, including the fraction of compensation eligible for match and the ceilings on contributions specified by the plan and the IRS, may have considerable influence on the level of 401(k) saving.

The results based on the effective contribution rates, shown in the last two columns of Table 2, are less striking, but they are still consistent with the assertion that the constraints are very important. By this measure, roughly half of all employees were at a kink or a corner, and 60 percent of all dollars contributed were received from such employees.

Individual Characteristics and 401(k) Contribution Behavior

Previous analysis of 401(k) contribution rates—for example Poterba, Venti, and Wise (1994, 1995) and Goodfellow and Schieber (1997)—has shown that, in household survey data, 401(k) participation and contribution rates are increasing functions of employee age and income. This is usually interpreted as evidence that the probability that a given individual will participate in a given plan, and the amount he or she will contribute conditional on participation, rises with age and income. The observed pattern in cross-section household surveys, however, could arise even if this description of individual behavior were false. If, for example, the plans available to older workers tend to be more attractive than the plans for younger workers, perhaps because of differences in the types of firms that employ older and younger workers, then we might observe rising age-participation profiles even if each individual's decision was independent of age. By analyzing data from a single 401(k) plan, we avoid the possibility that unobserved plan characteristics are confounding our interpretation of individual behavior.

Table 3 reports information on how 401(k) saving varied at the end of 1989 with the characteristics of individual employees. As suggested by previous work, participation rates (the upper panel) were greatest among higher-income workers. Fully 95 percent of those earning more than $40,000 were recorded as making contributions to the plan, and participation among those earning between $25,000 and $40,000 was almost as high. Age seems to be a relatively unimportant determinant of participation for these income groups, but it does seem to have been more important among those who earned less. In the $10,000–$25,000 income group, workers over the age of 45 participated at roughly the same rates as upper-income employees of all ages, but younger workers were much less likely to participate.[10]

Consistent with the evidence from other studies, contribution rates also varied across income and age categories, as the lower panel of Table 3 suggests. Among workers who earned more than $10,000, the average contribution rate was an increasing function of both income and age.

TABLE 3 Participation and Mean Contribution Rates by Age and Income, 1989

Income (thousands of $)	*Age*				
	<25	*25–45*	*45–65*	*>65*	*Total*
Participation rates (% of eligible population)					
<10	13.8	28.0	28.7	7.0	22.9
10–25	62.1	78.4	85.5	51.7	78.4
25–40	88.8	85.2	86.8	85.7	85.9
>40	95.6	94.5	96.6	90.6	95.3
Total	45.4	78.4	85.2	33.8	82.3
Contribution rates (% of eligible compensation)					
<10	3.4	4.3	5.3	3.3	4.4
10–25	4.7	5.1	6.1	5.9	5.4
25–40	4.9	5.2	6.5	6.7	5.7
>40	6.3	6.6	7.9	7.5	7.1
Total	4.7	5.6	6.9	6.4	6.0

Source: Authors' calculations using data provided by Buck Consultants.
Note: The population for the panel on contributions is *contributors* (i.e., the calculation is performed *conditional* on knowing that the individual has a positive contribution rate).

Indeed, among workers who earned more than $40,000 and were at least 45 years old, the average contribution rate was about 8 percent. On average, participants earning more than $40,000 contributed enough to exhaust the employer match. Among workers earning $40,000 or less, only those who were at least 45 years old contributed enough, on average, to exhaust the employer match.

Dynamics of Contribution Behavior

Our panel data afford us an unusual opportunity to examine the dynamics of individual contributions over time. In particular, they allow us to examine Papke, Petersen, and Poterba's (1996) conjecture that the high degree of persistence of participation and contribution rates at the plan level is the result of inertia in individual decisions. Table 4 examines the behavior of the 7,768 employees who were on the firm's payroll in all four years of the sample. It shows that relatively few of these employees altered their participation status during this period. Moreover, those changes that did occur tended to coincide with the swings in the match rate. Notably, between 1989 and 1990, a period when the match rate was relatively stable, only about 2 percent of the sample changed its status; more than 98 percent of the persons who made contributions in 1989 also made contributions in 1990, and 92 percent of noncontributors in 1989 remained noncontributors in 1990. The largest change in participa-

TABLE 4 Probabilities of Change in Contributor Status, 1988–1991

	Contribution behavior in next year (%)	
Base year and status	*Contributor*	*Noncontributor*
1988 contribution status		
Contributor (84.1%)	99.1	0.9
Noncontributor (15.9%)	63.0	37.0
1989 contribution status		
Contributor (93.4%)	98.4	1.6
Noncontributor (6.6%)	7.8	92.2
1990 contribution status		
Contributor (92.4%)	92.8	7.2
Noncontributor (7.6%)	3.7	96.3

Source: Authors' calculations using data provided by Buck Consultants.
Note: The sample population is the set of employees who were at firm all four years. Estimates of contribution status are based on dollars contributed during the year.

tion status occurred between 1988 and 1989, when the year-end match rate jumped from 65 percent to 150 percent, and 63 percent of the 1988 noncontributors joined the plan.[11]

A convenient way of summarizing the economic implications of the transition probabilities in Table 4 is to calculate the steady-state distribution of employees that would obtain if those transition probabilities described employee behavior forever. Straightforward calculations show that the transition probabilities for 1988–89, when the match rate was increasing sharply, are consistent with a steady state in which 98.5 percent of these long-term employees participate in the 401(k) plan. By contrast, the probabilities for 1989–90, when the match rate was about constant, are consistent with a steady state in which 83 percent of these employees participate in the plan. This is not much different from the average participation rate actually observed over our sample. Finally, the transition probabilities between 1990 and 1991, when the match rate was falling, are consistent with a steady state in which only 34 percent of employees contribute to our plan.

We also tabulated the participation rate for individuals who joined the firm during our sample to explore the possibility that new hires, many of whom leave the firm after a short period, exhibit different behavior from established employees. Not surprisingly, the participation rate among new hires was lower than that among other workers: only about half of this group participated, compared with an overall participation rate of about 80 percent. The participation rate among those new hires in 1989 who left the firm in 1990 was only 6.5 percent. This suggests that individuals may make decisions about 401(k) participation based in part on their expected longevity at the firm.

Conclusion

Our results demonstrate two important features of 401(k) plan participation. First, participants are heavily influenced by the various constraints on their contributions. Three-quarters of eligible employees at the firm we analyzed contributed nothing to the plan, or set their contributions equal either to the maximum amount they could contribute or to the amount at which the employer switched from matching to not matching contributions. Second, there is substantial inertia in individual 401(k) contribution decisions. Most workers do not change the fraction of their salary that they contribute to the plan from one year to the next, even when the marginal employer match rate changes from more than 100 percent to zero. In particular, contrary to the results of Andrews (1992) and Papke (1995), we see little evidence that workers respond to increases in the employer match rate by reducing their own contribution rate.

The data from Firm X also suggest that, once a worker participates in a 401(k) plan, he or she is unlikely to stop. This result supports the research strategy of studies such as Poterba, Venti, and Wise (1994, 1995) that have compared the wealth of households that have been eligible for 401(k) plans for different lengths of time to draw inferences about the net effect of these plans on household net worth. Our findings of contributor inertia suggest that, conditional on contributing when a 401(k) plan becomes available, a contributor is likely to contribute in most subsequent years. This suggests that years of eligibility should be strongly correlated with total contributions.

Our findings suggest that further research on the effect of employer match rates on contribution decisions must recognize the role of nonlinearities in the contribution opportunity set. The observation that most contributors are at corners or kinks on this opportunity set suggests that simple methods of calculating the elasticity of contributions with respect to the employer match rate or other parameters of the plan may yield rather unreliable answers. However, modeling the nonlinear budget set facing potential 401(k) contributors and applying the econometric methods described in Hausman (1985) and Moffitt (1990) is complicated by the fact that the budget set facing each 401(k) contributor is age-dependent. The rate of return an individual earns from tax-free accumulation depends in part on the number of years until he or she will withdraw the funds from the 401(k) account. One cannot therefore combine the simple model of 401(k) constraints presented in this chapter with simple models of individual intertemporal choice to estimate a structural model of 401(k) contributor behavior. Moreover, in order to implement a more sophisticated model in a satisfactory fashion, one would need data on the rest of the household balance sheet and income statement—data that are not available in the administrative records of any employer.

Finally, we close with a brief glimpse at the portfolio allocation behavior of employees at Firm X. As we noted earlier, these employees could invest their 401(k) balances in three types of instruments: a GIC, an S&P 500 stock index fund, and a fund wholly invested in the equity of the firm. Barely 20 percent of employees directed any of their own contributions into the S&P 500 fund. At the same time, nearly 25 percent of employees directed all of their contributions into the company stock fund, and another 22 percent directed half of their contributions into the company stock fund. These findings seem difficult to reconcile with standard portfolio theory. They raise questions about the financial acumen of at least some 401(k) participants.

We thank Richard Koski and Paul Euell of Buck Consultants for providing us with data, Stephen Helwig for research assistance, Regina Watson for assistance in preparing the manuscript, Olivia Mitchell for helpful comments, and the Center for Advanced Study in Behavioral Sciences, the Federal Reserve Board, the National Institute on Aging, and the National Science Foundation for research support. Opinions are those of the authors and are not necessarily shared by the Board of Governors or the other members of its staff.

Notes

1. Papke (1995) notes that employer contributions reported on the Form 5500 include any flat per-participant contributions made by the employer and "helper" contributions made to pass the IRS nondiscrimination tests. Such contributions offer the employee no incentive to raise his or her own saving at the margin.

2. If employers tend to adjust the fraction of salary that they will match at the same time that they adjust match rates, then the difficulties of interpretation noted above could apply to these results as well.

3. In focusing on individual-level records from a large employer, the current paper parallels a number of recent papers on defined-benefit pension plans and retirement decisions, such as Kotlikoff and Wise (1987, 1989), Lumsdaine, Stock and Wise (1990, 1992), and Stock and Wise (1990a, 1990b).

4. Eliminating the thrift plan appears not to have affected the aggregate participation and contribution rates for the 401(k) plan very much, in part because relatively few workers could "replace" the thrift plan by joining the 401(k) plan. More than 90 percent of the roughly 1,500 thrift plan members in 1988 also

contributed to the 401(k) plan. Roughly three-quarters of those who were participating in both plans were already contributing enough to the 401(k) to receive the full employer match, and many of them were at the contribution limit of 10 percent of salary. Of the 114 individuals who participated only in the thrift plan in 1988, nearly two-thirds joined the 401(k) in 1989.

5. We measure participation and contribution rates in two ways. The rates in the upper panel are based on each employee's contributions to his or her 401(k) over the course of a year, divided by that employee's "base salary," while those in the lower panel are based on the deferral percentage designated by the employee, as recorded with the plan at year end. The two measures of overall participation are essentially the same through 1990, but diverge sharply in 1991. The mean and median contribution rates are about the same when computed using the two approaches.

6. The stability of the participation rate in 1989 reflects two offsetting factors: an increase in participation among persons who worked at Firm X in 1988 but did not contribute to the 401(k) plan, and an influx of new workers who had very low participation rates. For employees who were at Firm X in all four years of our data, the participation rates based on contributions during the year were 84 percent (1988), 93 percent (1989), 92 percent (1990), and 86 percent (1991). Even for this group, the movements in participation are small.

7. Since the match rate is related to past earnings per share at Firm X, changes in the match rate may be associated with changes in the firm's future prospects. This makes the small response to match rate changes even more striking, since employees might associate reductions in the match rate with downward revisions in their future labor earnings.

8. A loan amount could not exceed the least of: $50,000; half of the vested amount; and 80 percent of the balance in the nonemployer account. The loan rate was tied to the prime rate, with interest credited to the borrower's own account. Borrowing did not limit the employee's ability to continue making 401(k) contributions or affect the firm's matching contribution.

9. When the balance is withdrawn, taxes are due on the original contribution, the employer match, and the investment return. In addition, withdrawals made before an individual reaches age 59½—for example, when he or she changes jobs—may be subject to a 10 percent federal penalty.

10. Twenty-three percent of workers with incomes below $10,000 belonged to the plan in 1989. Some members of this group may have worked at Firm X for only part of the year, so their reported income may understate their full-year earnings.

11. The elimination of the thrift plan was a small factor as well. Also, some of those who joined the 401(k) plan in 1989 may have been part-time workers who were hired in 1988 and who were not eligible to participate in the 401(k) plan until one year after they joined the firm.

References

Andrews, Emily S. "The Growth and Distribution of 401(k) Plans." In John Turner and Daniel Beller, eds., *Trends in Pensions 1992.* U.S. Department of Labor. Washington, D.C.: USGPO, 1992: 149–76.

Clark, Robert L. and Sylvester J. Schieber. "Factors Affecting Participation Rates and Contribution Levels in 401(k) Plans." This volume.

Goodfellow, Gordon P. and Sylvester J. Schieber. "Investment of Assets in Self-Directed Retirement Plans." In Michael S. Gordon, Olivia S. Mitchell, and Marc M. Twinney, eds., *Positioning Pensions for the Twenty-First Century*. Philadelphia: Pension Research Council and University of Pennsylvania Press, 1997: 67–90.

Hausman, Jerry A. "Taxes and Labor Supply." In Alan Auerbach and Martin Feldstein, eds., *Handbook of Public Economics,* Vol. 1, Amsterdam: North Holland, 1985: 213–63.

Hinz, Richard P. and John A. Turner. "Pension Coverage Initiatives: Why Don't Workers Participate?" This volume.

Ippolito, Richard A. "Selecting and Retaining High-Quality Workers." Washington, D.C.: Pension Benefit Guarantee Corporation, mimeo, 1993.

Kotlikoff, Laurence J. and David A. Wise. "The Incentive Effects of Private Pension Plans." In Zvi Bodie, John Shoven, and David Wise, eds., *Issues in Pension Economics*. Chicago: University of Chicago Press, 1987: 283–39.

——. *The Wage Carrot and the Pension Stick*. Kalamazoo, Mich.: W.E. Upjohn Institute, 1989.

Lumsdaine, Robin L., James H. Stock, and David A. Wise. "Efficient Windows and Labor Force Reduction." *Journal of Public Economics* 43 (1990): 131–59.

——. "Three Models of Retirement: Computational Complexity Versus Predictive Validity." In David A. Wise, ed., *Topics in the Economics of Aging*. Chicago: University of Chicago Press, 1992: 21–57.

Moffitt, Robert. "The Econometrics of Kinked Budget Constraints." *Journal of Economic Perspectives* 4 (1990): 119–40.

Papke, Leslie. "Participation in and Contributions to 401(k) Pension Plans: Evidence from Plan Data." *Journal of Human Resources* 30 (1995): 311–25.

Papke, Leslie, Mitchell Petersen, and James Poterba. "Did 401(k) Plans Replace Other Employer-Provided Pensions?" In David Wise, ed., *Advances in the Economics of Aging*. Chicago: University of Chicago Press, 1996: 219–36.

Poterba, James M., Steven F. Venti, and David A. Wise. "401(k) Plans and Tax-Deferred Saving." In David Wise, ed., *Studies in the Economics of Aging*. Chicago: University of Chicago Press, 1994: 105–42.

——. "Do 401(k) Plans Crowd Out Other Private Saving?" *Journal of Public Economics* 58 (1995): 1–32.

——. "How Retirement Saving Programs Increase Saving." *Journal of Economic Perspectives* 10 (1996): 91–112.

Shefrin, Hersh M. and Richard Thaler. "The Behavioral Life-Cycle Hypothesis." *Economic Inquiry* 26 (1988): 609–43.

Stock, James H. and David A. Wise. "The Pension Inducement to Retire: An Option Value Analysis." In David A. Wise, ed., *Issues in the Economics of Aging*. Chicago: University of Chicago Press, 1990: 205–24. 1990a.

——. "Pensions, the Option Value of Work, and Retirement." *Econometrica* 58 (1990): 1151–80. 1990b.

Thaler, Richard. "Psychology and Savings Policies." *American Economic Review* 84 (May 1994): 186–92.

United States Department of Labor (USDOL), Pension and Welfare Benefits Administration, *Abstract of 1992 Form 5500 Annual Reports. Private Pension Plan Bulletin* No. 5. Washington, D.C.: USGPO, Winter 1996.

Part II
Preserving Defined Contribution Pension Accumulations for Retirement

Chapter 6

Implications of the Shift to Defined Contribution Plans for Retirement Wealth Accumulation

William G. Gale and Joseph M. Milano

Pension wealth constitutes a sizable portion of households' retirement resources. Close to half of civilian nonagricultural workers participate in pension plans.[1] Future income flows from private pensions accounted for 20 percent of the wealth of households aged 65–69 in 1991 (Poterba, Venti, and Wise 1994, table 1). Thus the relation between pensions and other household wealth can have important implications for policy issues, such as how to raise the saving rate or assure adequate saving for retirement, as well as for more fundamental issues, such as how people make economic decisions about the future.

Over the past twenty years, the U.S. pension system has shifted toward defined contribution plans and away from defined benefit plans. This shift provides opportunities as well as risks. For example, workers typically possess more authority to determine participation, contribution levels, and portfolio choices in defined contribution plans than in defined benefit plans. The effects of such changes on the role of pensions in retirement wealth accumulation remains an open question.

This chapter examines these issues. The first section provides background on the shift toward defined contributions plans. The second section reviews evidence on the effects of pension wealth on households' nonpension wealth. An important shortcoming of that literature is the absence of a distinction between the potentially different roles of defined contribution and defined benefit plans. The third section discusses how DC and DB plans might differentially affect wealth accumulation. The fourth section presents estimates from the 1980s and the 1990s on these issues.

A final section provides concluding remarks. We find that understanding the implications for retirement saving of the trend toward defined contribution plans is a complex and unsettled issue for at least three reasons. First, the effects of pensions on wealth accumulation has proven to be complicated and difficult to untangle. Second, there are numerous differences between the features of defined contribution plans and those of defined benefit plans. Third, the nature of the plans and the samples of workers they attract have changed over the past decade and a half. Despite these difficulties, we note some relatively clear evidence of heterogeneity across workers in their response to different types of pensions, and highlight the uncertainties that remain.

The Rise of Defined Contribution Plans

By almost any measure, the U.S. pension system has shifted toward defined contribution plans over the past twenty years. The share of defined contribution plans rose from 67 percent to 87 percent of all plans from 1975 to 1992, from 29 to 60 percent of all active participants, from 35 to 72 percent of all contributions, and from 28 to 45 percent of all pension assets (USDOL 1996).[2] What is perhaps less well known is that at least part of the trend appears to predate the passage of ERISA in 1974. Among plans initiated before 1941 but still in effect in 1985, 10.4 percent were defined contribution plans (Clark and McDermed 1990). The figure rises to 16.8 percent for plans initiated in 1942–53, 24.8 percent for plans initiated in 1954–63, 31.3 percent for plans initiated between 1964–73, 47.4 percent for plans initiated between 1974–79, and 60.0 percent for plans initiated in 1980–85. A related trend is the recent growth in hybrid plans, which combine features of defined benefit and defined contribution plans. While less is known about these plans, they may be seen as an attempt to balance the costs and benefits of defined contribution and defined benefit plans (EBRI 1996; Rappaport 1996).

These trends have been attributed in varying degrees to increased regulation of defined benefit plans following the passage of ERISA in 1974, the changing composition of the work force, and other factors.[3] From 1984 to 1992, however, contributions to DC plans rose by $50 billion, while 401(k) contributions alone rose by $48 billion. Thus, explaining the growth of defined contribution plans since 1984 is in large part an effort to explain the growth of 401(k)s.

Ippolito (1993, 1995) provides a model of the advantages of 401(k)s. Workers with low discount rates—those who place a relatively high value on the future over the present—are assumed to be more productive than others. For example, they may place a higher value on future wages than would a high discounter, and so would work harder to develop a reputation as a reliable employee. A 401(k) plan can help firms retain low discounters and exclude high discounters. High discounters will find leaving the firm more attractive, because 401(k) balances can be cashed in upon exit. Low discounters will have incentives to stay because the matching provision of 401(k)s implies that they are in effect paid more than high discounters. Ippolito provides evidence consistent with these hypotheses. As discussed below, this model has important implications for examining the role of pensions on saving.

Effects of Pensions on the Accumulation of Wealth

Theoretical Concerns

In the simplest life cycle economic models, workers are posited to save only for retirement. Changing the form of workers' compensation from current wages to future pension benefits has no effect on consumption, and no effect on overall (pension plus nonpension) wealth or saving. Increases in pension wealth are offset completely by reductions in other wealth.

A number of issues, however, complicate the model when we move toward more realism. First, pensions are typically illiquid, tax-deferred annuities, unlike conventional taxable assets. Illiquidity implies that pensions may raise overall saving for households that cannot borrow as much as they would like (Hubbard 1986). Deferral of taxes raises the after-tax return on pension contributions relative to fully taxable saving. If pensions are the marginal source of saving, the higher return will generate income and substitution effects that work in opposite directions, so that the effect of pensions on overall saving is ambiguous. On one hand, if pension saving is inframarginal, raising the return on contributions should reduce overall saving. Also, as annuities, pensions provide insurance against uncertain lifespan, which would reduce overall saving (Hubbard 1987). As group annuities, pensions can provide more favorable terms than individual annuities, which will induce income and substitution effects in opposite directions (Feldstein 1978). On the other hand, pensions may also induce earlier retirement, which would be expected to raise saving among workers (Feldstein 1974). Therefore, even in a model where people save only for retirement, the effect of pension wealth on other wealth accumulation is ambiguous.

Also, people save for reasons other than retirement. Pensions will be poor substitutes for precautionary saving (Samwick 1994), intended bequests (Bernheim 1991), or saving for other nonretirement purposes. In such cases, changing a worker's compensation to include more pension wealth and less cash wages may not reduce other saving.

Additionally, a number of alternative models of saving have been proposed in which households are believed to make saving decisions based on psychological or behavioral models (Thaler 1990; Bernheim 1996) and frequently lack basic levels of economic literacy (Bernheim 1994, this volume). In these models, pension wealth may not reduce, and may even raise, nonpension wealth.[4]

Empirical Findings

Numerous studies have examined the impact of pensions on wealth.[5] Most of the studies suggest that an increased dollar of pension wealth reduces other wealth by at most 20 cents, and almost half of the studies suggest either that pensions have no effect at all on nonpension wealth or that pensions raise nonpension wealth. Previous empirical work, however, imposes a series of systematic statistical biases, which cause the studies to overstate the effect of pensions on other wealth (Gale, 1996). Some of the biases can generate an estimated positive effect of pensions on nonpension wealth, even when increases in pensions in fact reduce other wealth. These biases cast doubt on prior findings.

Correcting for none of the biases, Gale (1996) finds that a dollar increase in pension wealth reduces other wealth by 10 percent or less. After correcting for five (of the eight) biases, he finds that a dollar increase in pension wealth reduces other wealth by 40–80 cents, depending on the specification. Some estimates also suggest substantial heterogeneity in how households respond to pensions (Bernheim and Scholz 1993; Gale 1996). Thus, there remains substantial uncertainty concerning the impact of pensions on household wealth.

Studies of the impact of 401(k)s on saving have also produced discordant results[6] and also suffer from a series of econometric biases, most of which overstate the impact of 401(k)s on saving and at least one of which may lead to an understatement of the effects.

The Correlation Between Pension Coverage and Preferences for Saving

One of the clearest biases, and one of the most difficult to resolve, arises if households with pensions also have higher "tastes" or preferences for saving than households with similar observable characteristics that do not have pensions. This could occur in several ways. Firms where employees had stronger than average tastes for saving could face more demands to create pension plans. Alternatively, if firms provided pensions randomly, workers with stronger tastes for saving would naturally be more attracted to firms with better pension plans, other things being equal.

These patterns would bias the empirical relationship toward finding that pensions raise overall household saving. Some evidence suggest that pension coverage (or wealth) is positively correlated with tastes for saving, but the findings are not conclusive.[7] We consider this issue in greater detail below.

Distinctions Between Defined Contribution and Defined Benefit Plans

Studies of how pensions affect wealth have largely ignored differences between DB and DC plans. But differences in the features of the plans could have an impact on how pensions affect wealth; so the impact of pensions on wealth could be changing over time as the pension system evolves. This section highlights how several differences between the plan types might differentially influence wealth accumulation.[8]

Worker Choices and Sample Selection

At first glance, it may seem plausible that eligibility for 401(k)s is independent of household's tastes for saving. After all, as Poterba, Venti, and Wise (1995, p. 10) note, "eligibility is determined by employers." But while employers ultimately decide on the policy, the relevant issue is whether employers take employee preferences into account. In a survey of a broad range of employers, "perceived employee interest" was the second most frequently stated reason that a firm installed a 401(k) plan and was noted by 63.5 percent of respondents (Buck Consultants, 1989). This should not be surprising; it would be strange if employers created benefits without regard to employee preferences. Moreover, even if firms did provide 401(k)s randomly, we would expect workers with high tastes for saving to seek out firms with 401(k)s or to encourage their firms to provide 401(k)s. Either way, eligibility is likely to be positively correlated with tastes for saving.

Ultimately, this is an empirical issue. Poterba, Venti, and Wise (1995) present regressions showing that eligible households have about the same level of nonpension, non-401(k) financial assets as ineligible households, controlling for income and other factors. They conclude that 401(k) eligibility is exogenous with respect to tastes for saving. But Engen, Gale, and Scholz (1994, table 8), using the same data set, a slightly different test format, and a longer list of explanatory variables, find that eligible families have higher levels of nonpension, non-401(k) financial assets, net financial assets, and net worth. Moreover, Poterba, Venti, and Wise (1995) omit pensions. Families eligible for 401(k)s are between 24 and 33 percentage points more likely to be covered by a defined benefit pension plan than other families, controlling for other factors (Engen, Gale, and Scholz, 1994). Again, this implies that eligible households have higher non-401(k) wealth than ineligible households.[9]

The Poterba, Venti, and Wise test has another problem that creates a potentially large bias in favor of finding that eligibility is exogenous: the test ignores all 401(k) wealth and thereby *assumes* that all 401(k) saving is new saving. To determine whether 401(k) eligibility is exogenous requires knowing whether eligible families would have saved more than ineligible families in the absence of 401(k)s. Since no data sources track eligible families before 401(k)s were introduced, the exogeneity test used by Poterba, Venti, and Wise requires some assumption about what would have happened to 401(k) wealth had 401(k)s not existed. If x percent of 401(k) wealth would have existed anyway, an appropriate test of exogeneity compares the non-401(k) assets of ineligible families to the sum of non-401(k) assets plus x percent of the 401(k) wealth of eligible families. Clearly, assuming that all 401(k) saving is new saving (x=0) — as in the Poterba, Venti and Wise test — creates a strong bias in favor of finding that eligibility is exogenous. For all these reasons, we believe that 401(k) eligibility and participation are positively correlated with tastes for saving. This implies that cross-sectional tests of the effects of 401(k)s that do not control for households' tastes for saving will overstate the effects of 401(k)s on wealth accumulation.

A related issue is how the difference in tastes for saving between 401(k)-eligible and ineligible households has changed over time. Bernheim (1996) claims that the average "taste for saving" among eligible households has become diluted over time. The logic of the claim is that the most dedicated savers are most likely to become eligible for 401(k)s early on. As less dedicated savers became eligible, average tastes for saving fell among eligible households.

But the direction of the net bias caused by dilution is unclear. Over time, the most dedicated savers among *ineligible* households are the ones most likely to become eligible; so there is dilution among ineligible households, too. The key issue for estimation is the relative dilution of the two groups, not the absolute dilution in one group. Bernheim claims that trends in IRA participation are a "good indication" of dilution. But dilution concerns unobservable characteristics ("tastes for saving"), whereas IRA participation depends on observable and unobservable factors. Probit analysis using the SIPP shows that controlling for household characteristics, IRA participation among eligible households fell by only 1.3 percentage points relative to ineligible households from 1987 to 1991. Thus, changes in unobservable variables — the source of dilution — led to only a slight change in relative IRA participation.

If dilution of the sample of 401(k)-eligible workers were empirically important, the proportion of such workers making 401(k) contributions should have fallen over time. Instead, data from the Current Population Survey show that it rose from 57 percent in 1988 to 65 percent in 1993 (Bassett, Fleming, and Rodrigues 1996).[10] Also, workers with low tastes for saving can and frequently do liquidate their 401(k) upon leaving a firm (Bassett, Fleming, and Rodrigues 1996), which raises the average tastes for saving among eligible families and may reduce it among ineligible families. The model in Ippolito (this volume) also suggests a mechanism by which average tastes for saving among eligible workers could plausibly rise, not fall, over time. Thus, it is unclear whether the sample of eligible households became more or less diluted relative to ineligible households over this period.

A question still remains concerning whether DB pension coverage remains positively correlated with tastes for saving, now that 401(k) plans have expanded so greatly. It is worth noting that households with DB pensions have higher rates of 401(k) eligibility than those who do not have traditional pensions.[11] This suggests substantial overlap between households with 401(k)s and households with DB plans and suggests that households with DB plans may still have higher than average tastes for saving. But the degree of selection into these pension plans may have decreased over time.

Benefit Levels

It is often asserted that defined contribution plans are on average less generous than defined benefit plans. If so, then the impact of DC coverage should have a smaller (in absolute value) effect on other wealth than DB coverage would have. However, in a study of several hundred pension plans in existence in the 1980s, Samwick and Skinner (1993) conclude that defined contribution plans are on average about as generous as defined benefit plans.

Risks

DB and DC plans create different kinds of risks. In DB plans, benefits are linked to the highest few years of earnings, whereas in DC plans benefits are essentially a weighted average of earnings over many years. Thus, different patterns of earnings uncertainty will create different risk patterns across the two types of plans.

Rules regarding (nominal) benefits in a DB plan are set by the employer in advance. Benefits in a DC plan depend on the rate of return earned on pension assets, which depends on choices made by the participant. Both DB and DC benefits are subject to inflation risk.

Samwick and Skinner (1993) conclude that DC plans present less risk to participants than DB plans do.[12] If so, then DC plans may well engender less precautionary saving than DC plans do, and so have a larger negative impact on other saving.

Liquidity

Participants in DC plans can often borrow against their pension balance or access the funds for hardship reasons. Upon leaving a job, DC participants frequently roll over the balance into another pension or cash in the proceeds, subject to tax and penalty (Bassett, Fleming, and Rodrigues 1996). Although DB benefits have become increasingly liquid over time and can be cashed in upon exiting the firm in certain circumstances (mainly when the present value of future benefits is low), DB benefits are in general less liquid than DC benefits. Increased liquidity makes assets in DC plans better substitutes for household precautionary saving or for target saving, such as saving for downpayments or for college expenses, than DB plans are. This increased substitutability may raise DC contributions, but make those contributions more likely to be removed before retirement than would DB contributions. The net effect on retirement saving is ambiguous.

Visibility and Simplicity

Accruing balances are probably simpler to understand in DC plans for most participants. Whether increased visibility raises or reduces households' other saving depends in part on whether the household accrues more or less than it would otherwise have guessed in its DC plan. By providing periodic updates on balances, DC plans may more effectively remind households of the need to save for retirement. Of course, there is no reason why such updates could not also be provided in a DB plan.

In short, although the plans differ in several ways, it is difficult to identify unambiguous implications of these differences for how pensions affect wealth. Nevertheless, several items are worth emphasizing. The mechanisms through which pensions affect wealth can be exceedingly complex. There is no reason to expect the two types of plans to have identical impacts on the level or structure of household wealth, even if the benefit levels were held constant. There can be substantial variation within plan types as well as across plan types. And secular shifts in the pension system could be altering the way pensions affect retirement wealth accumulation.

Empirical Analysis

To analyze these issues further, we examine the relation between nonpension wealth, defined benefit coverage, and defined contribution coverage in two separate data sets from the 1980s and 1990s.

Evidence from the 1983 Survey of Consumer Finances

The 1983 Survey of Consumer Finances (SCF) contains interviews with 3,824 U.S. households in 1983, along with a supplemental survey of 438 high-income households. The SCF was designed specifically to collect data on household balance sheets. It also contains detailed information on pensions, demographic characteristics, income, and other variables.[13]

Ideally, the regressions would control for the present value of previous and future earnings and inheritances. Because it is not generally possible to construct earnings histories and futures with the available data, the regressions instead control for age of the household head, years of education (averaged over the head and spouse), earnings of the head and spouse, an interaction term between age and earnings, family size, marital status, and an indicator variable for the presence of two earners. These variables will be correlated with lifetime measures of wages and provide proxies for consumption demands as well.

The regressions also contain a variable that takes the value of 1 if either the head or spouse is covered by a defined benefit plan or defined contribution plan (this variable is called pension coverage) and a second variable indicating whether either the head or spouse has a defined contribution plan. The first variable shows differences between the population with pensions and those without and is meant to capture the effect of having a pension. The second captures the effect, conditional on having a pension, of having a defined contribution pension, and thus provides information on the difference between DC and DB plans on wealth accumulation. Of course, the DC variable will also pick up other differences between the two plans, such as differences in the types of households enrolled in each. Ideally, pension wealth measures would be used here. But using pension wealth introduces a number of additional biases, which are exacerbated when estimating the differential effects of DB versus DC plans (Gale 1995).

We explore the effects of pension coverage on two different measures of wealth: financial assets and nonpension private wealth, including housing (but not Social Security benefits). In each case, balances in defined contribution plans, profit-sharing plans, and so on are excluded from the measure of nonpension wealth, but trigger the pension variables to take the value 1. IRA and Keogh plans do not count as pension

TABLE 1 Sample Characteristics, 1983 Survey of Consumer Finances

	All households		*Households with IRA or Keogh*		*Households without IRA or Keogh*	
Variable	*Mean*	*Median*	*Mean*	*Median*	*Mean*	*Median*
Financial assets	65,699	8,875	149,185	36,187	26,075	3,098
Net worth	214,541	84,134	420,353	145,912	116,858	59,532
Age of head	50.1	50	51.8	52	49.3	48
Education	12.5	12	13.8	14	11.9	12
Family earnings	47,119	38,253	67,801	55,574	37,301	32,133
Family size	2.9	3	2.9	3	2.9	3
Married	0.650	—	0.747	—	0.603	—
Two earners	0.401	—	0.491	—	0.358	—
Have DB plan	0.615	—	0.658	—	0.594	—
Have DC plan	0.111	—	0.146	—	0.094	—
Have DB or DC plan	0.706	—	0.784	—	0.669	—
Have IRA or Keogh	0.322	—	1.000	—	0.000	—
Sample size	829		339		490	

Source: Authors' calculations using the 1983 Survey of Consumer Finances.
Note: All dollar figures are in 1995 dollars. "Financial assets" are defined as the sum of checking and saving accounts, money market accounts, certificates of deposit, bills and bonds, stocks, mutual funds, cash value of life insurance, balances in employment-related thrift accounts, and other financial assets. "Net worth" is defined as the sum of housing equity, financial assets, business equity, and other real estate, less unsecured debt. Other variables are defined in the text.

coverage and so are included in the measures of nonpension wealth. The literature indicates that using broader measures of wealth often produces larger estimates of the offset between pensions and other saving.[14] As discussed above, the pure life cycle model suggests that pensions should substitute for other retirement saving, but not necessarily for other saving. The problem in practice is determining what qualifies as a retirement asset: for example, should housing wealth be included as retirement wealth? Our view is that it is best not to prejudge or assume the answer. Thus, the most relevant measure for estimates of pension offset is the broadest possible measure of wealth.[15] For example, if most saving is nonretirement saving, that will show up in the estimates as little offset. However, the distinction, even at a conceptual level, is murky. Precautionary saving balances that do not get used up in the working years become retirement saving.

The sample focuses on households where the head is age 40 to 64, where the head works at least 1,000 hours per year and describes that activity as working full time, where no one in the household is self-employed, and where no one in the household is a farmer or farm manager. These restrictions were imposed to provide a sample of households with a minimum of extenuating circumstances regarding wealth accumu-

TABLE 2 Effects of Pension Coverage on Nonpension Wealth, 1983 Survey of Consumer Finances

Dependent variable	*Coefficient on . . .*	*LAD regression coefficients (t-statistics)* All families	Families with IRA or Keogh	Families without IRA or Keogh
Financial assets	DC coverage	18,028	23,437	2,604
		(1.91)	(1.11)	(0.59)
	Pension coverage	(27,349)	(61,411)	(8,535)
		(3.77)	(3.38)	(1.37)
Net worth	DC coverage	31,129	167,690	22,315
		(1.61)	(2.02)	(0.65)
	Pension coverage	(81,927)	(273,393)	(66,600)
		(5.25)	(2.27)	(1.27)
Sample size		829	339	490

Source: Authors' calculations using the 1983 Survey of Consumer Finances.
Note: All dollar figures are in 1995 dollars. "Financial assets" are defined as the sum of checking and saving accounts, money market accounts, certificates of deposit, bills and bonds, stocks, mutual funds, cash value of life insurance, balances in employment-related thrift accounts, and other financial assets. "Net worth" is defined as the sum of housing equity, financial assets, business equity, and other real estate, less unsecured debt.

lation. Hence, the results may not be applicable to the broader population. We also excluded households that could not say whether their pension was a DC or DB plan. The remaining sample consists of 829 households.

Two caveats are immediately relevant for this sample. The first is the relatively small sample size. The second is the finding in Mitchell (1988), based on a comparison of answers in the original SCF survey and in a supplemental pension provider survey, that a sizable minority of respondents appeared to misstate their pension type in the original survey.

Table 1 reports the means and medians of the variables used in the analysis. The sample is relatively affluent, most households are married, fewer than half have two earners. About 61 percent of the households have defined benefit coverage, while 11 percent have defined contribution coverage. There is remarkably little overlap: few households in the sample have both DB and DC coverage. About one-third of the sample holds an IRA or Keogh plan.

Table 2 reports the regression results for the effects of defined benefit and defined contribution pension coverage for the overall sample. Because there is substantial heterogeneity in households' tastes for saving, ordinary least squares estimation generates nonsensical results for estimates of pension offsets.[16] To address this issue, we use least absolute deviations estimators. These regressions indicate the effects of pensions on the typical, or median, household rather than the average (mean) household, and are thus much less sensitive to the presence of outliers in the data.

The results are shown in the first column of Table 2. The typical household with a pension accumulated about $17,000 less in financial assets than the typical household without a pension, controlling for other factors. This effect is statistically significant. Households with defined contribution plans had more nonpension financial assets than those with defined benefit plans, but still less than the typical household without a pension.

These results must be interpreted cautiously. While they suggest that DB plans displace more wealth than DC plans do, the finding could be due to differing selection processes into each plan, as well as a host of other issues.

Moreover, the estimates above require that each household have the same response to pension wealth. Households may respond differently, however, for a number of reasons. First, borrowing-constrained households may be unable to offset as much pension wealth as they would like (Hubbard 1986). Second, models that contain both retirement saving and precautionary saving suggest that the relative importance of the two motives changes over the life cycle (Engen and Gale 1993; Hubbard, Skinner, and Zeldes 1995; Samwick 1994). Pensions seem likely to be poor substitutes for precautionary saving, but may be good substitutes for other retirement saving. Third, some households may be poor planners, financially illiterate, or "rule of thumb" consumers. For these households, pension offset may be very small, suggesting that the offset should be related to factors that determine whether a household is in this category.

To capture these differences across households, we estimate separate equations for different groups, across which we expect the pension offsets to differ. Zeldes (1989) uses this strategy to test for the presence of borrowing constraints. A large number of additional studies of consumption and saving have followed similar strategies. In the current context, this strategy may help resolve two additional problems as well. First, the same reasoning that suggests that the coefficient on pension wealth will differ across groups also suggests that the response of wealth to *any* of the right hand side variables could vary as well. For example, a borrowing-constrained household may have a different response to pension wealth as well as a different age-wealth profile, so borrowing constraints would affect the coefficient on age as well as the pension offset. Second, under certain circumstances discussed below, estimating different equations for different groups may be a natural way to control for heterogeneity in unobservable tastes for saving and the potential endogeneity of such tastes with respect to pensions.[17]

The sample is divided into subsamples depending on whether the household has a positive balance in an IRA/Keogh. Households with positive saving incentive balances are less likely to be borrowing constrained,[18] more likely to be saving for retirement, and more likely to be financially literate. Thus, we expect households with saving incentives to exhibit more substitution between pensions and other wealth than other households would. There is of course no claim that this criteria splits the sample into two perfectly homogeneous groups. Rather, the idea is to split the sample such that households in one group differ systematically on average from households in the other group.

Although it allows for different groups to have different responses to pensions, the sample-splitting strategy we employ may generate a potential endogeneity problem. For example, households with IRAs exhibit stronger tastes for saving than other households, controlling for observable characteristics (Gale and Scholz 1994; Engen, Gale, and Scholz 1994). When the dependent variable is net worth, however, splitting the sample on the basis of tastes for saving may create sample selection bias. In any case, the direction of the bias for estimating pension offset is unclear, and the selection bias disappears under certain distributional assumptions.[19] Nevertheless, potential sample selection bias is an important caveat to all the results below that examine the heterogeneity of responses to pension wealth across groups. The smaller sample size created in each subsample is an additional caveat to these results.

The last four columns of Table 1 report means and medians for the samples with and without IRAs and Keoghs. Households holding such accounts are more affluent, more likely to be married and to have two earners, and more likely to have either a defined benefit or a defined contribution plan.

The last two columns of Table 2 show the results of splitting the sample. The negative effect of pensions on wealth is larger among households with IRAs or Keoghs than those without. This is consistent with more offset occurring in the group with IRAs or Keoghs, but could also be caused by those households' having larger pensions. In each case, the impact of DB plans is estimated to be larger in absolute value than the impact of DC plans.

Evidence from the Health and Retirement Study

The Health and Retirement Study (Wave I) contains interviews with 7,702 households where either the head or spouse was aged between 51

TABLE 3 Sample Characteristics, 1992 Health and Retirement Study

	All households		*Households with IRA or Keogh*		*Households without IRA or Keogh*	
Variable	*Mean*	*Median*	*Mean*	*Median*	*Mean*	*Median*
Financial assets	53,639	15,207	100,126	52,140	16,546	2,390
Net worth	152,942	84,510	245,146	164,023	79,374	43,450
Age of head	55.6	55	56.0	56	55.3	55
Education	12.6	12	13.5	13	12.0	12
Family earnings	44,796	39,105	55,509	49,967	36,248	31,501
Household size	2.3	2	2.3	2	2.3	2
Married	0.611	—	0.685	—	0.551	—
Two earners	0.369	—	0.452	—	0.304	—
Have DB plan	0.567	—	0.635	—	0.512	—
Have DC plan	0.361	—	0.471	—	0.273	—
Have DB or DC plan	0.711	—	0.799	—	0.641	—
Have IRA or Keogh	0.444	—	1.000	—	0.000	—
Sample size	2,641		1,053		1,588	

Source: Authors' calculations using the 1992 Health and Retirement Study.
Note: All dollar figures are in 1995 dollars. "Financial assets" are defined as the sum of checking and saving accounts, money market accounts, certificates of deposit, bills and bonds, IRA and Keogh balances, stocks, mutual funds, and investment trusts. "Net worth" is defined as the sum of housing equity, financial assets, business equity, and other real estate. Other variables are defined in the text.

and 62 in 1992. The HRS collected detailed data on households' wealth, health and disability status, income, and demographic factors. In the near future, a pension provider survey may be available, which will allow more detailed examination of pensions and wealth.[20]

The basic sample exclusions are similar to those using the SCF: all households where the head was working less than 1,000 hours per year, all farm households, all households where someone is self-employed, and all who did not know what type of pension they had. The remaining sample consists of 2,641 households.

Table 3 shows the means and medians of the variables used in the analysis. Like the 1983 SCF sample, the 1992 HRS sample is affluent. Defined benefit coverage is lower in the HRS, but defined contribution coverage more than tripled from 1983. A potentially important difference with the 1983 sample is that roughly 40 percent of defined contribution plans are held by families that also have defined benefit coverage. In the 1983 sample, there was virtually no overlap. This is an important caveat in comparing the coefficients across the samples.

The first column of Table 4 reports regression results for the overall sample. Financial assets are smaller for those with pensions than for those

TABLE 4 Effects of Pension Coverage on Nonpension Wealth, 1992 Health and Retirement Study

Dependent variable	*Coefficient on . . .*	*LAD regression coefficients (t-statistics)*		
		All families	*Families with IRA or Keogh*	*Families without IRA or Keogh*
Financial assets	DC coverage	6,477	1,993	234
		(4.69)	(0.48)	(0.49)
	Pension coverage	(3,814)	(8,505)	92
		(2.54)	(2.30)	(0.23)
Net worth	DC coverage	21,998	7,277	6,635
		(2.50)	(0.72)	(1.61)
	Pension coverage	(4,820)	(26,677)	13,528
		(0.28)	(1.60)	(3.23)
Sample size		2,641	1,053	1,588

Source: Authors' calculations using the 1992 Health and Retirement Study.
Note: All dollar figures are in 1995 dollars. "Financial assets" are defined as the sum of checking and saving accounts, money market accounts, certificates of deposit, bills and bonds, IRA and Keogh balances, stocks, mutual funds, and investment trusts. "Net worth" is defined as the sum of housing equity, financial assets, business equity, and other real estate.

without. But the typical household with a defined contribution plan has more wealth than the typical household with a defined benefit plan and even more than the typical household without a pension.

Table 3 also shows means and medians of variables for the samples with and without IRAs and Keoghs. The relative patterns are the same as in 1983. The sample with IRAs and Keoghs is much more affluent that households without either saving incentive.

The last two columns of Table 4 show the results of splitting the sample by saving incentive status. Pension coverage has a larger negative effect on households with IRAs and Keoghs than on other households. Controlling for pension coverage, the impact of defined contribution coverage on nonpension wealth is estimated to be positive but not significantly different from zero.

Discussion and Comparisons

These results present interesting patterns. First, the impact of pension coverage on nonpension wealth is consistently negative in 1983, but not in 1992. This could be due to shifts in the tastes for saving of households covered by pensions relative to those not covered by pensions. As discussed above, there are a number of reasons to think that the sample of 401(k)-eligible households raised their tastes for saving relative to ineligible households. Second, controlling for pension coverage, DC plans had a consistently positive coefficient in 1983, though not always significant. The effect in 1992 was generally smaller and less statistically significant.

Unfortunately, we are unable to conclusively identify just one interpretation of these results. They could be due to changes in relative tastes for saving among the groups, changes in the relative generosity of different plans, or the fact that DC plans in 1992 were much more likely to represent second plans. In addition, the SCF sample is somewhat younger than the HRS sample, which could also influence the results.

Conclusion

The long-term shift toward defined contribution plans could have important effects on how pensions interact with preparations for retirement. Each of the differences between DB and DC plans along dimensions of risks, liquidity, visibility, sample selection, and so on, has implications for how other saving should be affected. As described above, understanding the effects of pension on wealth is a complex task. Disentangling the differential impacts of DC and DB plans is even more difficult due to data limitations, shifts in unobserved variables (such as the tastes for saving among the pool of DC participants), and a large number of underlying models of saving behavior.

Against this backdrop, the empirical results developed here suggest that DB and DC plans can have different effects on wealth, that there is heterogeneity in responses to pensions, and that important endogeneity problems may be biasing the results. However, more definitive evidence on the precise nature of the links between pension type and wealth accumulation will have to await further developments of theory and data.

We thank Richard Ippolito, Olivia Mitchell, Nicholas Souleles, conference participants, and the referees for very helpful comments. The opinions are those of the authors and should not be ascribed to the trustees, officers, or staff of the Brookings Institution.

Notes

1. EBRI (1994, table 2). This participation rate includes salary reduction plans as well as more traditional defined benefit and defined contribution plans.

2. Other data provide further evidence on these trends. The proportion of the workforce with a defined benefit plan as the primary pension fell from 39 percent to 26 percent over the same period, while the proportion with primary defined contribution plans rose from 6 to 20 percent, and the proportion with supplemental defined contribution plans rose from 9 to 17 percent (USDOL 1996).

Defined contribution plans covered 80 percent of active participants in plans established since 1975, compared to 33 percent in plans established before 1975 (Beller and Lawrence 1992).

3. On the role of regulations, see Clark and McDermed (1990), Gale (1994), and Lichtenstein (1992). On the role of shifts in industrial composition and employment, see Gustman and Steinmeier (1992), Ippolito (1995) and Kruse (1991). See also Warshawsky (1995) for a related discussion.

4. An older tradition in the pension literature also advocates alternative models of saving, with similar findings. Cagan (1965) suggests that the provision of pensions makes workers realize the need to save for retirement, which raises their nonpension saving. Katona (1965) suggests that pensions raise nonpension saving because they make households feel that attaining a reasonable standard of living in retirement is more feasible, and because people tend to intensify their efforts (e.g., saving) as they come closer to achieving their goal (e.g., reasonable living standards in retirement).

5. See Gale (1995) for a review of the literature.

6. The literature is reviewed in Bernheim (1996), Engen, Gale, and Scholz (1996), and Poterba, Venti, and Wise (1996).

7. Johnson (1993), using experimental data from the first wave of the Health and Retirement Survey, finds that workers with higher risk aversion or lower time preference rates are more likely to be covered by pensions. Also see Ippolito (1993) and Allen, Clark, and McDermed (1993).

8. For further discussion, see Bodie, Marcus, and Merton (1988) and Samwick and Skinner (1993).

9. Along similar lines, Bernheim and Garrett (1995) find that 401(k) eligibility "raises" total wealth by about four times as much as it "raises" retirement wealth. Unless one is willing to believe that 401(k) contributions crowd in several times their value in non-401(k) saving, these findings suggest that eligibility is positively correlated with tastes for saving.

10. This increase is unlikely to be due to an increase in employer matching. In 1993, among eligible workers that did not receive a match, 60 percent contributed. Our own probit analysis using the SIPP indicates that between 1987 and 1991, controlling for household characteristics (including pension coverage), the 401(k) participation rate of eligible households rose by 8 percentage points, and the increase was statistically significant.

11. Data from the 1991 SIPP suggest that, controlling for a host of household characteristics, families with DB coverage are 25 percentage points more likely to be eligible for a 401(k) and 13 percentage points more likely to participate than observationally equivalent households without DB coverage.

12. This calculation does not include the risk that taxpayers face through possible pension bailouts by the Pension Benefit Guaranty Corporation.

13. For further information on the SCF, see Avery and Elliehausen (1988).

14. See Avery, Elliehausen, and Gustafson (1986) and Gale (1995). We estimate the effects of pension coverage on the level, rather than the log of wealth, for two reasons. First, some households have negative wealth, for which the log is undefined. Second, pension offset is an arithmetic effect—a dollar of pension wealth changes nonpension wealth by x cents—rather than a multiplicative effect. A result framed in terms of an elasticity of wealth with respect to pensions—say, that a 1 percent increase in pension wealth is associated with an x percent change in nonpension wealth—is not useful in determining pension offsets.

15. Engen, Gale, and Scholz (1996) and Gale (1995, 1996) provide extensive discussions of the value of examining the impact of pensions on broad measures of wealth.

16. Samwick (1994), for example, obtains ordinary least squares estimates that suggest that one dollar of pension wealth raises other wealth by as much as six dollars.

17. Another way to capture these different responses to pension wealth is to make the measured offset a function of household characteristics. This strategy is used, for example, by Venti and Wise (1990) and Gale and Scholz (1994) in analyses of how IRAs affect saving, but would be difficult to apply in the current context because it requires estimates of several additional parameters, which would not be feasible given the relatively small sample size.

18. Since the data are from 1983 and universal eligibility for IRAs was not present until 1982, "having an IRA" is likely to be closely correlated with "making an IRA contribution" in 1983, suggesting that those with IRAs are not likely to be borrowing constrained. Gale and Scholz (1994) provide further evidence on this issue.

19. For example, suppose tastes for saving are given by $e = v_1 + u$ for households with saving incentives and $e = v_2 + u$ for households without saving incentives, where the v's are constants, $v_2 > v_1$, u is normally distributed with mean zero, and the u's and v's are uncorrelated. Then, in separating the sample, the v's would be subsumed into the constant term in the regression and the expected value of u would be zero in each subsample.

20. For more information on the Health and Retirement Study see Gustman, Mitchell, and Steinmeier (1995) and the articles in Burkhauser and Gertler (1995).

References

Allen, Steven G., Robert L. Clark, and Ann A. McDermed. "Pensions, Bonding, and Lifetime Jobs." *Journal of Human Resources* 28, 3 (1993): 463–81.

Avery, Robert B. and Gregory E. Elliehausen. "1983 Survey of Consumer Finances: Technical Manual and Codebook." Washington, D.C.: Board of Governors of the Federal Reserve System, mimeo, 1988.

Avery, Robert B., Gregory E. Elliehausen, and Thomas A. Gustafson. "Pensions and Social Security in Household Portfolios: Evidence from the 1983 Survey of Consumer Finances." In F. Gerard Adams and Susan M. Wachter, eds., *Savings and Capital Formation.* Lexington, Mass.: Lexington Books, 1986: 127–60.

Bassett, William F., Michael J. Fleming, and Anthony P. Rodrigues. "How Workers Use 401(k) Plans: The Participation, Contribution, and Withdrawal Decisions." New York: Federal Reserve Board of New York, mimeo, 1996.

Beller, Daniel J. and Helen H. Lawrence. "Trends in Private Pension Plan Coverage." In John A. Turner and Daniel J. Beller, eds., *Trends in Pensions 1992.* Washington, D.C.: U.S. Department of Labor, 1992: 59–96.

Bernheim, B. Douglas. "How Strong Are Bequest Motives?" *Journal of Political Economy* 99, 5 (1991): 899–927.

——. "Personal Saving, Information, and Economic Literacy: New Directions for Public Policy." In *Tax Policy and Economic Growth in the 1990s.* Washington, D.C.: American Council for Capital Formation, 1994: 53–78.

——. "Rethinking Saving Incentives." Paper prepared for a conference titled

"Fiscal Policy: Lessons from Economic Research," sponsored by the Burch Center for Tax Policy and Public Finance at the University of California at Berkeley and held on February 2–3, 1996 (revised, March).

——. "Financial Illiteracy, Education, and Retirement Saving." This volume.

Bernheim, B. Douglas and Daniel M. Garrett. "The Determinants and Consequences of Financial Education in the Workplace: Evidence from a Survey of Households." Stanford, Calif.: Department of Economics, Stanford University, mimeo, 1995.

Bernheim, B. Douglas and John Karl Scholz. "Private Saving and Public Policy." In James M. Poterba, ed., *Tax Policy and the Economy,* Vol. 7. Cambridge, Mass.: MIT Press, 1993: 73–110

Bodie, Zvi, Alan J. Marcus, and Robert C. Merton. "Defined Benefit Versus Defined Contribution Pension Plans: What Are the Real Trade-offs?" In Zvi Bodie, John B. Shoven, and David A. Wise, eds., *Pensions in the U.S. Economy.* Chicago: University of Chicago Press, 1988: 139–62.

Buck Consultants, Inc. "Current 401(k) Plan Practices: A Survey Report." Secaucus, N.J.: Buck Consultants, 1989.

Burkhauser, Richard V. and Paul J. Gertler, eds., *Journal of Human Resources: Special Issue, The Health and Retirement Study, Data Quality and Early Results* 30 (supp.). Madison: University of Wisconsin Press, 1995.

Cagan, Philip. "The Effect of Pension Plans on Aggregate Saving: Evidence from a Sample Survey." National Bureau of Economic Research Occasional Paper No. 95. Washington, D.C.: NBER, 1965.

Clark, Robert L. and Ann A. McDermed. *The Choice of Pension Plans in a Changing Regulatory Environment.* Washington, D.C.: AEI Press, 1990.

Employee Benefit Research Institute (EBRI). "Employment-Based Retirement Income Benefits: Analysis of the April 1993 Current Population Survey." EBRI Special Report SR-25 and Issue Brief No. 153. Washington, D.C.: EBRI, 1994.

——. "Hybrid Retirement Plans: The Retirement Income System Continues to Evolve." EBRI Special Report SR-32 and Issue Brief No. 171. Washington, D.C.: EBRI, 1996.

Engen, Eric M. and William G. Gale. "IRAs and Saving in a Stochastic Life Cycle Model." Washington, D.C.: Brookings Institution, mimeo, 1993.

Engen, Eric M., William G. Gale, and John Karl Scholz. "Do Saving Incentives Work?" *Brookings Papers on Economic Activity* 1 (1994): 85–180.

——. "The Illusory Effects of Saving Incentives on Saving." *Journal of Economic Perspectives* 10, 4 (Fall 1996): 113–38.

Feldstein, Martin. "Social Security, Induced Retirement, and Aggregate Capital Accumulation." *Journal of Political Economy* 82, 5(1974): 905–26.

——. "Do Private Pensions Increase National Savings?" *Journal of Public Economics* 10, 3 (1978): 277–93.

Gale, William G. "Public Policies and Private Pension Contributions." *Journal of Money, Credit, and Banking* 26, 3 (1994): 710–32.

——. "The Effects of Pensions on Wealth: A Re-Evaluation of Theory and Evidence." Washington, D.C.: Brookings Institution, mimeo, June 1995.

——. "Comments on 'Rethinking Saving Incentives'." In Alan J. Auerbach, ed., *Fiscal Policy: Lessons from Economic Research.* Cambridge, Mass.: MIT Press, 1997: 313–30.

Gale, William G. and John Karl Scholz. "IRAs and Household Saving." *American Economic Review* 84, 5 (1994): 1233–60.

Gustman, Alan L. and Thomas L. Steinmeier. "The Stampede Toward Defined

Contribution Pension Plans: Fact or Fiction?" *Industrial Relations* 31 (1992): 361–69.

Gustman, Alan L., Olivia S. Mitchell, and Thomas L. Steinmeier. "Retirement Measures in the Health and Retirement Study." *Journal of Human Resources* 30 (1995): S59–S83 (suppl.).

Hubbard, R. Glenn. "Pension Wealth and Individual Saving." *Journal of Money, Credit, and Banking* 18, 2 (1986): 167–78.

——. "Uncertain Lifetimes, Pensions, and Individual Saving." In Zvi Bodie, John B. Shoven, and David A. Wise, eds., *Issues in Pension Economics.* Chicago: University of Chicago Press, 1987: 175–210.

Hubbard, R. Glenn, Jonathan Skinner, and Stephen P. Zeldes. "Precautionary Saving and Social Insurance." *Journal of Political Economy* 103, 2 (1995): 360–99.

Ippolito, Richard A. "Selecting and Retaining High-Quality Workers: A Theory of 401(k) Pensions." Unpublished paper. Pension Benefit Guaranty Corporation, Washington, D.C., 1993.

——. "Toward Explaining the Growth of Defined Contribution Plans." *Industrial Relations* 34, 1 (1995): 1–20.

——. "Disparate Savings Propensities and National Retirement Policy." This volume.

Johnson, Richard W. "The Impact of Worker Preferences on Pension Coverage in the HRS." Mimeo, U.S. Department of Labor, Washington, D.C., 1993.

Katona, George. *Private Pensions and Individual Saving.* Ann Arbor: University of Michigan Press, 1965.

Kruse, Douglas L. "Pension Substitution in the 1980s: Why the Shift Toward Defined Contribution Pension Plans?" National Bureau of Economic Research Working Paper No. 388. Washington, D.C.: NBER, 1991.

Lichtenstein, Jules H. "Pension Availability and Coverage in Small and Large Firms." In John A. Turner and Daniel J. Beller, eds., *Trends in Pensions 1992.* U.S. Department of Labor; Washington, D.C.: USGPO, 1992: 97–118.

Mitchell, Olivia S. "Worker Knowledge of Pension Provisions." *Journal of Labor Economics* 6, 1 (1988): 21–39.

Poterba, James M., Steven F. Venti, and David A. Wise. "Targeted Retirement Saving and the Net Worth of Elderly Americans." *American Economic Review* 84, 2 (1994): 180–85.

——. "Do 401(k) Contributions Crowd Out Other Personal Saving?" *Journal of Public Economics* 58 (1995): 1–32.

——. "How Retirement Programs Increase Saving." *Journal of Economic Perspectives* 10, 4 (Fall 1996): 91–112.

Rappaport, Anna M. "Family Concerns in Dealing with Retirement Planning." Pension Research Council Working Paper No. 96-16. Philadelphia: Wharton School, 1996.

Samwick, Andrew A. "The Limited Offset Between Pension Wealth and Other Private Wealth: Implications of Buffer-Stock Saving," Mimeo, Dartmouth College, Hanover, N.H., 1994.

Samwick, Andrew A. and Jonathan Skinner. "How Will Defined Contribution Plans Affect Retirement Income?" Mimeo, Dartmouth College, Hanover, N.H., 1993.

Thaler, Richard. "Anomalies: Saving, Fungibility, and Mental Accounts." *Journal of Economic Perspectives* 4, 1 (1990): 193–205.

U.S. Department of Labor (USDOL), Pension and Welfare Benefits Administration. *Abstract of 1992 Form 5500 Annual Reports, Private Pension Plan Bulletin,* No. 5. Washington, D.C.: USGPO, 1996.

Venti, Steven F. and David A. Wise. "Have IRAs Increased U.S. Saving? Evidence from Consumer Expenditure Surveys." *Quarterly Journal of Economics* 105, 3 (1990): 661–98.

Warshawsky, Mark J. "Determinants of Pension Plan Formations and Terminations." *Benefits Quarterly* (4th quarter 1995): 71–80.

Zeldes, Stephen P. "Consumption and Liquidity Constraints: An Empirical Investigation." *Journal of Political Economy* 97, 2 (1989): 305–46.

Chapter 7
Responses of Mutual Fund Investors to Adverse Market Disruptions

John D. Rea and Richard G. Marcis

Asset allocation by participants in 401(k) plans is critical to the contribution that these plans make in providing for retirement security. An important concern in this regard is how plan participants might react to adverse market developments, such as heightened market volatility or an extended bear market. This concern is relevant because the growth of 401(k) plans and assets during the last ten years has occurred when stock prices have trended upward and interest rates have trended downward. Consequently, many 401(k) participants have not yet had to cope with declining values in their 401(k) accounts.

Only limited information on asset allocation in 401(k) plans is available, and very little is known about how participants have reallocated plan assets or contributions in response to changes in stock prices and interest rates. Given the paucity of information on 401(k) participants, it may prove useful to examine the investment activity of mutual fund investors as an alternative. Mutual funds are a significant part of the 401(k) market, accounting for an estimated 37 percent of all assets held in 401(k) accounts at the end of 1995. In addition, the 401(k) market is a significant line of business for mutual funds, representing over 8 percent of all mutual fund assets at the end of 1995. Moreover, assets from all retirement-related accounts, including 401(k) plans, other defined contribution plans, and Individual Retirement Accounts (IRAs), accounted for an estimated 35 percent of all mutual fund assets at year-end 1995. Furthermore, between 1993 and 1995, about 30 percent of the net flow of new cash to mutual funds was from 401(k) plans and another 37 percent was from IRAs and other retirement plans.[1] Finally, an estimated 18.4 million households who owned mutual funds in mid-1995 had a family member participating in a 401(k) plan (Investment Company Institute

1996c). These households represented about 60 percent of all mutual fund owners and perhaps as many as 75 to 80 percent of all 401(k) participants. Of the 18.4 million households, approximately four out of five held mutual funds in their 401(k) accounts.[2]

In view of the overlap between mutual fund ownership and 401(k) participation and the high percentage of mutual fund assets and net flows arising from retirement-related accounts, this chapter reviews research on the response of mutual fund shareholders to short-term market disruptions and to longer-term declines in stock prices. This topic has received considerable attention lately, as concern has arisen over the possibility of a run on stock mutual funds in the event of a collapse in stock prices (Kaufman 1994).

To summarize the key findings, stock fund holders have not in the past liquidated their holdings en masse in response to stock market breaks or sharp sell-offs. They have, however, shown a sensitivity to cyclical and secular movements in stock prices. In addition, they displayed remarkable stability in 1994 in the face of market disruptions that included the tightening of monetary policy, derivative losses at taxable money funds, the bankruptcy of Orange County, and the Mexican peso crisis.

Although a run on mutual funds is not an impossibility, this evidence suggests that the probability is low. The low likelihood partly reflects the manner in which mutual funds are regulated. Assets of mutual funds must be marked to the market daily, and consequently shareholders cannot avoid losses associated with market developments by redeeming shares. In contrast, under similar circumstances, bank depositors have an incentive to make withdrawals because bank assets are not marked to market. Mutual funds must also hold readily marketable assets and disclose information about their investment objectives and investment strategies so that investors can assess the risks associated with mutual fund investments.

In addition to regulation, certain characteristics of mutual fund investors also contribute to the low likelihood of a run. Surveys of the shareholders show that most are seasoned investors with long-term investment horizons. Surveys also indicate that fund owners generally have not redeemed shares because of market developments and that they are not inclined to do so in the future. In addition, most shareholders have a basic understanding of investment risk and are aware that mutual funds are risky. As a result, they take risk into account when making purchase decisions, although they typically place it within a long-term investment horizon.

These characteristics of mutual fund shareholders suggest that participants in 401(k) plans may not act precipitately as well in response to market developments, although they may reallocate plan assets and contributions in response to longer-run changes in stock returns and interest rates. Further research is needed on the determinants of asset allocation in 401(k) plans, as this conclusion assumes that the activity of mutual fund investors generally is representative of that of 401(k) participants. In this regard, mutual fund shareholders with 401(k) plans do differ from those without plans in several respects. For example, those with 401(k) plans tend to be younger, less educated, and less wealthy. They also tend to have a higher proportion of their financial assets in 401(k) plans. In addition, those who only own mutual funds in their 401(k) plans appear to be much more dependent upon these plans for retirement income than other mutual fund owners. Such differences might be the source of different responses to market developments.

Profile of Mutual Fund Owners

Individuals are the primary owners of mutual funds, held either directly or indirectly through trusts or retirement plans. At the end of 1995, financial institutions, businesses, endowments, nonprofit organizations, and other types of nonpersonal entities held only 10 percent of the $2.8 trillion in mutual fund assets. Another 15 percent of mutual fund assets was held in fiduciary arrangements, such as trusts and custodial accounts for minors, a significant portion of which is for the benefit of individuals. Thus, depending upon the interpretation of fiduciary accounts, individuals owned or controlled at least 75 percent of all industry assets.

A survey of approximately 1,500 household owners of mutual funds conducted in 1995 showed that the typical financial decision maker in these households is 42 years of age; 54 percent have a college degree, 83 percent are employed, 15 percent are retired, and 77 percent have a working spouse (ICI, 1996b). Median household income is $55,000 and median financial assets—excluding real estate investments, life insurance policies, and retirement plan assets—are $40,000, of which 45 percent is in mutual funds (Table 1). Stock mutual funds are the most commonly owned mutual fund, being found in the portfolios of 72 percent of all households (ICI, 1996c). In addition, 52 percent of the households own money market funds, and 47 percent own bond funds. With regard to other types of financial assets, over half of the households own individual stocks, and roughly a quarter own individual bonds and annuities. Table 1 also highlights the importance of retirement-related, tax-advantaged accounts to mutual fund owners, of whom 62 percent have an IRA, and 60 percent participate in a 401(k) plan (ICI, 1996c). Of the 401(k) participants, 80 percent own mutual funds in the plan, whereas the remaining 20 percent holds no mutual funds in a plan. Of those

TABLE 1 Selected Characteristics of Households Owning Mutual Funds, by Ownership Through 401(k) Plans

Investor characteristic	*All owners*	*Owners with mutual funds in 401(k) plans*	*Owners with no mutual funds in 401(k) plans*
Median			
Age of financial decisionmaker	42	39	46
Household income	$55,000	$60,000	$52,500
Financial assets outside employer-sponsored retirement plans	$40,000	$30,000	$60,000
Mutual fund assets outside employer-sponsored plans	$18,000	$20,000	$20,000
Percent of respondents			
College degree	54	50	57
Employed, full- or part-time	83	93	74
Retired from lifetime occupation	15	6	23
Spouse employed*	77	83	71
Types of assets owned†			
Individual stocks	52	53	51
Individual bonds	23	20	26
Annuities	22	15	29
Types of mutual funds owned‡			
Stock	72	72	73
Bond	47	46	48
Money market	52	51	54
IRA	62	48	74

Source: Authors' computations using 1995 Investment Company Institute survey.
*Percent of married households.
†Multiple responses permitted.
‡Multiple responses permitted. Includes ownership in 401(k) plans.

owning mutual funds in a 401(k) plan, 55 percent also own mutual funds outside the plan.

Households with mutual funds in 401(k) plans differ in a number of respects from those that only own mutual funds outside these plans. Reflecting the relatively recent development of 401(k) plans, those households with plan mutual funds tend to be younger, and a higher proportion are employed, giving the group a higher median household income. The group with mutual funds in a 401(k) plan has accumulated smaller amounts of financial assets outside the employer-sponsored retirement plans and tends to have a higher percentage of financial wealth in mutual funds. In contrast, those households not owning mutual funds through a

TABLE 2 Selected Characteristics of Households Owning Mutual Funds Through 401(k) Plans, July 1995

Investor characteristic	*Owners with mutual funds only in 401(k) plans*	*Owners with mutual funds in and outside 401(k) plans*
Median		
Age of financial decisionmaker	37	41
Household income	$50,000	$60,000
Financial assets outside employer-sponsored retirement plans	$20,000	$50,000
Mutual fund assets in 401(k) plan	$12,000	$25,000
Percent of respondents		
College degree	40	60
Employed, full- or part-time	95	91
Retired from lifetime occupation	4	8
Spouse employed*	84	83
Types of assets owned outside of employer-sponsored plans†		
Individual stocks	43	62
Individual bonds	19	21
Annuities	8	22
Types of mutual funds owned†		
Stock	52	83
Bond	26	58
Money market	39	57
IRA	25	68
Employer-sponsored retirement plan other than 401(k) plan	32	65

Source: Authors' computations using Investment Company Institute data.
*Percent of married households.
†Multiple responses permitted.

401(k) plan — most of whom do not participate in a plan — show a higher frequency of ownership of IRAs and annuities.

Further distinctions can be made among those households who own mutual funds in a 401(k) plan, as described in Table 2. Those whose only holdings of mutual funds are in the plan are younger, have less education, have a somewhat higher concentration of financial assets in their 401(k) accounts, and are more conservatively invested than those 401(k) participants who also hold mutual funds outside 401(k) plans. In addition, a significantly smaller percentage of those households only owning mutual funds in 401(k) accounts is covered by another employer-sponsored retirement plan and has an IRA. Thus, these households would appear to be more dependent upon their 401(k) plans for retirement income (ICI 1996c).

Response of Mutual Fund Shareholders to Movements in Stock Prices[3]

The overlap in ownership of mutual funds in and outside 401(k) plans suggests that an analysis of the response of mutual fund owners to changing conditions in financial markets might indirectly provide some insight into how 401(k) participants might respond as well. To this end, this section and the next examine the response of mutual fund shareholders to movements in stock prices since 1944 and to a series of market disruptions in 1994. For this purpose, shareholder activity is measured as the net flow of cash to mutual funds, which is the difference between sales of mutual fund shares to investors and redemptions of shares by shareholders.

Stock Market Cycles and Sell-Offs

The post-World War II period provides a rich experience in which to examine the reaction of mutual fund owners to stock market developments. During this period, the stock market experienced fourteen major cycles, as measured by peaks and troughs in the monthly average of Standard and Poor's (S&P) 500 stock price index.[4] Figure 1 shows that eight of the cycles were associated with cycles in general business conditions, as dated by the National Bureau of Economic Research, and only the mild 1980 recession failed to produce a significant decline in stock prices. The other six stock market cycles were not associated with business cycles, although the contractions in 1961–62, 1966, and 1983–84 occurred in advance of slowdowns in economic activity (Table 3).

The stock market contractions differ considerably in length and severity. The duration of the fourteen contractions ranged from four to thirty-seven months, with the average downturn lasting fourteen months. With two exceptions, the shortest stock market contractions typically were not associated with business recessions, whereas the longest contractions occurred in conjunction with recessions. The largest decline in the S&P 500 index was 43.4 percent during the 1973–74 contraction, and the smallest decrease of roughly 10 percent occurred in the 1959–60, 1971, and 1983–84 contractions. The average decrease in the index for all contractions was 19.5 percent.

The fourteen cycles contain several short periods of sharp declines in stock prices. Because of the averaging of daily values, the largest one-month decline in the S&P 500 index occurred not in the October 1987 market break but in September 1946, when the index fell 14.7 percent. The second largest decline of 12.5 percent was in October 1987; three other contractions produced one-month decreases in excess of 10 per-

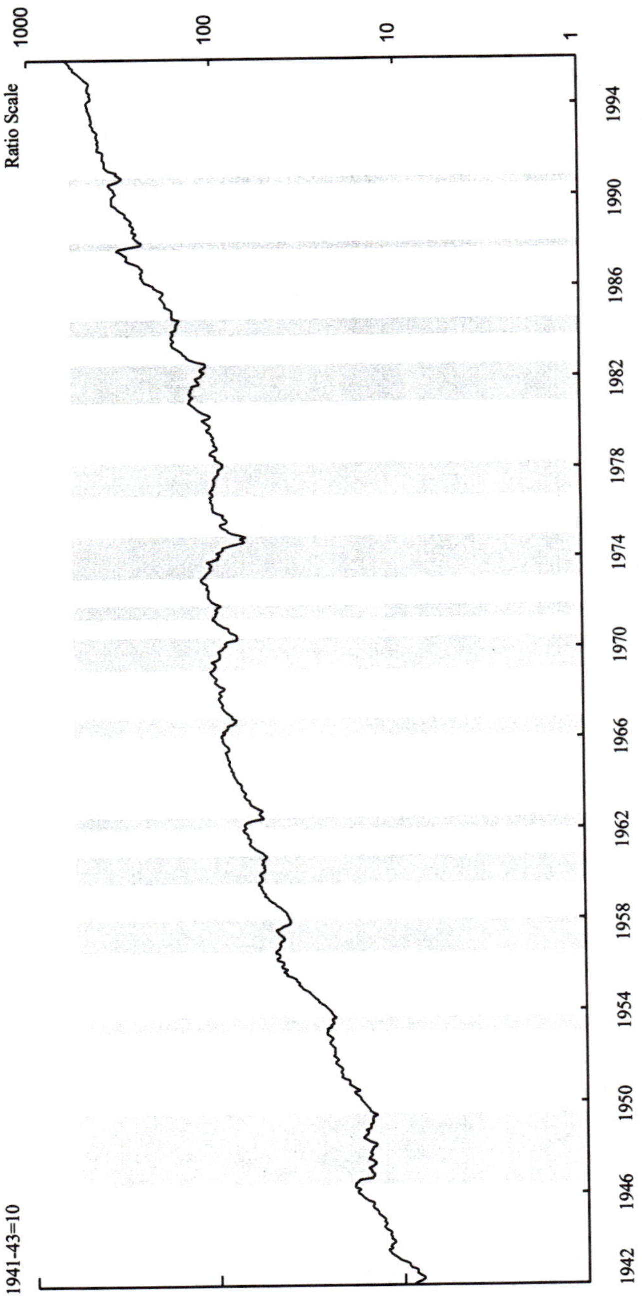

Figure 1. S&P 500 stock price index (monthly average of daily index, 1942–95). Shaded regions represent contraction phase of stock market cycle. Source: Rea and Marcis (1996).

TABLE 3 Stock Market Cycles, 1942–95

Cycle									
Expansion	*Contraction*		*Duration (months)*		*Change in S&P index (%)*		*Largest decrease in S&P index in contraction (%)*		
Trough	*Peak*	*Trough*	*Expansion**	*Contraction*†	*Expansion**	*Contraction*†	*One-month*	*Two-month*	*Three-month*
Apr. 1942	May 1946	Jun. 1949‡	49	37	138.5	−25.3	14.7	16.7	18.8
Jun. 1949	Jun. 1953	Sep. 1953‡	43	8	87.4	−11.1	4.9	5.6	7.9
Sep. 1953	Jul. 1956	Dec. 1957‡	34	17	109.6	−17.3	6.2	10.0	15.1
Dec. 1957	Jul. 1959	Oct. 1960‡	19	15	48.1	−10.1	4.0	5.6	6.8
Oct. 1960	Dec. 1961	Jun. 1962	14	6	33.5	−22.5	11.7	18.3	20.9
Jun. 1962	Jan. 1966	Oct. 1966	43	9	67.8	−17.3	6.0	9.4	10.2
Oct. 1966	Dec. 1968	Jun. 1970‡	26	18	38.1	−29.0	11.5	14.2	14.7
Jun. 1970	Apr. 1971	Nov. 1971	10	7	36.3	−10.0	4.6	6.7	4.6
Nov. 1971	Jan. 1973	Dec. 1974‡	14	23	27.6	−43.4	10.4	17.8	24.1
Dec. 1974	Sep. 1976	Mar. 1978	21	18	57.2	−15.8	3.8	5.2	6.4
Mar. 1978	Nov. 1980	Jul. 1982‡	32	20	52.7	−19.4	8.8	7.6	10.6
Jul. 1982	Oct. 1983	Jul. 1984	15	9	53.3	−9.9	5.5	5.4	5.3
Jul. 1984	Aug. 1987	Dec. 1987	37	4	118.0	−26.8	12.5	23.1	25.6
Dec. 1987	Jun. 1990	Oct. 1990‡	30	4	49.6	−14.8	8.1	12.4	14.7
Average			28	14	65.6	−19.5	8.1	11.3	13.3

Source: Rea and Marcis (1996).
*Trough to peak.
†Peak to trough.
‡Contraction associated with business recession.

cent. Over a two-month period, the largest decrease was the 23.1 percent drop in the 1987 contraction. Sizable two-month declines also were posted in the 1962 and 1973–74 contractions. Over a three-month period, the 25.6 percent decrease in the index between October and December 1987 was the largest for all postwar contractions but was not much greater than the 24.1 percent drop between June and September of 1974. Substantial three-month decreases also occurred in the 1946 and 1962 downturns.

Net Flow During Expansions and Contractions

Shareholder activity in stock funds generally has not fluctuated between inflows during periods of rising stock prices and outflows during periods of falling stock prices.[5] Indeed, such a pattern has been the exception rather than the rule (Figure 2). Of the thirteen stock market cycles for which complete data are available for both the expansion and contraction, only three—those in 1970–71, 1984–87, and 1987–90—showed this pattern; that is, only in these three cycles was net flow positive over the expansion and negative over the contraction (Figure 3). Of the remaining ten cycles, three experienced a net outflow in both the expansion and contraction, and seven posted a net inflow in both the expansion and contraction. The fourteenth cycle from 1942 to 1949, for which data are only available since 1944, most likely was of the last type, as net flow was positive from 1944 through 1949.

With only three minor exceptions, the eight contractions with positive, cumulative net flows experienced a net inflow in each month. That is, the inflow does not mask a short period of outflows (Table 4). Although no significant net outflows occurred during these eight contractions, two of the largest one-month and two-month declines in the S&P stock price index were recorded during the 1946–49 contraction and during the 1961–62 contraction. Neither of these market breaks, however, was associated with net redemptions, either during the break or in subsequent months.

In the six contractions with net outflows, none cumulated over the course of the entire contraction to a high level, ranging from 0.9 percent of equity fund assets to 13.1 percent (Figure 3). The largest occurred in the relatively mild 1976–78 contraction, and the net outflow in the 1987 downturn was 3.5 percent of assets.

The relatively low rate of net outflows over the entire course of the six contractions would not necessarily rule out substantially higher rates of net outflows within a shorter time interval. Despite the possibility, net outflows measured over one-month, two-month, and three-month intervals were never large. The largest one-month net outflow was in October

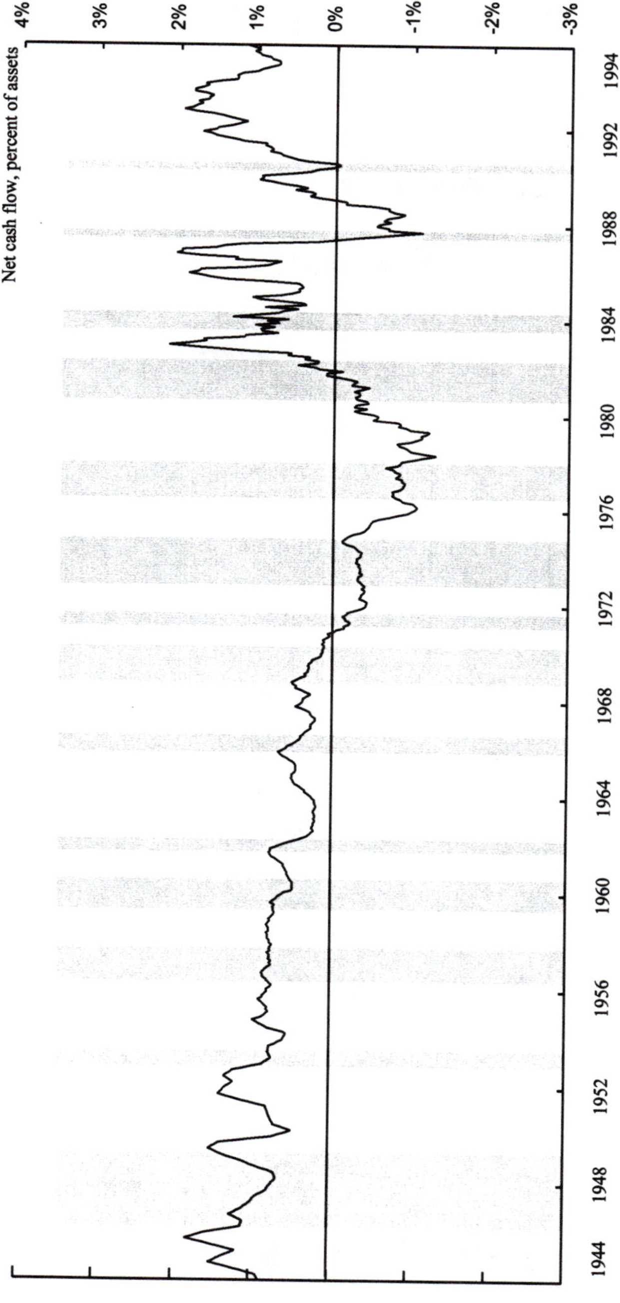

Figure 2. Net flow to equity mutual funds (monthly, six-month moving average, 1944–95). Shaded regions represent contraction phase of stock market cycle. Source: Rea and Marcis (1996).

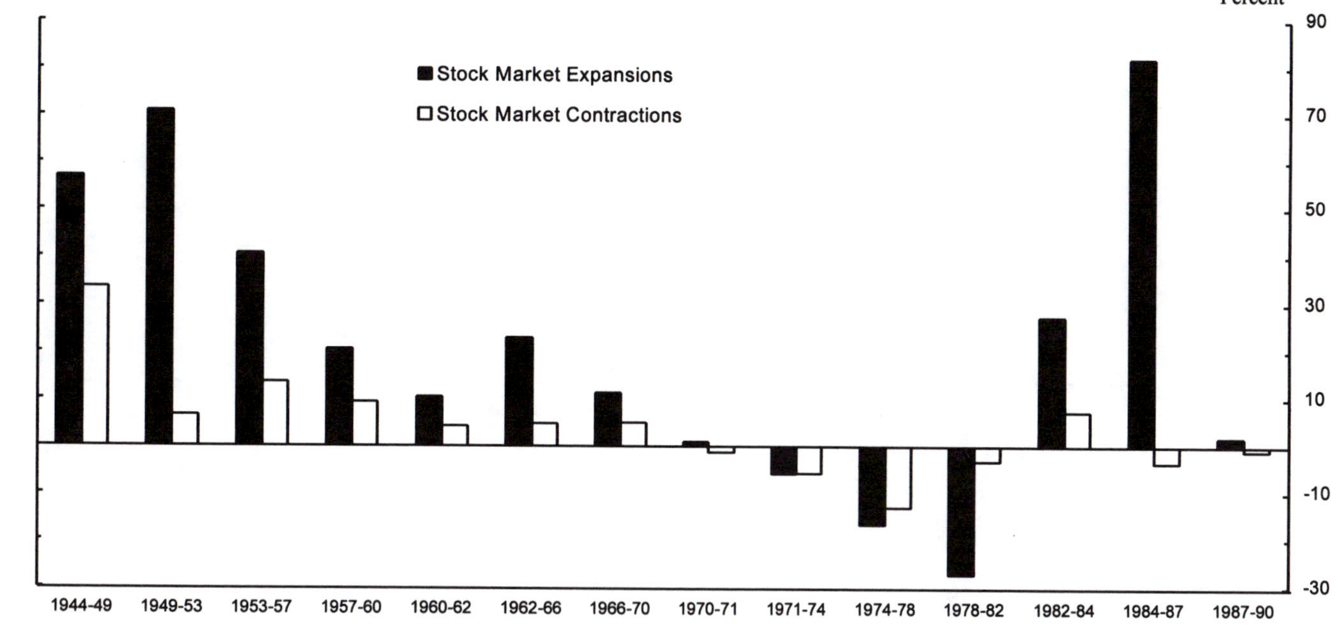

Figure 3. Net flow to equity mutual funds during stock market expansions and contractions, 1944–90 (percent of assets). Net flow is expressed as a percent of assets at trough for stock market expansions, as a percent of assets at peak for contractions. Source: Rea and Marcis (1996).

TABLE 4 Minimum and Maximum Monthly Net Flow to Equity Funds During Stock Market Contractions, 1946–90 (% of assets in previous month)

Contraction			
Peak	*Trough*	*Minimum*	*Maximum*
May 1946	Jun. 1949	0.6	1.3
Jan. 1953	Sep. 1953	0.7	1.0
Jul. 1956	Dec. 1957	0.6	1.2
Jul. 1959	Oct. 1960	0.4	0.9
Dec. 1961	Jun. 1962	0.4	1.0
Jan. 1966	Oct. 1966	0.3	0.8
Dec. 1968	Jun. 1970	−0.1	0.8
Apr. 1971	Nov. 1971	−0.5	0.1
Jan. 1973	Dec. 1974	−0.6	−0.1
Sep. 1976	Mar. 1978	−1.0	−0.4
Nov. 1980	Jul. 1982	−1.1	0.9
Oct. 1983	Jul. 1984	−0.1	1.9
Aug. 1987	Dec. 1987	−3.1	0.6
Jun. 1990	Oct. 1990	−1.0	0.3

Source: Rea and Marcis (1996).

1987 and represented only 3.1 percent of stock fund assets (Table 4). This contraction also produced the largest two- and three-month net outflows, but even over the three-month period, the outflow represented little more than 4.0 percent of assets. The next largest outflows for these time intervals ranged from 1.1 percent for the one-month period to 2.8 percent for the three-month period.

The 1987 Stock Market Break

On a monthly basis, the net outflow of $7.5 billion in October 1987 was the highest on record, and it resulted primarily from an increase in share redemptions and secondarily from a drop-off in sales of new shares. The outflow in October reversed a $1.5 billion net inflow in September and followed an average monthly net inflow of $3.2 billion during the first nine months of 1987.

The net outflow in October likely was concentrated in the second half of the month and could have been as high as $8.2 billion.[6] Information from thirty large complexes—which at that time held 80 percent of equity fund assets—implies that perhaps $1.6 billion occurred on October 16, $2.7 billion on October 19 (the day of the break), and $1.3 billion on October 20.[7] The three-day estimate of $5.6 billion is nearly 70 percent of the net outflow between October 16 and the end of the month.

Despite the record level of net redemptions in October 1987, several aspects of the redemption activity suggest that it was not large in a relative sense. At most, the net outflow in the last half of October amounted to no more than 4.5 percent of assets.[8] In addition, the burst in net redemptions was largely confined to October 16, 19, and 20. After averaging nearly $2.0 billion per day over these three days, the net outflow moderated to an estimated $325 million per business day over the remainder of the month and then tapered off to $60 million per business day in November and December. For each of these two months, the net outflow represented about 0.7 percent of assets.

Furthermore, mutual fund shareholders did not characterize themselves as having liquidated shares heavily during and shortly after the market break. In a survey of households owning stock funds conducted in November 1987, only 5 percent had redeemed shares during and since the break (ICI 1988). In a follow-up survey taken in May 1988, this figure had risen only to 11 percent. The May survey, however, did reveal that mutual fund shareholders had become more conservative in their investments and were exercising restraint in making new purchases of mutual fund shares.

Perhaps reflecting this cautiousness, the net flow to equity funds remained negative through the first quarter of 1989 even though stock prices were rising. The net outflow resulted, however, not from a pickup in the pace of redemptions but rather from a slowdown in sales. In fact, monthly redemptions as a percent of assets declined, on average, about one percentage point between the first nine months of 1987 and the period from January 1988 to March 1989.

The 1976–78 Contraction and Long Waves in Net Flow

The net outflow of 13.1 percent in the 1976–78 contraction, which included several monthly net redemptions of 1.0 percent of assets and a three-month net outflow of 2.8 percent between March and May 1977, occurred in the period extending from 1971 through mid-1982, when equity funds experienced net redemptions in almost every month (Table 5). In comparison with net outflows in the expansions during this period, the net outflow in the 1976–78 contraction was not, however, especially large. For example, the cumulative net outflow in the 1978–80 expansion was 27.2 percent of assets, more than double that in the 1976–78 contraction, and the cumulative net outflow in the 1975–76 expansion also exceeded that in the 1976–78 contraction. In addition, both of these two expansions had numerous months in which the net outflow was more than 1.0 percent of assets, and the largest net outflow, 4.5 percent, for any three-month period since 1944 occurred during the 1978–80 expansion.

TABLE 5 Largest Net Outflows in Stock Market Contractions over One-, Two- and Three-Month Periods

Period	*Percent of assets in previous month*
One-month	
October 1987	3.1
March 1977	1.1
January 1981	1.0
May 1977	1.0
August 1977	1.0
December 1977	1.0
December 1981	1.0
May 1982	1.0
August 1990	1.0
Two-month	
October–November 1987	3.6
March–April 1977	1.9
December 1980–January 1981	1.8
June–July 1981	1.4
August–September 1990	1.2
Three-month	
October–December 1987	4.1
March–May 1977	2.8
June–August 1981	2.2

Source: Rea and Marcis (1996).

Furthermore, from the trough in S&P index in March 1978 through October 1978, equity funds experienced a net outflow of 9.0 percent of assets, even as the S&P index increased 13.2 percent.

This period of eleven and one-half years in which equity funds were out of favor with the investing public stands in marked contrast to the preceding period, dating back to 1944, when equity funds experienced net inflows in virtually every month of each expansion and contraction. Stock prices in the 1944–70 period trended strongly upward, with the S&P index increasing at an 8.4 percent compound annual rate between the cyclical peaks in May 1946 and December 1968. In contrast, the 1970s were a period of stagnation in the stock market. The S&P index reached a record high in December 1968, pushed briefly above that level in late 1972 and early 1973, but never saw it again until late 1979. The compound annual rate of increase in the S&P index between the cyclical peaks in December 1968 and November 1980 was only 2.1 percent.

The period spanning the 1970s and early 1980s also contrasts with the subsequent decade and a half in which stock prices generally rose and stock funds again experienced persistent net inflows, apart from the eighteen months after the 1987 market break. This relationship between the long-run movement in net flow and stock returns, along with that observed between the late 1940s and early 1970s, suggests that mutual fund investors are sensitive to long-term rates of return on equity. The 1970s and early 1980s were a period of high inflation, making investments in real assets more attractive than those in financial assets, whereas the high stock returns before and after this period likely contributed to households' investing in equities through mutual funds.

The 1973–74 Contraction

The nearly 25 percent drop in the S&P 500 index over the third quarter of 1974 was second in size only to the decline registered in the 1987 stock market break. Nonetheless, the pace of net outflows ticked up only slightly during the three-month sell-off, averaging a modest 0.4 percent of assets. After the fall in stock prices subsided in the fourth quarter, net redemptions moderated significantly, declining to less than 0.1 percent of assets, and did not rise again until several months after stock prices turned up in January 1975. As stock prices continued to advance thereafter, net outflows rose further, reaching 1.2 percent of assets in the spring of 1976, a figure that was about double the largest monthly net outflow in the 1973–74 contraction.

Other Market Sell-Offs

Movements in net flow to equity funds during other periods with significant short-term declines in the S&P 500 index have been mixed. In some instances, such as the market downturn sparked by Iraq's invasion of Kuwait in August 1990, net flow turned negative by a small margin for a month or two. Net flow also was negative for a two-week period with the heightened market volatility in the spring of 1994 (Marcis, West, and Leonard-Chambers 1995). In all these instances, the largest monthly outflow amounted to no more than 1.1 percent of stock fund assets.

During other market sell-offs, such as the outbreak of the Korean War in June 1950 and the sharp sell-off between August and October 1957, net flow either declined slightly and remained positive or continued at the same pace posted in preceding months (Bullock 1959). And, in the market decline in the spring of 1980, net flow actually turned from negative to positive.

Other Cyclical Patterns

Although net flow has not generally fluctuated from positive in the expansion phase of the stock market cycle to negative in the contraction phase, several recurrent patterns are observable in the cyclical movement of net flow, measured as a percent of assets. To identify these patterns, the expansion and contraction phases of the stock market cycle have been divided into two stages. For the expansion, the first stage includes all months other than the last six and the second stage covers the last six months. For the contraction, the first stage is the first six months, and the second is the remaining months, although not all contractions extend into the second stage.[9]

Net flow has tended, on average, to rise during the expansion phase and to decline during the contraction phase. For all fourteen cycles, the average of monthly net flows, as a percent of assets, increases from 0.38 percent in the first stage of the expansion to 0.58 percent in the last six months of the expansion (Table 6). Thereafter, the average declines to 0.25 percent for the first six months of the contraction, about the value in the remaining months of the contraction.

The absence of variation in net flow between the two stages of the contraction is the result of three of the contractions being so short that they do not contain the second stage. Eliminating these three from the computations of stage averages reveals a tendency for net flow to decline as the contraction progresses. During the first six months of the contraction for the eleven complete cycles, net flow averaged 0.36 percent, as compared with 0.26 percent for the remaining months.

The cyclical pattern in net flow results from a similar pattern in sales of shares rather than share redemptions. Sales, as a percent of assets, tend to rise during the expansion and to fall during the contraction (Table 7). In contrast, the redemption rate has generally remained unchanged, except in the second stage of the contraction, when it declines slightly (Table 8).

From the pattern of sales and redemption rates, it would appear that, to the extent stock fund owners respond to cyclical movements in stock returns, they do so by adjusting the pace of new share purchases rather than by changing the pace of redemptions. That is, stock fund owners have tended to buy more intensively when stock prices are rising and to become more restrained when prices are falling. Even so, the cyclical variation in the pace of sales is not particularly large, ranging from an average low of 1.2 percent in the last part of the contraction to 2.0 percent in the last six months of the expansion. Furthermore, the sales rate in the last six months of the expansion exceeds that in the first stage of

TABLE 6 Net Flow to Equity Mutual Funds During Expansion and Contraction Phases of Stock Market Cycles (percent of assets, period average, 1944–90)

Cycle			*Expansion*		*Contraction*	
Expansion	*Contraction*					
Trough	*Peak*	*Trough*	*Other than last six months*	*Last six months*	*First six months*	*Remaining months*
Apr. 1942	May 1946	Jun. 1949	1.21*	1.66	1.10	0.93
Jun. 1949	Jan. 1953	Sep. 1953	1.05	1.31	0.83	0.78
Sep. 1953	Jul. 1956	Dec. 1957	0.79	0.80	0.86	0.75
Dec. 1957	Jul. 1959	Oct. 1960	0.80	0.76	0.72	0.55
Oct. 1960	Dec. 1961	Jun. 1962	0.55	0.72	0.71	—
Jun. 1962	Jan. 1966	Oct. 1966	0.32	0.54	0.59	0.44
Oct. 1966	Dec. 1968	Jun. 1970	0.34	0.39	0.42	0.23
Jun. 1970	Apr. 1971	Nov. 1971	0.13	0.07	−0.21	−0.02
Nov. 1971	Jan. 1973	Dec. 1974	−0.34	−0.39	−0.31	−0.31
Dec. 1974	Sep. 1976	Mar. 1978	−0.47	−1.04	−0.76	−0.81
Mar. 1978	Nov. 1980	Jul. 1982	−0.91	−0.25	−0.32†	−0.07
Jul. 1982	Oct. 1983	Jul. 1984	1.11	1.17	1.03†	0.34
Jul. 1984	Aug. 1987	Dec. 1987	1.06	1.42	−0.97	—
Dec. 1987	Jun. 1990	Oct. 1990	−0.25	0.94	−0.23	—
Average						
All cycles			0.39	0.58	0.25	0.26
Eleven complete cycles			0.37	0.46	0.36	0.26

Source: Rea and Marcis (1996).
*January 1944 to May 1946.
†Four months.

TABLE 7 Sales of Shares of Equity Mutual Funds During Expansion and Contraction Phases of Stock Market Cycles (percent of assets, period average, 1944–90)

Cycle			*Expansion*		*Contraction*	
Expansion	*Contraction*					
Trough	*Peak*	*Trough*	*Other than last six months*	*Last six months*	*First six months*	*Remaining months*
Apr. 1942	May 1946	Jun. 1949	2.08*	2.62	1.90	1.55
Jun. 1949	Jan. 1953	Sep. 1953	1.89	1.79	1.36	1.22
Sep. 1953	Jul. 1956	Dec. 1957	1.39	1.27	1.23	1.12
Dec. 1957	Jul. 1959	Oct. 1960	1.22	1.26	1.11	1.01
Oct. 1960	Dec. 1961	Jun. 1962	1.14	1.14	1.20	—
Jun. 1962	Jan. 1966	Oct. 1966	0.87	1.08	1.15	0.97
Oct. 1966	Dec. 1968	Jun. 1970	0.98	1.11	1.15	0.88
Jun. 1970	Apr. 1971	Nov. 1971	0.72	0.81	0.68	0.75
Nov. 1971	Jan. 1973	Dec. 1974	0.71	0.69	0.62	0.57
Dec. 1974	Sep. 1976	Mar. 1978	0.52	0.48	0.59	0.55
Mar. 1978	Nov. 1980	Jul. 1982	1.05	1.82	1.88	2.09
Jul. 1982	Oct. 1983	Jul. 1984	4.22	3.89	3.55	2.56
Jul. 1984	Aug. 1987	Dec. 1987	4.46	6.14	4.48†	—
Dec. 1987	Jun. 1990	Oct. 1990	3.19	4.08	3.01†	—
Average						
All cycles			1.75	2.01	1.71	1.21
Eleven complete cycles			1.42	1.53	1.38	1.21

Source: Rea and Marcis (1996).
*January 1944 to May 1946.
†Four months.

TABLE 8 Redemptions of Shares of Equity Mutual Funds During Expansion and Contraction Phases of Stock Market Cycles (percent of assets, period average, 1944–90)

Cycle			*Expansion*		*Contraction*	
Expansion	*Contraction*					
Trough	*Peak*	*Trough*	*Other than last six months*	*Last six months*	*First six months*	*Remaining months*
Apr. 1942	May 1946	Jun. 1949	0.87*	0.96	0.80	0.61
Jun. 1949	Jan. 1953	Sep. 1953	0.85	0.48	0.53	0.44
Sep. 1953	Jul. 1956	Dec. 1957	0.60	0.46	0.37	0.36
Dec. 1957	Jul. 1959	Oct. 1960	0.42	0.49	0.39	0.46
Oct. 1960	Dec. 1961	Jun. 1962	0.59	0.43	0.48	—
Jun. 1962	Jan. 1966	Oct. 1966	0.55	0.55	0.56	0.52
Oct. 1966	Dec. 1968	Jun. 1970	0.66	0.72	0.74	0.64
Jun. 1970	Apr. 1971	Nov. 1971	0.57	0.74	0.89	0.75
Nov. 1971	Jan. 1973	Dec. 1974	1.06	1.08	0.93	0.86
Dec. 1974	Sep. 1976	Mar. 1978	0.99	1.53	1.35	1.35
Mar. 1978	Nov. 1980	Jul. 1982	1.95	2.06	2.20	2.17
Jul. 1982	Oct. 1983	Jul. 1984	3.12	2.72	2.53	2.23
Jul. 1984	Aug. 1987	Dec. 1987	3.40	4.71	5.45†	—
Dec. 1987	Jun. 1990	Oct. 1990	3.44	3.14	3.24†	—
Average						
All cycles			1.36	1.43	1.46	0.94
Eleven complete cycles			1.06	1.07	1.03	0.94

Source: Rea and Marcis (1996).
*January 1944 to May 1946.
†Four months.

the expansion, on average, by only 0.25 percentage points. This is also about the same amount as the drop-off in the sales rate during the first six months of the contraction phase of the cycle relative to the last six months of the expansion.

In moving from the contraction phase of one cycle to the expansion phase of the next, both the sales rate and the redemption rate have tended to increase. The average rate of sales in the first stage of the expansion has exceeded the average sales rate in the last part of the previous contraction by 0.26 percentage points. In addition, the average redemption rate in the first stage of the expansion has exceeded that in the last part of the previous contraction by 0.14 percentage points.

The Response of Mutual Fund Shareholders to Market Disruptions in 1994

A series of market disruptions in 1994 provides further insight into the response of mutual shareholders to financial developments.[10]

Tightening of Monetary Policy

The year 1994 produced a variety of financial shocks that had the potential to undermine investor confidence in mutual funds generally or in specific types of mutual funds. The first of these occurred in February, when the Federal Reserve initiated the first of six increases in the federal funds rate in 1994. Interest rates moved upward over the course of the year, producing significant losses for bondholders, including those in bond mutual funds. The movement in interest rates also likely contributed to stock prices' posting only small gains during the year.

The first and subsequent increases in interest rates were associated with outflows from domestic bond funds. These began in February 1994 and continued in each month for the remainder of the year; in contrast, the net flow to these funds had been strong since 1990 as households allocated a greater share of net purchases of financial assets to bond funds in response to the steeply sloped yield curve and declining interest rates. The outflows in 1994 induced by the increase in interest rates and the flattening of the yield curve, however, were not concentrated within a short span of time but rather were spaced over the course the year. The largest outflow occurred in March 1994 in conjunction with a heightened market volatility but amounted to less than 2.0 percent of all assets held by domestic bond funds. Relatively heavy outflows also occurred in the fourth quarter, most likely as households redeemed shares to realize capital losses for tax purposes.

The net outflows that occurred in 1994 were similar to those in 1987

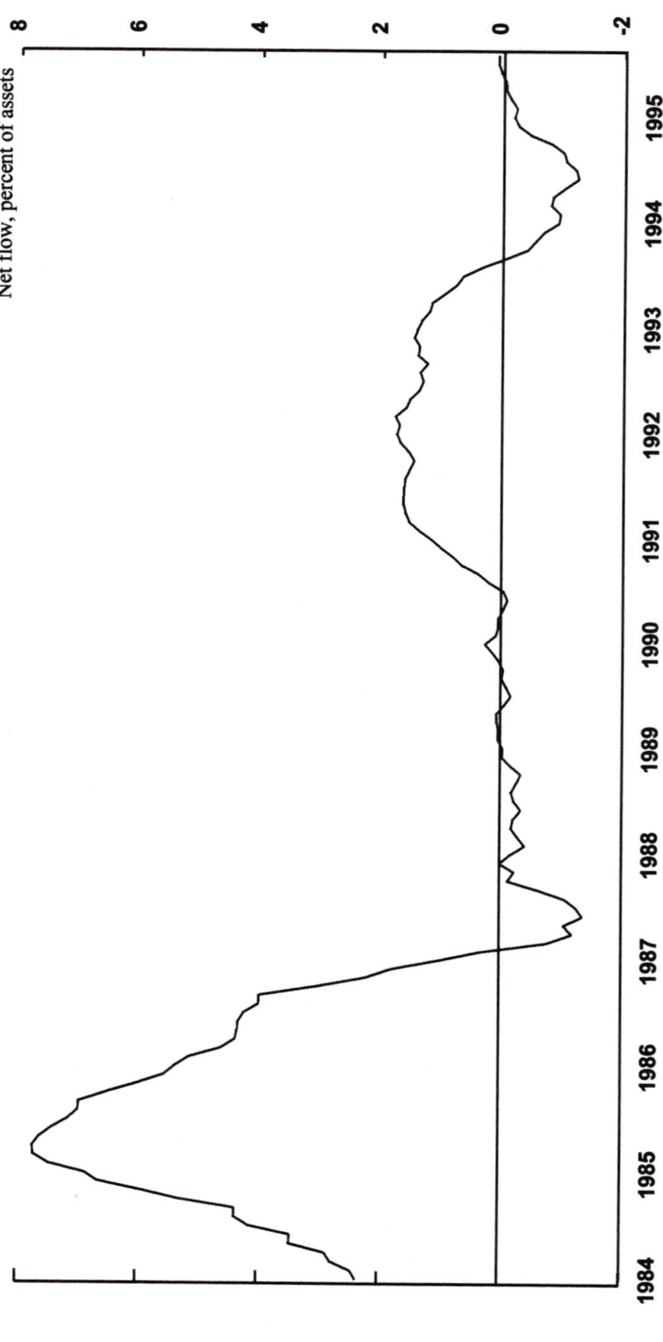

Figure 4. Net flow to domestic bond and income mutual funds (monthly, six-month moving average, 1984–95). First observation is July 1984; last is February 1996. Source: Marcis, West, and Leonard-Chambers (1995).

that began in April of that year in response to the tightening in monetary policy (Figure 4). As in the most recent experience, the outflows in 1987 had been preceded by two years of heavy inflows, brought on by declining interest rates. This experience, along with that in 1994, indicates that the demand for bond funds depends upon the level of interest rates and the slope the yield curve, and thus the net flow to bond funds is likely to have a pattern that relates to fluctuations in interest rates.

In contrast to the outflow from bond funds, equity fund owners did not respond to the tightening in monetary policy by redeeming shares on balance. In fact, the net inflow to stock funds in 1994 was, at that time, the second highest on record and only 7.9 percent below the record set in 1993. This occurred despite a lackluster performance of the stock market. The only evidence of any response came in late March and early April, when equity funds posted a small net outflow during a period of increased stock price volatility.

Derivatives Losses at Taxable Money Market Funds

Between May and September of 1994, increases in interest rates caused a number of taxable money market funds to experience losses on structured notes and other derivative instruments that threatened to cause their share prices to fall below $1.00. Rather than allow the funds to "break the buck," their sponsors or investment advisors provided capital support, thereby permitting the share prices of the funds to remain at $1.00. The only exception was a small fund that liquidated its portfolio at a 6 percent loss.

Despite the publicity given to the injections of capital, shareholders did not reduce their holdings of money fund assets. In fact, assets increased 5.3 percent from the end of April through year end. Assets of the sponsor-supported funds, however, declined 20.9 percent over this period, suggesting that shareholders distinguished between the two types of funds. The overall reaction, however, was not long lived, as assets generally began to increase at sponsored-supported funds three months after the announcement of the capital injection.

The Bankruptcy of Orange County

The filing for bankruptcy by Orange County, California in early December 1994, caused by losses in an investment pool managed by the county for other California municipalities, raised concern among investors about the value of outstanding Orange County securities, as well as obligations of participants in the investment pool of other California issuers managing similar investment pools. Because of the uncertainty regarding the value of Orange County securities, many tax-exempt money funds entered into support agreements with their sponsors or advisers to ensure that the funds could maintain a stable share price of $1.00.

In response to these developments, shareholders reduced their holdings over the remainder of December in tax-exempt money funds that only held obligations of California issuers. In addition, California-only tax-exempt bond funds experienced a pickup in the pace of outflows relative to those of tax-exempt bond funds during December. These reactions, however, were short lived, as assets at California tax-exempt money funds began to increase in January 1995 and the net flow to California bond funds came in line with those at other municipal bond funds in February 1995.

Devaluation of the Mexican Peso

The devaluation of the Mexican peso in late December and the resulting sharp decline in Mexican securities prices produced sizable losses for holders of Latin American mutual funds and, as the effects spilled over to other developing countries, for holders of emerging market funds generally. For example, in the last two weeks of December, Latin American equity funds dropped over 15 percent in value, and they suffered another 30 percent loss during the first quarter of 1995.

The reaction of shareholders in Latin American and emerging market funds to these events was subdued. These funds experienced net outflows during the last half of the month, but they were small in size and not sustained. For example, the net outflow from Latin American equity funds was less than 2.0 percent of assets in the last two weeks of December. The net outflow ended in March, and by the beginning of May, the cumulative net inflow had more than offset the net outflow posted in the aftermath of the devaluation. Other emerging market equity and bond funds had a similar experience, although the net inflow from the bond funds was larger than that from equity funds.

Reasons for Shareholder Response to Market Developments

The above evidence indicates that mutual fund investors have been sensitive to changes in interest rates and stock returns, but they have not responded precipitately to market developments. The explanations for the absence of runs are of two types: one involves the regulation of mutual funds,[11] and the other concerns characteristics of mutual fund owners.

Regulation of Mutual Funds

In examining the potential for a run on mutual funds, it is natural to superimpose the experience with bank runs upon mutual funds. Doing so, however, is inappropriate because banks, for several reasons, are more susceptible to runs than are mutual funds. One reason is that bank deposits are redeemable at par value unless the bank is insolvent. Thus, in the event of a financial or economic shock that reduces the value of bank assets, it is rational for depositors to attempt to make withdrawals to avoid possible losses that would be sustained if the bank became insolvent. Those withdrawing first are more likely to succeed, as the bank can meet the redemptions with cash on hand and not be forced to realize losses through asset sales.

In contrast, a mutual fund is required to value portfolio securities daily and to reflect the valuation in the price at which it sells and redeems shares. As a consequence, declines in the prices of the assets held by a mutual fund are immediately reflected in the share price of the mutual fund, thereby eliminating any opportunity for shareholders to avoid losses through redemptions.[12] Mutual fund shareholders thus do not have the same incentive as bank depositors to redeem shares immediately after a sharp drop in asset prices.[13]

A second reason banks are more susceptible to runs than mutual funds is that a substantial portion of bank assets are illiquid loans about which depositors generally have little information. This serves to increase the uncertainty about the value of bank assets after a financial shock because depositors may not know what loans are held by the bank and because forced sales of the loans to meet deposit withdrawals are almost certainly at a substantial discount from the values that could be realized with greater time to conduct transactions (Calomiris 1993). The illiquidity and nontransparency of bank assets contrast sharply with assets held by mutual funds, the vast majority of which must be readily marketable. More specifically, for at least 85 percent of the assets in a bond or stock mutual fund and at least 90 percent in a money market fund, the fund must be able to sell the securities within a seven-day period at approximately the prices at which they had been valued by the fund. In addition, mutual funds are required to disclose sufficient information about their investments to enable investors to evaluate the risk and prospective return associated with investing in the fund.

To protect depositors against loss because of insolvency and to mitigate the risk of a run, banks are subject to a set of prudential regulations, the purpose of which is to limit asset losses. One of the most important aspects of such regulation is the requirement that banks hold a minimum level of capital as a buffer to absorb asset losses (Haberman 1987). In addition, bank liquidity is enhanced by allowing banks to borrow from the Federal Reserve. And, as a further safeguard against sudden withdrawals arising from investor uncertainty about a bank's solvency or liquidity, the federal government insures bank deposits against loss up to specific limits.

With only one exception, prudential regulation is not imposed upon mutual funds, as investors in mutual funds are, by design, to be exposed to investment risk. Mutual funds are heavily regulated,[14] but the purpose is to ensure adequate disclosure, asset liquidity, and accurate asset valuation. In addition, mutual fund regulation safeguards the assets and activities of a mutual fund from potential conflicts of interest that might arise between the fund and those organizations providing services to it, such as the investment manager.

The exception involves money market mutual funds. Although they are not required to do so by law or regulation, money fund managers have a stated objective of attempting to maintain a constant share price of $1.00. This investment objective, along with the practice thus far of sponsors' providing capital support when the share price of $1.00 is threatened, has led the public to expect money market funds to have a stable value. As a consequence, even though they must disclose that the share price can deviate from $1.00, money funds are more susceptible to a run than other types of mutual funds. In view of the public's expectation, money funds are subject to regulations designed to minimize the potential for share price fluctuations arising from credit losses and illiquidity.

Shareholder Characteristics

In addition to the regulatory features that mitigate the potential for a run, mutual fund owners have a number of characteristics that likewise work against a precipitate reaction to adverse market developments. Most shareholders see themselves as long-term investors saving for retirement, their children's education, or some other long-range goal. And they hold mutual funds as a means of achieving these objectives (ICI 1993, 1994a, 1994b, 1996a; Morgan 1994). Consistent with this view, the typical shareholder in a survey of those who had redeemed shares in 1991 had been invested in the mutual fund for five years, and the vast majority making a full redemption did so not because of market developments but primarily because of a change in investment strategy. As a result, most of those who closed an account in 1991 reinvested the proceeds in another mutual fund. Finally, those making a partial redemption typically used the proceeds to finance purchases of goods or services or to pay outstanding bills (ICI 1993).

Shareholders' responses to questions about their probable response to market developments also point toward a long-range investment orientation. For example, most indicate that they would not adjust their portfolios if the stock market dropped precipitously or if interest rates rose significantly (ICI 1994b). Of those that would take action after a decline in stock prices, the responses tend to be split about evenly between those who would redeem shares and those who would purchase additional shares. This is not an overwhelming endorsement of the widely held view among analysts that mutual fund owners consider market sell-offs to be "buying opportunities." At the same time, however, the evidence suggests that the vast majority would not regard stock market declines as "selling opportunities." In contrast to the response to declines in stock prices, most of those who would adjust their portfolios if interest rates rose significantly would redeem shares and place the proceeds in certificates of deposit (ICI 1994b).

Mutual fund investors generally recognize that investing in mutual funds entails risk, and the vast majority have some degree of tolerance for investment risk. They also tend to review the risk of a mutual fund before purchase and consider risk over a time horizon in excess of five years (ICI 1996a, 1997). Most shareholders report having a basic understanding of investment risk, acknowledging an awareness of the relationship between expected return and risk and recognizing the importance of diversification in reducing risk; many also assess prospective purchases of new funds within the context of their entire portfolio (ICI 1996a).

Mutual fund investors are not, however, a homogeneous group, and there is evidence that some have only a limited knowledge of mutual funds and have little awareness of some specific types of risks, such as interest rate risk. And, even though many have indicated that they are comfortable with the risk level that they perceive to exist in their holdings of mutual funds, some shareholders have investment portfolios that may be inconsistent with their tolerance for risk (ICI 1994a). Those showing gaps in their understanding of mutual fund risk are not, however, necessarily doomed to making poor investment decisions, as the majority of these shareholders purchases mutual funds through brokers and financial advisers (ICI 1996b, 1997).

Mutual fund shareholders are generally experienced investors and are not, for the most part, new to investing either in mutual funds or stocks and bonds. Of those households in 1995 representing the more than three-quarters of all household shareholders who own mutual funds outside a 401(k) plan, an estimated 68 percent made their first purchase of a mutual fund before 1990. Twenty percent initially invested in a mutual fund between 1990 and 1992, and only 12 percent since then.[15] In addition, the majority of those having only recently made their initial fund purchase owned stocks, bonds, and annuities before investing in mutual funds, suggesting that many of new owners of mutual funds had some experience with investment risk[16] (ICI 1994b). Furthermore, those without previous investment experience were not necessarily making their initial purchase without advice, as the majority transacted through brokers and financial advisers.

Conclusion

Based on past evidence, mutual fund investors are unlikely to react precipitously to sharp sell-offs in stock prices. Because 60 percent of household owners of mutual funds participate in a 401(k) plan, by implication, plan participants too would seem to be unlikely to withdraw en masse from stock mutual funds during market downturns. Mutual fund investors generally have behaved as long-term investors and consequently have shown greater sensitivity to long-run stock returns than to short-run returns. Although direct evidence on 401(k) participants is needed, the overlap between plan participants and mutual fund owners points to participants similarly taking a long-term approach to their 401(k) investments.

Research assistance was provided by Monica Bennsky, Srinivas Pulavarti, and Jianguo Shang.

Notes

1. These estimates for 401(k) and other retirement assets have been prepared by the Investment Company Institute.
2. These estimates for mutual owners participating in 401(k) plans and their plan investments are based upon a survey of 1,500 randomly selected mutual fund owners conducted in July 1995. The estimates should be interpreted with caution, as they likely overstate the actual numbers. Some respondents may not have been able to distinguish a 401(k) plan from other types of employer-sponsored plans, and some may have reported other types of pooled investments as mutual funds.
3. The material in this section is based on Rea and Marcis (1996).
4. A peak in the S&P 500 index is identified as a cyclical high that is followed either by a three- or four-month period over which the index declined at least 20 percent or by a period of five or more months over which the index declined at least 9 percent. The cyclical low or trough marks the end of the downturn from which the index begins a sustained increase. The use of monthly averages conforms to the method used by the Bureau of Economic Analysis to date stock market cycles (U.S. Department of Commerce 1989). Monthly averages also smooth out transitory movements in the index that would affect daily, weekly, or month-end data.

5. Net flow is the difference between sales of shares by mutual funds to investors and redemptions of shares by shareholders. Sales include those due to exchanges from bond, income, and money market funds into equity funds but do not include those from the reinvestment of income and capital gains distributions. Redemptions include exchanges out of equity funds into bond, income, and money market funds. The first year for which data on sales and redemptions are available is 1944. Data are quarterly from 1944 through the third quarter of 1954 and are monthly thereafter. In those instances in which monthly data are required, a monthly estimate is obtained for each month of the quarter by dividing the quarterly data by three. From 1944 through 1975, data of sales due to reinvested dividends have been estimated. Between 1944 and 1960, data on exchanges are not available; no estimates have been made as the volume of exchange transactions was small. From 1944 through 1959, separate data for stock, bond, and income funds are not available; however, stock funds constituted the vast majority of mutual funds during this period.

6. This estimate assumes that a net inflow continued through October 15 at the daily rate recorded in September. The estimate is consistent with information reported by thirty mutual fund complexes for the period October 16–26 (Silver 1987). For this period, these complexes, which held 80 percent of equity fund assets, had a net outflow of $4.6 billion. If we assume that the average net outflow over October 22, 23, and 26 of $330 million for the thirty complexes continued over the remaining four business days of the month, the estimated net outflow would be $5.9 billion for the thirty complexes over the last half of October. If their 80 percent share of equity assets also represents their share of equity fund net flow, we get an estimated net outflow of $7.4 billion for all stock funds between October 16 and 31.

7. These estimates apply the proportions of the net outflow for the thirty complexes to the estimated total net outflow of $8.2 billion.

8. For the thirty complexes, the net outflow of $4.6 billion recorded between October 16 and October 26 represented 3.3 percent of their assets. If the net outflow over the remaining four days of the month was $330 million per day, we get an estimated 4.4 percent of assets.

9. A six-month period before and after the peak was selected for the purpose of determining whether net flow as percent of assets tended to accelerate near market peaks and to decelerate shortly after market peaks.

10. This section is based upon Marcis, West, and Leonard-Chambers (1995).

11. For a discussion of the potential for a run on mutual funds, see Edwards (1996).

12. To be more specific, an order from an shareholder to redeem shares must be executed by the mutual at the time of the next pricing or valuation of the fund's portfolio.

13. The decline in securities prices might cause some investors to redeem shares because the event might have caused their expectations about future securities prices to differ from expectations now embedded in securities prices. This is not to say that shareholders can avoid those losses caused by the financial shock through the redemption but rather that they may redeem because of anticipated further losses. By the same token, expectations could have been altered to cause other investors to view the existing level of securities prices as representing a buying opportunity, triggering purchases of mutual fund shares.

14. At the federal level mutual funds are regulated by the Securities and Ex-

change Commission under the provisions of the Investment Company Act of 1940. Mutual funds also are subject to the Securities Act of 1933, the Securities Exchange Act of 1934, and the Investment Advisers Act of 1940.

15. This information is from a survey that asked questions about investment experience only of those participants owning mutual funds outside a 401(k) plan. Those owning mutual funds only through a 401(k) plan differ in a number of respects from other shareholders, as described above. From the standpoint of investment experience, since the expansion of the number of 401(k) participants has largely occurred within the last ten years, households only owning funds through a 401(k) likely have had less investment experience. Nonetheless, the investment experience for many is not solely limited to mutual funds, as a significant number own stocks and bonds outside of the plan (Table 2).

16. This information is based upon a survey conducted in mid-1994 of owners who made their first purchase outside a 401(k) plan since January 1, 1992.

References

Bullock, Hugh. *The Story of Investment Companies.* New York: Columbia University Press, 1959.

Calomiris, Charles M. "Is the Discount Window Necessary? A Penn-Central Perspective." National Bureau of Economic Research Working Paper No. 4573. Washington, D.C.: NBER, 1993.

Edwards, Franklin R. *The New Finance: Regulation and Financial Stability.* Washington, D.C.: AEI Press, 1996.

Haberman, Gary. "Capital Requirements of Commercial and Investment Banks: Contrasts in Regulation." *Quarterly Review* (Federal Reserve Bank of New York) 12, 3 (Autumn 1987): 1–9.

Investment Company Institute (ICI). "After the October 1987 Market Break: An Industry and Investor Perspective." Washington, D.C.: ICI, 1988.

———. "Understanding Shareholder Redemption Decisions." Washington, D.C.: ICI, 1993.

———. "Piecing Together Shareholder Perceptions of Investment Risk." Washington, D.C.: ICI, 1994. 1994a.

———. "Profiles of First-Time Buyers." Washington, D.C.: ICI, 1994. 1994b.

———. "Shareholder Assessment of Risk Disclosure Methods." Washington, D.C.: ICI, 1996. 1996a.

———. "Mutual Fund Shareholders: The People Behind the Growth." Washington, D.C.: ICI, 1996. 1996b.

———. "Shareholders with 401(k) Plans Invested in Mutual Funds." *Fundamentals* (May/June 1996). 1996c.

———. "Understanding Shareholders Use of Information and Advice." Washington, D.C.: ICI, Spring 1997.

Kaufman, Henry. "Structural Changes in Financial Markets: Economic and Policy Significance." *Economic Review* (Federal Reserve Bank of Kansas City) 79, 2 (second quarter 1994): 5–15.

Marcis, Richard, Sandra West, and Victoria Leonard-Chambers. "Mutual Fund Shareholder Response to Market Disruptions." *Perspective* (Investment Company Institute) 1, 1 (July 1995).

Morgan, Donald P. "Will the Shift to Stocks and Bonds By Households Be Destabilizing?" *Economic Review* (Federal Reserve Bank of Kansas City), 79, 2 (second quarter 1994): 31–44.

Rea, John and Richard Marcis. "Mutual Fund Shareholder Activity During U.S. Stock Market Cycles, 1994–95." *Perspective* (Investment Company Institute), 2, 2 (March 1996).

Silver, David. Letter to David Ruder, Chairman of the Securities and Exchange Commission, November 27, 1987.

U.S. Department of Commerce. *Business Conditions Developments.* Washington, D.C.: USGPO, December 1989.

Chapter 8
Trends in Retirement Income Plan Administrative Expenses

Edwin C. Hustead

The purpose of this analysis is to examine changes in the costs of administering U.S. retirement income plans since the enactment of the Employee Retirement Income Security Act (ERISA). For the purposes of this study, pension administrative costs are defined as all expenditures not for the direct provision of benefits for the members of the retirement income plan: these include in-house administrative costs, consultant fees, and Pension Benefit Guaranty Corporation (PBGC) premiums. The figures do not include investment expenses or one-time costs to conform to changes in regulations.

Our analysis compares the administrative cost of typical defined benefit and defined contribution plans. The defined contribution plans are those created under section 401(k) of the IRS code. The defined benefit plans are standard single-employer qualified plans. An earlier analysis for the Pension Benefit Guaranty Corporation compared administrative costs from 1981 through 1990 (Hay Huggins 1990). The current analysis examines pension plans from 1981 through 1996.

The chapter begins with a description of the methods and assumptions used in this study. All dollar values are presented in 1996 dollars. Inflation and wage trends are those used by the Social Security Trustees. Assumptions on the units of effort and unit cost were developed by Hay based on consultant experience.[1] We then describe the major changes in environment that have affected the cost of administration of retirement income plans since ERISA. Most of the changes resulted from innovations in the law governing qualified plans. However, a Supreme Court decision mandating unisex benefits and changes in accounting rules also increased the cost of administering retirement income plans. I then collect findings. Appendix Tables 1 and 2 summarize the assumptions used in this study.

Methodology and Assumptions

The approach is to examine costs for four typical retirement income plan populations. Four plan types were developed by the Academy of Actuaries (Committee on Pension Actuarial Principles and Practices 1985) in an earlier study prepared for the Financial Accounting Standards Board. Three pension plan specifications were used directly, with 75,500, and 10,000 active lives. In addition, plans of 15 lives were investigated. Since proration of the 15 lives in the smallest case would have resulted in fractional lives in each cell, the 15 lives were assigned to cells to achieve the same overall distribution.

Cost comparisons were conducted for 1981 forward. The baseline cost for 1981 was determined by examining the units and costs of services required to administer the plan in that year. Units and costs of additional services were assigned to each change in the environment. Our consultants estimated the unit costs and number of services based on their past experience and discussions with clients. Initial salaries, consultant fees, and changes in consultant fees are derived from professional experience of Hay Group consultants. Changes in salaries and inflation were based on economic experience published by the Social Security Trustees report.[2] PBGC base premiums do not include any risk-related premium: the basic annual PBGC premium is $19 per participant per year. Many pension plans also pay an additional premium because the plan is underfunded according to criteria established by the federal government.

The tables below give results for defined benefit plans with 15, 75, 500, and 10,000 active employees. Findings are also reported for 15 and 10,000 life defined contribution plans (I do not indicate results for 75 and 500 life defined contribution plans). As noted above, the reader should also note that the study does not include one-time costs related to implementation of law changes.

The administrative costs reported here are computed for a plan sponsor that has only one well-funded retirement plan that covers all the employees of the sponsor; costs will be significantly greater for more complex situations. For example, costs will be much higher for a sponsor who offers a wide range of defined benefit and defined contribution plans to employees across different divisions or in different countries.

Changes in the Pension Regulatory Environment

It has been argued in previous studies that pensions in general, and defined benefit plans in particular, have become increasingly costly to administer over time. One reason this may be so is that there have been numerous regulatory changes over time, driving up plan administration costs. The major impacts of the many changes in defined benefit plans are described below. The year shown for each law is the year that law was enacted. In many cases, the impact in cost was spread over several years after enactment.

Tax Equity and Fiscal Responsibility Act of 1982

- Determined the effect of the reduced limits on benefits and contributions for individuals. This calculation was particularly onerous for an employer with both a defined benefit and a defined contribution plan. The top-heavy rules affected all plans because of the need for at least a nominal amendment. However, small plans with highly compensated participants had to change their plans substantially.

Deficit Reduction Act of 1984

- Mandated further changes in the benefit and contribution limits. Administrative costs were increased because of the need to notify older employees of distribution.

Retirement Equity Act of 1984

- Required preretirement survivor annuities and spousal notification, which increased the cost of administration and benefits. Reducing the age and service requirements increased the cost of benefits and required amendments.

Single Employer Pension Plan Amendments Act of 1986

- Mandated increase in Pension Benefit Guaranty Corporation premium.

Tax Reform Act of 1986 (major changes)

- Required minimum coverage tests and general nondiscrimination tests, resulting in substantial administrative costs and redesign for controlled-group situations.
- Required definition of "highly compensated employee," which increased record keeping.
- Required minimum vesting standards and present value of benefit rules, leading to changes in most plans. This change increased benefits as well as administrative costs.
- Called for new integration rules, which required review and probably revision of most integrated plans and resulted in substantial costs for

the analysis and possible increases in benefits cost for the resulting plan changes.

Age Discrimination in Employment Act of 1986

- Increased administrative and benefits costs by requiring that credit be given after Normal Retirement Age.

Omnibus Budget Reconciliation Act of 1987

- Increased administrative costs to conform to Omnibus Budget Relations Act requirements.
- Increased PBGC premium.

Technical and Miscellaneous Revenue Act of 1987

- No major change for most plans.

Omnibus Budget Reconciliation Act of 1989

- No major change except for plans that had used a three-year valuation cycle. The incidence of funding was changed for many plans, but there was no direct effect on the ultimate cost.

Omnibus Budget Reconciliation Act of 1990

- No major change for ongoing plans. The excise tax on asset reversions was increased and employers were permitted a one-time transfer of "excess" assets to a retiree health account.

Unemployment Compensation Amendments of 1992

- Required sponsor to withhold 20 percent of any distribution that was not rolled over to a qualified plans. The sponsor was required to provide a written explanation of the distribution options.

Omnibus Budget Reconciliation Act of 1995

- Reduced limit on compensation considered for benefits to $150,000.

Uniformed Services Employment and Reemployment Rights Act of 1994

- Required sponsors to credit certain military service.

Retirement Protection Act of 1994 (General Agreement of Tariffs and Trades) (major changes that affected administration)

- Changed cash out rules.
- Required standard mortality table for some purposes.
- Set up special funding rules for underfunded plans.
- Added plan liquidity requirements.

Financial Accounting Standards Board Statements 87 and 88

- Added administrative costs to provide additional valuation.

Manhart, Norris—Decisions of the Supreme Court

- Led to administrative cost of modifying plan and actuarial equivalent factors.

Findings

Administrative pension expenses by year computed for each of the plans in the study are given in Tables 1 and 2. The results, shown in 1996 dollars and as a percent of payroll, include all in-house administrative and consultant costs as well as basic PBGC premiums, but exclude investment expenses. In 1996, current costs for defined benefit plans ranged from 3.10 percent of pay, or $9,300, for the smallest plan in the study to 0.23 percent of pay, or $680,000, for the largest plan. Costs for defined contribution plans ranged from 1.44 percent of payroll, or $4,300, for the smallest plan to 0.16 percent of payroll, or $490,000, for the largest plan.

The cost of 3.1 percent of payroll for the small employer defined benefit plan compared to 1.4 percent for the defined contribution plan is particularly significant when we consider that benefit costs for a typical small employer plan total around 5 percent of payroll. As a result, small employers rarely even consider offering a defined benefit plan when installing a retirement income plan. On the other hand, since administrative costs for large plans are relatively small, it is unlikely that the extra defined benefit plan administrative costs, by themselves, would cause a large employer to replace a defined benefit plan with a defined contribution plan.

It will be noted from Table 1 that administrative costs for the smallest defined benefit plans are higher than for defined contribution plans. This has been true over time, mainly because of the high fixed expenses associated with a defined benefit plan (such as the need for an actuarial

TABLE 1 Annual Administrative Costs in 1996 Dollars

	Defined benefit employees ($)				*Defined contribution employees ($)*	
Year	*15*	*75*	*500*	*10,000*	*15*	*10,000*
1981	$2,920	10,423	33,927	233,231	2,057	257,109
1982	2,992	10,666	34,571	233,659	2,113	262,121
1983	3,160	11,253	36,275	241,185	2,231	277,490
1984	3,486	11,822	38,217	249,602	2,351	291,351
1985	3,937	13,077	42,880	315,678	2,591	332,078
1986	4,614	15,005	51,006	433,530	2,768	351,783
1987	4,827	15,643	58,890	447,278	3,309	376,772
1988	7,942	19,849	69,967	578,769	3,456	389,737
1989	7,617	21,874	75,853	637,201	3,785	442,998
1990	7,899	22,561	77,722	638,473	3,935	456,897
1991	8,234	23,605	81,583	678,720	4,071	467,282
1992	8,422	24,019	82,863	683,921	4,119	474,090
1993	8,492	24,182	83,114	678,232	4,158	476,041
1994	9,128	25,511	85,911	688,187	4,217	482,351
1995	9,226	25,754	86,477	686,606	4,268	487,796
1996	9,299	25,926	86,810	683,258	4,308	491,868

Source: Author's computations using Hay Group data.

valuation). However, the cumulative effect of the changes in the regulatory environment has been to increase the cost of a defined benefit plan from around 140 percent of the defined contribution plan cost in 1981 to more than 210 percent in 1996.

In 1980, administrative costs for the 10,000 life defined benefit plan were actually lower than those of the defined contribution plan. During the 1980s, however, defined benefit plan costs grew much more rapidly than defined contribution plan costs; indeed, they grew to exceed defined contribution plan costs after 1985. By 1996, the defined benefit administrative costs for the 10,000 life case were almost 40 percent greater than the costs of a defined contribution plan.

Costs of administration of pension plans increased steadily over the 16 years of the study. The increase was partly due to wages and consulting fees increasing more rapidly than inflation. The largest increase, however, was attributable to changes in the regulatory requirements for pension plans. And these regulatory increases were substantially greater for defined benefit plans than for defined contribution plans. Thus the largest increase in cost for defined benefit plans, both absolutely and relative to defined contribution plans, occurred in the late 1980s as plans absorbed the impact of TRA-1986 and REA-1984. The defined benefit

TABLE 2 Annual Administrative Costs as Percentage of Payroll

	Defined benefit employees (%)				*Defined contribution employees (%)*	
Year	*15*	*75*	*500*	*10,000*	*15*	*10,000*
1981	1.11	0.64	0.26	0.09	0.79	0.10
1982	1.14	0.65	0.26	0.09	0.80	0.10
1983	1.18	0.67	0.27	0.09	0.83	0.10
1984	1.25	0.68	0.27	0.09	0.84	0.10
1985	1.40	0.75	0.31	0.11	0.92	0.12
1986	1.59	0.83	0.35	0.15	0.95	0.12
1987	1.64	0.85	0.40	0.15	1.13	0.13
1988	2.38	1.07	0.47	0.20	1.17	0.13
1989	2.59	1.19	0.51	0.22	1.28	0.15
1990	2.69	1.23	0.53	0.22	1.34	0.16
1991	2.83	1.30	0.56	0.23	1.40	0.16
1992	2.83	1.29	0.56	0.23	1.38	0.16
1993	2.89	1.32	0.57	0.23	1.42	0.16
1994	3.08	1.38	0.58	0.23	1.42	0.16
1995	3.09	1.38	0.58	0.23	1.43	0.16
1996	3.10	1.38	0.58	0.23	1.44	0.16

Source: Author's computations using Hay Group data.

cost also increased substantially as PBGC premiums increased as provided in SEPPAA-1986 and OBRA-1987.

Figures 1 and 2 compare plan administrative expenses for the 15 and 10,000 life cases across plan type. Though we do not estimate administrative costs for defined contribution plans for 75 and 500 lives, it is likely that the two middle plans do as well since the end point plans have substantially higher defined benefit plan costs.

Figure 3 shows the trend in cost for all four defined benefit cases expressed as a percentage of payroll. The 15 life defined benefit plan costs increased from 1.1 to 3.1 percent of payroll between 1981 and 1996. The costs for the 10,000 life case doubled, but the cost at the end of the period was only 0.2 percent of payroll. The cost for the defined contribution plans in 1996 ranged from 1.4 percent for the smallest plans to 0.2 percent of payroll for the largest plans.

The time trend in relative level of administrative costs parallels that of the prevalence of defined benefit plans. Annual *Hay/Huggins Benefits Report* surveys (1980–82) showed that the percentage of employers providing a defined benefit plan dropped steadily from 90 percent prior to 1980 to 66 percent in 1992. The drop occurred over a period in which the relative cost for a small defined benefit plan increased from 142 percent

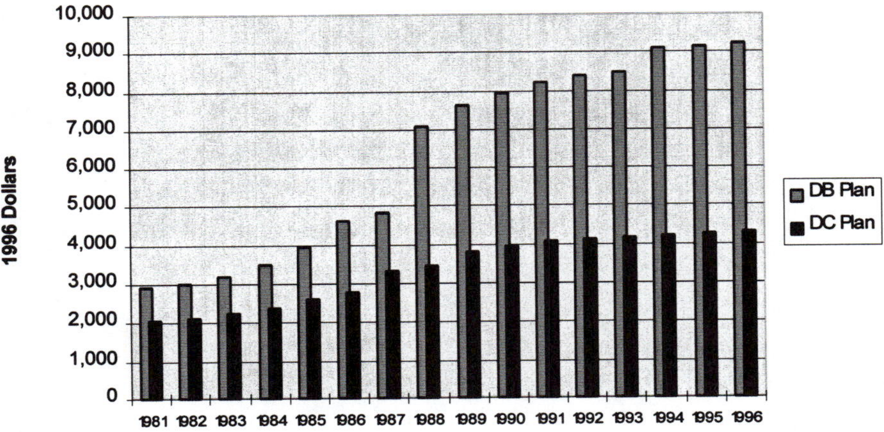

Figure 1. Administrative costs of 15 life retirement plans. Source: Author's computations using Hay Group data.

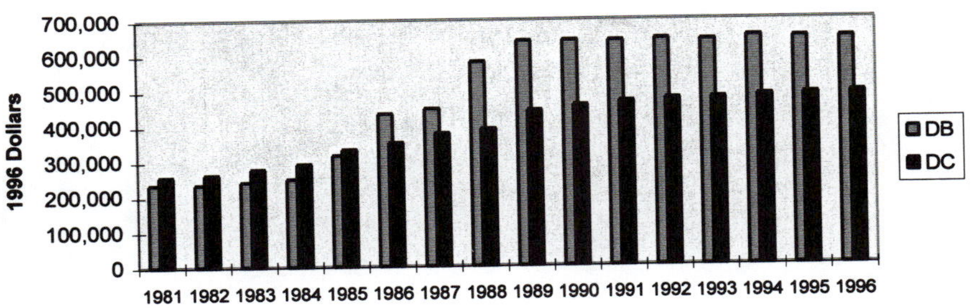

Figure 2. Administrative costs of 10,000 life retirement plans. Source: Author's computations using Hay Group data.

to 204 percent of the cost of a defined contribution plan. The relative cost for a large defined benefit plan grew from 91 percent to 136 percent of a defined contribution plan in that period. There was no significant drop in the prevalence of defined benefit plans between 1992 and 1996. During that period the relative cost of a small defined benefit plan grew to 216 percent of the defined contribution plan and the cost of a large defined benefit plan grew to 139 percent of the defined contribution plan.

Table 3 shows the details of the cost by category. Most of the admin-

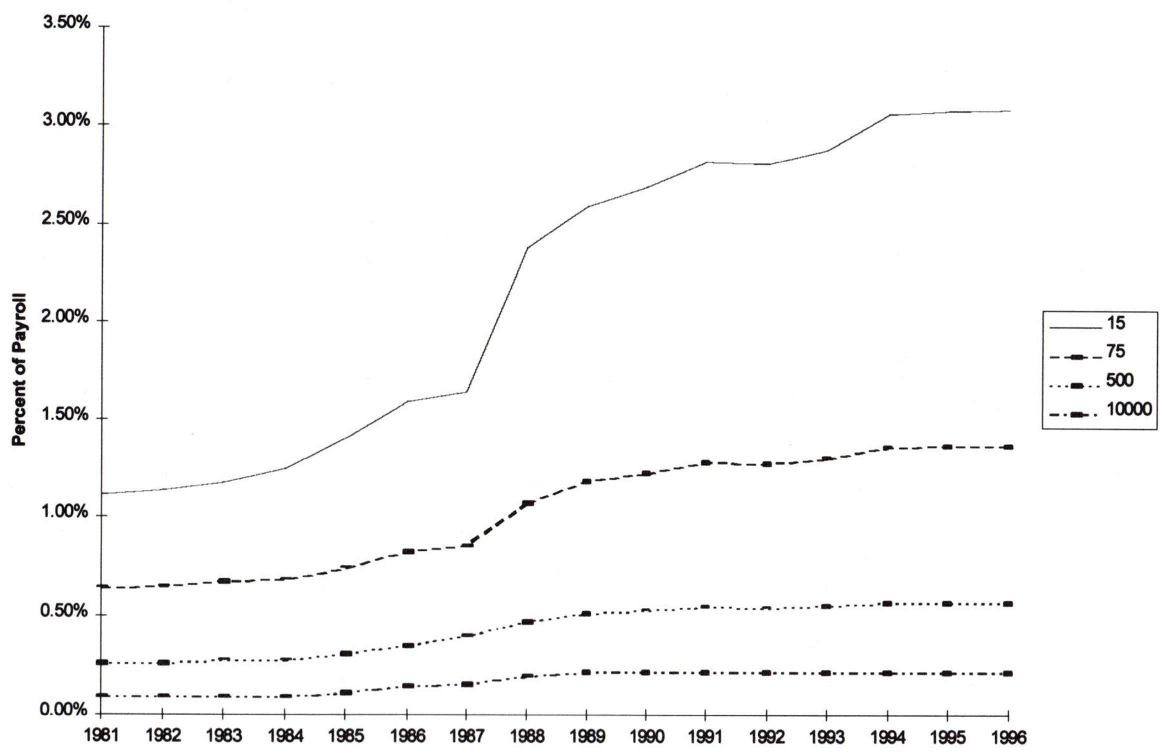

Figure 3. Administrative costs as percentage of payroll. Source: Author's computations using Hay Group data.

TABLE 3 Administrative Cost by Category (1996 Dollars)

	In house	*Actuary*	*Attorney*	*Auditor*	*PBGC*	*Total*
15 Life DB						
1981	125	2,538	194	0	71	2,928
1996	477	7,996	465	0	304	9,242
75 Life DB						
1981	833	8,291	973	0	357	10,454
1996	1,551	20,848	1,758	0	1,489	25,647
500 Life DB						
1981	4,941	17,889	2,721	6,126	2,348	34,026
1996	7,993	47,501	5,306	14,287	9,872	84,959
10,000 Life DB						
1981	93,882	70,785	10,108	12,252	46,884	233,912
1996	135,151	258,471	30,502	25,092	197,087	646,304
15 Life DC						
1981	360	3,586	224	0	0	4,170
1996	367	3,710	231	0	0	4,308
10,000 Life DC						
1981	96,329	144,224	5,055	12,252	0	257,860
1996	137,473	317,534	15,250	21,610	0	491,868

Source: Author's computations using Hay Group data.

istrative cost for small plans is attributable to consultant costs, which have increased because of the growing complexity of services required from consultants. While relatively more of the cost of the large plans is for in-house services, costs for consulting services are still greater than for in-house services. The actuarial column for the defined contribution plans includes the record-keeping function. The major reason for the cost increase for large defined benefit plans has been the rising Pension Benefit Guaranty Corporation premium that defined contribution plans do not pay. Defined benefit plan administrative expenses for large plans have therefore surpassed and now greatly exceed the cost of defined contribution plans.

Conclusion

The cost of administering retirement plans has continuously increased since the enactment of ERISA in 1974. This is particularly true for defined benefit plans, where costs have tripled in constant dollars and doubled as a percentage of covered payroll between 1981 and 1996. While the costs of defined contribution plans have also risen, the increases have been less than for defined benefit plans.

Administrative costs of defined benefit plans, which were close to those defined contribution plans in 1981, are now more than double those of defined contribution plans for smaller employers. As a result, the great majority of small employers adopt defined contribution plans as the simplest and least expensive approach to provide tax-deferred retirement income. The almost exclusive adoption of defined contribution plans by small employers today will have a ripple effect in the future as small employers grow and become part of the medium to large employer universe of the future.

The author acknowledges invaluable assistance from Kevin Binder, Melissa Rasman, and Roslyn Silverman.

Notes

1. Neither the present analysis nor the report that preceded this study (Hay Huggins 1990) used a survey of actual plan administrative costs.

2. The previous (Hay Huggins 1990) report on pension plan expenses included the same series of economic assumptions, but some of these were estimates. Actual numbers have been substituted for those estimates so minor adjustments to the 1990 study results are used in the present analysis.

References

Board of Trustees, Federal Old-Age and Survivors Insurance and Disability Insurance Trust Funds. *Annual Report of the Board of Trustees of the Federal Old-Age and Survivors and Disability Insurance Trust Funds.* Washington, D.C.: USGPO, April 3, 1995.

Committee on Pension Actuarial Principles and Practices. *Pension Cost Method Analysis.* Washington, D.C.: American Academy of Actuaries, 1985.

Hay Huggins Company. *Hay/Huggins Benefits Report.* Philadelphia: The Hay Group, various years. 1980–95.

——. *Pension Plan Expense Study.* Report to the Pension Benefit Guaranty Corporation, Washington, D.C., September 1990.

Appendix Table 1 Assumed Average Hourly Rates for Administrative Costs, 1996

Level of work	*In-house administration*		*Actuarial*		*Accounting/attorney*	
1	Clerk/sec.	$15.23	Clerk/sec.	$47.45	Clerk/sec.	$47.45
2	Tech. assoc.	$21.32	Tech. assoc.	$101.23	Tech. assoc.	$75.92
3	Mgr.	$30.45	Assoc. act.	$158.17	Assoc.	$158.13
4	Bnft. mgr.	$45.68	Conslt.	$316.33	Prtnr.	$316.33

Source: Author's computations using Hay Group data.

Note: The PBGC premiums were as scheduled in the law that applied to each of the years. These rates were $2.60 per participant in 1981; $8.50 beginning in 1986; $16.00 beginning in 1989; and $19.00 beginning in 1991. Before 1985, the premiums excluded employees under age 25. These employees were added to the PBGC base in 1985 since REA required that they be covered. There were no employees in the model under age 21. It was assumed that there would not be any additional risk-related PBGC premium.

Appendix Table 2 Economic Assumptions

Year	*CPI increase (%)*	*Wage growth (%)*
1981	10.3	9.8
1982	6.0	6.5
1983	3.0	5.1
1984	3.4	7.3
1985	3.5	4.3
1986	1.6	5.1
1987	3.6	4.7
1988	4.0	4.8
1989	4.8	4.4
1990	5.2	5.0
1991	4.1	2.9
1992	2.9	5.4
1993	2.8	1.3
1994	2.5	3.5
1995	2.7	3.5
1996	3.0	3.5

Source: Board of Trustees (1995); 1995 and 1996 estimated by the author.

Appendix Table 3 Average Salary Assumptions

Number of employees	*Average salary ($)*
15	20,000
75	25,000
500	30,000
10,000	30,000

Source: Author's computations using Hay Group data.

Chapter 9
Emerging Problems of Fiduciary Liability

Brian T. Ortelere

With the passage of the Employee Retirement Income Security Act of 1974 (ERISA), Congress included a provision—section 404(c)—designed to shift to participants the losses stemming from their exercise of control over their investments in defined contribution plans. Until recently, and notwithstanding the remarkable growth in the prevalence of these plans, there has not been any judicial guidance on the meaning of this crucial provision. Section 404(c), nestled among the general fiduciary prudence requirements, carves out defined contribution plans (or individual account plans) for special treatment:

> (c) Control over assets by participant or beneficiary.
>
> In the case of a pension plan which provides for individual accounts and permits a participant or beneficiary to exercise control over the assets in his account, if a participant or beneficiary exercises control over the assets in his account (as determined under regulations of the Secretary)—
>
> (1) such participant or beneficiary shall not be deemed to be a fiduciary by reason of such exercise, and
>
> (2) no person who is otherwise a fiduciary shall be liable under this part for any loss, or by reason of any breach, which results from such participant's or beneficiary's exercise of control.[1]

While bearing witness to the remarkable growth of such plans, fiduciaries have uneasily awaited the courts' rulings on the meaning and scope of this ERISA provision.

The decision of the United States Court of Appeals for the Third Circuit in *In re: Unisys Savings Plan Litigation*[2] represents the federal courts' first foray into the fiduciary responsibility issues surrounding the administration of these defined contribution pension plans. The Court in

Unisys has impressed upon fiduciaries a host of new obligations that may ultimately threaten the availability of this increasingly popular method of delivering retirement income.

The *Unisys* opinion adopted a stringent standard of review for determining the prudence of investment decisions, while ignoring both the discretion owed the fiduciaries in such circumstances and the causation requirements in ERISA. With the adoption of such a standard for determining the prudence of plan investments, the Court of Appeals will require a trial on the fiduciary breach claims every time an investment does not perform as anticipated. Further, and perhaps most troubling for plan sponsors, the opinion requires that fiduciaries rebroadcast public information on the status of plan investments, contrary to the explicit Department of Labor regulations excusing fiduciaries from any such obligation. Indeed, the *Unisys* opinion adopts a disclosure standard higher than that contemplated under federal securities law, which are similarly predicated upon the law of trusts.

Background of the Litigation

Defendants in the *Unisys* matter are the fiduciaries of the Unisys Savings Plan, the Unisys Retirement Investment Plan, and the Unisys Retirement Plan II (collectively the "Plan").[3] The Plan is an employee-directed defined contribution plan under ERISA sections 3(34) and 404(c), 29 U.S.C. §§ 1002(34), 1104(c). Of course, in a defined contribution plan (such as the Unisys Savings Plan), "employees are not promised any particular level of benefits, instead, they are promised only that they will receive the balances in their individual accounts."[4]

The employee-investors, participants in defined contribution plans, not the fiduciaries, bear the risk of loss. Two commentators described the risk allocation in these plans:

> Defined contribution and defined benefit plans allocate investment risk oppositely. Under a defined contribution plan, the employee bears the burden of disappointing investment results and pockets the gains from good results. Under a defined benefit plan, the employer bears the investment risk. Since the employer has promised to provide benefits at a certain level, the employer remains liable to pay the benefits even if the fund turns up short. (Fischel and Langbein 1988, 1112–13)

To facilitate the management of their investments, the Unisys Plan offered participants the opportunity to direct their money to any of six investment options and, further, subject to certain restrictions, to transfer their money monthly between these six funds. According to the Third Circuit:

Like its predecessors, the Unisys Savings Plan established an individual account for each participant and offered several fund alternatives into which a participant could direct contributions on a tax-deferred basis: the Diversified Fund; the Indexed Equity Fund; the Active Equity Fund; the Unisys Common Stock Fund; the Short Term Investment Fund; and the Insurance Contract Fund.[5]

In 1987 and 1988, Unisys purchased three five-year "guaranteed investment contracts" for inclusion in the Sperry Fixed Income Fund and the Unisys Insurance Contract Fund.[6] These contracts were issued by Executive Life Insurance Company of California and were then rated AAA and A+ by two nationally recognized insurance ratings services, Standard & Poor's and A. M. Best.[7] On April 11, 1991, California regulators imposed a conservatorship, the insurance equivalent of a Chapter 11 corporate reorganization, on Executive Life.[8] Immediately thereafter, plaintiffs in these consolidated proceedings filed twelve class action complaints in the district courts of Minnesota and Pennsylvania, alleging that their Executive Life investments were a total loss.

The district court granted Unisys's motion for summary judgment and dismissed plaintiffs' claims, holding that the fiduciaries selection of Executive Life GICs was based upon "solid, respectable and typical grounds."[9] Moreover, because the participants had adequate information from which to make informed choices regarding their investments, the district court ruled that, pursuant to ERISA section 404(c), 29 U.S.C. § 1104(c), the fiduciaries could not be liable for the alleged losses.[10]

The Third Circuit reversed the district court's ruling and remanded the matter for trial. As to the initial investment, that Court held that the prudence of the Unisys decision to purchase the Executive Life GICs could not be determined without a trial.[11] More specifically, the Court held that the prudence of the fiduciaries' primary reliance on the insurance ratings services, in selecting the Executive Life GICs, could not be resolved on summary judgment.[12] While the Third Circuit described the general prudence standards to guide the district court on remand, the Court failed to address squarely the causation prong of the analysis, required by ERISA, which looks to whether the fiduciaries' actions caused the alleged losses.

Moreover, while the Third Circuit held that Unisys may rely on ERISA section 404(c), 29 U.S.C. § 1104(c), in defense of the participants' claims, the Court ruled further that Unisys' disclosures to participants on the status of their investments could not be examined in the larger context of publicly available information then available on Executive Life.[13] Section 404(c) recognizes that participants in such plans enjoy the right to direct their investments as they see fit and, further, excuses fiduciaries from losses associated with those investment instructions. To determine whether Unisys gave participants adequate information regarding their investments, the Court of Appeals rejected Unisys' argument, grounded in both the practical aspects of defined contribution plan administration and the explicit Department of Labor regulations, that the fiduciaries need not republish public information on these investments. In other words, and equally troubling for plan administrators, the Third Circuit's ruling requires defined contribution plan fiduciaries to somehow collect, assess, and then republish public information on each of the many hundreds of investments that may comprise a typical 401(k) plan portfolio.

Fiduciary Discretion

The Third Circuit's ruling on the investment decision squarely raises the issue left open in the Supreme Court's ruling in *Firestone Tire and Rubber Co. v. Bruch,*[14] that is, whether fiduciary decisions should be scrutinized under the "arbitrary and capricious standard," particularly when plan documents afford the fiduciaries discretion in such matters (and the statutory scheme impresses investment risk on participants). However, to the extent the *Unisys* Court announced an exacting standard of review of investment decisions, that portion of the Third Circuit's ruling has arguably been overruled in the Supreme Court's recent decision in *Varity Corp. v. Howe.*[15]

The *Unisys* opinion is also at odds with then Judge, and now Justice, Scalia's opinion in *Fink v. National Savings and Trust Co.,*[16] and its Circuit Court progeny, recognizing that ERISA's causation requirements compel the dismissal of fiduciary breach claims where there is indisputable objective evidence of the prudence of the fiduciary's actions. Adoption of either the *Firestone/Varity* or *Fink* approach works to avoid a full trial on the prudence of fiduciary investment decisions each time any plan investment falls short of expectations. The *Unisys* ruling presents such a nightmare for fiduciaries (Schultz 1996).

Moreover, and as more fully discussed below, the Court in *Unisys* impressed upon fiduciaries disclosure obligations inconsistent with ERISA. The Third Circuit held that Unisys' disclosures to participants on the status of their investments could not be read in the context of the variety of publicly available information on Executive Life. In so holding, the Court refused to follow the Department of Labor's regulations on the issue, some 18 years in the making. Further, the Third Circuit's ruling runs counter to the uniform standard on disclosures necessary under the federal securities laws.

Given the relationship between 401(k) plans and securities markets, the Third Circuit's ruling may have untoward consequences for the nation's economy (Williams 1996). To impress additional costs on defined contribution plan sponsors and fiduciaries may result in the curtailment of the availability of such plans, to the detriment of both workers and financial markets.[17]

Although the Unisys Plan documents granted the fiduciaries discretion in making the initial investment choice, and ERISA recognizes that discretion is the hallmark of fiduciary activity, the Third Circuit, on remand, ordered the district court to apply strict scrutiny to the prudence question.[18] Examining a decision of another administrative body or lower judicial tribunal, a court will, at the threshold, select an appropriate "standard of review." The level of scrutiny employed by that reviewing court will often determine the outcome of a dispute.

The Supreme Court in *Firestone* held that, in certain instances, an ERISA fiduciary's actions will be evaluated pursuant to the deferential "arbitrary and capricious" standard of review. In other words, the Supreme Court recognized that judicial scrutiny of a fiduciary's decision on a participant's claim for plan benefits need not be exacting. The Third Circuit's opinion raises the question whether such a deferential standard of review is appropriate in addressing fiduciary breach claims under ERISA section 502(a)(2), 29 U.S.C. § 1132(a)(2), like imprudent selection of investments and failure to disclose material information, as well as benefits claims under ERISA section 502(a)(1)(B), 29 U.S.C. § 1132(a)(1)(B).[19] The Courts of Appeals have not uniformly resolved this question.

As the Supreme Court held in *Firestone,* "ERISA's legislative history confirms that the Act's fiduciary responsibility provisions . . . 'codif[y] and mak[e] applicable to [ERISA] fiduciaries certain principles developed in the evolution of the law of trusts.' "[20] Further, and particularly important to the determination of the appropriate standard of review:

> Trust principles make a deferential standard of review appropriate when a trustee exercises discretionary powers. *See* Restatement (Second) of Trusts § 187 (1959) ("Where discretion is conferred upon the trustee with respect to the exercise of a power, its exercise is not subject to control by the court except to prevent an abuse by the trustee of his discretion").
>
> * * *
>
> Hence, over a century ago we recited that "When trustees are in existence, and capable of acting, a court of equity will not interfere to control them in the exercise of discretion vested in them by the instrument under which they act."[21]

Indeed, the Supreme Court's very recent opinion in *Varity* holds that the standard applied to benefits claims should also govern the resolution of fiduciary breach claims:

> [C]haracterizing a denial of benefits as a breach of fiduciary duty does not necessarily change the standard a court would apply when reviewing the administra-

tor's decision to deny benefits. *After all, Firestone, which authorized deferential court review when the plan itself gives the administrator discretionary authority, based its decision upon the same common-law trust doctrines that govern standards of fiduciary conduct.*[22]

Although *Varity* seemingly compels the adoption of a deferential standard of review of the fiduciary breach claims at issue in *Unisys,* the final resolution of that question must await a ruling from the Supreme Court. Unisys' *certiorari* petition, however, was denied on October 7, 1996.[23]

Prior to *Varity,* the Courts of Appeals disagreed on whether discretionary review is appropriate in resolving fiduciary breach claims under ERISA section 502(a)(2). According to the Third Circuit:

[W]e believe that after *Firestone,* trust law should guide the standard of review over claims, such as those here, not only under section 1132(a)(1)(B) but also claims filed pursuant to 29 U.S.C. § 1132(a)(2) based on violations of the fiduciary duties set forth in section 1104(a). After all, section 1104(a) also abounds with the language of trust law, and the Supreme Court previously has noted that "Congress invoked the common law of trusts to define the general scope of [fiduciaries'] authority and responsibility."[24]

The Second Circuit, on the other hand, has limited *Firestone's* reach to the review of benefits claims under ERISA section 502(a)(1)(B):

We reject the argument that *Firestone*'s arbitrary and capricious standard applies to [defendants'] conduct in this matter. *Firestone* involved the denial of benefits, and the Court stated that if the terms of the plan accorded the administrator discretion in such matters, the decision should be upheld unless arbitrary and capricious. However, we decline to apply the arbitrary and capricious standard to the fiduciary conduct at issue because this case does not involve a simple denial of benefits, over which the plan administrators have discretion.[25]

As Unisys explained to the Court of Appeals, both the Department of Labor and the Pension Benefit Guaranty Corporation (PBGC), during the relevant time period, established a flexible standard for the purchase of insurance annuities upon the termination of a defined benefit pension plan, pursuant to ERISA section 4041(b)(3)(A)(i), 29 U.S.C. § 1341(b)(3)(A)(i). In other words, to satisfy an individual's pension benefit from one insurance company for his or her lifetime, both of these regulatory agencies required only that the insurance company selected by state licensed.[26] This standard applies notwithstanding the fact that the fiduciaries typically labor under a conflict of interest in such circumstances; that is, they stand to recoup any available defined benefit pension plan surplus.[27]

Aside from the fact that Executive Life was licensed by the State of California, it had, at the time of Unisys' purchase, an AAA rating from Standard and Poor's and an A+ rating from A. M. Best.[28] Moreover, it is undisputed that no conflict of interest arose with the purchase of the Executive Life GICs, and Executive Life was but one of the many insurers in the Plan's portfolio. Mindful of the abundance of proof suggesting the reasonableness of the selection of Executive Life, proper application of the *Firestone/Varity* "arbitrary and capricious" standard would likely have absolved Unisys from plaintiffs' claim to damages, without the need for a trial.

Causation Requirements

The Third Circuit's *Unisys* opinion also ignores the express command of ERISA section 409, 29 U.S.C. § 1109, and other Circuit opinions, requiring that plaintiffs bringing fiduciary breach claims prove that the fiduciary's actions caused loss. Following then Judge Scalia's lead in *Fink v. National Savings and Trust Co.,*[29] other federal judges have adopted the "hypothetical prudent fiduciary" analysis to summarily resolve fiduciary breach claims. These courts, properly accounting for the deference owed fiduciaries and the statute's explicit causation requirements, recognize that, if some objective proof of the prudence of a fiduciary's actions can be mustered, no finding of liability is proper.[30] Similarly, the *Firestone/Varity* analysis—application of the "hypothetical prudent fiduciary" test, required by a close reading of ERISA—would curtail the number of fiduciary breach claims to the benefit of *both* fiduciaries and participants.[31]

After describing the general prudence standard, then Judge Scalia observed that a second step is needed. ERISA's causation requirement, contained in section 409, compels an inquiry into whether there is objective evidence of prudence. In such circumstances, a fiduciary cannot be held liable in damages:

> I know of no case in which a trustee who had happened—through prayer, astrology or just blind luck—to make (or hold) objectively prudent investments (e.g., an investment in a highly regarded "blue chip" stock) has been held liable for losses from those investments because of his failure to investigate and evaluate beforehand.[32]

The Eighth Circuit, building on Judge Scalia's opinion in *Fink,* explained further: "Even if a trustee failed to conduct an investigation before making a decision, he is insulated from liability if a hypothetical prudent fiduciary would have made the same decision anyway."[33]

Although the Third circuit cited both *Fink* and *Roth* on the general prudence standard, the *Unisys* opinion makes no mention of the causation requirement and requires a trial, despite Unisys's proffer of an abundance of indisputable objective evidence showing the prudence of the fiduciaries' actions.

Fiduciary Disclosures

The Third Circuit's opinion also requires defined contribution plan fiduciaries to retransmit publicly available information on the status of participants' investments, contrary to the Department of Labor's explicit regulatory command excusing fiduciaries from such an obligation. Indeed, by tying this obligation to ERISA section 404(a), the Third Circuit has unwittingly supplanted the Department's detailed regulatory scheme for such plans, spanning, along with its "preamble," some thirty-one pages of the *Federal Register.*[34] In effect, the *Unisys* opinion requires defined contribution plan fiduciaries to run a "clipping service" for participants, collating and rebroadcasting the multitude of public information on plan investments, cobbled only from ERISA's general fiduciary obligation to act prudently.[35]

The Third Circuit properly held that, on remand, Unisys may seek to prove, pursuant to ERISA section 404(c), 29 U.S.C. § 1104(c), that the participants in this "individual account plan" caused the alleged losses. In other words, the Court recognized that the Plan fiduciaries cannot be held liable if the alleged losses "result[ed] from such participant's or beneficiary's exercise of control."[36] Consistent with the design of many 401(k) plans, featuring varied investment options and participant transfer rights, ERISA section 404(c) works to circumscribe fiduciary liability upon a showing that the participant's personal investment decisions gave rise to the claimed losses.

Nevertheless, the Court went beyond section 404(c), to the general prudence obligations of section 404(a), to define the fiduciary's disclosure obligations in administering plans governed by 404(c). Building upon a line of unrelated Third Circuit fiduciary disclosure cases, construing the prudence standard of section 404(a), the Court reached the alarming conclusion that Unisys was obligated to broadcast to participants public information on the status of their investments, limited only by the materiality standard apparently borrowed from federal securities law:

> In our view, while Unisys was not obligated to share with participants everything it knew about GICS and Executive Life, it was obligated to impart to participants material information of which it had knowledge that was sufficient to apprise the average plan participant of the risks associated with investing in the Fixed Income and Insurance Contract Funds in view of the purchase of the Executive Life GICs and the financial condition Executive Life presented in 1990. *Moreover, in this regard, we do not, as Unisys urges, distinguish between "public" and "non-public" information nor do we limit Unisys' duty to disclose to the latter.*[37]

Oddly enough, and further clouding the fiduciaries' obligations, the Third Circuit's opinion does not resolve "whether Unisys had a duty under section 1104(a) to communicate anything at all to the Plans' participants about these matters in the first place."[38]

The Third Circuit now seemingly requires that fiduciaries comport their disclosures with an amorphous standard derived from a mixed bag of decisions involving everything but defined contribution pension plans. Indeed, to look to the general fiduciary obligations of section 404(a), to define the disclosures needed under 404(c), runs counter to the limited nature of ERISA's explicit disclosure requirements, spelled out in ERISA sections 101, 102, 103 and 104, 29 U.S.C. §§ 1021–24.[39]

In that regard, the Supreme Court's holding in *International Brotherhood of Teamsters, Chauffeurs, Warehousers and Helpers v. Daniel,*[40] underscores the Third Circuit's error. *Daniel* emphasized the particularized nature of the disclosures required under ERISA, as opposed to federal securities laws:

> Unlike the Securities Acts, ERISA deals expressly and in detail with pension plans. ERISA requires pension plans to disclose specified information to employees in a specified manner, . . . in contrast to the indefinite and uncertain disclosure obligations imposed by the antifraud provisions of the Securities Acts.[41]

Cast adrift from ERISA's statutory moorings, the Third Circuit, contrary to *Daniel,* has fashioned a new "rule" threatening the very existence of defined contribution plans.

More specifically, the Third Circuit's opinion is directly at odds with the Department of Labor's 404(c) regulations. To keep defined contribution plan administrative costs down, the regulations explicitly relieve fiduciaries of the disclosure obligation announced in *Unisys.* Under the regulations, a participant's exercise of control under ERISA section 404(c) will not be deemed "independent" if:

> (ii) *A plan fiduciary has concealed material non-public facts regarding the investment from the participant or beneficiary,* unless the disclosure of such information by the plan fiduciary or beneficiary would violate any provision of federal law or any provision of state law which is not preempted by [ERISA].[42]

Admittedly, the 404(c) regulation, by its terms, did not directly apply to the *Unisys* dispute.[43]

Nevertheless, that fact only further highlights the problems facing fiduciaries in the wake of the *Unisys* opinion. By grounding the disclosure obligation in section 404(a), as opposed to 404(c), the *Unisys* holding applies equally to fiduciary conduct arising before and after the effective date of the regulations. In other words, fiduciaries must now harmonize the Third Circuit's opinion, based on section 404(a), and the Department's 404(c) regulation. Because the two approaches are irreconcilable, the fiduciaries must either adhere to the *Unisys* ruling (at tremendous cost), or terminate the plan.

Moreover, and despite this Court's warning in *Daniels,* the *Unisys* opinion's disclosure requirements *surpass* that required under the federal securities laws. It is a basic principle of corporate law that a corporation's directors owe fiduciary duties to the corporation's stockholders.[44] Despite this fiduciary relationship, the federal securities laws do not require the dissemination of public information regarding a corporation's securities.[45] While corporate law and ERISA share the same fiduciary underpinnings, the Third Circuit has, without any basis in law or logic, announced a more stringent standard governing disclosures on investments held on behalf of participants in ERISA plans.

The 404(c) Regulations

The Department of Labor, in 1992, issued the regulations called for in ERISA section 404(c). Although the regulations themselves are exceptionally intricate and defy ready characterization, a couple of highlights bear mention. To bring itself within the "safe harbor" contemplated by ERISA section 404(c), the defined contribution plan must offer participants at least three investment alternatives, each of which is diversified and "has materially different risk and return characteristics."[46] Participants must also be able to transfer their money between these investment vehicles, or funds, "with a frequency which is appropriate in light of the market volatility to which the alternative may reasonably be expected to be subject."[47]

While the regulations include a laundry list of required information to be disclosed to participants, so that the participants can exercise the "control" contemplated by the statute, the plan sponsor need not distribute publicly available information on the status of plan investments.[48] As noted above, however, the Third Circuit's *Unisys* ruling is to the contrary.

Moreover, the regulations mandate that the operative documents specifically warn participants that the fiduciaries may be relieved from any losses associated with the plan's investments. In other words, the fiduciaries may not invoke the 404(c) defense unless the participants are given:

> [A]n explanation that the plan is intended to constitute a plan described in section 404(c) of the Employee Retirement Security Act, and Title 29 of the *Code of Federal Regulations* Section 2550.404c-1, and that the fiduciaries of the plan may be relieved of liability for any losses which are the direct and necessary result of investment instructions given by such participant or beneficiary.[49]

Lastly, and as should be clear by now, because the Third Circuit in *Unisys* grounded its disclosure obligations in the statute, rather than the DOL regulation, it remains to be seen whether, in the future, a fiduciary's compliance with the regulations alone will effectively cut off liability for investment losses.

Conclusion

In sum, the Third Circuit's *Unisys* opinion: (1) adopts a standard of review for determining the prudence of an investment that ignores the discretion owed fiduciaries in such circumstances; (2) fails to analyze the explicit causation requirements in ERISA; and (3) dictates disclosure standards higher than those adopted by the Department of Labor (and required under federal securities law). The practical effect of the ruling is to require fiduciaries to keep participants abreast of the status of the hundreds, if not thousands, of investments in a typical 401(k) plan, at a time when regulatory burdens already threaten the availability of such plans. To so engraft on section 404(c) duties derived from section 404(a) will, contrary to the legislative intent, dramatically drive up the costs of administering such a plan while circumscribing the availability of the congressionally mandated affirmative defense. All told, fiduciaries can expect to see an increase in fiduciary breach claims, whenever defined contribution plan investments do not perform as anticipated.

It should be noted that the author and his firm have represented the Unisys defendants since the inception of this dispute.

Notes

1. 29 U.S.C. § 1104(c). The corresponding definitional section, 1002(34), limits the application of this defense to certain enumerated plans:

> (34) The term "individual account plan" or "defined contribution plan" means a pension plan which provides for an individual account for each participant and for benefits based solely upon the amount contributed to the participant's account, and any income, expenses, gains and losses, and any forfeitures of accounts of other participants which may be allocated to such participant's accounts.

29 U.S.C. § 1002(34). Although ERISA was passed in 1974, the regulations called for in section 404(c) were not issued until 1992.

2. 74 F.3d 420 (3d Cir. 1996).

3. The three plans were "identical" and, as such, will be together described as a singular plan (*In re: Unisys Savings Plan Litig.*, 74 F.3d 420, 426–27 [3d Cir. 1996]).

4. *Pension Benefit Guar. Corp. v. LTV Corp.*, 496 U.S. 633, 637 n.1 (1990). Such plans have enjoyed phenomenal growth in the last ten years, eclipsing the use of defined benefit plans to deliver income to retirees:

> Since the mid 1970s, the private pension system in the United States has undergone considerable change. The most notable development has been the increasing reliance on defined contribution plans over the traditional defined benefit plans. Between 1980 and 1985 alone, the number of primary defined contribution plans increased by 71 percent and the number of participants rose by 83 percent; in contrast, primary defined benefit coverage showed virtually no growth.

(Clark and McDermed 1990).

5. *Unisys,* 74 F.3d at 426.

6. A guaranteed investment contract (GIC) is a contract, issued by an insurance company, "under which the issuer is obligated to repay the principal deposit at a designated future date and to pay interest at a specified rate over the duration of the contracts" (ibid., 426). The Unisys Savings Plan emerged from the merger of the Sperry Retirement Program—Part B and the Burroughs Employees Savings Thrift Plan (id.). Following the merger of the two plans, the Sperry fund ceased to accept new contributions, but proceeds from contracts in that fund were reinvested in the Unisys Insurance Contract Fund (id.).

7. Ibid., 427.

8. Ibid., 431.

9. *In re: Unisys Savings Plan Litig.,* No. 91-3067, 1995 WL 29048, at *4 (E.D. Pa. Jan. 26, 1995). Summary judgment is a means by which a court may, in the absence of a dispute over a fact in a civil lawsuit, summarily grant a judgment in favor of a party to that suit (without the need for a trial).

10. Ibid., *3.

11. *Unisys,* 74 F.3d at 434–37.

12. Ibid., 435–36.

13. Ibid., 443.

14. 489 U.S. 101 (1989).

15. No. 94-1471, 1996 U.S. LEXIS 1954 (U.S. March 19, 1996).

16. 772 F.2d 951, 961–65 (D.C. Cir. 1985) (Scalia, J., concurring in part and dissenting in part).

17. Indeed, the mischief of the *Unisys* opinion will extend beyond the borders of the Third Circuit. ERISA's expansive jurisdictional provision allows for suit wherever a defendant "may be found" or where the "breach took place" (29 U.S.C. § 1132[e][2]). Hence, future plaintiffs, by suing in the Third Circuit, may readily circumvent unfavorable circuit authority elsewhere, so long as the defendant is found to have minimum contacts with the Third Circuit (an easy task given the number of Delaware corporations) or the plaintiff resides there (e.g., *Varsic v. United States District Court,* 607 F.2d 245, 248 [9th Cir. 1979] ["Congress' choice of this term ['found'] for inclusion in the ERISA venue provision further supports our conclusion that the provision is intended to expand, rather than restrict, the range of permissible venue locations"]).

18. *Unisys,* 74 F.3d at 433–37.

19. The Supreme Court's opinion in *Firestone* was limited to the standard governing judicial review of benefits claims under ERISA section 502(a)(1)(B). According to Justice O'Connor:

> The discussion which follows is limited to the appropriate standard of review in § 1132(a)(1)(B) actions challenging denials of benefits based on plan inter-

> pretations. We express no view as to the appropriate standard of review for actions under other remedial provisions of ERISA.

(*Firestone,* 489 U.S. at 101).

20. Ibid., 110.

21. Ibid., 111. The commentary to section 187 of the Second Restatement of Trusts, the section relied on in *Firestone,* extends this discretionary authority to investment decisions. See Restatement (Second) of Trusts § 187, comment c (1959) (the discretionary authority "is applicable not only to powers to lease, sell or mortgage the trust property or to invest trust funds, but also to powers to allocate the beneficial interest among various beneficiaries, to determine the amount necessary for a beneficiary's support, or to terminate the trust").

22. *Varity,* 1996 U.S. LEXIS 1954, at * 45 (emphasis added).

23. A trial in this matter was concluded in the fall of 1997.

24. *Moench v. Robertson,* 62 F.3d 553, 565 (3d Cir. 1995) (quoting *Central States, Southeast and Southwest Areas Pension Fund v. Central Transp., Inc.,* 472 U.S. 559, 570 [1985]). *See also Mahoney v. Board of Trustees,* 973 F.2d 968, 971–73 (1st Cir. 1992) (rejecting "strict standard of review" because " 'Where discretion is conferred upon the trustee with respect to the exercise of a power . . . the trust's 'exercise is not subject to control by the court, except to prevent an abuse by the trustee of his discretion' ") (quoting Restatement [Second] of Trusts § 186).

25. *John Blair Communications, Inc. Profit Sharing Plan v. Telemundo Group, Inc. Profit Sharing Plan,* 26 F.3d 360, 369 (2d Cir. 1994).

26. See 29 C.F.R. § 2617.2, 2617.4, 2617.22(d)(8) (Pension Benefit Guaranty Corporation standard); 29 C.F.R. § 2510.3–3(d)(2)(ii)(A)(1) (Department of Labor standard).

27. E.g., *Riley v. Murdock,* 890 F. Supp. 444, 458–59 (E.D.N.C. 1995) (purchase of Executive Life annuities ancillary to termination of defined benefit pension plan not a breach of fiduciary obligation, even if selection of annuity maximizes reversion of plan surplus).

28. *Unisys,* 74 F.3d at 427.

29. 772 F.2d 951, 961–61 (D.C. Cir. 1985) (Scalia, J., concurring in part and dissenting in part).

30. *Kuper v. Quantum Chemicals Corp.,* 852 F. Supp. 1389, 1397–98 (S.D. Ohio 1994) ("Indeed, evidence that independent, professional observers of market trends differed in their projections of future Quantum stock performance merely underscores the fact that circumstances then existing would not have compelled reasonable persons to a singular conclusion about the stock's future prospects. . . . Defendants cannot be said to have been objectively imprudent for having acted in the same manner as impartial observers had recommended").

31. Cf. H.R. Rep. No. 533, 93d Cong. 2d Sess. (1974), reprinted in 1994 U.S. Code Cong. & Admin. News 4639, 4640 (ERISA designed to "promote a renewed expansion of private retirement plans and increase the number of participants receiving private retirement benefits"). See also *Mertens v. Hewitt Assocs.,* 113 S. Ct. 2063, 2071 (1993) ("ERISA [is] an enormously complex and detailed statute that resolved innumerable disputes between powerful competing interests—not all in favor of potential plaintiffs").

32. *Fink,* 772 F.2d at 962.

33. *Roth v. Sawyer-Cleator Lumber Co.,* 16 F.3d 915, 919 (8th Cir. 1994). See also *Kuper v. Iovenko,* 66 F.3d 1447, 1459 (6th Cir. 1995) ("[A] fiduciary's failure to investigate an investment decision *alone* is not sufficient to show that the decision

was not reasonable") (emphasis in original); *Diduck v. Kaszycki & Sons Contractors, Inc.*, 974 F.2d 270, 279 (2d Cir. 1992) ("Proof of a causal connection . . . is required between a breach of fiduciary duty and the loss alleged").

34. *See* 57 Fed. Reg. 46906–37.

35. Unisys collected for the Court of Appeals a sample of the public materials then available on Executive Life, from such sources as the *Wall Street Journal, Forbes,* the *New York Times,* the *Los Angeles Times,* the *San Francisco Chronicle,* the United Press International, and the Associated Press. According to the Court of Appeals, "[d]uring this time, Executive Life's condition was widely reported in the financial press" (*Unisys,* 74 F.3d at 431).

36. 29 U.S.C. § 1104(c)(2).

37. *Unisys,* 74 F.3d at 443 (emphasis added). The opinions from which the Third Circuit's new disclosure rule was derived speak nothing of the circumstances unique to the administration of defined contribution pension plans (*Unisys,* 74 F.3d at 440–41). See *Unisys Corp. Retiree Medical Benefit "ERISA" Litig.,* 57 F.3d 1255 (3d Cir. 1995) (modifications to retirement medical plan), *petition for cert. filed,* 64 U.S.L.W. 3167 (U.S. Sept. 8, 1995); *Curcio v. John Hancock Mut. Life Ins. Co.,* 33 F.3d 226 (3d Cir. 1994) (claims for life insurance and accidental death and dismemberment benefits); *Bixler v. Central PA Teamsters Health and Welfare Plan,* 12 F.3d 1292 (3d Cir. 1993) (participant inquiries regarding medical benefits); *Fischer v. Philadelphia Elec. Co.,* 994 F.2d 130 (3d Cir.) (early retirement "window" afforded defined benefit pension plan participants), *cert. denied,* 114 S. Ct. 622 (1993).

38. *Unisys,* 74 F.3d at 442–43.

39. In so holding, the *Unisys* opinion also runs afoul of the Supreme Court's repeated admonition that ERISA cannot be construed to create new rights and obligations, absent an explicit congressional directive. E.g., *Mertens v. Hewitt Assoc.,* 113 S. Ct. 2063, 2071 (1993) ("[V]ague notions of a statute's 'basic purpose' are nonetheless inadequate to overcome the words of its text regarding the specific issue under consideration"). Prior to *Unisys,* all assumed that a 404(c) plan fiduciary need not look beyond that section to discern its responsibilities in administering such a plan. (Sacher et al. 1991).

40. 439 U.S. 551 (1979).

41. *Daniel,* 439 U.S. at 569. See also *Curtiss-Wright Corp. v. Schoonegjongen,* 115 S. Ct. 1223, 1231 (1995) (regarding ERISA's statutory disclosure requirements—"This may not be a foolproof informational scheme, although it is quite thorough. Either way, it is the scheme that Congress devised").

42. 29 C.F.R. § 2550.404c-1(c)(2)(ii) (emphasis added).

43. 29 C.F.R. § 2550.404c-1(g)(1) ("[T]his section is effective with respect to transactions occurring on or after the first day of the second plan year beginning on or after the first day of the second plan year beginning on or after October 13, 1992").

44. "A director is a fiduciary" (*Twin-Lick Oil Co. v. Marbury,* 91 U.S. 587, 588 [1875]). So is a dominant or controlling stockholder or group of stockholders (*Southern Pacific Co. v. Bogert,* 250 U.S. 483, 492 [1919]). Their powers are powers in trust. See *Jackson v. Ludeling,* [88 U.S. 616,] 21 Wall. 616, 624 [1874] ("[The] standard of fiduciary obligation is designed for the protection of the entire community of interests in the corporation—creditors as well as stockholders").

45. *Sailors v. Northern States Power Co.,* 4 F.3d 610, 613 (8th Cir. 1993) ("The securities laws require disclosure of information that is not otherwise in the public domain") (quoting *Acme Propane, Inc. v. Tenexco, Inc.,* 844 F.2d 1317, 1323

[7th Cir. 1988]); *Hillson Partners Ltd. Partnership v. Adage, Inc.*, 42 F.3d 204, 212 (4th Cir. 1994) (same).

46. 29 C.F.R. § 2550.404c-1(b)(3)(B).
47. 29 C.F.R. § 2550.404c-1(b)(2)(B)(2)(ii)(C).
48. 29 C.F.R. § 2550.404c-1(c)(2)(ii).
49. 29 C.F.R. § 2550.404c-1(b)(2)(B)(1)(i).

References

Clark, Robert L. and Ann A. McDermed. *The Choice of Pension Plans in a Changing Regulatory Environment.* Washington, D.C.: AEI Press, 1990.

Fischel, Daniel and John H. Langbein. "ERISA's Fundamental Contradiction: The Exclusive Benefit Rule." *University of Chicago Law Review* 55 (1988): 1105–60.

Sacher, Steven J., Jeffrey L. Gibbs, and Howard Shapiro. *Employee Benefits Law.* Washington, D.C.: Bureau of National Affairs, 1991.

Schultz, Ellen E. "So Your 401(k) Had a Loss? Try Suing Your Boss." *Wall Street Journal,* February 16, 1996: B1.

Williams, Fred. "Managers Hold Firm in Soaring Markets." *Pension & Investments,* February 19, 1996: 1.

Chapter 10
The Changing Paradigm of 401(k) Plan Servicing

Ronald D. Hurt

If one examines the changes in the employee benefit plans offered by American companies over the past decade, it would be difficult to judge whether medical or retirement plans had changed more dramatically. Medical plans have undergone much change (including managed medical care, "flexible" benefits, and the shifting of medical plan costs to employees), but developments in the world of retirement benefits have been significant as well.

In both cases, employers have turned rapidly to new ways to pay for these benefits, primarily looking to limit their financial exposure and make more predictable their short- and long-term liabilities. Employers have begun to ask their employees to pay part or even all the cost of these benefits, and this shift has been rationalized using a variety of now-common workplace mantras: employee empowerment, the freedom to choose what's best for the individual, and personal control. In medical plans, it is called managed care; in retirement, it is called defined contribution.

While the introduction of managed care plans has begun to redefine the nature of healthcare in this country, the shift in retirement plans from defined benefit (the traditional "pension" plan) to defined contribution (primarily 401[k]) plans may well alter the retirement landscape even more significantly in the years to come.

Consider the following. The ability of the social security system to continue to fund workers' retirements meets with widespread skepticism in the workplace, in part because of fears of an encroaching national debt and in part by aging baby boomers who must depend on fewer young workers to support them during retirement. At the same time, however, approximately 25 percent of employees who have a defined contribution retirement plan do not participate.[1] Of those who do, on average they are saving no more than about 5 percent or 6 percent of their salaries, an amount most experts agree will not provide a significant replacement income at retirement (Foster Higgins, Inc. 1993). This is only exacerbated by the fact that many employees eligible for such plans do not begin saving until they are in their late thirties or early forties, weakening the power of compound earnings (Access Research, Inc. 1995). And, by and large, 401(k) savers put a disproportionate percentage of their savings in stable value funds, which many experts say will not provide the growth necessary to build an inflation-proof nest egg (Hewitt Associates, cited in EBRI 1995).

Finally, what savings do exist are often depleted years before retirement, as job-changers take advantage of an IRS loophole that permits access to their accumulated 401(k) assets. When employees change jobs, they are offered a choice: to take a "distribution" from their 401(k) plans (in short, to "get the cash") or to transfer the money—or a portion of it—to another IRS-qualified retirement plan. In alarming numbers, employees have simply taken the money, even though they will have to pay taxes and, in most cases, a 10 percent penalty for early withdrawal. In 1990 alone, according to the Employee Benefit Research Institute, *more than $40 billion of preretirement lump-sum distributions was not rolled over* into any other qualified plan, significantly diminishing those employees' hopes for a richer retirement (EBRI 1994).[2] One survey (Burkhauser and Salisbury 1993) suggests that only 13 percent of recipients "roll over" lump sum preretirement distributions into qualified retirement instruments and 40 percent of the recipients use some of the funds for consumption.

In short, many employees do not have access to any defined contribution retirement plan, and those who do are not all participating, are saving at low rates, are investing unwisely, and are squandering their savings at the first opportunity. Few if any American companies are creating new pension (defined benefit) plans, and the benefits from existing ones are being trimmed.[3]

Given all this, it looks as if the once stable world of American retirement security may be in for some significant and unprecedented change (see Table 1). The purpose of this chapter is to demonstrate that these changes are also having a significant and long-term effect on the way employers' 401(k) plans are administered and serviced by financial intermediaries, primarily banks, mutual funds, and insurance companies. In fact, the shift away from defined benefit plans, the growing emphasis on employee involvement, and the increased use of sophisticated information technology are all changing the basic paradigm of client service, which is in turn changing how major portions of the financial services industry do business and service clients.

TABLE 1 The Evolution of 401(k) Features: How Plan Design, Account Information, and Client Service Are Moving from an Institutional to an Individual Focus

	First wave: focus on the institutional plan sponsor	*Second wave: a retail orientation for a retail customer*	*Next wave: total participant interaction facilitated by technology*
Employee access to plan information	Limited primarily to Summary Plan Description	Prospectuses, sales literature, toll-free 800 access, meetings, financial planning assistance	Internet, technology-driven, total access to information and assistance, data-based information
Investment options	"Mystery" funds, limited choices, fees hidden	Mutual funds (with no-load pricing), brokerage options, asset allocation funds, daily transfers, increased number of options	Commoditization of funds, individual securities, unlimited access, personally managed portfolios, lowered expense ratios, custom-built needs-based portfolios
Valuation of individual accounts	Quarterly at best, often annually	Daily or monthly	Daily, or on-demand pricing (with individually traded securities)
Employee access to account information	Limited: annual or semi-annual statements	Monthly or quarterly statements; statements on-demand. 24-hour access via 800 number	Access via Internet
Ability for employees to transfer among investments	Monthly at best, often quarterly	Moving to daily, via 800 #; many still limited to monthly	Daily, via Internet
Definition of client	Plan sponsor; investment/pension committee	Still focused on plan sponsor but increased awareness of participant	Participant

The First Wave: Intense Focus on the "Institutional" Sponsor

Until the mid-1980s, many American companies provided to their employees benefit packages (medical, dental life insurance disability, pension, etc.) that permitted almost no employee choice about individual benefits or levels of coverage. The prevailing institutional view of benefits packages was that "one size fits all." This attitude was seen as appropriately "paternalistic" at the time, and employees appeared to be content under such a system, in essence surrendering individual choice (if it were ever even contemplated by the average employee) in exchange for a comprehensive package of benefits.

The paternalistic attitude about benefits was also evident in employers' approaches to providing retirement security through the traditional defined benefit (pension) plan. Again, as with other benefits, one size fit all, and employee choice was almost absent from a plan's ongoing existence, except as the eventual recipient of this paternalistic largesse.

Until about 10 years ago, an employer offering a retirement plan designed it in consultation with professional benefits consultants and actuaries. Employers made annual contributions to "fund" the plans (usually), and they handled investment of the plan's assets with the help of money managers (primarily banks and insurance companies). It was the rare employer that disclosed to employees any useful information about the financial workings of the plan (Hurley et al. 1995). Employees were told of the plan's existence, but often knew nothing else, except perhaps that the company would calculate the pension amount based on a complicated formula based on "years of service" and "final average pay" (Hurley et al 1995). Of course, the official "Summary Plan Description" was available upon request, but it was infrequently requested and certainly less frequently read or understood. Employees were not encouraged to ask questions, and it was generally the case that the employer would not assume that the employees had any need to know much more than the fact that the company had a pension plan.

Because the plan sponsor—the employer—was identical for both defined benefit (DB) and defined contribution (DC) plans, it should be no surprise that in the earliest days of DC plans, roughly the early 1980s, employers administered them in very much the same way that they had administered their companies' DB pension plans. Again, here, the third-party administrators and money managers hired by plan sponsors continued to think of the employer as the client, justifiably, and continued to manage the relationship the way they managed their traditional pension clients. There was little focus on the employee, if any. Employers asked insurance companies, banks, and investment management companies to manage the assets of the DC plan (the employees' money), often in nonretail "separate" accounts (Hurley et al. 1995). Separate accounts are an unregistered pool of investments managed separately from the investment manager's "general" accounts. They are not registered mutual funds. Employee records were kept primarily by banks and insurance companies, and an account statement—a new wrinkle from the traditional pension plan!—distributed to participants once a year was the norm. (It is entirely possible, given the newness of these plans, the small balances, and the history of sparse plan information, that many employees expected little more.)

Limited Information for Participants

Prior to a decade ago, the plan information employees did receive was often limited to that mandated by federal pension regulations (primarily through the Employee Retirement Income Security Act, ERISA). In the case of 401(k) plans, this was usually no more than a wordy, legal "Summary Plan Description" and an enrollment form to initiate contributions through payroll deduction (Hurley et al. 1995). Separate accounts, unlike mutual funds, do not have prospectuses, so descriptions to potential investors, the participants, were often inconsistent and incomplete. Some employers explained the 401(k) plan to newly hired employees during their "orientation" program, but because most plans required an eligibility period of one year, the explanation was often perfunctory and employee interest low. Few employees understood the plans well, but, again, it was not at all clear that that mattered much to employees accustomed to benefit paternalism.

"Mystery" Funds with Infrequent Valuations

Taking a cue from their DB plans, employers generally offered separate-account investment options, not mutual funds, as noted above. With such investments, very little "public" information is either required or available. On the other hand, one clear difference between DB and DC plans is that participants' accounts have to be "valued" and that value has to be communicated to participants. In the early days of 401(k) plans, this task usually given over to the outside administrator or fund manager, but semi-annual or annual valuations were felt to be sufficient.

Limited Ability to Move Money Among Investment Options

Transfers of accumulated assets within a participant's account were limited, typically, to the valuation frequency. As noted, this was almost never more often than once a quarter. To make the process even more onerous, employees had to plan and formally request a transfer well in advance of the plan's deadline for such activity, usually at least a month before the valuation date, and based on information that was usually at least two months old. A decade ago, employees also had little flexibility to increase or decrease contributions from their pay or change how those contributions were allocated among the plan's investment options.

Little or No Investment Choice

Early 401(k) plans introduced to employees the ability to direct the investment of their contributions to their retirement accounts. Even ten years ago, however, there were often no more than a handful of investment options available: a stable value option (fixed income), a balanced (stock and bond) option, and sometimes company stock (*Financial Planner* 1994). Even today, investment options can be rather limited in 401(k) plans: it is not uncommon to find a plan with a single investment option of company stock, resulting in single-security "portfolios" that a professional financial planner would consider quite risky.

Alternatively, the investments were insurance company separate accounts, including the highly popular stable value, or fixed interest, account, often so called Guaranteed Investment Accounts (GICs). With these accounts, employees received a rate of return that was fixed, and announced in advance, for a specified period of time, commonly a year. The principal and interest were "guaranteed" by the insurance company. Because of the guarantee and the declared earnings, these options have always been very popular with employees, often capturing as much as 50 percent of the typical plan's assets (Hewitt Associates, cited in EBRI 1995). This remains so today, despite the highly publicized failures of several insurance companies.

Emphasis On the Needs of the Plan Sponsor

The focus of these plans, and the subsequent delivery of support services by third-party providers, was almost exclusively on the "institutional" client, the plan sponsor. Even contact with the sponsor by the service provider was infrequent: annual performance reviews, perhaps, or annual "rate re-sets" on the stable value options. There was next to no contact with, or access by, employees. Employees received limited information, about both the plan and the investment options, and much of what they received was dated, complex, and not meant to be helpful or supportive of decision making. This appears to have been based on a sort of "Pandora's Box" theory of employee communication: "The less they know, and the less we remind them of this plan, the fewer headaches I'll have to deal with!"

In short, DC plans originated with the focus on the institutional sponsor, and the services provided to the sponsor by third-party administrators, recordkeepers, and investment managers were essentially driven by the institutional relationship forged by the pension business. Employees were quite secondary to the business, despite the obvious fact that, without their active participation, the plans simply did not exist.

The Second Wave: Employee "Empowerment" and a Retail Investment Orientation Brings More Information and Access

By the late 1980s, a number of economic, market, and even social forces were converging on the 401(k) business that would change forever the way these plans were designed and administered. These forces would even begin to redefine for service providers who their "client" was and, therefore, would also begin to reshape the nature, type, and variety of services provided to both plan sponsors and participants.

One major reason these "Dark Ages" of 401(k) plans drew to a close what that the large mutual fund companies started to notice the growth in "assets under management" within these plans by the late 1980s. In 1986, the total assets within 401(k) plans was $155 billion; by 1988, that figure had grown 48 percent to $230 billion and, by 1990, it had grown another 30 percent to $300 billion (Access Research 1995). In 1996, assets in 401(k) plans approached $690 billion, an increase of 345 percent from their levels just 10 years before (Access Research 1995). Clearly, as more companies began to introduce 401(k) plans, and as more employees began to contribute to them, and as earnings began to build up with them, they became more and more attractive to a wider variety of service providers. In short, to paraphrase the late Senator Everett Dirksen, "pretty soon we started to talk about serious money."

Mutual Fund Companies Enter the Picture

When the big mutual fund companies began to enter the market, they brought with them their "retail" approach to investments. Their funds often had "brand" names and came with prospectuses, which made sponsors and participants more comfortable than the mysterious separate accounts. Their funds were valued daily, and information on them was available through a toll-free 800 telephone number or in daily newspapers. The fund companies had resources to staff their telephone service centers with people to answer participants' questions. Additionally, the insurance companies lost some luster when several company failures reduced GIC values in the late 1980s. In 1989, the 401(k) market share enjoyed by mutual fund companies was estimated to be 15 percent; by 1995, it had more than doubled to 33 percent (Access Research 1996). In the same period of time, the 401(k) market share of insurance companies shrank from 39 percent to 29 percent, and that of banks dropped from 31 percent to 24 percent (Access Research 1996).

Retail Approach Influences the Institutional Market

As the mutual fund companies began to capture more and more 401(k) market share, their retail orientation also began to redefine the nature of service and the definition of "the client." Previously, the approach was "institutional," and provider services were directed toward the plan sponsor. Now, the approach became much more "retail," and services began to be directed toward the individual consumer (the participant). For example, since mutual fund companies already provided quarterly or even monthly statements to their investors, they began to offer this service to 401(k) plans' participants, as well. Fund companies had glossy marketing information and sales literature for their funds, and they even began to offer sophisticated materials on financial planning and investment decision making. These materials could be readily adapted to meet the special issues of 401(k) plans, and the mutual fund companies began to use their availability for employees as a marketing tool with the plan sponsor.

More and more 401(k) plans being introduced in the late 1980s also began to feature the fact that mutual funds were valued and traded daily. This feature allowed participants to conduct daily transactions among the plan's investment options. Today, more than a third of all 401(k) plans, regardless of size, have daily valuation, and, among large plans (at companies with more than 1,000 employees), the number approaches 50 percent, with the trend accelerating over the past several years (Access Research 1996). While many plan sponsors were initially concerned about the advisability of offering daily transaction capability within a long-term savings and retirement account, their fears about market timing and frequent trading have not been borne out in practice. Recordkeepers and money managers report little or no increase in participant transactions following the introduction of daily valuation. In fact, some have postulated that having less opportunity to trade—say, in a quarterly valued plan—puts more pressure on participants to actually do so, since they know that if a transaction is not initiated another quarter will have to pass before the next transaction window opens.[4] Daily trading appears to have been accepted easily by employee investors, and it is becoming the norm. Some sponsors, however, have introduced daily valuation of their plan investments but limited their participants to less frequent transactions, usually monthly or quarterly. Finally, mutual fund companies were also used to providing toll free telephone access to customer service representatives for their retail investors, so this feature was introduced to 401(k) plans, as well. The participant could call essentially 24 hours a day to get up-to-date account balances, conduct transactions, check on the status of transactions, and ask questions about the plan's various investment options or administrative details.

In short, partly because of the mutual funds' entry into the 401(k) market, participants became a much more important part of the service equation. And the plan providers—again, mutual funds, insurance companies, and large recordkeepers—began to think about keeping the individual participant happy as a way to keep their institutional client happy. The result was that participants began to enjoy much broader access to their accounts and much improved information about the plan and about information about the investments within the plan.

Whither the Plan Sponsor?

Interestingly, the trend toward focusing on the needs of the individual participant began at about the same time that plan sponsors were becoming less paternal about benefits in general *and* at about the same time that these plans were becoming much more important for most workers' retirements than the traditional defined benefit pension plan.

Employers Introduce Employee Choice and Limit Exposure to Rising Benefit Costs

At the end of the 1980s, employers began to rethink the comprehensive benefits packages they had provided, driven in part by the rising cost of medical benefits. Rather than provide a one-size-fits-all package, employers began to employ the concept of so-called "flexible" benefits: providing a specified dollar amount to cover benefit costs and then letting the employee choose which benefits to "buy" and at what levels. The employee who wanted the most coverage or the richest plans might have to pay for those benefits him or herself. This provided a very effective way for the employer to define and predict the annual expenditures required for employee benefits. This was in sharp contrast to the traditional method of covering benefit costs, through which the employer paid regardless of how high benefit costs might go in any given year. The concept was often explained in a variety of ways. New lifestyles required new kinds of benefits packages. Employees were being "empowered" to manage their own benefits packages. Modern employees wanted more personal choice. In particular, employees were told that these new benefits packages gave them the flexibility to *not* purchase benefits in which they had no interest and then use those freed-up "benefits dollars" to pay for other benefits that were attractive to them. Using the concept of so-called "total compensation" (which conceives that the employer provides compensation comprised of salary and benefits, including holidays and paid time off), some flexible benefits packages (primarily from larger corporations) even allow employees to buy and sell vacation days, which means an employee willing to trade in higher benefits can have more time off the job, and vice versa.

The effect of this trend was to introduce to employees the idea that they were responsible for their own benefits, that they might have to pay for higher levels of benefits, and that they had the right to choose what they wanted. Clearly, this worked in close parallel to the changes in retirement benefits: the shift from traditional employer-managed pension plans to employee-directed DC programs.

"Downsizing," "Outsourcing," and Other Business Trends Converge to Focus on the Employee

Other forces within business were also beginning to shape the delivery of benefits in general and 401(k) plans in particular. Many large employers began to reduce their total number of employees, and often the "nonessential" or "nonline" benefits or human resources staff were among the first to go (*Institutional Investor* 1994). Sometimes, these companies turned to outside vendors to provide traditional benefits services, further weakening the institutional ties. In fact, many employers began to look at "total" benefits outsourcing, by which they meant contracting with outside vendors to provide benefits and administrative services that were traditionally managed within the employer's own workforce.

Also, employers began to shift to employees some of the responsibility for funding benefit programs, including retirement benefits, and rationalized the change under the umbrella of employee empowerment. There was even some interest among employers in a concept called "total compensation," which meant that an employer would provide as compensation a fixed-dollar amount to employees, who would then decide how to divide it up among such things as current pay, vacation, health benefits, and retirement savings.

These forces combined to change the long-standing paradigm that the plan sponsor was solely in charge of retirement benefits and that the participant was a secondary player whom it was best to keep in the dark.

The Next Wave: Focus on Interaction and Information, Driven by Technology

Now that employers have empowered employees, given them open and on-request access to information, and authorized them to make decisions about their financial well-being in retirement, the cat, as it were, may be out of the bag. It seems that employees will be satisfied with traditional employer responses to investment flexibility, instant information, access to account transactions, and education that goes well beyond plan-specific communications. Furthermore, as account balances grow in DC plans—the six-figure 401(k) account is no longer uncommon—employees may simply no longer be willing to let the management and servicing of such significant assets be driven by what the employer deems appropriate.

Employees are already demanding more and faster information, different investment options, and increased flexibility within the plan itself. Loan features are common. Employees' accounts are "portable": they can take their accounts with them if they change jobs. And there are even some service providers offering brokerage options within the 401(k) plan. With such an option, the participant could invest in hundreds of different no-load mutual funds and even trade individual securities. These are not common, but as investors become more sophisticated and balances increase, there will surely be more demand for this type of flexibility.

But the real demand from employees is for more information, and not just about the plan itself or the plan's investment options. Employees want to know how make decisions about financial-planning issues, how to manage money, and how to prepare for a financially sound retirement. And service providers appear to be willing to provide this increased information in order to increase assets and keep the business.

Changing Government Policy in the 401(k) Market

In the mid-1990s, even the federal government has begun to contribute to this movement toward increased investment flexibility, plan information, and investment education. In 1995, the U.S. Department of Labor (DOL) launched a national public relations campaign called "Save! Your Retirement Clock Is Ticking!" in conjunction with plan sponsors and 401(k) service providers (EBRI 1995). The point of the campaign is to encourage employees to understand that they now have personal financial responsibility for much of their financial well-being during retirement and to continue the general education of employees on financial planning, investment basics, and financial decision making.

The campaign was followed very quickly by an "exposure draft" in December 1995 of the DOL's Interpretative Bulletin on Internal Revenue Code (IRC) Section 404(c), with the final Bulletin released in June 1996. This provides for plan sponsors a "safe harbor" from employees who may want to hold their employer liable for poor investment performance or other shortcomings within the sponsor's 401(k) plan (USDOL 1996). Essentially, 404(c) affords such protection if, generally, the employer provides (1) a reasonable selection of investment options (three distinctly different options is the minimum), (2) the ability for individuals to have reasonable access to their accounts for the purpose of moving assets among options, (3) certain information about the plan and its investments, and (4) sufficient information that the employee can make an "informed" decision about participation, contribution levels, and the management of individual accounts. The Interpretive Bulletin also makes it clear that it is permissible for employers—that is, that liability for damages is not increased—to provide generic financial planning information, including such things as asset allocation, risk/reward, and the projection of individual account balances based on assumptions of investment performance by asset class. In other words, increased access and information *for the participant* are not only now protected, they are even mandated, by federal regulatory statutes.

Given the lack of information sponsors have traditionally provided and the mystery funds they once structured, even in the recent past, one can now ask, Whither the plan sponsor? Is not the participant the new client for 401(k) service providers? And, further, will not this new client demand new products and services that the industry may be unused to providing?

The Role of Technology in Participant Service

Clearly, one of the most important tools to facilitate the movement toward increased attention on the participant will be technology, primarily through its ability instantaneously to provide access to, and to update, individual account information.

This movement began with daily valuation and the use of toll free voice-response technology, but it has already moved well beyond that initial arrangement. Service providers now offer investment and financial planning information through the Internet, and a handful have even begun to permit transactions within that medium. (Security remains a concern for many providers, but the direction is clear.) The on-line employee can easily download mutual fund prospectuses or call up third-party evaluations of various funds' current and long-term performance. Retirement planning software—in both diskette and CD-ROM formats—are widely available and often provided free of charge by providers expecting greater participation and contributions (assets under management). There are providers who have developed financial education seminars "attended" by thousands of employees in dozens of locations across the nation through video teleconferencing facilities. To support 401(k) enrollment meetings, employers for years have asked service providers to provide technology-based communications tools like videos, audiovisual aids, and cassette tapes, and there are even software programs that allow employers to enroll employees by entering data into a personal computer and then electronically transmitting the information to the record keeping department, payroll system, and other employer divisions. Employees are now also able to enroll in their 401(k) plans over the 800 telephone lines maintained by service providers: no paper, no delay, no hassles.

An Example: Paperless Loan Transactions

Providers also now offer 401(k) loans directly through voice-response, touch-tone telephone systems. This process directly bypasses the plan sponsor, who, in the past, had to: (1) distribute loan forms to employees requesting them, (2) receive the forms from the employee, (3) check the forms' accuracy, (4) forward the loan forms to the service provider, (5) distribute the promissory note to the employee, (6) return the signed promissory note to the service provider, and (7) sometimes even hand-carry the check to the participant. This process is just one of many that clearly demonstrates how the new service paradigm puts the focus squarely on the participant and eliminates the role of the plan sponsor entirely, except for the initial design of the loan feature (which may have taken place years ago) and for monitoring ongoing management reports from the providers. In fact, this process was not driven by participants, many of whom did not know how cumbersome the loan process was, but by the sponsors themselves, who are asking service providers for more and better ways to save them time and effort by refocusing their service on the participant.

This move to a "paperless" environment, one that uses technology as a means to provide information, investment education, account transactions, instant access to account balances, and investment flexibility, is now the most powerful force shaping the future of 401(k) communications and administration.

Conclusion

Given the new focus on employee-directed retirement plans, driven by the broad range of factors noted above, the old paradigm of the primacy of the "traditional" plan sponsor and the definition of sponsor service may be rapidly changing. At least three assertions can be made based on the trends discussed:

First, service providers (mutual fund companies, insurance companies, third-party administrators, etc.) are now fully involved in the business of employee communications, whether they recognize that fact or not, and whether they do it well or not. Record keeping, administration, and even investments are becoming commodities. The most powerful differences in client service will be the providers' ability to motivate employees, their power to communicate with them, their ability to understand employee needs, and the resources to link technologies as a tool to facilitate participant interaction.

Second, success in capturing DC market share will be driven to a large part by providers' ability to blend effective employee communications with the power and efficiency of technology. The traditional factors driving a plan sponsor's decision to purchase services from a provider (stability, fixed-income expertise, administrative, and record-keeping expertise) appear to be diminishing.

Finally, once having been "empowered" to shape their own financial well-being during retirement, employees will continue to demand products and services different from those their employers may have selected in traditional defined-benefit plans. In the future, it is quite conceivable that major 401(k) plan features and the nature of plan servicing will be driven by neither sponsors nor providers, but by the ever-increasing number of true clients, the participants. The sponsor's ability to provide attractive and competitive 401(k) plans, and the provider's ability to capture market share and assets may well depend on their willingness and ability to listen to employees and where *they* want these plans to go.

Notes

1. The average rate of participation among employees eligible for 401(k) plan participation was 76 percent in 1995, according to Access Research, Inc. (1996).

2. The figure cited includes both defined benefit and defined contribution preretirement lump-sum distributions.

3. "[O]ne recent study reported that [DB] coverage had slipped to 43 percent. For those who are covered, the defined benefit has been defined every more skimpily. Cost-of-living adjustments disappeared years ago. The percentage of salary that a worker could get at retirement stopped rising. In the past five to ten years, more and more employers have switched from a final-average-pay formula

to a career average. Because the new formula draws on the earlier years of a career when a worker earns less, a pension based on it may be only half as rich as one calculated with the old formula, according to Dennis Kass, a managing director at J.P. Morgan Investment Management and the chief Federal pensions administrator before [David] Walker, . . . [and w]here defined benefit plans used to provide 50 to 60 percent of preretirement income, says David Veeneman, a consultant with Hewitt Associates, they now make up only 25 to 40 percent" (*Institutional Investor* 1994: 51).

4. Revealed in unpublished employee surveys and focus group research conducted in 1995 and 1996 by the author for several large clients (with employee populations in excess of 5,000) of the Metropolitan Life Insurance Company Defined Contribution Group of New York.

References

Access Research, Inc. "Participant Attitudes and Behavior." Report prepared for members of the Society of Professional Administrators and Recordkeepers. Windsor: Access Research, 1995.

———. "1996 Marketplace Update." Report prepared for members of the Society of Professional Administrators and Recordkeepers. Windsor: Access Research, 1996.

Burkhauser, Richard V. and Dallas L. Salisbury, eds. *Pensions in a Changing Economy.* Washington, D.C.: Employee Benefit Research Institute, 1993.

Employee Benefit Research Institute (EBRI). Issue Brief, February 1994.

———. "Can We Save Enough to Retire? Participant Education in Defined Contribution Plans." Issue Brief No. 160, April 1995. 1995a.

———. "Highlights of the Department of Labor's Public Education Campaign on Pensions and Retirement Savings." 16, 6, June 1995. 1995b: 3.

Financial Planner. "Fiddling with 401(k)s." (February 1994): 64.

Foster Higgins, Inc. "Survey on Employee Savings Plans, 1993." Chicago: Foster Higgins, 1993.

Hurley, M., S. Meers, B. Bornstein, and N. Strumingher. "The Coming Evolution of the Investment Management Industry: Opportunities and Strategies." New York: Goldman Sachs & Co., October 1995: 28.

Institutional Investor. "The Pension Officer: More Work, Same Staff," January 1994: 54.

U.S. Department of Labor (USDOL). "Interpretative Bulletin 96-1: Participant Investment Education." Rules and Regulations, Pension and Welfare Benefits Administration (PBWA). *Federal Register* 61, 113 (June 11, 1996).

Part III
Retirement Policy and Defined Contribution Plans

Chapter 11
The Importance of Variable Annuities in a Defined Contribution Pension System

P. Brett Hammond

Variable annuities are an increasingly popular retirement vehicle in the U.S. A variable annuity is a mechanism by which a person's current savings can be turned into a future retirement income (i.e., transfer assets from the present to the future). Often tax-advantaged, a variable annuity is one of two major classes of annuities that provide insurance against financial insecurity in retirement by pooling the assets of many savers and then paying a lifetime or long-term income to people in the pool based on the size of their assets and mortality expectations. The other annuity class—the *fixed* annuity—also offers insurance features, but a fixed annuity differs from a variable annuity in that it *guarantees* to preserve principal and provide a modest return (by law, at least 90 percent of principal plus 3 percent per annum) based on savings invested in assets such as bonds, mortgages, and real estate held in an insurance company's general or separate account (i.e., not marked to market).

Variable Annuities and Mutual Funds

A variable annuity is like a mutual fund in that it does not guarantee the principal or a return. Rather it is a fund that pools individuals' savings and gives them a variable return on those savings, depending how well the underlying investments perform minus various management fees. Like a mutual fund, a variable annuity enables individuals to obtain the benefits of a professional investment manager, who is supposed to reduce risk and increase overall returns by spreading their savings among a variety of stocks or bonds purchased on their behalf.

But an annuity differs from a mutual fund in that it provides insurance

TABLE 1 Characteristics of Variable Annuities vs. Mutual Funds, 1995

	Stand alone product		*Held inside qualified plan or IRA*	
	Variable annuities	*Mutual funds*	*Variable annuities*	*Mutual finds*
Tax Status of contributions	Taxed	Taxed	Most are deferred	
Tax Status of accumulations	Deferred	Taxed	Deferred	
Tax Status of distributions	Earnings taxed	Exempt	Taxed	
Major emphasis	Income	Savings	Income	Savings
Annual contribution limit	No	No	Yes, Varies	
Availability of fixed rate fund	Yes	No	Yes	No
Investment management fees average*	0.79%	1.30%	0.79%	1.30%
Annuity/insurance fees average*	1.27%	None	1.27%	None
Commissions	Common	No	Common	No
Actuarial & investment guarantees	Some	No	Some	No
Front-end or sales charges	Rare	Some	Rare	Some
Early withdrawal penalties	Yes	No	Yes	No
Exit penalties/surrender charges	Common	Rare	Common	Rare
Can be annuitized at retirement	Yes	Must be cashed in	Yes	Must be cashed in
Regulation	SEC; state insur. depts.	SEC	ERISA agencies; SEC; state insur. depts.	ERISA agencies; SEC

Source: Lipper (1995)

with two parts or phases. In the first, or accumulating phase (a *deferred* annuity), typically, a percentage of an employee's before-tax salary is paid by him or her (or, on the employee's behalf, by the employer) as a periodic premium into an annuity that may offer certain guarantees, such as a guaranteed death benefit, and impose certain restrictions, such as surrender charges. In the second, or retirement phase (an *immediate* or *payout* annuity), a person uses her accumulated savings to purchase a lifetime or long-term income through an annuity that offers a significant additional form of insurance not found in a mutual fund, namely a way to receive a guaranteed term or lifetime retirement income through pooling the savings and the mortality risk of many retirees. An insurance company can guarantee income to a large number of annuity purchasers, because some individuals die before getting back the full accumulated value of their variable annuity investment while others live longer than average and receive much more than the accumulated value of their variable annuity investment. In this sense, annuities may be classified as either group (employer-sponsored tax-qualified) or individual (individually purchased qualified or unqualified) annuities, but in practice, the distinction between group and individual annuities isn't always clear (Gentry and Milano 1996). Somewhat more distinct—and similar to mutual funds when used as retirement vehicles—is the difference between qualified and unqualified annuities. Qualified annuities shelter all contributions and earnings from taxes until they are withdrawn. Nonqualified annuities require taxes to be paid on contributions, but not on subsequent earnings until they are withdrawn. Table 1 compares the significant features of variable annuities and mutual funds.

Mutual funds and variable annuities are not mutually exclusive. A person can invest after-tax or before-tax savings in a qualified-plan mutual fund or accumulating annuity and then at retirement remove those savings plus the earnings in order to purchase an immediate payout annuity. Moreover, variable annuities can be based on mutual funds; that is, variable annuity savings can be invested in mutual funds and pooled along with non-tax-deferred savings of other investors.

Growth and Size of Variable Annuities

Variable annuities are an increasingly popular retirement vehicle for Americans. Although there is some disagreement about what proportion of the annuity market is held in variable assets as opposed to fixed assets (e.g., Krawcheck and Hicks 1995 vs. *National Underwriter* 1996), variable annuities are now believed to be over $400 billion of the more than $650 billion in total annuity assets (*National Underwriter* 1996, p. 3). This compares to over $4 trillion of financial assets held in public and private

TABLE 2 Changes in the Variable Annuity Market over Time, 1975–95

	1975	*1980*	*1985*	*1990*	*1995*	*Annualized growth rate (%*
Variable annuity sales (millions)			5.3	17.3	51.5	28.9
Fixed annuity sales			23.6	47.8	47.3	8
Number of companies offering variable annuities	5	6	34	73	104	
Number of variable annuity policies	5	9	47	105	244	
Number of variable annuity accounts	14	27	198	624	2575	

Source: LIMRA (1995), sales; Morningstar (1995), numbers.

pension plans in 1992 (EBRI 1995, p. 190). Variable annuity assets grew by about 300 percent between 1990 and 1995, while the broader, more visible mutual fund market (about $2.75 trillion at the end of 1995) increased by about 150 percent during that time. Perhaps reflecting the stock market runup, variable annuity purchases reached an all-time high of $52.5 billion in 1995, up from $4.5 billion in ten years (*National Underwriter* 1996, p. 14). Table 2 shows sales growth from 1985 to 1995 for variable and fixed annuities (a portion of this reported growth may be accounted for by rollovers from one annuity to another). Growth in non-tax-qualified variable annuity sales has averaged 48.2 percent per year since 1985, compared with 23.4 percent per year for tax-qualified variable annuities. Flows into the mutual fund market totaled $300 billion in 1995, some of that via variable annuities using mutual funds as investment vehicles.

Growth in the institutional capacity of the variable annuity industry also has been spectacular, as illustrated by Table 2, which shows changes since 1975 for several indicators, including the number of variable annuity companies, policies, and separate accounts. Table 3 shows the 35 largest variable annuity providers in the United States along with the nonfixed, nonguaranteed variable annuity assets they manage. In comparison, the mutual fund industry has grown to over 5,000 funds (Hurley et al. 1995). But in the 401(k) market, traditionally thought of as the province of mutual funds, as much as about 40 percent of large plan assets are held by insurance companies (Goldstein et al. 1995). Of course, insurance companies may offer mutual funds and mutual fund companies may offer or have ties to variable annuity products.

Recent analysis suggests that the investment management industry—in particular, variable annuities and mutual funds—could experience

TABLE 3 35 Largest Variable Annuity Providers by Assets, 1995

Rank	*Insurance company*	*Total assets in variable annuity accounts ($ millions)*
1	College Retirement Equities Fund (CREF)	79,250.58
2	Hartford Life Insurance	19,937.43
3	Lincoln National Life Ins.	14,566.00
4	IDS Life Insurance	12,486.05
5	Nationawide Life Insurance	11,141.10
6	Allianz Life Ins of North Amer	7,700.23
7	Equitable Life Assur Soc of US	6,930.50
8	Prudential Ins of America	6,643.90
9	Anchor National Life Insurance	5,484.70
10	North American Sec Life Ins	5,128.63
11	Sun Life Assur of Canada (US)	5,075.63
12	Fidelity Investments Life Ins	4,421.80
13	American Skandia Life Ins	4,111.22
14	Merrill Lynch Life Insurance	3,941.59
15	Travelers Insurance	3,740.68
16	Variable Annuity Life Ins Co	3,536.24
17	Metropolitan Life Insurance	3,451.21
18	Guardian Insurance & Annuity	3,379.01
19	Aetna Life Insurance & Annuity	3,229.61
20	John Hancock Mutual Life Ins	3,088.03
21	Massachusetts Mutual Life Ins	2,962.35
22	Lutheran Brotherhood Var Ins Prod	2,677.91
23	SMA Life Insurance	2,605.48
24	Phoenix Home Life Mutual Ins	2,056.26
25	Western Reserve Life Assur of OH	1,933.01
26	Security Benefit Life Ins	1,810.32
27	Life Insurance of Virginia	1,738.30
28	MONY Life of America	1,668.05
29	Kemper Investors Life Insurance	1,641.74
30	Providian Life & Health Insurance	1,479.06
31	Fortis Benefits Insurance	1,380.83
32	New England Mutual Life Ins	1,168.32
33	Connecticut Mutual Life Ins	1,085.30
34	United Investors Life Ins	1,055.55
35	Mutual of America Life Insurance	956.50
Total for 104 companies		255,000.00

Source: Morningstar (1995)

slower growth in the near future (Krawcheck and Hicks 1995; Hurley et al. 1995), perhaps because the baby boom won't start entering its peak annuity purchasing years for another ten years. If the baby boom behaves like its predecessors, however, the long-term growth prospects for variable annuities are positive.

An Era of Individual Choice

The unique characteristics, market size, and growth in recent years of variable annuities are alone enough to justify a close examination of their place within the pension system, but it is the rush toward individual freedom and responsibility for retirement in America that compels a closer examination of the use of variable annuities. For example, in contrast to traditional defined benefit plans, defined contribution plans require a high degree of employee rather than employer responsibility. Overall growth in employer pension plans over the past decade can be entirely attributed to an increase in the number of defined contribution plans that has more than offset a decline in the number of defined benefit plans (USDOL 1996, p. 59). Some observers attribute this to changing employer and employee preferences, while others cite contrasting legal and regulatory treatment of defined benefit and defined contribution plans (Warshawsky 1995; Gentry and Milano 1996). In either case, the proportion of workers covered by some kind of defined contribution plan has increased dramatically in the past two decades (EBRI 1994b).

Although the trend toward greater individual responsibility for retirement security is clear, not all plan participants treat the attendant freedoms similarly. Bernhein, elsewhere in this volume, has shown that individuals' financial knowledge is far from extensive. In response to a poll (EBRI 1994a), over a third of employees say they would spend their defined contribution accumulation or put it in a personal savings account rather than transfer it to a new plan if they changed employers. More than half would do so if the sum was small or they lost their job.

Major U.S. national policy changes and proposals promise further to devolve control of retirement savings into the hands of individuals. Calls to privatize the social security system through the use of individually directed investment accounts are growing more numerous and are attracting considerable attention (SSAC 1997). Recent legislation (H.R. 3448, Small Business Job Protection Act of 1996) aims to protect Americans in an era when workers can expect to change jobs during their careers by strengthening pension portability and reducing the legal and regulatory distinctions among types of defined contribution pensions. The consequences of any policies that would increase individual responsibility for retirement are only amplified by demographic changes that have and will occur over the next 20 years (Biggs 1994; Shoven 1995).

At the same time, the Department of Labor has issued regulations requiring employers to improve defined contribution pension savings and investment education (USDOL 1995). Although Clark and Schieber (this volume) show that education programs can affect individual pension investment choices, it remains to be seen whether such programs will ensure adequate retirement income in retirement for all or most employees.

Indeed, the crucial pension policy issue most relevant to variable annuities is how much of a person's retirement savings and accumulations ultimately becomes available to support a retirement income stream. Reductions in retirement savings for whatever reason, either through reduced savings rates or through removing assets from retirement savings, thereby reduces the future retirement income stream and runs the risk of leaving a retiree with insufficient income. There have always been opportunities for people covered by certain defined benefit and defined contribution plans to remove retirement savings when they leave a job. But solid statistics on the proportion of people or funds that disappear from tax-sheltered and taxable retirement savings are hard to come by. With changes in the tax laws in the 1980s, penalties for taking cash from certain types of plans were increased, but as the experience of TIAA-CREF will show, sufficient avenues remain for persistent people to get at their retirement assets prior to retirement.

In light of these important issues, what viable experience is available for better understanding how defined contribution pension systems do or should work in an era of individual responsibility? Considerable attention has been paid to the savings side of the individual retirement responsibility equation, but not to the income side. Recent reforms and education campaigns have promoted incentives and education for increased retirement savings, the power of regular investments and compounding, time diversification, portfolio construction and allocation, and other issues associated with preretirement savings and investment.

Such a focus is most appropriate when considering issues such as the inadequate national savings rate and the long lead time needed for accumulating sufficient retirement savings under defined contribution plans. But concerns about retirement savings need to be matched with concerns about retirement income and other arrangements. We need to focus on (1) savings as they affect retirement payouts and (2) retirement income design and adequacy. In this vein, more attention should be given to variable annuities as a model for individual retirement security and national retirement security policy.

The rest of this chapter uses the variable annuity experience to examine the following questions:

What policies are necessary to insure adequate retirement income in a defined contribution system?

How should Americans choose to receive retirement income?

How can we educate Americans to make the "right" choices?
What should workers pay for management of their retirement funds, both before and after retirement?
What is the best way to insure pension portability?
How does the variable annuity experience inform current and proposed policy reforms that continue to shift responsibility for retirement security to individuals and their families?

This chapter addresses these questions by examining in depth the experience with variable annuities at TIAA-CREF, the company that invented the variable annuity and that is still the world's largest provider of them.

TIAA-CREF's experience argues that national retirement security policy—particularly policies for defined contribution pension systems and proposals for Social Security reform—should not lose sight of the full spectrum of the retirement life cycle: retirement income arrangements as well as retirement savings and accumulations. As such, national policy should continue to encourage and support payout annuities that ensure an adequate income over a worker's retirement life.

Variable Annuities and TIAA-CREF

TIAA-CREF invented the modern variable annuity in 1952 and is now the world's largest private pension and variable annuity provider. The invention of the variable annuity was the culmination of several decades of development of a defined contribution pension system for higher education starting in 1905 (this history is provided in Greenough 1990). In that year, prior to the founding of the Teachers Insurance Annuity Association (TIAA) in 1918, Andrew Carnegie established a $15 million revolving fund (a "free pension system") that was used to provide a retirement income for each faculty member at 96 colleges and universities. His gift recognized that higher education had difficulty attracting and keeping faculty with the low salaries and lack of benefits then prevailing. This grant led to creation of the Carnegie Foundation, which, among other responsibilities, provided faculty who attained age 65 a retirement benefit of $400 plus half of the faculty member's final salary. Unfortunately, this defined benefit plan quickly failed, because liabilities exceeded assets during a period of rapid salary increases and because the plan did not foresee the large number of eligible faculty and their widows.

Consequently, the Carnegie Corporation sought advice on a retirement system for higher education that could remain solvent. In 1917, an independent commission called for creation of an insurance company established under the laws of New York. In response, the nonprofit

Teachers Insurance and Annuity Association of America (TIAA) was founded in 1918 with a grant of $1 million from the Carnegie Corporation; it was chartered to provide pensions to serve the education and research communities based on a system of individual annuities invested in fixed assets.

Other features of the system, many of which were new then but now in widespread use, included full funding, contractual rights for policyholders, multiple employers and portability (to allow movement by faculty among employers), full and immediate vesting, no cash values, contributions on the part of participants, and nonagency, low-cost distribution. These elements allowed the company to insure pensions for faculty for more than two decades based on fixed accumulating and payout annuities.

What led TIAA to consider other pension options was post World War II inflation. Before 1940, rising investment income and the increasing number of new faculty followed by falling prices in the 1930s allowed TIAA to provide an adequate income for its retirees. World War II's aftermath—and those of later wars, hot and cold—helped transform inflation into a serious permanent concern. In the late 1940s, inflation increased and coincided with a steep rise in salaries as well as the first big wave of faculty retirements. These new retirees had spent most of their careers at lower salaries covered by TIAA fixed annuities whose investments were based primarily on corporate bonds held to maturity and real estate. This group found that fixed retirement annuity benefits could not keep up with rapidly rising inflation. Even benefits based on many years of service were low. Fixed annuity rates had remained relatively high during the Depression but had declined after the World War II, and contributions of newly retired faculty had of course been based on many years of low preinflation salaries. As a result, retirement benefits as a proportion of preretirement salary dropped substantially for most faculty in the immediate postwar period. Many colleges and universities felt obliged to supplement fixed income annuity benefits with additional payments.

By the early 1950s, the difficulties posed by simultaneous high inflation, low interest rates, and low benefits, prompted TIAA to re-examine the role of traditional annuities in defined contribution plans. Other pension providers were faced with similar circumstances, but in the case of defined benefit plans, employers rather than employees faced the challenge of meeting the promises they'd made with eroding real assets and revenues.

Under William C. Greenough, then TIAA vice president, the company launched studies to discover how an annuity plan could respond more effectively to a variety of investment and inflation conditions. By tracing the performance of common stocks over the previous 70 years, a TIAA study team found the key: a completely new instrument—christened a variable annuity—with a 100 percent equity investment base. The resulting separate legal, actuarial, and investment entity was called the College Retirement Equities Fund, or CREF (Greenough 1951).

Greenough's 1951 report proposing the variable annuity sought a way to "overcome some of the troubles inflicted by inflation" and concluded that adding an annuity plan investing in a broad range of common stocks over the period studied—1880 to 1950—would have provided better returns and better purchasing power than from fixed income investments over most periods:

> This economic study should result in a basic change in planning retirement systems in the future. The factors of inflation and deflation have pretty generally been disregarded in past planning, with unfortunate results. This study shows that common stock would have provided better returns than those available from fixed-income investment in most periods. (Greenough 1951, p. 6)

Variable annuities are so common today that it is hard to realize that they were a new invention in 1952. Common stock and mutual fund ownership by individuals was not nearly as widespread as it is today, especially in the aftermath of the Depression. This may have prompted some powerful insurance industry interests initially to oppose the concept.

Almost as important an invention as CREF itself was the education initiative that went with it. Meetings with educational associations, college boards of trustees, college administrators, and TIAA participants, all aided substantially in introducing and supporting the new variable annuity.

Plan Design and Individual Choice

CREF's creation represented a truly significant expansion of investment choice for retirement savers and annuitants. TIAA-CREF was the first to offer to its plan participants the option of choosing how much of their premiums to allocate to the fixed-annuity account and how much to the new variable annuity. And on retirement, annuitants faced a similar choice about what proportion of their retirement income they wished to receive from the fixed or the variable account. Along with new choices, retirement savers and annuitants also faced new risks, because neither their principal nor their earnings were guaranteed in exchange for the possibility of greater returns on equities purchased through variable annuities.

Expansion of choice has continued in the TIAA-CREF system. Since 1988, the company introduced a number of new options for accumulating participants and retired annuitants. On the investment side, colleges and universities were given the chance to offer their employees more options: a money market account, an account for corporate bonds, then global, growth, and indexed equities accounts, and a social choice account. Finally, in 1995 TIAA introduced a separate account for real estate. On the payout side, as new accounts were added to CREF for premiums and accumulations, they were also added as options for payout annuities as well.

Traditional Lifetime Annuity Options

To accommodate different family situations and preferences for receiving retirement income, TIAA-CREF now provides a variety of annuity income options. Annuitants may select a one-life option, that provides to the annuitant an income for life, or a two-life option, that provides an income for both the primary annuitant and a second annuitant (e.g., a spouse) for both lifetimes. Under the two-life option, there are some additional choices. For example, upon the death of one of the annuitants, the annuity can be designed to pay the remaining annuitant a full benefit or two-thirds of the original benefit. In addition, for both one-life and two-life annuities, retirees can add to lifetime benefits a guaranteed period (10, 15, or 20 years).

TIAA-CREF also offers different payment methods. Under the TIAA standard payment method, an annuitant's first year's income is based on a full payout dividend rate that reflects current TIAA investment earnings (recently this has been about 7 percent). Subsequent income will continue to reflect total TIAA earnings, that can vary from year to year (changes in payout rates are made by the TIAA Board of Trustees). This continues for the life of the annuity. The CREF payment method is similar, but initial annuity income is set at an assumed investment rate of 4 percent. Again, depending on investment performance in comparison with the 4 percent assumed rate, subsequent income is periodically adjusted up or down. To supplement the CREF and TIAA standard payment methods, in 1982 the company introduced the TIAA Graded Payment Method. Under this method, annuity payments in the first year are based on an assumed interest rate of 4 percent—higher than the TIAA minimum 2.5 percent guarantee, but lower than the total interest rate used for the TIAA standard method. This assumed interest rate is less than the full anticipated rate to allow for increases in which a portion of each year's earnings are added to the "annuity reserve" (which can be thought of as assets) in order to purchase additional annuity income for the following year. The remainder is paid as current income. The proportional benefit increase each year is close to the difference between a 4 percent rate and the total interest rate earned. Thus, new retirees face a choice between higher initial income through the TIAA standard method or a better chance at inflation protection but lower initial income through CREF or the TIAA graded method.

Alternatives to Traditional Lifetime Annuities

More recently, the pension plan introduced several additional options for obtaining retirement income and direct cash prior to or in lieu of a lifetime or long-term payout annuity in response to changing tax and benefit laws and to participants' expressed desires. The following alternatives are governed by a wide variety of laws, regulations, institutional rules, and TIAA-CREF policies:

Minimum distribution option (MDO). In response to 1980s legislation that affected private sector pension accumulations and payouts, TIAA-CREF has since 1991 offered MDO, which is a temporary or permanent substitute for a traditional annuity that allows an individual reaching age 70½ to take a required minimum payment each year based on the size of his or her accumulation and an actuarial calculation specified in the tax regulations.

Transfer payout annuity (TPA). This allows an individual to transfer funds from the fixed annuity TIAA account in equal amounts over a 10-year period either to a CREF account, to another company's retirement account, or directly to the individual as a cash payment.

Cash withdrawals. Subject to the employer's rules, withholding, taxes, and, in some cases, IRS penalties, a higher education employee, after leaving a job, may take a cash withdrawal from his or her tax-deferred group annuity account after age 59½. For example, a former employee over the age of 59½ who takes a cash withdrawal will pay income taxes on the amount in the year in which the payment is made. In contrast, if that employee had chosen to annuitize those same funds, she would pay income taxes only on the amount received each year (possibly at a lower rate, since each yearly payment would be smaller than the full cash withdrawal). Institutions in higher education have set a wide variety of rules for their employees in this area, but of approximately 5,500 participating institutions in TIAA-CREF, only about 700 prohibit any sort of cash. Even in those cases, individuals can obtain cash from their own voluntary supplemental annuities (known as SRAs or TDAs).

Transfers and rollovers. Under certain circumstances, participants may transfer some or all of their accumulations to another retirement funding vehicle or roll their savings over to an individual retirement account (IRA). Transfers continue to be treated as retirement funds. IRA accounts are not subject to withholding imposed on direct cash withdrawals and can, therefore, be used in a two-step process to obtain cash.

Loans. Similarly, employees may take loans against their accumulations in voluntary supplemental retirement annuities (SRAs). When these are repaid, the accumulations remain available to support retirement income. If these are not repaid, they are subject to penalties and taxes and, most important, are lost from the tax-deferred retirement account.

In addition to these income and cash options, TIAA-CREF introduced in 1996 the ability for annuitants to make postretirement transfers (no more than once a year) among most of the CREF accounts and to TIAA, thus enabling them to change the source of their income throughout retirement. Although this is not an income option, it underscores that, today, TIAA-CREF participants and retirees face a large number of choices about their premium allocations, preretirement investments, annuity income, and annuity investments.

Results of Individual Choice

Some of TIAA-CREF's accumulating participants and retired annuitants have responded to these changes by choosing one or more of the new options for retirement savings, investment, and retirement income. We next summarize these responses and offer suggestions about the implications of this changing behavior.

We note, however, that TIAA-CREF's participants are concentrated in higher education and research institutions. Hence, they are not representative of the U.S. working population, nor are they fully representative of workers covered by pension plans. Further, these results are from the past, not the future. Therefore, they must be taken with the appropriate cautions before they are used to predict or even suggest how the entire future U.S. workforce might respond to similar options that could be part of private pension reform or social security privatization. For example, the full-time higher education workforce is older and has a higher proportion of women, than the rest of the full-time private sector U.S. workforce. Higher education employees are more likely to work in an institution that offers a pension plan than employees in other private sectors (94.5 percent to 71.5 percent). And they are more likely to participate in the pension plan (by 79.8 percent to 59.1 percent, the preceding numbers were computed by Mark Warshawsky and John Ameriks 1996, from the 1993 Current Population Survey). They also have higher working incomes, wealth, and retirement incomes than employees in other sectors. Of course, TIAA-CREF participants, by definition, have nearly 100 percent participation rates and so are even less representative of the entire U.S. working population. But because of this latter difference, the TIAA-CREF experience does show how individuals *might* behave as defined contribution plans grow increasingly popular in the public and private sectors or under social security-sponsored individual retirement accounts.

Results of Individual Choice I: Retirement Savings

In defined contribution plans, retirement income depends on the choices individuals make about allocating their premiums and their accumulations, and then how all those savings perform as assets.

Returns on Accumulations. Overall, what is the investment experience with CREF variable annuities as retirement savings vehicles? Figure 1 shows that CREF Stock has outperformed inflation since 1952 by an average of 6.5 percent per year (investment experience with other CREF funds has been good to excellent, but they are too new to allow long-term measurement). Although CREF and TIAA (the fixed annuity) have enjoyed superior returns overall, both are subject to return variations. Figure 1 also shows that CREF stock accumulations failed to keep up with inflation during the 1970s and early 1980s. TIAA-CREF's participants and annuitants were directly affected: for those still saving for retirement, it reduced for a time the expected value of future retirement income based on pension savings and the earnings on those savings. Of course, it did offer the advantage of some valuable dollar cost averaging, and in fact CREF performed well in the 1980s and 1990s.

Savings Allocation Decisions. How have TIAA-CREF participants allocated their savings? Table 4 shows preretirement premium and savings accumulation allocations between TIAA and CREF over the past 25 years. Among other things, this table reflects long-term changes in the stock and bond markets. Poor performance of the stock market in the 1970s likely discouraged participants from holding assets or allocating premiums to CREF. As interest rates moderated and the stock market performed well in the 1980s, allocations to CREF began to increase.

We can also take a snapshot that shows how individual demographics affect the allocation choices people make. Table 5 shows preretirement saving and premium allocations for retirement plan participants by age, income, sex, occupation, and education. (These figures are from a 3,602-person sample of TIAA-CREF participants in 1993; the sample has been weighted to match key characteristics of all TIAA-CREF participants.)

Age. As might be expected, the average size of a participant's annual premium payments and accumulations increases with age, but the use of the CREF fund declines with age. The proportion of premiums going to all CREF accounts diminishes from 68 percent for those under age 35, to

**(1952 = $1.00)

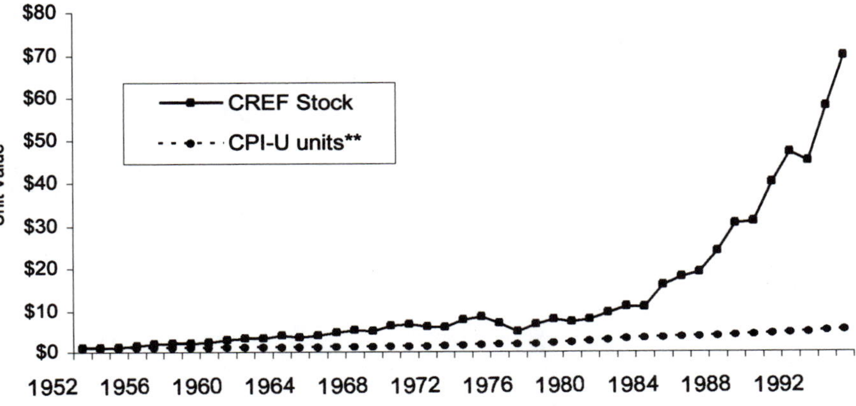

*(1972 = $1.00)

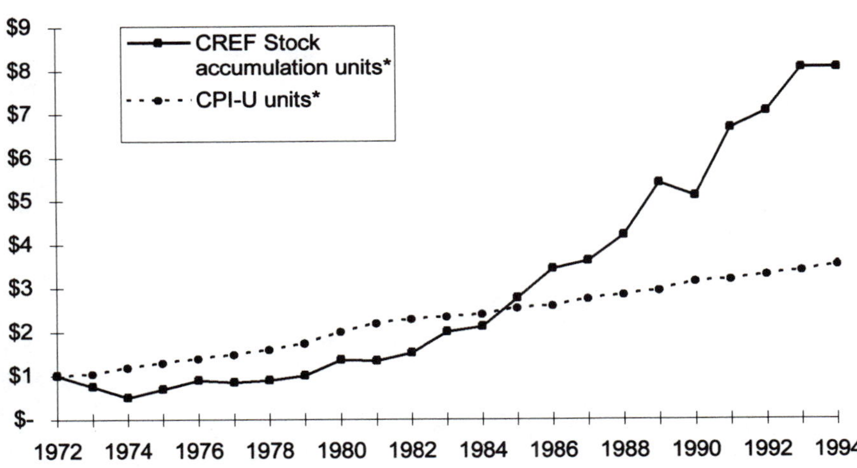

Figure 1. CREF stock and stock accumulation unit values versus inflation. Source: Authors' computations.

TABLE 4 Changes over Time in the Proportion of Premiums, Accumulations, and Annuity Income and Annuity Reserves Allocated Between TIAA and CREF, 1982–95

	Accumulating annuities (%)				*Payout annuities (%)*			
	Premiums		*Accumulating annuity reserves*		*Income*		*Reserves*	
	TIAA	*CREF*	*TIAA*	*CREF*	*TIAA*	*CREF*	*TIAA*	*CREF*
1982	57.6	42.4	49.8	50.2	74.4	25.6	58.9	41.1
1985	60.4	39.6	48.0	52	73.2	26.8	58.1	41.9
1990	54.4	45.6	52.1	47.9	72.9	27.1	64.6	35.4
1995	39.0	61.0	42.6	57.4	70.4	29.6	58.8	41.2

Source: Author's computations using TIAA-CREF data.

47 percent among those age 65 and above. Younger participants allocate a greater proportion of their accumulations to CREF, while older participants allocate greater percentages to TIAA.

Sex. Men's average total preretirement accumulations are more than double women's, although women's total annual premiums are about 70 percent of men's. Both men and women allocate a markedly higher proportion of their premiums and accumulations to variable annuities as compared to fixed annuities, although men allocate somewhat more than women to variable annuities. This difference, we believe, is a function of accumulation size as well as sex differences in risk aversion.

Occupation and institution type. Faculty and senior administrators strongly prefer CREF variable annuities to TIAA fixed annuities. Although their premium payments and accumulations are far lower than faculty and administrators, professional/technical staff make almost identical choices. Only clerical and maintenance staff prefer TIAA to CREF for their basic retirement plan. Only small variations in allocations, accumulation, and premium totals are evident by type of institution.

Household income. Total accumulations and premiums show a predictable increase with income, as does the preference for CREF. Although the preference for CREF varies with income, it is nearly universal. The only exception are households with income under $25,000, where participants allocate about half their premiums and 53 percent of their assets to TIAA.

Education. Total accumulations, premiums, and the use of variable annuities all increase with education. More highly educated participants allocate a greater proportion of their funds to CREF.

Although not presented in this table, neither marital status nor the

TABLE 5 Percent of 1995 Accumulations and Premiums Invested by Non-Retirees in TIAA-CREF RA/GRA Accounts by Selected Demographic Characteristics, 1993 (N = 3,602)

	Average accumulations	*Accumu-lations in TIAA (%)*	*Accumu-lations in CREF (%)*	*Average total premium*	*In TIAA (%)*	*In CREF (%)*
Total	$115,402	44	56	$ 7,000	38	62
Age						
Under 35	$ 21,004	37	63	$ 4,370	32	68
35 to 44	$ 58,671	44	56	$ 6,202	37	63
45 to 54	$147,214	45	55	$ 8,026	38	62
55 to 64	$243,255	49	51	$ 8,856	44	56
65+	$290,552	57	43	$ 9,653	53	47
Sex						
Men	$160,697	41	59	$ 8,277	35	65
Women	$ 70,761	47	53	$ 5,742	41	59
Occupation						
Teaching Faculty	$158,798	42	58	$ 8,064	37	63
Senior Admin.	$156,942	43	57	$ 9,405	36	64
Prof./Technical	$ 74,697	44	56	$ 6,315	37	63
Clerical Support	$ 44,356	53	47	$ 3,766	46	54
Income						
Under $25K	$ 21,829	53	47	$ 2,550	50	50
$25K–$34K	$ 28,285	45	55	$ 3,898	41	59
$35K–$49K	$ 62,864	46	54	$ 5,073	39	61
$50K–$74K	$102,541	44	56	$ 6,285	39	61
$75K–$99K	$147,784	42	58	$ 8,088	35	65
$100K+	$224,514	40	60	$11,699	34	66
Risk tolerance						
Substantial risk	$ 89,011	25	74	$ 6,276	20	80
Above average	$106,975	35	65	$ 7,171	28	72
Risk						
Average	$125,623	49	51	$ 7,034	44	56
Below average	$119,775	62	38	$ 7,018	58	42

Source: Author's computations using TIAA-CREF data.

presence of children seems to be associated with differences in allocation percentages.

This table is drawn from data on participants in the basic retirement plans at TIAA-CREF. Many participants also have the option of starting and maintaining a separate voluntary supplemental retirement annuity (SRA or a "tax-deferred annuity"), which is a voluntary salary reduction plan that uses the participant's before-tax dollars (subject to a $9,500 per year limit or less, depending on other defined contribution plan usage). We combined the data from the 1993 survey with SRA data information, and detect variations in allocations similar to those for the basic retirement plan. However, for almost every variable, participants allocate more of their premiums and accumulations to CREF as opposed to TIAA. Allocations to CREF range from about 60 percent to about 75 percent. One hypothesis is that participants are more risk tolerant with their voluntary tax-deferred accounts than with their basic retirement accounts.

Retirement and Financial Education. Other than demographics, what might affect allocation decisions? At least one attitudinal characteristic does seem to affect behavior: participants' willingness to take on investment risk. Table 5 shows that participants willing to take on substantial risk (i.e., participants who are relatively risk tolerant) allocate over 80 percent of their premiums and over 70 percent of their accumulations to CREF, while those who are most conservative in their approach to risk allocate about 60 percent of their premiums and accumulations to TIAA.

In turn, risk tolerance may be affected by education, both by general education levels and by specific education about finance and retirement. It is likely that education about savings, risk, return, retirement annuities, and related concerns can help individuals make choices appropriate to their changing circumstances. The company has a long-standing commitment to and has made significant investments in participant education through brochures, books, seminars, individual counseling, sponsorship of financial programs on television and radio, retirement planning software, specific illustrations of retirement income for individuals, and other means. Although the exact effects of these programs are hard to measure, the company is known as a leader in retirement planning education.

As an example, TIAA-CREF suggests in its literature that many, if not most people will be able to balance risk and return by allocating half of their premiums to TIAA fixed funds and half to the CREF variable annuity funds. While participants do not, in the aggregate, allocate 50 percent of their premiums to CREF, they do tend to behave as one might predict. That is, younger, more highly compensated and educated risk takers, are more likely to allocate premiums and assets to CREF, while their opposites are more likely to put their funds into the fixed account.

Such a result suggests that, with substantial retirement-awareness education, people roughly follow the pattern that many financial planners think they should: allocate a greater proportion of retirement savings to higher-risk, higher-return stocks when younger and reduce those allocations with time. The one discordant note here is that lower-income and clerical/support staff allocate less of their premiums and accumulations to CREF than any other group.

Of course, it is difficult to draw a causal connection from this data, since these demographic variables are likely to be highly correlated and it is unclear how much of the variation we see is due to age versus cohort effects. The next step in this research will be to assess the relative contribution of each factor to allocation decisions. Another step should be to track more precisely the effects of demographic variables and risk tolerance over time.

Results of Individual Choice II: Retirement Income

A key question driving pension and social security policy is whether workers will be able to meet their retirement income goals, which could be defined as total retirement income that lasts as long as needed, that provides for a spouse or other beneficiaries in case the retiree dies first, and that is adequate in amount. In practice, a combination of an employer pension, social security benefits, and personal savings should enable a retiree to (1) provide income for the retiree's remaining lifetime, (2) have provisions for covering a beneficiary, and (3) replace an adequate portion of preretirement income.

Traditional lifetime annuity choices. While TIAA-CREF participants have traditionally chosen lifetime annuities when they retire, since 1990, some participants have elected to take advantage of other income options, such as minimum distribution, systematic withdrawals, IRA rollovers, and lump sum withdrawals. Although starting an annuity doesn't necessarily equal retirement, we know when TIAA-CREF participants choose to begin retirement annuities. Figure 2 and Table 6 show changes in TIAA-CREF annuity starting ages for both men and women over time. Reflecting general shifts in the U.S. economy and specific changes in laws affecting retirement, first-time annuitants have bifurcated: more are now older and younger than age 65. In 1979, nearly 42 percent of new annuitants were age 65, while in 1994 about 21 percent of new annuitants were age 65. However, since peaking at 18.8 percent in 1991, the proportion of participants age 70 and over starting payout annuities dropped to 14.8 percent in 1994 (due to the availability of the minimum distribution option, as described below). Although not required by law, two-life annuities have become more popular among all age groups since 1978. The popularity

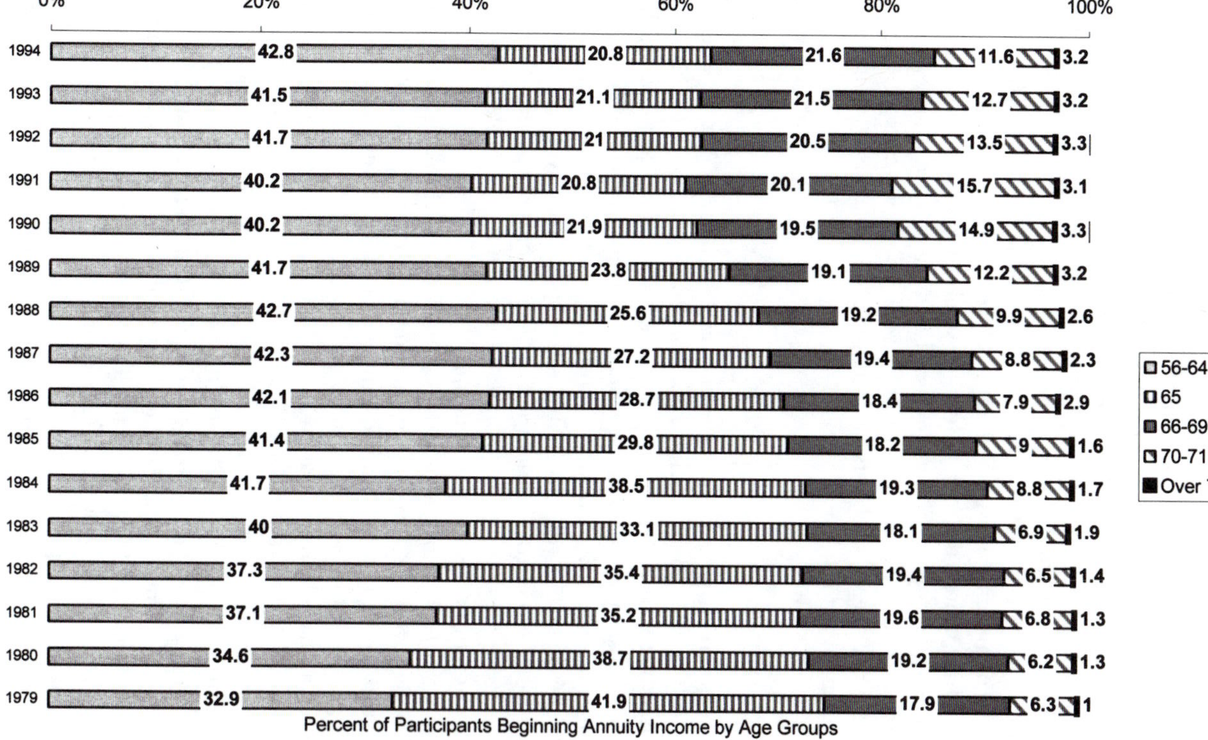

Figure 2. TIAA-CREF annuity income starting ages. Source: Authors' computations using TIAA-CREF data.

TABLE 6 Selection of One-Life and Two-Life Annuity Income Options by Age at Retirement

	Male primary annuitants (%)		*Female primary annuitants (%)*	
Age annuity started	*One-life*	*Two-life*	*One-life*	*Two-life*
1978	43.5	56.5	81.1	18.9
1983	36.8	63.2	73.1	26.9
1986	27.8	72.2	69.2	30.8
1990	25.6	74.4	66.0	34.0
1994	26.0	74.0	67.8	32.2

Source: Author's computations using TIAA-CREF data.

of one-life annuities has declined, but they remain relatively popular among younger male retirees. Women are more likely than men to choose one-life annuities at all ages. In addition, there is a wealth effect in annuity choice: annuitants with larger total accumulations are more likely to select two-life annuities than those with smaller totals.

New Income and Cash Options. Finally, and most important, significant changes have occurred in participants' preference for nontraditional income options. Recalling that the percentage of participants starting one-life or two-life annuities dropped between 1991 and 1994, Table 7 combines for those years the numbers of TIAA and CREF life annuity and minimum distribution option (MDO) contracts issued. MDO contracts were first offered in 1991 as an alternative way of dealing with federal requirements that participants reaching age 70½ begin to take a minimum distribution. Since then, MDOs have grown from 2.2 percent of total TIAA income contracts issued to 17.3 percent in 1994, while CREF MDOs have increased from 3.4 percent of all contracts in 1991 to 21.2 percent in 1994. Total MDOs increased by 49 percent from 1993 to 1994. MDOs issued where no other premiums are being paid under the employer plan—a presumption that the recipient is truly retired or is now working at a non-TIAA-CREF employer—totaled 12.2 percent of TIAA contracts and 15 percent of CREF contracts issued in 1994 (King 1996).

Even for those taking traditional income options, the use of the TIAA graded method and CREF have both increased at the expense of the TIAA standard payout method. A separate analysis reveals that this change may reflect an interest in inflation protection and the ability of people with larger accumulations to take a reduction of income in the short run in exchange for an increase in income later on.

Similarly, the use of transfer payout annuities (TPAs) has increased rapidly since their introduction in 1991. This is a popular vehicle for

TABLE 7 TIAA and CREF Life Annuity and Minimum Distribution Contracts Issued

	1990		*1991*		*1992*		*1993*		*1994*	
Type of contract	*Number*	*Percent*	*Number*	*Percent*	*Number*	*Percent*	*Number*	*Percent*	*Number*	*Percent*
TIAA (total)	20,400		21,558		22,197		20,860		21,296	
Standard		93.4		90.7		82.4		78.4		70.9
Graded		6.6		7.1		8.8		9.7		11.7
Minimum distribution		—		2.2		8.8		12.0		17.3
CREF (total)	8,877		9,801		11,538		12,073		13,616	
Stock		93.6		89.2		81.2		76.8		67.6
Money market		6.4		7.0		5.3		4.4		3.7
Social choice		—		0.3		0.9		1.9		1.9
Global		—		—		<0.1		1.5		5.2
Growth		—		—		—		—		0.3
Equity index		—		—		—		—		0.1
Minimum distribution†		—		3.4		12.2		15.3		21.2

Source: Author's computations using TIAA-CREF data.
Note: Except for payments under the Minimum Distribution Option, all contracts are for Immediate Life Annuities.
*Percentages in the Minimum Distribution subgroups may not add to totals because of rounding.
†Includes Minimum Distributions from all types of CREF accounts.

moving accumulation from TIAA to CREF over a ten-year period. TPAs also allow individuals to receive payments directly or to transfer funds to another pension provider. In 1994, about 13 percent of TPAs were used to transfer accumulations to another pension provider, 16 percent took direct cash payments, and the rest transferred to a CREF variable annuity account. Since only 2 percent of all 1994 TPA cash participants also settled a portion of their accumulations as life annuities, taking cash through this method seems to be, in most cases, an alternative to a traditional annuity.

In the 1990s, TIAA-CREF's participating institutions have been allowed to offer participants the option of removing funds from accumulating (preretirement) contracts. Overall, approximately 80 percent of institutions allow individuals to withdraw all accumulations after terminating employment, while another 5 percent allow partial withdrawals. In addition, within legal, institutional, and TIAA-CREF guidelines, individuals at most institutions may receive funds from CREF accounts by transferring them to another carrier's retirement plan or by rolling them over to an IRA (since 1991). Finally, participants may take a direct cash withdrawal from an SRA (beginning in 1990 for people no longer working at the college concerned and in 1993 for some people still working). Cash withdrawals and some IRA rollovers (which then allow individuals to take cash without the withholding penalty) represent funds being removed from retirement savings, thus diminishing the amount of money available to support a participant's retirement annuity. As with MDOs and TPAs, the use of these options has increased in the past few years.

In sum, TIAA-CREF has traditionally offered and encouraged its participants to take lifetime payout annuities. The growing popularity of two-life annuities supports the goal of spousal coverage and the growing popularity of the TIAA graded method supports the goal of inflation protection. However, as nonlifetime annuity options have become available, there has been a rapid increase in their use. This trend suggests, at least in the short run, that a proportion of participants are interested in removing cash from their tax-deferred savings prior to retirement and in receiving income that is not guaranteed for life after retirement. Offsetting this, as we will see below, are increases in the average accumulation size, which may allow some individuals to take cash and still replace a significant portion of their preretirement income through traditional annuities.

Through new non-traditional income and lump sum options, traditional annuities could begin to be affected by adverse selection. Warshawsky and Friedman (1990) have shown that adverse selection does play a role in the choices individuals make. Depending on the flexibility offered in a retirement plan—that is, opportunities for exercising adverse selection—it could affect the entire pool of annuitants. With its large pool of 1.8 million participants and annuitants, TIAA-CREF's traditional annuities have not been affected by new options. However, the design of pension reforms, including private pension systems as well as possible social security privatization, will need to confront demands by participants for flexibility in income and cash options (Mitchell and Zeldes 1996).

TIAA-CREF retirement income experience. Although TIAA-CREF variable annuities have for most periods performed well, payments have varied along with market performance. For example, prior to the 1970s and again in the 1980s, people did very well with accumulating and payout annuities based on CREF. But as Figure 1 shows, CREF annuity income rates dropped seven times between 1972 and 1982. Since that time, CREF annuity income rates have risen substantially and, over the long haul, have provided a good, if variable source of income for retirees depending on their savings rate and the length of time they were able to accumulate assets. Thus, participants and annuitants who rely on variable annuities are not immune from ups and downs in the real value of their portfolios.

Other things being equal, initial annuity-based retirement income can be a good predictor of later retirement income. Figure 3 shows, for new annuitants, the average annualized initial annuity payments for TIAA, CREF, and the total for TIAA and CREF for each year from 1980 to 1994. The average total initial payment has increased by 10.9 percent per year, well ahead of inflation over that time. For 1992–1994, however, the increase is only 2.6 percent per year; this reflects increased use of CREF annuities and the TIAA graded method, which use an initial interest rate assumption of 4 percent (lower than the TIAA standard method initial interest rate for the same period). For example, the proportion of new annuitants selecting the TIAA graded method or CREF variable annuities increased from 45 percent in 1990 to nearly 60 percent in 1994. Figure 4 further shows the relationship between size of accumulation and preference for CREF payout annuities in 1994. As size of accumulation rises, so does the preference for CREF payout annuities and the TIAA graded method.

Initial and subsequent retirement income also depends on the size of accumulation at retirement, as well as subsequent earnings on that income. Based on a survey of TIAA-CREF retirees, Table 8 provides a snapshot for 1993 of retirees' annualized annuity income (payments were annualized for those individuals who started a payout annuity during 1993) and "average payout reserves" (i.e., a present value, actuarial calculation that is the functional equivalent of remaining assets or accumulations). These numbers do not indicate what proportion of pre-

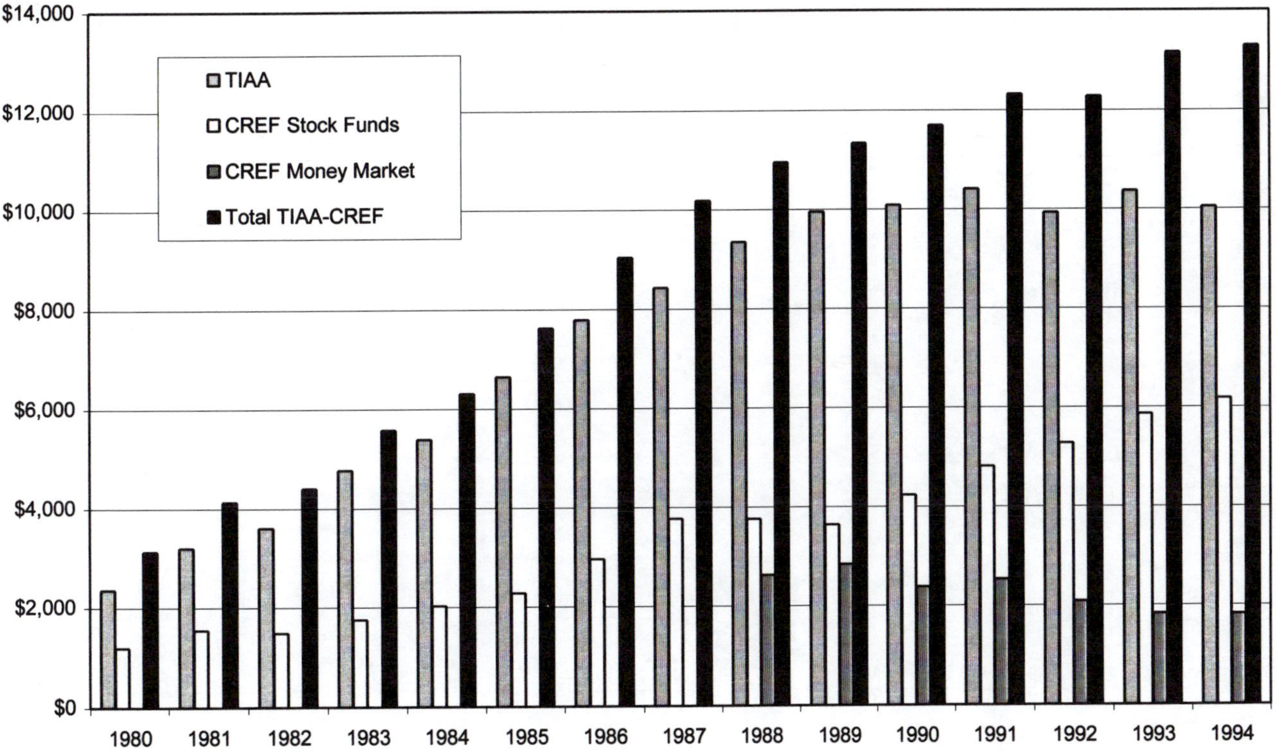

Figure 3. Average TIAA-CREF initial annuity payment per person, 1980–94. Source: Authors' computations using TIAA-CREF data.

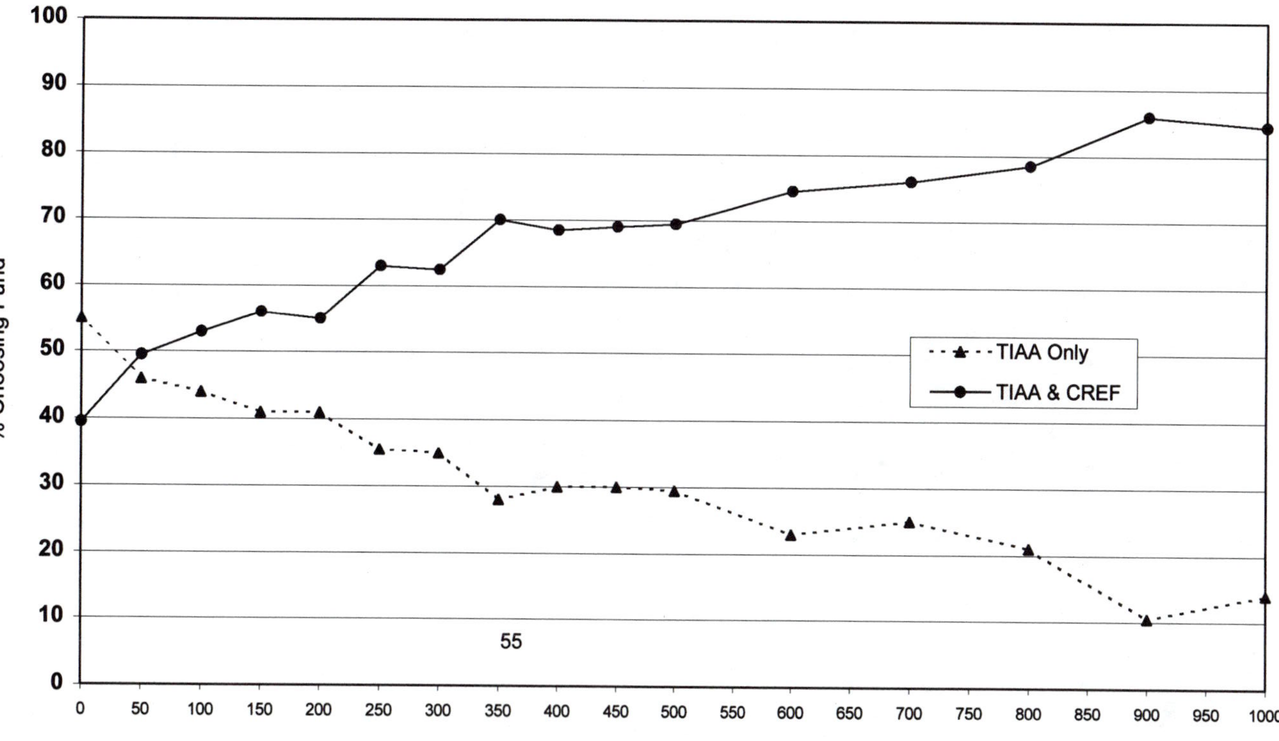

Figure 4. Payout annuity fund elections by accumulation amount (average 1994 accumulation: TIAA, $124,160; TIAA-CREF $210,000). Source: Authors' computations using TIAA-CREF data.

ABLE 8 Estimated Annualized Annuity Payouts and Total Reserves from TIAA and CREF Accounts by Selected Demographic Characteristics, 1993

	Average annualized annuity payments	*% Average annualized TIAA payments*	*% Average annualized CREF payments*	*Average payout reserves*	*% Average TIAA payout reserves*	*% Average CREF payout reserves*
otal	$11,677	66.9	33.1	$114,029	58.7	41.3
ge						
nder 65	$10,733	76	24	$125,237	68.3	31.7
5 to 70	$11,703	74.5	25.5	$127,262	65.1	34.9
1 to 75	$14,071	72.5	27.5	$136,258	63.4	36.6
6+	$10,103	50.3	49.6	$ 82,138	39.4	60.6
ex						
Ien	$15,186			$152,459		
Vomen	$ 7,976			$ 73,487		
ducation						
ome College	$ 5,751			$ 53,833		
ollege Graduate	$ 9,736			$ 98,712		
ost Grad Work	$11,392			$111,415		
Iasters Degree	$10,294			$ 98,609		
octorate	$16,893			$169,432		
rofessional	$22,503			$229,601		
otal household income/annuity payments as of % of Total Income						
Inder $25K	$ 4,219		≥18%	$ 36,840		
25K–$34K	$ 7,262		21–29%	$ 67,876		
35K–$49K	$10,773		22–31%	$106,137		
50K–$74K	$14,740		20–29%	$148,198		
75K–$99K	$20,318		21–27%	$207,651		
100K +	$25,770		≤26%	$250,284		

ource: Author's computations using TIAA-CREF data.

retirement income is being replaced, but annualized TIAA-CREF income is seen to represent only about 20 to 30 percent of total reported household income in 1993, for nearly all income groups. We speculate that social security income represents a substantial proportion of the remaining income for lower-income annuitants, while other income sources—earned income, other private pensions, and personal savings—contribute to the total for higher-income annuitants.

Annuity income for these retirees is split about two-thirds to one-third between TIAA and CREF annuities, and the split varies little by demographic characteristics. The exception seems to be people aged 76 and

TABLE 9 Average Household Wealth Held in Tax-Deferred Accounts Among Retired TIAA-CREF Annuitants, 1995

		If owned, assets held in . . .			Total
	Owned	*Stock*	*Fixed-income*	*Cash*	*invested*
401(k) salary reduction plan	(n=28)	47%	47%	7%	$155,661
TIAA-CREF individual annuities	(n=477)	36%	63%	1%	$132,763
403(b) salary reduction plan	(n=31)	38%	61%	1%	$86,441
Other thrift savings plans	(n=58)	58%	25%	22%	$75,258
Individual retirement account	(n=319)	56%	22%	22%	$72,231
Other tax-deferred annuities	(n=162)	22%	48%	30%	$67,091
KEOGH account	(n=18)	49%	29%	22%	$52,017
Average, all respondents					$100,254
Average, all respondents (non-TIAA-CREF)					$75,081

Source: Author's computations using TIAA-CREF data.
Notes: Number of persons reporting any amount in parentheses. Persons reporting a total amount for an account type but reporting no amount for an asset class within the account are assumed to hold $0 in that asset class for purposes of calculating above averages. Totals are averages over account types within each asset class, weighted by the number of persons reporting a total for each account type.

older who derive a larger proportion of their income from CREF annuity contracts (of course, annuitants whose responses are reflected in this table could choose how to allocate their retirement reserves only at the time a payout annuity was established). The overall conclusion is that annuitants tend to diversify risk. Based on other data, nearly 95 percent of CREF stock participants chose to balance the volatility of the variable annuity by electing the fixed annuity (TIAA) as part of their retirement portfolio, while nearly 54 percent of TIAA participants choose to diversify into CREF.

Annuitants may also diversify their other retirement assets. Preliminary responses to a November 1995 survey of the assets reported by 487 retired annuitants show that reported assets held in TIAA and CREF appear roughly comparable to the average totals and percentages as measured by company records. However, as Mitchell (1988) has shown elsewhere, self-reports on retirement plans can be inaccurate. In any event, the TIAA annuitants report total household assets of $581,355, including $200,000 in real estate holdings, and net worth of $555,213. Turning to retirement-related assets, Table 9 provides average household wealth reported by these respondents for a range of tax-deferred accounts, including TIAA-CREF. The number of individuals reporting that they hold an asset is given in parentheses. One interesting result is that although their

TIAA and CREF assets are split two-thirds to one-third in favor of fixed annuities, respondents report that they hold a greater proportion of their other retirement wealth in variable (e.g., stock) funds. The survey also shows that 47 percent of these same respondents hold stocks and 47 percent (not necessarily the same people) hold stock mutual funds, while 30 percent hold bond mutual funds and 80 percent hold corporate bonds. In addition, about a third of the annuitants surveyed say they are covered by a defined benefit plan and 17 percent report that their spouse is likewise covered. Aside from employer plans, individual retirement accounts are the most popular form of personal retirement savings. Sixty-five percent of annuitant households surveyed list IRA assets. Unfortunately, we do not yet know whether people who hold one kind of asset are more or less likely to hold another kind of asset. Still, it is likely that these annuitants diversify their retirement assets as well as other assets they hold.

Other data show that there are distinct differences between male and female annuity income-related behavior, but this is mainly due to differences in time spent in the accumulation phase. In 1994, males in our sample used on average over $200,000 to purchase payout annuities, over twice as much as women that year. Females comprised over 40 percent of the total population who annuitized in 1994, but they represented less than 10 percent of those who annuitized an amount over $500,000. These proportions have remained roughly the same (in real terms) since the early 1980s.

Size of accumulation depends most on length of time spent in the our pension system. Women spend less time (17 years on average) in the accumulation phase than men (23 years). Thus, male annuitants are likely to have higher accumulations, even in those cases where salary histories are comparable. Table 10 shows the distribution of new annuitants in 1994 according to time in the TIAA-CREF system. Women are far more likely than men (44.5 percent to 25 percent) to have been in system 15 years or less when they start an annuity. In recent years, however, the proportion of females starting new annuity contracts has increased, and there is some evidence that they remaining in the system longer than they did previously. Thus, the male-female split in annuity payouts may begin to migrate toward equality in the future. The lesson is that in a defined contribution, variable annuity setting, time spent in the accumulation phase is crucial to income adequacy. Factors affecting time spent accumulating include the age at which a person begins accumulating savings, the age of retirement, and the time during which retirement saving is suspended (e.g., sabbatical, unemployment or employment outside of a pension plan, family obligations, etc).

TABLE 10 Distribution of TIAA-CREF Annuitants by Years in TIAA-CREF Systems—1994 Issues

	Male annuitants		*Female annuitants*		*All annuitants*	
Years in system	*Percent of annuitants*	*Cumulative percent of annuitants*	*Percent of annuitants*	*Cumulative percent of annuitants*	*Percent of annuitants*	*Cumulative percent of annuitants*
0–5	5.07	5.07	6.97	6.97	5.84	5.84
6–10	9.72	14.79	16.82	23.79	12.59	18.43
11–15	10.31	25.10	20.71	44.50	14.52	32.95
16–20	11.98	37.08	22.70	67.20	16.32	49.27
21–25	18.52	55.60	17.90	85.10	18.27	67.54
26–30	21.39	76.99	9.12	94.22	16.42	83.96
31–35	14.64	91.63	3.96	98.18	10.32	94.28
36–40	6.72	98.35	1.39	99.57	4.56	98.84
41–45	1.53	99.88	0.40	99.97	1.07	99.91
46–50	0.12	100.00	0.03	100.00	0.09	100.00
Total	100.00		100.00		100.00	

Source: Author's computations using TIAA-CREF data.

Costs

In addition to individual behavior and annuities, a issue critical to the retirement adequacy question is how much it costs individuals for pension asset management. This is especially important because even relatively small charges have a significant effect on accumulations. For example, over a 30-year accumulation period, an individual could invest $100 per month in an account with an annual expense fee of .35 percent, and the same amount in an account with a 1 percent annual expense charge—with both funds earning the same 10 percent per annum. The account with the lower expense fee would yield $22,852 more.

Variable annuities are expensive when compared with mutual funds, but they do offer additional products and services, so, direct cost comparisons must be made carefully. Table 11 shows average annual expense charges for variable annuity accounts and mutual funds. A small number of variable annuity accounts have no surrender charge and a few have a front end load. About a third of mutual funds have a front or back end load. Even so, the basic investment management fees for mutual funds and variable annuities are similar. But the extra insurance feature makes annuity product fees average more than double those for mutual fund products. Variable annuities include insurance for the risk of providing lifetime income (i.e., in managing a population of annuitants, there is unpredictability associated with future mortality). Some variable annuities also guarantee principal and offer other features. But the most

TABLE 11 Average Expenses for Variable Annuities and Comparable Mutual Funds by Objective, 1996 (does not include sales charges, withdrawal charges, or annual contract charges)

	Variable annuities			*Mutual funds*	*CREF*
	Fund expense	*Total insurance expense*	*Total expenses*	*Total expense*	*Total expense*
Equity index	—	—	—	0.53	.30
Growth	0.82	1.25	2.07	1.13	.37
Growth and income	0.64	1.26	1.91	0.97	.32
International stock	1.10	1.26	2.35	1.56*	.40
Balanced	0.79	1.26	2.06	1.08	.31
Corporate bond	0.68	1.24	1.92	0.93	.29
Money market	0.51	1.26	1.78	0.65	.29
Average†	0.79	1.27	2.06	1.06‡	.33

Source: Morningstar (1996) Lipper (1996)
*Global Funds
†Average includes types of funds not shown
‡Excluding Equity Index

interesting issue is that the fee variation among variable annuities is far greater than the variation between variable annuities and mutual funds; thus, variable annuity expense rates range from 0.29 percent to 3.43 percent per year. Some annuity issuers are able to charge rates that are less than a tenth of the most expensive rates. Variable annuities would be very attractive as vehicles for social security individual accounts, if they were to be managed for fees at the low end of scale. At the high end of the scale, savers would experience considerable erosion of earnings.

How is possible to manage variable annuities with a cost structure near the bottom of the scale, even below average mutual fund fees, like TIAA-CREF does? Table 11 shows total expenses for the CREF variable annuity accounts, and, CREF account expenses also compare favorably with mutual fund expenses. This is probably because CREF funds are internally managed, are committed to low sales and marketing costs (such as low advertising costs and the absence of a sales force with commissions), have economies of scale in investment management, enjoy nonprofit status, and avoid some of the insurance charges associated with other variable annuities.

Variable Annuities as Part of the TIAA-CREF System

Variable annuities, the CREF side of TIAA-CREF, are now the largest part of the nation's largest private retirement system. Experience shows that

TIAA-CREF participants face a large number of choices about whether and how to use variable annuities for savings and income. Currently, the range of choices could be seen as confusing or even overwhelming, but, in general, individuals seem to have made sensible choices within the limits imposed by law, employers, and the plan structure itself.

This conclusion should be tempered in two ways. First, as alternatives to traditional annuities and annuitization have appeared, people have begun to take advantage of opportunities to take money out of TIAA-CREF's retirement system. Some portion of this money is being used for current consumption or in lieu of a lifetime annuity. Second, since most of the increase in options for investment choice and for taking nonannuity funds has appeared within the last 10 years or less, it is too early to tell how these new options will affect retirement income adequacy several decades from now.

Implications for Pension Policy

This chapter began with a set of questions about variable annuities and how experience with them might inform private pension policy. Among other things, the recent pension simplification bill extends the use of defined contribution pension savings to nonprofit organizations and small employers. It also limits requirements that older workers begin to draw down their retirement savings at age 70, and it encourages pension portability for workers who change jobs.

But like most of the public attention paid to pensions in recent years, it focuses primarily on the savings side of the pension equation. Consequently, despite the growing popularity of variable annuities, many people in defined contribution pension plans receive little encouragement and education regarding retirement income options. The questions addressed in this chapter argue for an additional pension policy focus on the retirement income side of the equation. Specifically, public policy should encourage annuitization as a mechanism for receiving retirement income as an important component of the shift toward individual responsibility for retirement. At the very least, this will help avoid the impact of mortality illusion — that is, an increasing number of people outliving their retirement savings. With support for annuitization, variable annuities can be a powerful means of linking retirement security and individual choice.

Can defined contribution pension plans replace the insurance component of defined benefit pension plans? There is an inherent tradeoff between the built-in insurance component of defined benefit pension plans, where the employer bears much of the risk of providing adequate retirement income, and the freedom of choice associated with many defined contribution pension plans where the individual bears these risks. On the one hand, defined benefit plans reduce participants' exposure to market risk, investment risk, inflation risk, mortality risk, and other risks. On the other hand, defined contribution plans offer the opportunity to obtain higher returns associated with equity investment, and they avoid the larger and longer-term risk that individual companies might devalue or not honor their promises.

Variable annuities are designed to provide many of the insurance guarantees promised by defined benefit plans, while retaining individual choice about investments. Variable annuities can be purchased that protect against risks such as mortality and loss of principal. Few variable annuities currently provide inflation protection as currently designed. Most of all, variable annuities can be designed to provide guaranteed lifetime or term income and are thus superior to mutual funds in these respects.

What should workers pay for management of their retirement funds, both before and after retirement? The biggest drawback to variable annuities is their cost, which averages twice that of the typical mutual fund. However, the lowest-cost variable annuities (e.g., TIAA-CREF) and mutual funds (e.g., Vanguard) are about a third of the average cost of mutual funds, mainly because of low marketing and sales expenses. If other providers can find ways to limit such expenses, variable annuities could become an even more attractive vehicle for retirement savings and income. Unfortunately, the difficulty for some providers may be constitutional: reliance on a sales force structure that builds costly commissions into expense charges.

What policies are necessary to ensure adequate retirement income in a defined contribution system? If adequacy is defined as a lifetime retirement income that replaces a significant proportion of preretirement income, then the TIAA-CREF experience illustrates the importance of variable annuities in assuring adequacy. Aided by pension law, TIAA-CREF actively encourages employers and employees to save regularly and steadily, to invest those savings in well-managed, low-cost funds, and then to purchase retirement annuities that guarantee lifetime income. On the other hand, some people will opt out of a lifetime or even a long-term retirement income in favor of cash if given the chance. Since few people have good information about their own mortality, some will live longer than their assets and thus could become a burden on the rest of society. Although an economic analysis of the costs and benefits to society of allowing relatively easy access to retirement cash is beyond the scope of this chapter, there is a need for policy-oriented analysis and discussion that focuses on the retirement income side of the pension equation, not just on the savings side. Future pension policy should go beyond concerns such as adequate savings, nondiscrimination, portability, and investment issues, in order to address the need for lifetime income, availability of annuities and their design, limits on removing funds from retirement accounts prior to annuitization, limits on retirement income options other than lifetime annuities, and retirement savings, investment, payout income education, and cost control.

How should Americans choose to receive retirement income? An era of individual responsibility for retirement is just that: Americans are increasingly on their own, rather than dependent on an employer or—if Social Security is privatized—on the federal government, to ensure an adequate retirement income for life. The TIAA-CREF experience suggests that it is possible to design a private retirement system that permits individual choice, when the choices include a range of savings vehicles, well-managed funds, and sensible retirement income options. But we also have argued that much education is needed to support annuitization, and adverse selection probably raises the cost of privately purchased annuities.

How can we educate Americans to make the "right" choices? The U.S. Department of Labor has actively encouraged employers to increase the level and amount of pension and investment education provided to defined contribution pension participants. Here, too, the emphasis has been on adequate savings and the risks and returns on investment choices. TIAA-CREF's experience shows that education works, at least for most people, regarding the retirement payout side as well as the savings side. Payout issues must be central to any pension reform program involving increased individual responsibility.

What is the best way to insure that retirement accounts are portable? American workers today perceive that job changes may be more likely than in the past, so pension portability is a way to accommodate these changing realities and perceptions. TIAA-CREF pioneered pension portability and has been able to adapt it to changing circumstances, including the presence of other carriers in its market.

Conclusion

The current trend to allow Americans to remove funds from their private pensions for important purposes (housing, college, or hardships) undermines pension plans' ability to provide adequate retirement income. Even more important, proposals to reform the social security program to replace part of the current defined benefit system with a system of individual investment accounts exposes participants to a host of new risks. For instance, to ask all Americans to bear investment and market risks and then be willing to live with the results is unrealistic. The few or many who suffer under this system will undoubtedly attract considerable sympathy when markets experience a downturn. Even more, should we support pension reforms that make it likely some *will* suffer the consequences of their actions? There is no solution that allows for complete freedom, but that ensures complete protection. The appropriate balance may be to encourage education and wise choice prior to retirement, and to provide strong mechanisms, such as annuitization, for ensuring continuing retirement income when individuals are less likely to have the financial flexibility to make up for income. Future pension reform must give attention to the sorts of risks, individual behaviors, and protection policies that have been confronted in the TIAA-CREF experience.

The author wishes to thank those who provided data and helpful comments, including John Ameriks, Richard Eggers, Michael Heller, Francis King, Joan Lambe, Joseph Liuzzo, David Rubel, Elliot Schechter, Lawrence Scheinson, Mark Warshawsky, and Howard Young. The views and interpretations expressed in this paper are those of the author alone, and do not necessarily reflect positions taken by TIAA-CREF.

References

Bernheim, B. Douglas. "Financial Illiteracy, Education, and Retirement Savings." This volume.

Biggs, John H. "Implications of Demographic Change for the Design of Retirement Programs." *Research Dialogues* (TIAA-CREF) No. 39 (February 1994).

Clark, Robert L. and Sylvester J. Schieber. "Factors Affecting Participation Rates and Contribution Levels in 401(k) Plans." This volume.

College Retirement Equities Fund, Accumulation Unit Data, 1952–1994.

——. "Retirement Program Lump-Sum Distributions: Hundreds of Billions in Hidden Pension Income." *EBRI Issue Brief* No. 146 (February 1994). 1994a.

——. "Salary Reduction Plans and Individual Savings for Retirement." *EBRI Issue Brief* No. 155 (November 1994). 1994b.

Gentry, William M. and Joseph Milano. "Taxes and the Increased Investment in Annuities." Working Paper, Brookings Institution. Washington, D.C., 1991. 1991b.

Goldstein, Michael L. et al. *The Future of Money Management in the Americas.* 1995 ed. (NY Bernstein Research, February 1995).

Greenough, William C. *A New Approach to Retirement Income.* New York: TIAA-CREF, 1951.

——. *It's My Retirement Money: Take Good Care of It.* Homewood, Ill.: Pension Research Council and Irwin, 1990.

Hurley, Mark P. et al. *The Coming Evolution of the Investment Management Industry: Opportunities and Strategies.* New York Goldman Sachs Investment Management Group, October 1995.

King, Francis. "Trends in the Selection of TIAA-CREF Life Annuity Options." *Research Dialogues* (TIAA-CREF) No. 48 (July 1996).

Krawcheck, Sallie L. and Weston M. Hicks. *The Annuity Market: The Slowing of a Most Excellent Adventure.* New York: Bernstein Research, August 1995.

Life Insurance Marketing and Research Association LIMRA. *Insurance Industry Data Disk.* Atlanta: Limra, 1995.
Mitchell, Olivia S. "Worker Knowledge of Pension Provisions." *Journal of Labor Economics* 6, 1 (1988): 21–39.
Mitchell, Olivia S. and Stephen P. Zeldes. "Social Security Privatization: A Structure for Analysis." *American Economic Review* 86, 2 (May 1996): 363–67.
Morningstar. *Principia for Variable Annuity/Life Insurance,* Chicago, 1975–95.
National Underwriter. "Annuity Market Takes Another Leap." February 19, 1996: 3.
Schieber, Sylvester. "Individual Retirement Accounts." Presentation to the Social Security Advisory Council Washington, D.C.: Social Security Advisory Council, December 1995.
Shoven, John B. "The Retirement Security of the Baby Boom Generation." *Research Dialogues* (TIAA-CREF) No. 43 (March 1995).
U.S. Department of Labor (USDOL), Pension and Welfare Benefits Administration. *Interpretive Bulletin,* September 1995. USGPO Washington, D.C.
——. *Abstract of 1992 Form 5500 Annual Reports. Private Pension Plan Bulletin* No. 5 USGPO Washington, D.C.: USGPO, Winter 1996.
U.S. House of Representatives. H.R. 3448, Small Business Job Protection Act of 1996.
U.S. Social Security Advisory Council. Social Security Advisory Council *Report of the 1994–1996 Advisory Council on Social Security.* Washington, D.C.: USGPO, 1997.
Warshawsky, Mark J. "Determinants of Pension Plan Formations and Terminations." *Benefits Quarterly* (4th quarter 1995): 71–80.
Warshawsky, Mark J. and John Ameriks. "Pension and Health Benefits for Workers' Higher Education." *Research Dialogues* (TIAA-CREF) No. 49 (August 1996).
Warshawsky, Mark J. and Benjamin M. Friedman. "The Cost of Annuities: Implications for Saving Behavior and Bequests." *Quarterly Journal of Economics* 105, 1 (February 1990): 135–54.

Chapter 12
Disparate Savings Propensities and National Retirement Policy

Richard A. Ippolito

In this chapter, I consider an underlying theme that is implicit in much of the discussion of national retirement policy—the disinclination of some individuals to save for retirement. Put differently, if all individuals had sufficient foresight and self-control to save for their own retirement periods, the need for a national retirement policy would be minimal. If some individuals do not save, however, they are destined to be impoverished in old age, a result that poses an important problem for society. In this chapter, I touch on some of the principles of 401(k) plans, which is the main focus of several other chapters in the volume, but my main thrust is to explore why the tax treatment of savings is important, both to national income and consumption levels during old age.

In this context, the drift away from defined benefit plans portends a growing old age problem. Historically, most pension coverage took the form of defined benefit pensions. In these plans, typically, covered workers have no choice but to earn accruals in the pension. Furthermore, these plans typically pay benefits in the form of annuities, diminishing the chances that recipients can spend down assets prior to their old age. In 401(k) plans, however, even if the firm offers workers the opportunity to participate in the plan, and though it may offer some substantial rewards for their participation (in the form of matching employee contributions), a significant portion of workers will not contribute to the pension. And these plans typically pay benefits in the form of lump sums, increasing the chances that some recipients will spend their pension monies long before they become old.

In reality, firms are not motivated to be inclusive in their pension coverage, and may have incentives to exclude workers from pensions who otherwise do not care to participate. These incentives are magnified if the qualities of being a "spender" are correlated with attributes that make a lower-quality worker.

The trend toward 401(k) plans redoubles the need for a national retirement policy that encourages participation by all individuals in some kind of savings arrangement for old age. I do not provide specific policy recommendations, except for the sake of illustration. Rather, I concentrate on the principles that characterize an efficient solution to the "nonsaver problem."

The Nature of the Problem

I start by separating the population into two groups, low discounters and high discounters. High discounters downplay the future. They prefer immediate gratification. Low discounters attach more value to future outcomes and thus are more likely to choose options with long-term payoffs. If two otherwise identical people are offered \$100 today or \$100 + *x* one year in the future, the "high discounter" requires a higher value of *x* to choose the delayed payment compared to a "low discounter."[1] The differences in internal discount rates across the population can have some profound effects on the well-being of a society.

Low discounters, while young, anticipate their standard of living when they reach old age and thus save sufficient amounts to support old age consumption. High discounters attach less importance to their economic condition far in the future and thus are inclined to devote their earnings to support higher current consumption. Other things being the same, low discounters have high savings propensities; high discounters have low savings propensities.[2]

A conflict is predictable. High discounters will be impoverished in old age, and low discounters will be wealthy. As long as society supports old age consumption at some reasonable level, it is rational for low discounters to anticipate the need to "share" their retirement savings with high discounters. This prospect is akin to a tax on savings that diminishes low discounters' incentive to accumulate wealth for retirement.

As a general proposition, high discounters naturally gravitate toward firms that award compensation immediately, and thus tend to avoid pension firms. Unless information is perfect and workers have job choices among a large number of alternatives, however, some high discounters enter firms that offer pensions, creating incidental pension coverage of some high discounters.

To the extent that incidental coverage has characterized the pension market, it is expected to wane owing to the growing share of pension coverage by defined contribution plans (Gustman and Steinmeier 1992). These plans embody incentives to encourage high discounters to voluntarily quit pension firms and/or permit them to voluntarily exclude themselves from 401(k) savings (Ippolito 1998). These outcomes may be desirable from the perspective of firms trying to maximize productivity and of high discounters trying to maximize the present value of their own welfare. In the long run, however, the systemic exclusion of high discounters from pension coverage will lead to a growing portion of the population that saves "too little" for their retirement.

As long as high discounters can vote in democratic elections, and governments have the power to redistribute income, high discounters' disinclination to save poses a potential economic burden on low discounters in the long run. Unless public policies (which themselves are influenced by a democratic vote) can resolve the natural conflict between high and low discounters, the result can degenerate to an equilibrium characterized by a lower standard of living for high and low discounters, particularly in old age.

I first consider the high discounter from the corporate perspective and show that firms, individually, have little incentive to include high discounters in pension plans. I then consider the problem from the public perspective. Here, I consider how low discounters as a group can solve the high discounter problem without importantly reducing output and savings in the economy. The general idea is that instead of accepting the prospects of a tax on their own wealth when old, low discounters are better off subsidizing high discounters' savings, thereby diminishing high discounters' incentive to hold up low discounters when they reach old age.

The Corporate Perspective

Discount Rates and Worker Quality

Managers operate firms to maximize returns for investors. Unless pensions can increase the firm's market value, for example, by increasing labor productivity or reducing turnover and the like,[3] each firm individually has no stake in its workers' savings behavior, including their pension participation. Firms, however, may have an economic interest in workers' underlying internal discount rates. If workers greatly discount the future, they may be inclined to behave in the workplace in ways that reduce productivity. In this sense, firms may have an interest in workers' overt savings behavior because it is a signal of workers' underlying internal discount rates.[4]

It is natural to think that individuals with low discount rates are more productive. Just as low discounters attach more value to the long-term benefits of financial savings, so do they attach more value to investments in their human capital. These investments reveal themselves in a large array of decisions—including many workplace decisions. The behavior of individuals with low discount rates is influenced by the long-term implications of their current work performance.

For example, low discounters are less likely to take a day off on a whim or quit in a "huff," instead valuing the long-term implications of their reputation for reliability and thus economizing on firms' expenditures on duplication and hiring. They are less likely to mistreat machines and equipment, because they recognize the long-term benefit of being labeled a "low-cost" employee. They are less likely to value the short-term gains from shirking over the long-term consequences of getting caught and are more likely to be motivated to work hard to gain the benefits of promotions. In all these ways, low discounters economize on firms' monitoring costs.

In contrast, high discounters are influenced disproportionately by benefits realized in the short term. The firm either must expend resources to discipline their behavior or accept the implications of high discounters' short-term perspective. In either case, high discounters are less valuable as workers compared with low discounters.[5]

If values of marginal product are importantly related to internal discount rates, competition will drive firms to identify low discounters. The identification, however, is not trivially accomplished because information in the labor market is imperfect. While firms can observe some telltale signs of job applicants' discount rates, notably education attainment or other training, much of the variation in internal discount rates is unobservable.[6]

Firms do not all attach the same value to employing low discounters. Firms that can monitor output cheaply, and/or do not face significant costs from absenteeism, quitting, and the like, will offer compensation schemes more attractive to high discounters. Firms that attach higher value to employing low discounters will use compensation packages that put more emphasis on deferred pay. The competitive process ensures that low discounters receive compensation commensurate with their higher value of marginal product. But their compensation must be reduced by the costs incurred by firms to identify low discounters. Firms that find the most efficient mechanisms to sort low discounters attract a higher-quality work force and earn higher profits.

Presumably, if it expends sufficient monitoring resources, the firm can align pay and productivity across the spectrum of discount rates characterizing workers in its employ. I consider a more interesting issue: whether the firm can find efficient sorting devices that allocate high and low discounters to their best uses without incurring monitoring costs.

More specifically, I pursue one part of the compensation package that is naturally suited to low discounters, namely, the pension plan.

Selecting in Low Discounters

If information is perfect and workers can choose jobs from a large array of compensation packages, high discounters will not take jobs in firms that offer pensions. When job search is costly, some high discounters inadvertently enter pension firms.

The problem of workers entering the "wrong" firm is not easily dismissed because it is endemic to workers with high discount rates. Job shopping is inherently an investment activity. Search costs incurred early in the career result in the long-term benefits of finding the "right" job. Low discounters should thus invest more in the search process and have a greater likelihood of selecting a firm that values their long-term outlook (Lippman and McCall 1976). High discounters presumably are less careful job shoppers and thus more frequently take jobs at firms with production functions designed for low discounters.

The entry of some high discounters poses a problem for firms designed for low discounters. The firm can address the high discounter problem in several ways. It can accept the inefficiency of having some high discounters in the firm, or incur monitoring costs to identify high discounters and transactions costs to fire them, or erect a mechanism to encourage high discounters to leave the firm voluntarily early in their tenure. Plain defined contribution plans are ideally suited to perform the sorting out function.

Sorting Out High Discounters: Defined Contribution Plans

Consider a defined contribution plan in its simplest form. The firm contributes a fixed percentage of pay, denoted by s, into each worker's account. Vesting is immediate.[7] Upon quitting, the worker takes a lump sum (it is eligible for rollover into an individual retirement account[8]); otherwise, he has no access to his account.

Suppose that workers have identical attributes except for their internal discount rates, and that these rates have a dichotomous distribution. Low discounters have zero discount rates and a desired savings rate, s. High discounters have an infinite discount rate, and a zero desired savings rate.

Assume that firms know the overall proportions of high and low discounters in the labor market, but do not know individual workers' discount rates. They simply hire all workers who apply for a job and rely on sorting devices to influence the composition of their workforces. Workers know their own discount rates, but have imperfect information about the labor market.

The firm wants to employ low discounters because they economize on monitoring costs.[9] Owing to their lackluster job search, some high discounters enter the no-monitoring firm. I characterize their gain from entering as j_H which is positive for some high discounters.[10]

The Economics of Quitting a Defined-Contribution Firm

Consider the efficacy of a defined contribution pension in correcting hiring errors. At the end of period 1, workers make a decision whether to quit the firm. Assuming they have the same knowledge of the labor market as they did at the beginning of period 1, the economics of joining and staying are the same, with one important difference. Upon quitting, workers obtain the lump sum amount s after period 1: If they stay, *s* is payable in some future period. For low discounters, the value of s is the same whether or not it remains in the pension plan, and thus the gains from staying are the same as for joining. For high discounters, the perceived net gains from staying, g_H, are lower by the added value of obtaining the available pension amount immediately: $g_H = j_H - s$.

An economic function for defined contribution plans emerges. The lump sum they provide upon quitting encourages high discounters to select themselves for early departure from the firm. In effect, the plan continually sifts the workforce for high discounters; thereby improving the composition of the firm's workforce over time. High discounters with the smallest values of j_H quit after period 1. At the end of the next period, the available lump sum is $2s$, and after the third period, $3s$, and so on. Gradually, most of the high discounters find it economic to depart the firm.

Paying Less to High Discounters: 401(k) Plans

In plain defined contribution plans, the firm periodically contributes a fixed amount, often a percentage of pay, to each worker's account. In 401(k) versions of these plans, the firm might make an unconditional contribution. More often, workers choose some voluntary savings rate in the plan, and the firm often matches these contributions on an *m*-to-one basis. It is easy to understand the appeal of voluntary contributions in these plans: they facilitate a more efficient pattern of savings across workers. Explaining the matching mechanism is more problematic.

An oft-cited candidate to explain matching is the Internal Revenue Code. The Code specifies "discrimination rules" that regulate the size of contributions of higher-paid workers to the 401(k) plan compared to lower-paid workers. In this explanation, matching elicits more contributions from lower-paid workers, which permits more tax-favored contributions by higher-paid workers. I have shown elsewhere, however, that matching generates potential tax benefits that are inconsequentially small, and impose costs on the firm by misaligning wages and values of marginal product across its workforce (Ippolito 1998).

One could alternatively postulate that firms have a stake in the timely retirement of older workers. Even if they do not use defined benefit plans, presumably firms would attain earlier retirement patterns if its workers had access to funds sufficient to finance their earlier retirement. In this sense, the match could be interpreted as an incentive to encourage more pension savings in its workforce. But if this goal were important, the firm could use a simple defined contribution plan, thereby requiring some pension savings for all workers.

The economics of matching is captured by a simple observation: Firms pay a premium to workers solely on the basis of their decisions to contribute to 401(k) plans. In the context of a sorting theory, a 401(k) plan with matching encourages workers to align their pay and productivity without imposing monitoring costs on the firm. Instead of encouraging high discounters to depart, 401(k) matching schemes simply pay high discounters less than low discounters.

The pay difference is not necessarily limited to the match amounts. Once the firm infers workers' internal discount rates from observing 401(k) contribution rates, it can use this information in selecting workers for more important jobs. In this way, the implications of sorting go beyond the wage differences established from the matching amounts.

Summary

Firms ought to be indifferent to pension participation unless it affects their market value. If premature quitting and late retirement ages reduce productivity in the firm, pension participation (especially in defined benefit plans) adds value to the firm. If firms use production functions designed for low discounters, but are not necessarily concerned with long tenure, firms may have incentives to effectively exclude high discounters from pension savings vehicles, particularly in 401(k) plans. In this sense, the growth of defined contribution plans in place of defined benefit plans suggests lower pension coverage rates for high discounters.

If pensions do not affect performance, the only reason firms offer pensions is to confer tax advantages to workers.[11] In a pure tax model, firms are disinterested savings agents. Firms individually have no inherent interest in their workers' living standard during their retirement. Similarly, low discounters individually have no stake in programs that force high discounters to engage in long-term savings. Each low discounter wants flexibility to attain his desired pension savings even if it means zero participation by high discounters.

From a broader perspective, firms as a whole—as corporate taxpayers—and low discounters as a whole—as income tax payers—have a stake in the savings behavior of high discounters. If high discounters do not save for retirement then, as long as society provides public monies to support high discounters' retirement, taxpayers face the prospects of transferring part of their wealth to finance high discounters' retirement consumption. It is inevitable that, in a free market, high discounters will pose problems for society in their old age. In this sense, there is a need for some public savings mechanism that is inclusive; otherwise, the incentives for low discounters to save may also wane, as I will show below.

In the next section, I develop a simple model of a democracy with a government function that can be used to redistribute income. The model, though highly simplified, illustrates some of the implications of high and low discounters coexisting in the same society, and illustrates how cooperative solutions can be found to diminish the adverse consequences that arise when high discounters do not save for retirement.

The Public Perspective

If an economy is comprised of either all high discounters or all low discounters, the results are predictable. Economies dominated by high discounters will have low levels of investment in human and physical capital, and thus will be poor. Economies dominated by low discounters will have high levels of investment in human and physical capital, and thus will be rich.[12]

The interesting question is whether a democratic society with a mix of high and low discounters can become rich. Individuals with disparate internal discount rates accumulate different wealth positions. A government can perform a valuable function in this society by establishing property rights and providing police and court functions to ensure stability of ownership. At the same time, through enactment of comprehensive income or wealth taxes, the government also can "legitimately" tax private property, or some stream of income derived from property. If high discounters can gain more votes than low discounters, a government can be transformed from a protector of property rights to a facilitator of transfers from voters who have wealth to those who do not.

The conundrum for this society is simply put: The incentive to save and invest must be sufficient to encourage low discounters to follow their natural inclinations to save; yet, the unequal distribution of wealth that inevitably ensues must be sustainable. In this section, I pursue the nature of contracts between high and low discounters that can provide for a self-enforcing equilibrium level of savings and transfers.

Natural Outcomes

Consider a two-person, two-period model. Both individuals have identical attributes except for their internal discount rates.[13] The low discounter has a zero discount rate. The high discounter has some positive discount rate, $r >> 0$.

The individuals are born to zero wealth, have no children,[14] and produce output worth $1 in period 1 when they are young. Owing to a natural deterioration of productive capacity, both can produce zero in period 2 when they are old. Death occurs at the end of period 2. Both individuals have full information. The only reason to save is to support retirement consumption. In general, savings can generate productivity improvements, but initially, I assume that the only benefit of savings is smoothing lifetime consumption; thus, savings are goods set aside in period 1 for consumption in period 2.

I assume that utility is a log function of consumption that is identical and separable across individuals and periods. Unless some output is saved in period 1, consumption and utility in period 2 is zero. When the individuals live separately, each chooses a savings rate S_j that maximizes discounted lifetime utility:

(1) $$U = \log\,[1 + C_{j1}] + \log\,[1 + C_{j2}]/(1 + r_j), j = L, H,$$

subject to the constraints:

(2) $$C_{j1} = 1 - S_j;\ C_{j2} = Sj, \text{ and } r_L = 0;\ r_H = r >> 0.$$

where C_{jt} is consumption by the jth individual in period t, and the subscripts L and H denote low and high discounter.

The optimal savings rates for the low and high discounter, S_L and S_H respectively, are:

(3) $$S_L = 1/2 \quad \Rightarrow C_{L1} = C_{L2}, \quad \text{and}$$
$$S_H = [1 - r]/[2 + r] \geq 0, \quad \Rightarrow C_{H1} > C_{H2} \geq 0.$$

The low discounter equalizes consumption in both periods, and thus has a 50 percent savings rate. The high discounter consumes output disproportionately in period 1: If his discount rate is at least 100 percent ($r = 1$), he consumes all his income in period one and thus saves nothing. In this case, consumption in period 2 is zero, and thus, the individual is impoverished in old age.

Mixing High and Low Discounters

I now consider savings decisions when high and low discounters are mixed in a democracy. For simplicity, I assume that production is unaffected by commingling workers in the same economy. I assume that the only function of the government is to assign and protect property rights, and that this function is effected at zero cost. The assignment of property rights depends on groups' abilities to influence voting outcomes.

I employ a model of political economy that mimics the essence of a government transfer mechanism in a democratic society, but which is free of unnecessary complexities. The model reflects the principle that the majority is favored to win each vote but that political outcomes are uncertain due to other factors (for example, nonlinear utility functions, asymmetric information, different production functions to influence voting, and so on). Thus, minorities can win voting outcomes, albeit with a lower probability.

More specifically, I use a simple stochastic voting outcome model. The "government" is an urn filled with p balls marked H and $1-p$ balls marked L. Conflicts between the high and low discounter that cannot be resolved to their mutual self-interest result in a draw from the urn. Either individual can make the draw, but there can be only one draw per period. If an H-ball is drawn, all wealth existing in that period goes to the high discounter. The all-or-nothing outcome simplifies the problem but is not critical to the basic thrust of the model.[15] If an L-ball is drawn, all wealth goes to the low discounter. The outcome is enforced at zero cost.[16]

First-Round Effects

Savings patterns that prevail when the high and low discounter live in separate societies may not be sustainable in a democracy. To illustrate, assume that the high discounter's discount rate is sufficiently high so that his savings rate is zero.[17] Thus, the high discounter consumes all his wealth in period 1, and faces dire prospects in period 2.

In period 2, the high discounter has an incentive to try to take the low discounter's wealth, and thus to make a draw from the urn: he has nothing to lose, and some probability p that he can take the low discounter's wealth.

The low discounter must decide whether to make an offer to the high discounter to dissuade him from playing the lottery. If the low discounter does nothing, he faces some chance (with probability p) of having zero consumption in period 2. His alternative is to give some portion, t, of his wealth to the high discounter so as to dissuade the high discounter from making a draw. The transfer, tS_L, must be sufficiently large so that the high discounter's utility from certain consumption of this amount is higher than expected utility of attempting to take the low discounter's entire wealth:

(4) $$\log [1 + tS_L] \geq p \log [1 + S_L], 0 < t < 1.$$

When condition (4) is satisfied, the high discounter has no incentive to risk losing the transfer amount, tS, in exchange for a chance, p, of obtaining the low discounter's cache S_L; and thus, the lottery is not used.

Second-Round Effect

Knowing in period 1 that a hold-up is inevitable, the low discounter does not save the amount S_L. He views the hold-up in period 2 as a de facto tax on savings, where the tax rate is t. If the low discounter saves the amount S_L, he will consume the amount $(1 - t) S_L$ in period 2 and transfer the amount tS_L to support the high discounter's period-2 consumption. When the low discounter sets his savings rate in period one, he maximizes his utility in expression (2) subject to the following income constraints:

(5) $$C_{L1} = 1 - S_L; C_{L2} = [1 - t] S_L.$$

The low discounter's optimal savings rate is either positive or zero depending on the tax rate:

(6) $$S_L^* = 1 - 1/[2(1-t)] > 0, \text{ all } t < ½, \text{ and}$$
$$S_L^* = 0, \qquad \text{all } t \geq ½.$$

If the de facto tax rate is zero ($t = 0$), the savings rate is 50 percent, which reflects the low discounter's natural preference. If the tax rate is positive, the low discounter's savings rate falls. If the tax rate is sufficiently high ($t =$ ½ in the illustration), the solution degenerates, so that savings are zero: the low discounter is better off by consuming all his wealth in period 1. Thus, in this simple model, a necessary condition for positive savings is that the tax rate is not "too high." In addition, the condition in (4), which ensures a sustainable income distribution, must be satisfied. In this model, it turns out that there is no tax rate, t, and consequent savings rate, S_L, that satisfies (4): a period-2 hold-up attempt is inevitable. The low discounter therefore saves nothing,[18] and both the high and low discounter are impoverished when old.

The solution is not general in the sense that a savings tax always leads to zero savings. The general result is that systems that depend on a tax on savings to redistribute income lead to lower savings levels. While the tax is designed to alleviate a savings deficiency for part of the population, in fact, it leverages the problem to the entire population: it exacerbates the low savings problem. If instead income is redistributed by subsidizing the high discounter's savings, a cooperative solution can be found that is characterized by lower transfers, making the low and high discounter better off.

Subsidizing the High Discounter's Savings

I now pursue a savings subsidy solution to the high discounter problem. In place of penalizing low discounters from following their natural inclination to save, high discounters are offered a subsidy to participate in savings. Low discounters still award a transfer to high discounters, but because high discounters save some portion of their earnings in response to the subsidy, the transfer is lower, and the distribution of income during retirement is more likely to be sustainable.

To keep the illustration simple, I consider a solution where low discounters subsidize the high discounters. In the model, these types of individuals are readily identified. In reality, discount rates are not observable, and so the savings subsidy must be offered to everyone, including low discounters. This complicates the solution, but the overall thrust of the outcome is the same.[19]

Suppose that for each dollar saved by the high discounter, the low discounter adds the amount s. The high discounter chooses a savings rate, S_H^o, that maximizes his lifetime utility in (1) subject to the constraints:

$$C_{H1} = 1 - S_H, \text{ and } C_{H2} = S_H (1 + s). \tag{7}$$

In general, S_H is weakly positive in s.[20]

The low discounter chooses his savings rate, S_L^o, so as to maximize lifetime utility in (1), subject to his new income constraints.[21] The low discounter's optimal savings rate is:

$$S_L^o = \tfrac{1}{2} (1 - s\, S_H^o). \tag{8}$$

Equilibrium Conditions

Consider the equilibrium subsidy rate. The low discounter must set the subsidy rate at least at the minimum that guarantees a sustainable income distribution, say, s^o. In period 2, the high discounter must find it in his interest not to try to take the low discounter's wealth.[22] Beyond this level, the equilibrium subsidy rate cannot be determined without putting more structure on the model. To avoid the complexities of gaming solutions, I simply assume that the low discounter can choose the subsidy rate so as to maximize his utility, subject to the period-2 stability condition.[23] Hence,

'ABLE 1 Comparing Outcomes When Savings Are Either Taxed or Subsidized

	Consumption period 1		*Consumption period 2*		*Savings*		*Utility period 2*		*Utility period 2*	
'ategory	*LD*	*HD*	*LD*	*HD*	*LD*	*HD*	*LD*	*HD*	*LD*	*HD*
solation	.50	1.0	.50	0.0	.50	0.0	.81	.69	.40	.00
)emocracy: Tax on savings (degenerate solution)	1.0	1.0	0.0	0.0	0.0	0.0	.69	.69	.36	.28
)emocracy: s^o=.5 (savings subsidy solution)	.44	.77	.44	.33	.44	.33	.73	.72	.36	.28

'ote: The table shows the consumption rates, savings rates, and utility levels for period 1 (work period) nd period 2 (retirement period) for low and high discounters. Illustrative solutions are based on the ssumptions that there is one low discounter (LD) with a zero discount rate, one high discounter HD) with a discount rate equal to 100 percent (r= 1), and a zero productive return on savings. The ariable s^o is the minimum level of the subsidy rate offered by low discounters on each dollar saved by igh discounters that ensures a stable distribution of income.

the low discounter's optimal choice of subsidy rate also is the minimum necessary to stave off a period-2 hold-up, namely, s^o.[24]

It turns out that when the high discounter's discount rate is 100 percent, the value of s^o is 50 percent. In this solution, the high discounter voluntarily saves 22 percent of his income. He receives a subsidy from low discounters equal to one-half of this amount, so that his savings rate, gross of the subsidy, is .33, which finances his period-2 consumption. Notably, the high discounter ends up with higher income (namely, 1.11) than the low discounter (namely, .89). Clearly, the high discounter is better off compared to living in isolation, particularly in "old age."

The low discounter is always worse off compared to living in isolation because some transfer is required to ensure sustainable property rights. In this sense, there is an inherent cost to being a low discounter. The low discounter is better off, however, offering to subsidize the high discounter's savings, compared to a solution that depends on the threat of a hold-up in period 2. The gains to a cooperative solution are always positive in this sense, but the gains are especially large when the hold-up solution produces a degenerate equilibrium.

Table 1 summarizes these solutions for the simple case. In the appendix, I consider the results when high discounters have discount rates different than 100 percent, and when the numbers of high and low discounters are unequal. The results confirm intuition that solutions with positive savings are easier to find when low discounters are more numerous than high discounters, and when high discounters are more like low discounters (that is, when their discount rates are closer to zero than 100 percent).

A Positive Return on Savings

In the above solutions, the value of savings stems solely from diminishing returns to consumption. A productive return to savings raises the stakes to finding a cooperative solution.

Suppose that if an individual sacrifices consumption in the amount S in period 1, he is rewarded with consumption in period 2 in the amount $(1 + i)S$, where i is the productive return to savings.[25] For illustration, I set i equal to 50 percent. I set the high discounter's discount rate to 200 percent to ensure a zero savings rate for this level of return. In isolation, the high discounter saves nothing, and thus has a zero period-2 consumption. The low discounter naturally saves two-thirds of his period-1 output, and enjoys consumption in period 2 equal to 1.0.[26]

I now reconsider the hold-up solutions (tax on low discounters' savings) and the cooperative solutions (subsidy on high discounters' savings). The new solutions are shown in Table 2; they are comparable to those in Table 1 except national income is a function of the savings rate.[27]

The first row shows the outcomes when both individuals live in isolation. The second and third row shows the solutions under either the tax or subsidy approach. Recall that I award all the bargaining power to the low discounter. Thus, the low discounter chooses the tax or subsidy rate that maximizes his utility, subject to the condition that the period-2 wealth distribution is sustainable. In this solution, the savings tax rate is 45 percent ($t^* = .45$). The low discounter saves 39 percent of his period-1 product and transfers 18 percent of his income to the high discounter.

Alternatively, in the savings subsidy solution, the equilibrium subsidy rate is 80 percent ($s^o = .8$). The high discounter saves 22 percent of his income and, inclusive of his subsidy, has gross savings of 38 percent of income. The low discounter sets his own savings rate to 56 percent of income. Per capita savings per capita are twice as high as the in the tax solution; per capita income increases from 1.10 to 1.23. Compared to a redistributive tax on savings, the low discounter clearly is better off offering to subsidize high discounters' savings.

Figure 1 shows how the results change with different proportions of high and low discounters. (Details are presented in the appendix.) The figure shows per capita savings and output under the tax and subsidy solutions. There are two striking features of the results.

TABLE 2 Tax and Subsidy Solutions, Given a Positive Return on Savings

Category	*Tax/ subsidy solution*	*Savings LD*	*Savings HD*	*Transfer per LD*	*Utility LD*	*Utility HD*	*Output per capita*	*Savings per capita*
Isolation outcome	—	.66	.00	.00	.98	.69	1.16	.33
Democratic solution	$t^* = .45$	.39	—	.18	.75	.77	1.10	.20
$L=H=1$	$s^o = .80$	.58	.22	.16	.86	.73	1.24	.48

Note: L is the number of low discounters and H is the number of high discounters. The high discounter (HD) has a 200 percent discount rate ($r = 2$), the low discounter (LD) has a zero discount rate, and the return on savings is 50 percent ($i = .5$). The variable t^* denotes the minimum tax rate on the low discounter's savings that ensures a stable distribution of income; the variable s^o is the minimum level of the subsidy rate offered by low discounters on each dollar saved by high discounters that ensures a stable distribution of income. Lifetime utility is discounted to period 1 using each individual's discount rate.

First, the equilibrium outcomes depend importantly on the share of low and high discounters in the population. If there are "too many" high discounters, no interior solution exists: low and high discounters consume all their output in period 1 and are impoverished in period 2. In the illustration, the critical low discounter share is approximately 30 percent. If low discounters are a smaller minority, savings are zero and per capita consumption in period 1 is 1.

As low discounters increase their proportions beyond this level, interior solutions are feasible, which dramatically affect per capita output.[28] Per capita income increases with the proportion of low discounters in the economy.

Second, per capita savings and income are always higher using a subsidy solution to the high discounter problem rather than a tax solution. Solutions that encourage high discounters to act more like low discounters lead to more savings and output than solutions that discourage low discounters from following their natural inclinations to save. The difference in these outcomes is always positive, but is largest when low discounters do not dominate the population.

Figure 2 shows high and low discounters' utility levels under the savings subsidy solutions. Lifetime utility is discounted to period 1 using each individual's personal discount rate. High discounters do not attach a high value to the prospect of higher period-2 consumption, and thus their lifetime utility is dominated by consideration of period-1 consumption.

Viewed from the perspective of period 2, however, high discounters' utility is substantially higher in the cooperative solution. Compared to zero savings and zero period-2 consumption in the isolated solution, high

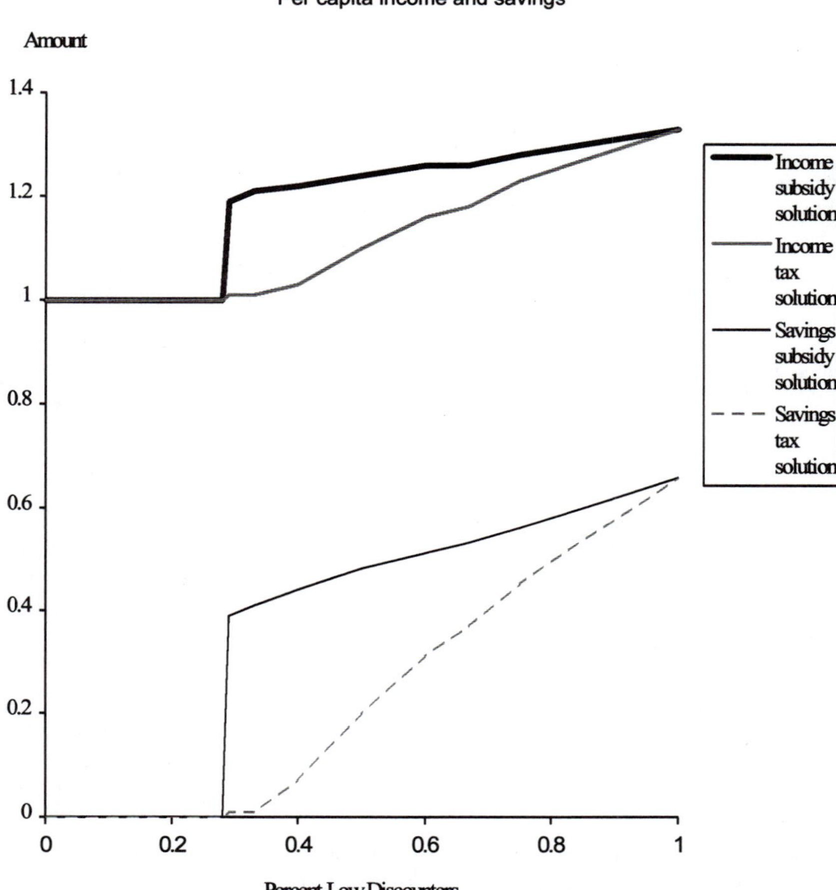

Figure 1. How per capita income and saving vary with the share of low discounters. High discounter's discount rate is taken as 2.0%, low discounter's as 0.5%.

discounters enjoy higher consumption in old age. In return for generating relatively high period-2 consumption for high discounters, low discounters enjoy a relatively high (and sustainable) consumption level in period 2.

Starting from equilibrium solutions when low discounters dominate the population, high discounters clearly are better off if they can increase their relative numbers in the population. Their higher share gives them

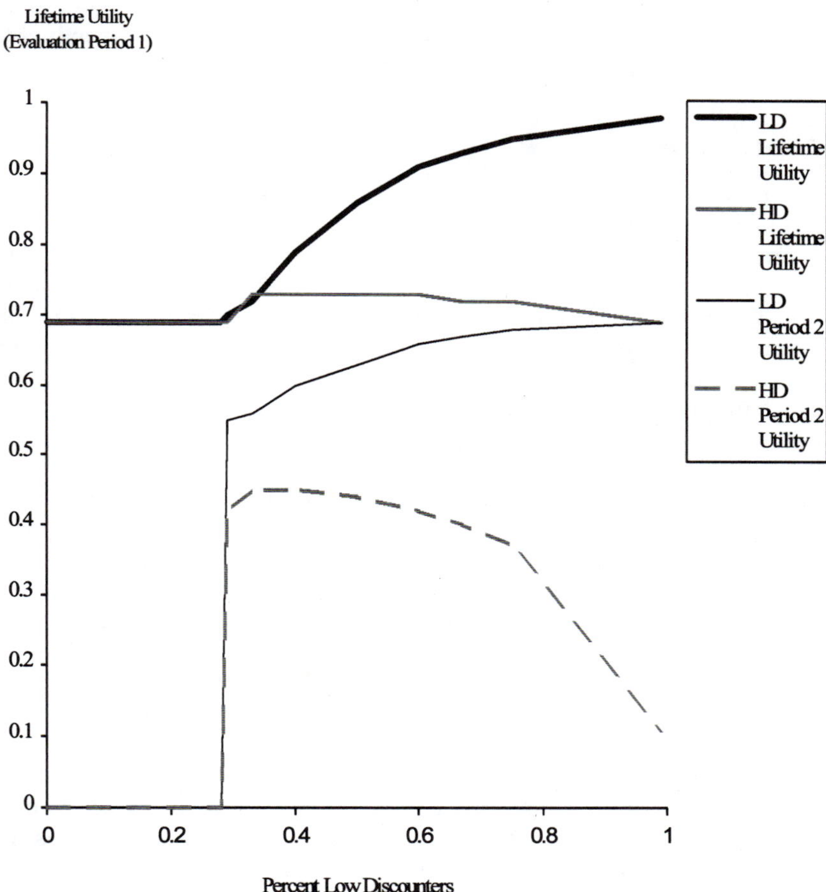

Figure 2. How utility levels vary with the share of low discounters (assuming a savings subsidy cooperative solution). Utility = log $(1 + C_1)$ + log $(1 + C_2) / (1 + r)$; $r = 0$ for LD and 2.0 for HD; return on savings is 0.5.

more leverage to collect transfers from low discounters who attach substantial value to ensuring a sustainable income distribution. As their numbers grow beyond some critical point, however, there are "too few" low discounters to support economical transfers, and a degenerate equilibrium is inevitable.

Low discounters are always somewhat worse off compared to a world in which they dominate the population. But as long as there are not "too many" high discounters, low discounters can have a high standard of living when young and old that is not threatened by an unsustainable distribution of wealth.

Conclusion

When low discounters are mixed with high discounters, different wealth positions develop, giving rise to a "high discounter problem:" low discounters accumulate wealth, and high discounters do not. The ability of high discounters to vote to effect a redistribution of income gives rise to prospects for a hold-up in later periods. To thwart the hold-up, low discounters can "share" their wealth—that is, incur a wealth tax to redistribute income to high discounters. This outcome is problematic because the threat of a redistributive tax discourages savings. In effect, the defacto tax on savings encourages low discounters to act more like high discounters.

A more efficient solution arises if low discounters can alter the form of a transfer from a tax on their savings to a subsidy on high discounters' savings. The subsidy encourages some savings by high discounters and gives them a stake in the economy's wealth position. In effect, high discounters are encouraged to act more like low discounters. Per capita savings and output increase, partly financing the transfers to high discounters. Old age consumption is higher for both low and high discounters compared to solutions that depend on a hold-up potential.

The model has implications for tax, regulatory, and national retirement policy. Existing pension policy is partly driven by an attempt to expand coverage (for example, vesting rules, anti-discrimination rules, and participation rules). The model suggests that this approach is unlikely to be fruitful: high discounters have a natural tendency to avoid firms that defer part of compensation; and firms that offer pensions more likely seek to hire and retain low discounters. In this sense, profit-maximizing incentives in the market work in tandem with high discounters' natural aversion to save. The rise of 401(k) plans further diminish the prospects for forced coverage in the private market.

The thrust of the comprehensive income tax in the United States essentially conforms to the tax solution discussed above. The general rule in the tax system is that income diverted to savings are "doubly taxed"; effectively income devoted to savings is taxed at higher rates than income devoted to immediate consumption.[29] By penalizing savings, the tax code discourages low discounters from following their natural inclination and redoubles high discounters' natural aversion to savings.

Exceptions in the tax code are made for pension vehicles, but even here, defined contribution plans are treated more favorably than defined benefit plans. The distortion occurs because the latter plans are denied the opportunity to fund their plans at the same level as defined contribution plans.[30] Moreover, so-called antidiscrimination rules in the Internal Revenue Code are chiefly designed to prevent highly-paid workers from saving "too much," rather than toward encouraging more participation by those otherwise not inclined to save.

An unfunded social security system such as that used in the United States has some of the elements suggested by a cooperative solution: there is a requirement to participate in the program, but formulas are set up to subsidize those least likely to voluntarily accumulate wealth for old age. The same principles could apply to a funded system, whether defined benefit or defined contribution. Nevertheless, the social security system penalizes those who save and rewards those who save little or nothing for old age.[31] In a broad sense, it is far more likely that a consumption tax approach—which eliminates the special added taxes on savings—combined with more subsidies to some levels of savings for retirement, would generate higher national income, more resources for consumption in old age, and a more sustainable distribution of income across society.

Appendix: The Role of the High/Low Discounter Mix and Discount Rate Spreads

The chapter considers a case where there is one low discounter and one high discounter. When the proportions of high and low discounters vary, the transfers from each low discounter are aggregated and spread over the population of high discounters. As such, the conditions for a sustainable income distribution are altered, and this is the subject of this appendix. Here, I recalculate the minimum tax rates and subsidy rates that generate a sustainable equilibrium on the assumption that the probability of winning a voting outcome is proportional to high discounters' proportion in the voting pool ($p = H/[L + H]$).[32]

No Productive Return to Savings

Appendix Table 1 shows the outcomes for the low and high discounter under several conditions when the productive return savings is zero. The top portion of the table shows the expected outcome when each individual lives in isolation. The bottom portion shows various outcomes in a democratic society. The values in the second column are the minimum tax rate (t^*) and minimum subsidy rate (s^o) that generate a sustainable income distribution under either a savings tax approach or a subsidy approach.

APPENDIX TABLE 1 Comparing Savings and Tax Outcomes When There Is No Productive Return on Savings

Category	*Tax/subsidy solution*	*Savings LD*	*Savings HD*	*Transfer per LD*	*Utility LD*	*Utility HD*
Isolation outcome	—	.50	.00	.00	.81	.69
Democratic outcomes						
$L = 1$	$t^* =$ ds	.00	—	.00	.69	.69
$H = 1$						
$r = 1$	$s^o = .5$	.44	.22	.11	.73	.72
	$t^* = .2$	.37	—	.07	.75	.79
$L = 3$						
	$s^o = .45$	.48	.21	.03	.79	.71
	$t^* = .15$	.42	—	.06	.76	.74
$r = ½$						
	$s^o = .2$	.47	.30	.06	.77	.73
	$t^* =$ ds	.00	—			
$H = 2$						
	$s^o =$ ds	.00				
	$t^* =$ ds	.00	—			
$r = 1½$						
	$s^o = .8$	.43	.17	.14	.72	.71

Note: The table shows the savings rates, utility levels, and transfers from low to high discounters, assuming alternatively that high discounters' retirement savings are enhanced by either a tax on low discounters' savings or a subsidy on high discounters' savings. In either case, the tax and subsidy rates are chosen to maximize low discounters' utility, subject to a stable distribution of income. L is the number of low discounters; H is the number of high discounters. The high discounter (HD) has a discount rate equal to $r > 0$, the low discounter (LD) has a zero discount rate, and the productive return on savings is zero. The variable t^* denotes the minimum tax rate on the low discounter's savings that ensures a sustainable income distribution. The variable s^o is the minimum level of the subsidy rate offered by low discounters on each dollar saved by high discounters that ensures a sustainable distribution of income. Lifetime utility is discounted to period 1 using either the low or high discounter's discount rate, as appropriate. The notation ds depicts a degenerate solution: There is no tax (or subsidy) solution that makes low discounters better off, and ensures a sustainable income distribution. Thus, overall savings are zero.

The other columns report the savings rates of the low and high discounter, the amount transferred from the low discounter to the high discounter, and the discounted utilities for both individuals under these solutions, evaluated in period 1. In the cooperative solution, the transfer is the matching amount, and thus is part of aggregate savings.

The first row of democratic outcomes shows the solution discussed in the text when there is one low discounter with discount rate zero and one high discounter with a discount rate of 100 percent ($r = 1$). The cooperative solution is clearly superior to the potential for a period-2 hold-up. The subsidy rate is set to 50 percent. The high discounter voluntarily saves 22 percent of his income. The low discounter has a net savings rate of 44 percent, and transfers 11 percent of his income to the high discounter. Aggregate savings in this solution is 38 percent of aggregate period-1 output, which exceeds the solution where individuals live in isolation.[33] Both individuals are better off compared to the hold-up solution; the high discounter is better off in the democracy (he consumes 55.5 percent of total output, inclusive of the transfer).

Moving down the table, the solutions show that low discounters tend to fare better, the higher their proportions in the population, and the more closely high discounters resemble low discounters in the level of their discount rates. The second and third democratic solutions reflect situations where low discounters are three times more numerous than high discounters; and high discounters have a more modest discount rate (namely ½ instead of 1).

In the last two rows, I show solutions less favorable to low discounters, namely, when high discounters are twice as numerous as low discounters, and when high discounters have an even higher discount rate ($r = 1.5$ in place of $r = 1$). Except for a subsidy solution in the latter case, these cases are dominated by degenerate solutions (that is, there is no positive savings rate that makes low discounters better off and ensures a sustainable income distribution).

Productive Return to Savings

Appendix Table 2 shows similar solutions when the productive return on savings is 50 percent and the high discounter's discount rate is 200 percent. The solutions are reported for various portions of the population that are low discounters (where a denotes the low discounter percent of total population).

The results show that when high discounters outnumber low discounters two to one ($a = .33$), the savings rate is negligible in a tax solution. But the savings subsidy solution produces a savings rate of approximately 40 percent. Compared to the tax solution, per capita income increases from 1.01 to 1.21. Finding conditions that generate a sustainable solution with positive savings is an important determinant of income and utility in the model.

Per capita income increases with the proportions of low discounters. If there are two low discounters for every three high discounters, interior solutions can be found for both the savings tax and subsidy approaches, but the subsidy outcome produces higher savings and per capita income.

APPENDIX TABLE 2 Tax and Subsidy Solutions When There Is a Positive Return on Savings

Category	*Tax/subsidy solution*	*Savings LD*	*Savings HD*	*Transfer per LD*	*Utility LD*	*Utility HD*	*Output per capita*	*Savings per capita*
Isolation outcome	—	.66	.00	.00	.98	.69	1.16	.33
Democratic outcomes								
$a = .33$	$t^* = .65$	.05	—	.04	.70	.69	1.01	.00
	$s^o = .75$	.50	.21	.32	.72	.73	1.21	.41
$a = .4$	$t^* = .60$	.17	—	.10	.71	.74	1.03	.07
	$s^o = .75$	.54	.21	.24	.79	.73	1.22	.44
$a = .5$	$t^* = .45$	.39	—	.18	.75	.77	1.10	.20
	$s^o = .75$	.58	.22	.16	.86	.73	1.24	.48
$a = .6$	$t^* = .30$	.52	—	.16	.83	.79	1.16	.31
	$s^o = .70$	.61	.21	.10	.91	.73	1.26	.51
$a = .67$	$t^* = .25$	.55	—	.14	.85	.81	1.18	.37
	$s^o = .65$	.63	.20	.06	.93	.72	1.26	.53
$a = .75$	$t^* = .15$	.61	—	.09	.90	.81	1.23	.45
	$s^o = .60$	.65	.19	.04	.95	.72	1.28	.56

Note: The table shows the solutions when a savings tax or savings subsidy approach is used to address the high discounter problem. a is the percent of low discounters in the population ($a = L/(L + H)$, where L is the number of low discounters and H is the number of high discounters. The high discounter (HD) has a 200 percent discount rate ($r = 2$), the low discounter (LD) has a zero discount rate, and the return on savings is 50 percent ($i = .5$). The variable t^* denotes the tax rate on the low discounter's savings that generates a sustainable income distribution. The variable s^o is the level of the subsidy rate offered by low discounters on each dollar saved by high discounters that ensures a sustainable distribution of income. Lifetime utility is discounted to period one using the individual's internal discount rate.

The difference between the tax and subsidy outcomes is greater, the more the population is dominated by high discounters.

The views expressed in this chapter do not reflect the official views of the Pension Benefit Guaranty Corporation.

Notes

1. The individual is indifferent between \$100 now and \$100 + x in one year when \$100 = (\$100 + x) / (1 + r) where r is the individual's discount rate. Thus,

the higher that x needs to be to create the equality, the higher must be the discount rate he attaches to payoffs one year into the future.

2. The implications of heterogeneous savings propensities on wealth accumulation can be found in Poterba, Venti, and Wise (1995) and Engen and Gale (1996). Savings propensities also can differ across workers owing to different amounts of information about the consequences of savings behavior (Bernheim and Garrett 1995).

3. For example, the firm may wish to use defined benefit pension plans to discourage quitting and to encourage earlier retirement.

4. This idea is developed more fully in Ippolito (1995).

5. The argument makes the assumption that capital markets are imperfect, that high discounters cannot borrow against the promise of higher income in the future. As long as borrowing is not possible, productivity decisions will be influenced by their internal discount rate.

6. Some low discounters may not have opportunities to pursue education; some high discounters may attain education because it is financed by parents, and so on.

7. In the United States, cliff vesting can be no more than five years. While five-year cliff vesting is almost universal in defined benefit plans, it typically is much shorter in defined contribution plans. The firm can and sometimes does use immediate vesting.

8. If the individual does not roll over the monies, he pays an excise tax of 10 percent and takes the lump sum into immediate taxable income.

9. The firm does not use a defined benefit plan because it does not find a deferred wage scheme to be economic; that is, the benefits of deferred wages are outweighed by the indenture premium.

10. For example, suppose that the high discounters's imperfect information is described by a perceived alternative wage in a no-monitoring firm of $1 + e$, where e is an error term with mean zero. For high discounters with large, negative values of e, the perceived alternative wage is less than the wage in the monitoring firm, and thus, the gains from entering the monitoring firm are positive: $j_H = w_0 - s - [1 + e] > 0$, for some $e < 0$.

11. The full tax advantages of pensions are afforded only in plans offered by firms. Individual retirement accounts permit only $2,000 per annum in contributions.

12. The mobility of physical capital from low- to high-discount economies is hampered because property rights are more tenuous in economies dominated by high discounters. That is to say, high discounters perceive the immediate gains of holding up low discounters without appreciating the long-run consequences on lower future capital investment. Thus, if rich nations make specialized investments in economies dominated by high discounters, they face the risk that their capital will be expropriated.

13. I later expand the results to allow varying proportions of high and low discounters.

14. Thus, there are no prospects for intergenerational transfers.

15. The qualitative results are similar if a significant portion of wealth is transfer upon winning a draw.

16. In reality, government outcomes need not be all or nothing, and production functions for influencing outcomes generally goes beyond a random draw concept (Becker 1983; Peltzman 1976).

17. In terms of condition 4, zero savings occur if the discount rate is 100 percent or higher.

18. To be complete, I need to show that the low discounter prefers certain consumption of all his income in period 1 compared to saving some portion to be contested in a period-2 lottery: $\log(2) > \log(2-S_L) + (1-p)\log(1+S_L)$. In fact, this condition is satisfied.

19. If the subsidy is made available to all, then low discounters also respond to the incentive, creating some transfers from low discounters to themselves, and creating an inefficiency from encouraging low discounters to "too much" savings. In practice, the solution might involve a subsidy over some initial levels of savings, diminishing at higher levels of savings.

20. Maximizing (1) subject to the constraints in (7), the high discounter's optimal savings is:

$$S_H^o = (2z - 1)/(1 + s + z), \text{ where } z = (1+s)/(1+r),$$

and thus consumption in period 2 is

$$C_{H2}^o = S_H^o\,[1 + s].$$

Consider the case when the high discounter's discount rate is 100 percent (r=1). Without the subsidy (s=0), the high discounter saves nothing. If the discount rate is sufficiently high, the high discounter will maintain zero savings within the range of subsidy rates that makes the low discounter better off.

21. These constraints are: $C_{L1} = 1 - S_L - sS_H$; and $C_{L2} = S_L$.

22. The minimum value of s that guarantees stability is s^o: $\log\,[1 + (1+s^o)\,S_H^o] = p \log\,[1 + (1+s^o)\,S_H^o + S_L^o]$.

23. See note 22.

24. I also make this assumption in developing savings tax solutions that compete with the subsidy scheme.

25. For example, suppose work in period 1 takes the form of expending effort to search for food. Savings in this simple model might take the form of using some period-1 time to develop plants that yield food without an expenditure of effort. This process may yield a superior solution compared to spending all of period 1 collecting food for both periods.

26. The new income constraints are:

$$C_{j1} = 1 - S_j \text{ and } C_{j2} = S_j\,(1 + i).$$

Maximizing (1) subject to these constraint gives the optimum savings rates:

$$S_j = [2(1+i) - (1+r_j)]/(1+i)(2+r_j),\ j = L, H.$$

27. In the case of the tax solution, the income constraints for the low discounter are:

$$C_{L1} = 1 - S_L;\ C_{L2} = d\,S_L,\ d = (1-t)(1+i),$$

and thus the low discounter's savings rate is:

$$S_L^* = 1 - 1/2d.$$

The stability condition is the same as expression (4) except that S_L^* is replaced by $(1+i)\,S_L^*$.

In the case of the savings subsidy to the high discounter, the high discounter's constraints are

$$C_{H1} = 1 - S_H \text{ and } C_{H2} = S_H \lambda, \text{ where } \lambda = (1+i)(1+s),$$

where s is the per dollar subsidy offered by low discounters to high discounters' savings. Thus, the high discounter's optimal savings rate is:

$$S_H^o = [2\lambda - (1+r)]/\lambda(2+r).$$

The low discounter faces the constraints:

$$C_{L1} = 1 - S_L - s S_H \text{ and } C_{L2} = S_L(1+i),$$

where s is the subsidy rate offered to high discounter's savings. Thus, the low discounter's optimal savings rate is

$$S_L^o = [(1+i)(2 - sS_H) - 1]/2(1+i).$$

The stability condition is the same as in footnote 19 except that S_j^*, $j=L, H$ are replaced by $(1+i)S_j^*$.

28. In this model, when the return on savings is .5 and the high discounter's discount rate is 200 percent, equilibrium degenerates when the share of low discounters in the population falls below 30 percent of the population.

29. The double tax refers to the income tax applied at the time wages are earned; then again as the individual tries to save these monies to finance future consumption. See Ippolito (1990) for a fuller discussion.

30. A special full funding limit was enacted in 1987 that sharply limits funding of defined benefit pensions, particularly those that have lots of workers and few retirees. See Ippolito (1990).

31. These rules include special taxes on social security benefits to individuals who have other sources of income during retirement, the availability of nursing home care to those without assets, and so on. A menu of reforms for social security and pensions along the lines discussed here are provided in Ippolito (forthcoming).

32. In the tax solution, the expression for the low discounter's savings choice is the same, given some tax rate t against savings (see expression 6). The high discounter's period-2 consumption becomes:

$$C_{H2} = (1+i)\,[l\,t\,S_L + S_H],\ l = L/H.$$

Thus, the period-2 stability condition is

$$\log[1 + (1+i)(l\,t\,S_L + S_H)] \geq p \log[1 + (1+i)(l\,S_L + S_H)],\ p = H/(L+H).$$

In the subsidy solution, for any subsidy rate, s, high discounters solve for the same level of savings. Since the subsidy amount to H high discounters, HsS_H, is spread across L low discounters, the optimum savings rate for each low discounter is

$$S_L = [(1+i)(2 - sS_H/l) - 1]/2(1+i).$$

The period-2 stability condition becomes:

$$\log (1 - \lambda S_H) \geq p \log [(1 + \lambda S_H + l (1 + i) S_L), \lambda = (1{+}i)(1{+}s).$$

33. Savings are .44 for the low discounter, .22 for the high discounter, plus the transfer amount of .11; since total output is 2 then (.44 + .33 + .11) / 2 = .38.

References

Becker, Gary. "A Theory of Competition Among Pressure Groups for Political Influence." *Quarterly Journal of Economics* 98 (August 1983): 371–400.

Bernheim, B. Douglas and Daniel Garrett. "The Determinants and Consequences of Financial Education in the Workplace: Evidence from a Survey of Households." Stanford University, unpublished working paper, 1995.

Engen, Eric and William Gale. "The Effects of Fundamental Tax Reform on Savings." Washington, DC: Brookings Institution, unpublished working paper, 1996.

Gustman, Alan and Thomas Steinmeier. "The Stampede Towards Defined Contribution Plans." *Industrial Relations* 31 (Spring 1992): 361–69.

Ippolito, Richard A. *An Economic Analysis of Pension Tax Policy in the U.S.* Philadelphia: Pension Research Council and University of Pennsylvania Press, 1990.

——. "Explaining the Growth of Defined Contribution Plans." *Industrial Relations* 34 (January 1995): 1–20.

——. *Pension Plans and Employee Performance.* Chicago: University of Chicago Press, 1998.

Lippman, Steven A. and John J. McCall. "The Economics of Job Search: A Survey." *Economic Inquiry* 14, 2 (1976): 155–89.

Peltzman, Sam. "Toward a More General Theory of Regulation." *Journal of Law and Economics* 19, 2 (August 1976): 211–40.

Poterba, James, Steven Venti, and David Wise. "Do 401(k) Contributions Crowd Out Other Personal Savings?" *Journal of Public Economics* 58 (September 1995): 1–32.

Chapter 13
The Future of the Defined Contribution Revolution

Sylvester J. Schieber, Richard Dunn, and David L. Wray

This volume explains why and how the U.S. employer-based retirement system underwent a structural revolution in the last twenty years. Most analysts recognize that the environment changed from one dominated by defined benefit plans to one that today is more evenly balanced between defined benefit and defined contribution plans. The shift toward greater balance has occurred in several different ways. In some cases, new companies starting up a pension for the first time chose the DC mode to begin with, valuing its flexibility, relatively low cost, and employee appeal. In other cases, employers previously sponsoring DB plans terminated them and substituted DC plans in their place. In still other cases, companies continued to sponsor existing DB plans, but also added a DC plan as a supplement to the basic pension. In the latter case, some employers curtailed the generosity of their defined benefit plan as they added the DC plan, while others offered a defined contribution plan in lieu of enhancements to the existing defined benefit plan.

Supporting these recent trends toward the DC environment are other indicators suggesting that this pension plan type will grow more popular in the future. Around the world, we have seen increasing reliance on DC arrangements as the preferred mechanism to provide for workers' retirement security. Chile led the way in the early 1980s with the creation of a defined contribution system financed solely by employee contributions, designed to replace their old national social security system. More recently, Australia has mandated a system that has certain similarities with that in Chile, except that it is primarily funded by employer contributions (Schieber and Shoven 1996). Mexico, Argentina, and Peru have taken a similar path toward a national DC pension system, though each with individual country variants. Sweden is in the process of modifying its social security program from a pay-as-you-go defined benefit plan to a pay-as-you-go defined contribution plan. In the latter case, workers will accumulate a notional account balance over their working careers based on contributions made to the system based on their covered wages although there will not be an actual accumulation of financial assets behind the balances. The notional accounts will be credited with interest during workers' careers at the rate of growth in average wages in the economy. At retirement, the account balance will be converted to an annuity based on the life expectancy of a worker's birth cohort and the worker's own actual retirement age. Even in the United States, there is a growing debate over whether public policymakers should seriously consider reforming the nation's social security program to include some defined contribution components.

While the shifting of national retirement systems from traditional DB pensions to DC arrangements may be having the most significant impact on national retirement systems, there are also signs that employers in every country are moving more toward DC arrangements to the extent that they sponsor retirement plans for their workers.

Recently several large U.S. employers that traditionally sponsored DB pensions have amended their pensions to create a DC promise inside the structure of a DB funding arrangement. These so-called "cash balance" plans attribute contributions to notional accounts held in workers' names. These accounts accrue interest at some rate specified in the plan. In many cases, the employee perceives he or she has a plan with DC characteristics, but the sponsor can still fund the plan in the same fashion that a traditional defined benefit plan is funded. Along the same lines, so-called "pension equity" plans define their benefits on an accumulating percentage of final salary and the number of years a worker has been a participant in the plan. Once again, workers covered by these plans perceive they are participating in a DC plan although it is funded like a traditional DB pension.

These patterns represent a partial DB to DC conversion, but there is also early evidence suggesting that some large firms are beginning to consider making the wholesale shift to DC plans. Growing concerns over an aging workforce and the funding structure of defined benefit plans are making some plan sponsors wary of the potential future obligations they might face with their traditional pensions. In addition, even for large employers, administrative costs for DB plans are higher than those for defined contribution plans. Finally, many employers have found that the perceived value of DC plans is greater than that of a DB plan of comparable cost. Like many other phenomena that businesses have experienced in recent years, if a few large employers shift completely away from their defined benefit plans to offer only DC plans, it is likely that many others will follow suit.

The Changing Nature of Defined Contribution Plans

Along with the fact that more workers are covered by DC plans, the pension plans themselves are undergoing structural change. Such reconfigurations are partly explained by the growing importance of 401(k) plans, accompanied by employees' perception that the money in their DC plan is truly "their own money." This perception is largely attributable to the growing dependence of employers on voluntary contributory plans, as described in Chapter 1 of this volume. In simple terms, workers making their own contributions to a plan tend to think of the money they contribute as theirs, and this is not surprising since it *is* their own money.

Another factor leading to plan redesign is plan sponsors' desire to minimize their risks relative to potential losses in plan values because of adverse investment experience. In the United States, Section 404(c) of ERISA provides for fiduciary relief for plan sponsors when they allow plan participants to direct the investment of their own plan assets. If participants are permitted to direct their own DC investment accounts, plan fiduciaries are not held legally liable for losses resulting from participants' exercise of control over their own assets. In order to achieve this relief from the fiduciary requirements, however, participants must be able to "exercise independent control" of their assets. This means that participants must be able to move their assets between a number of investment options sufficient to let them affect the returns on their assets and to manage their portfolio risk through asset diversification. In terms of specific investment options, the plan must offer at least three alternatives, not including the sponsor's own securities. If only three options are offered, each must have materially different risk and return characteristics from the others. Participants must be provided sufficient information to make informed investment decisions among the various investment options available to them. Finally, participants must be able to move their assets between the investment options in the plan frequently enough that they can respond to expected market volatility.

As DC plans grow more widespread, employers have increasingly allowed and in some cases required workers to direct their own pension portfolio asset allocation decisions. This tendency flows in part from participants' perception that 401(k) assets are "owned," and arises partly because plan sponsors seek to shift investment risk so as to avoid potential liability. Table 1 shows that, between 1978 and 1994, the fraction of companies that permitted workers to direct the investment of their own DC plan contributions rose from 16 to 94 percent, and those that permitted

TABLE 1 Characteristics of Defined Contribution Plans, 1978 and 1994

Plan characteristic	*1978*	*1994*
Average account balance in 1994 dollars	$30,061	$59,200
Companies permitting voluntary participant contributions	46%	70%
Companies permitting participant direction of the assets in the plan		
Employees' own contributions	16%	94%
Employers' contributions	10%	74%
Number of plan investment alternatives		
One fund	51%	12%
Two funds	28%	7%
Three funds	13%	9%
Four funds	4%	15%
Five or more funds	4%	58%

Source: Data supplied to authors by Profit Sharing Council of America.

workers to direct the investment of company contributions rose from 10 to 74 percent. Nearly three-quarters of the participants in DC plans today have the opportunity to invest their retirement savings in a diversified portfolio of investment choices, including four or more funds.

Changes in the Pension Arena Not Universally Hailed

Greater reliance on DC pension plans arouses concern in some observers, including long-time pension critic Karen Ferguson, who decries the shift to a DC system dependent on voluntary employee contributions as "do it yourself" pensions. Among the problems cited with the shift to 401(k) and similar plans is that employers may contribute less to DC plans than they do to traditional DB plans, making them a "cheap treat" for the plan sponsors. Second, it is argued that the money contributed to a DC plan may be more susceptible to preretirement distribution and consumption, as compared to the money benefit accrued under a DB. A third issue is that the investment of the assets in self-directed accounts is often more conservative than the investment of assets in professionally managed DB plans. A fourth concern is that moderate- and lower-wage workers may tend not to participate in a DC plan because they often cannot afford to save regularly. Fifth, the advantages of the tax incentives and the matching contributions that are accorded these plans are largely directed at higher-wage workers eligible to participate in them. Finally, benefits tend to be paid in lump sums rather than through the annuity form provided by traditional DB plans (Ferguson and Blackwell 1995).

Although the criticisms of the shift to a retirement system that is more dependent on voluntary participation by workers are often discounted by those preferring DC plans over DB pensions, even strong advocates of DC plans acknowledge these views deserve consideration. Indeed, much public criticism concerning the shift from DB to DC plans conveys a sense of angst on the part of professionals who have spent their careers working on the design or administration of retirement plans, and in the public policy arena that governs them. Their comments should be taken seriously.

Nevertheless, no matter how fondly pension specialists might think on the "old days" when DB plans paid annuities to long-service workers, forward-looking managers must recognize that the world of the next century will be inevitably different from times gone by. It will be a world where workers do not spend lifetime careers with single employers. To the extent that the trends are apparent, they suggest that pension designers and pension experts must expect to place even greater reliance on defined contribution plans, and less on defined benefit plans. Not only are "entitlements" likely to be downsized, but ultimately the responsibility for retirement income security will increasingly rest on workers' shoulders.

Understanding the New Reality

Having concluded that employers are moving toward DC plans and curtailing their defined benefit promises, this presents pension policymakers with a powerful new challenge. Specifically, the question arises: how can pensions be adapted to the new perspective emphasizing individual responsibility for retirement saving, while at the same time providing retirement security across the income spectrum? In our view, it is probably most productive to respond to this challenge by working to make DC plans more effective than they have been in the past, rather than looking backward to the old DB environment.

Several of the studies in this volume support the practical experience of plan administrators and advisors who work with savings programs on a daily basis. At the firm level, we have come to understand that appropriate savings and investment behavior by workers will not be achieved until the cultural environment is in place to support it. There are some notable success stories, in both large and small firms. At Exxon, for example, a successful saving culture is based in part on the proposition that everyone from the truck driver to the CEO is offered the same benefit plans. Exxon has a 95 percent voluntary participation rate in its DC pension plan, partly because rank-and-file workers see the senior executives in the firm participating in the plan and thereby perceive that it is in their own interest to do so as well. General Electric boasts almost universal participation in its pension fund, which requires a posttax contribution as a condition for participation. High participation rates are reported even among production employees in these firms, partly because union stewards and senior workers make it a point to personally encourage young workers to participate in the plans.

It is perhaps inevitable that some people will never save as long as the act is voluntary. In part, these people are the high discounters that Ippolito has described above. In other cases, however, people who do not save are unable to do so, perhaps because they are barely ahead of the sheriff seeking child support or face foreclosure on an overdue mortgage. While it is reasonable to expect that some workers may not be able to save during portions of their careers, for most workers saving should be a habit that is developed within their cultural environment. It is here that society needs to do more in creating an environment that encourages appropriate behavior.

In our view, part of the explanation for low saving rates in the United States today is that the population is deeply enmeshed in a culture that encourages consumption rather than saving. For better or worse, most workers receive information about the world through television, radio, and print media—and communication networks are inevitably financed by companies selling consumer services or products. For consumers a little short on cash to meet these stimulated consumption appetites, credit is freely available to support living beyond current means (at least for a while). Nowhere are adults (as well as children) taught the importance of saving to cover anticipated retirement needs.

Related to this problem is a well-founded concern about workers taking preretirement distributions from DC plans, often spent rather than saved (Schultz 1993). In some regards, this pattern might also be attributable to the same myopia or high discounting behavior that results in many workers not even participating in pensions in the first place. In this book we have shown that an effective communications program encourages participation in voluntary contributory plans, and may also discourage premature consumption of retirement savings. Clearly this is an important issue for DC plan sponsors, but it is not limited to this plan type: increasingly, defined benefit plans are permitting lump sum cashouts as well, with similar results.

From a worker's perspective, however, the comparison between DB and DC plans looks somewhat different than to the employer. Consider the case of the employee who changes jobs at age 30, after 10 years of employment. Under the DC approach, this worker can take his or her lump sum and either roll it into an alternative retirement saving vehicle or consume some or all of it prior to retiring. If it is consumed, then its value as retirement saving is lost.[1] It must be recognized, however, that the same worker covered under a DB plan would have also received very little. This is particularly troublesome when the DB plan provides no benefits until the worker reaches the normal retirement age under the plan. In both cases, the worker changing jobs would lose considerable pension value.

Concerns regarding workers being too conservative in their investment of self-directed retirement assets can, in our view, be thought of as two separate issues. One problem is that workers appear to many to be excessively risk averse, and will probably end up with inadequate retirement income as a result of conservative investment behavior. The second, and related, concern is that sponsors of plans must contribute more to meet a specific retirement income target when employees are controlling the investment of plan assets, than when the designated professional asset manager controls the investments. Fortunately, research shows that there is something that can be done to resolve the inconsistency between disposition and behavior, in that financial education might go a long way toward making workers more informed about investment options and the consequences of investment behavior. Both Bernheim's analysis and that of Clark and Schieber (this volume) focus on how pension information influences participation in voluntary contributory plans. In previous work (Goodfellow and Schieber 1997) it was found that older workers were quite conservative in their pension holdings, allocating around 60 percent of their assets in fixed income funds, whereas people in their twenties invested only about 40 percent of their savings plan accumulations in fixed income funds. Though the fraction in fixed income assets in all cases might be higher than professional investment advisors would suggest, it is not far off, and the inverse correlation with age is exactly what most advisors would suggest. One result of older workers investing more conservatively than younger workers, however, is that it creates a bias toward overall plan assets being conservatively invested. The natural distribution of assets in these plans along with the more conservative investment behavior of older workers partially accounts for the generally conservative structure of self-directed plan assets (Goodfellow and Schieber 1997).

It seems likely that communicating about pension investments can only induce workers to think more carefully about retirement plan savings patterns. And employers have incentives to provide this education, since if they do not it is likely that conservative investment patterns will yield too little retirement security. Of course in a DC plan, the ultimate benefit level is not the sponsor's responsibility as it is in a DB situation; sponsors do not directly assume pension investment risk.

Some have argued that moderate- and lower-waged workers cannot afford to take advantage of the financial incentives available to them in voluntary contributory saving plans, but this ignores the fact that many workers with similar wage levels do participate in these plans. Partly, workers' failure to participate in these plans is the result of the fact that it is not popular to extol the virtue of thrift. Nevertheless this behavioral characteristic does not mean that we should abandon employer-sponsored voluntary contributory retirement savings plans; indeed, such plans are often workers' only means of saving for retirement. And it is far from obvious that a return to a DB environment (were it possible) would offer much in the way of retiree benefits for those at the bottom of the wage distribution. Employers can only pay workers their worth. The cost of providing a worker a pension is a compensation cost directly associated with hiring and retaining that worker; it is only different in form from cash wages. This means that implementing a DB plan would likely result in a reduction in consumable compensation while that worker is covered under the plan. In that regard, having a DC or a DB plan reduces cash pay in exactly the same way.

One as yet understudied issue raised by DC plans is that most such plans pay retirees in the form of lump sums rather than in the form of annuities, of the type that DB plans traditionally offered. Some analysts consider this a problem because people cannot predict their life expectancy with any precision. If a retiree taking the lump sum benefit payout were to live longer than expected, he or she would quite possibly live so long as to deplete retirement savings. This is particularly a problem in the family context, as noted by Rappaport (1996).

To deal with the problem of outliving one's accumulated retirement savings, individuals can and sometimes do purchase annuities on their own. Nevertheless, private annuity markets appear to suffer from adverse selection, such that these annuities are quite costly to purchase. For example Paul Wenz (1996) has suggested that there are cost savings achievable by purchasing annuities under a group pension plan rather than as an individual, savings amounting to additional income of 2 to 6 percent per year (see Table 2). These savings result when a plan requires all participants to take an income-paying annuity with life contingencies; otherwise there would be adverse selection of annuities by participants expecting to live longer than average, reducing the amount of annuity income available to retirees. The problem is that when pensions permit lump sum cashouts to some retirees, the loss of risk pooling is a cost imposed on all retirees. As a result, most retirees tend to shy away from this market, exacerbating the problem.

One possible answer to this market problem is to have workers purchase variable annuities in their retirement plans, a practice described by Hammond (this volume). It also must be acknowledged, of course, that DB plans are increasingly offering lump sum cashouts as well, and consul-

TABLE 2 Illustration of Monthly Annuity Income Using Individual Versus Group Mortality Rates

	Age			
	55	*60*	*65*	*70*
Life annuity				
Using indiv. mortality	$594	$635	$693	$778
Using group mortality	+3%	+4%	+5%	+6%
Life annuity w/installment refund				
Using indiv. mortality	$583	$618	$665	$730
Using group mortality	+3%	+3%	+4%	+5%
50% survivorship annuity w/installment refund*				
Using indiv. mortality	$563	$593	$634	$693
Using group mortality	+2%	+3%	+4%	+5%

Source: Wenz (1996).
Note: The figures assume a $100,000 deposit and a 6 percent interest rate. All coannuitants are assumed to be three years younger than the annuitant. Individual rates based on Individual Mortality Table (Table "a" weighted 50% male, 50% female); Group rates based on GAM83 projected mortality table (also weighted 50/50). No expenses assumed.

tants report that in these instances, the overwhelming majority of participants take the lump sum form of benefit. This may be because employers offering DB plan annuities are offering them on terms more favorable than those that are offered anywhere in the commercial annuity markets. A subsidized lump sum may be financially sensible due to the fact that mandatory government insurance premiums need not be paid after retirees' benefit obligations are retired, a result that lump sum cashouts accomplish. If this as yet anecdotal evidence proves to be generally true, the demand for annuities may be significantly lower in the future than now.

Given the potential implications of this shift toward lump sum payouts in defined benefit plans, it is important that we better understand the underlying dynamics of this shift and how workers are reacting to it. First, we need to understand better the reasons employers are offering this form of benefit payment to retirees. Second, we need to understand why retirees are taking the lump sum benefits when so many retirement policy analysts believe that it would be in their best interest to accept annuities instead. Perhaps many people take lump sum payments in lieu of annuities because they underestimate life contingencies and the relative value of alternative benefit forms. If true, this is another case where more education and communication might prove to be the vital ingredient to assure the success of our new age retirement system. For certain, the annuitization issue will be of increasing policy importance as the baby boomers approach retirement. In any event, it is no longer an issue confined to the "DB versus DC" debate.

Conclusion

In recent years, much of the discussion about the evolution of the U.S. retirement system has focused on the relative merits of defined benefit and defined contribution systems. The debate has its international counterparts, since the United States is not unique in its push for DC pension plans. Indeed, in the 1980s a handful of countries including Chile implemented DC-type retirement savings programs, plans widely touted as new models for retirement accumulation vehicles. The decade of the 1990s saw defined contribution pensions legislated nationally in Argentina, Bolivia, Mexico, Peru, and Uruguay, and currently several Eastern European nations are fashioning their own versions of DC pension reforms. This trend has been encouraged by the World Bank (1994) and other financial institutions, on the argument that privately managed DC pension plans can play a key role in national growth and development.

During this debate, employers in the United States and abroad have increasingly grown to depend on DC plans, and on modifications of existing DB plans so they take on attributes of DC plans. For all practical purposes, the fact of worldwide increasing dependence on DC plans has eclipsed an older debate over which is the "best" form of plan. While some lament the passage of an era, the old defined benefit plan is one that many workers and employers no longer support given the exigencies of modern labor and capital markets. Indeed, the task before us now is to figure out how to maximize the probability that evolving pension plan structures assure the retirement income security of current and future generations of workers.

Note

1. It is possible that the accumulation could be used to finance education or a home that might accumulate in value over time, in which case the value would not be lost. While such expenditures might be technically counted as consumption, they are in fact a means of preserving the capital that had been accumulated in the plan.

References

Bernheim, B. Douglas. "Financial Illiteracy, Education, and Retirement Saving." This volume.

Clark, Robert L. and Sylvester J. Schieber. "Factors Affecting Participation Rates and Contribution Levels in 401(k) Plans." This volume.

Ferguson, Karen and Kate Blackwell. *Pensions in Crisis*. New York: Arcade Publishing, 1995.

Goodfellow, Gordon P. and Sylvester J. Schieber. "Investment of Assets in Self-Directed Retirement Plans." In Michael Gordon, Olivia Mitchell, and Marc Twinney, eds., *Positioning Pensions for the Twenty-First Century*. Philadelphia: Pension Research Council and University of Pennsylvania Press, 1997.

Hammond, P. Brett. "The Importance of Variable Annuities in a Defined Contribution Pension System." This volume.

Ippolito, Richard. "Disparate Savings Propensities and National Retirement Policy." This volume.

Rappaport, Anna M. "Family Concerns in Dealing with Retirement Planning." Pension Research Council Working Paper No. 96-16, Wharton School, 1996.

Schieber, Sylvester J. and John B. Shoven. "Social Security Reform: Around the World in 80 Ways." *American Economic Review* 86, 2 (May 1996): 373–77.

Schultz, Ellen E. "Your Money Matters: Raiding Pension Money Now May Leave You Without a Piggy Bank for Retirement." *Wall Street Journal*, April 7, 1993, sec. C, p. 1.

Wenz, Paul. "Payout Design Issues in Defined Contribution Plans." Pension Research Council Working Paper No. 96-14, Wharton School, 1996.

World Bank. *Averting The Old Age Crisis*. Policy Research Report Series. Oxford and New York: Oxford University Press, 1994.

Contributors

B. Douglas Bernheim is the Lewis and Virginia Eaton Professor of Economics at Stanford University. His work focuses on taxation and fiscal policy, the determinants of personal saving, insurance issues, antitrust policy, labor market issues, and topics in mathematical economics. Professor Bernheim is a Research Associate of the National Bureau of Economic Research and a member of the Board of Directors of the American Council for Capital Formation, the Center for Policy Research, and the Commission on Savings and Investment in America. He received the bachelor's degree from Harvard University and the Ph.D. from MIT, both in economics.

Robert L. Clark is Professor of Economics and Business Management at North Carolina State University. He is the author of numerous articles and books on retirement and pension policy, economic responses to population aging, the economic well-being of the elderly, and international pensions. Professor Clark serves as Senior Fellow at the Center for the Study of Aging and Human Development at Duke University and as Senior Research Fellow at the Center for Demographic Studies at Duke University. Dr. Clark earned the bachelor's degree from Millsaps College and the Ph.D. degree in economics from Duke University.

Richard Dunn is Program Manager for Qualified Plans at General Electric Company, responsible for over $40 billion in assets. An attorney by training, Mr. Dunn has more than two decades of pension and related tax experience. He has advised many large corporations and pension trusts, lectures on employee benefit issues, and has testified on pensions and retirement. He is affiliated with several industry organizations including the Erisa Industry Council.

William G. Gale is a Senior Fellow and the Joseph A. Pechman Fellow in the Economic Studies Program at the Brookings Institution. His research focuses on saving behavior, pensions, and tax policy. Dr. Gale has written on how saving incentives affect private and national saving. He earned the bachelor's degree from Duke University and the Ph.D. in economics from Stanford University. He also studied for a year at the London School of Economics.

P. Brett Hammond is Director of Strategic Research at the Teachers Insurance Annuity Association-College Retirement Equities Fund (TIAA-CREF). His research publications are in the areas of pensions, higher education, science and technology, finance, and health policy. Dr. Hammond receiver the bachelor's degree in economics and politics from the University of California, Santa Cruz and the Ph.D. in public policy from MIT.

Richard P. Hinz is the director of the Office of Research and Economic Analysis in the Pension and Welfare Benefits Administration at the United States Department of labor. He directs a program of research on policy issues related to the private employee benefits system within the jurisdiction of the ERISA. His office provides comprehensive statistics on ERISA plans through a variety of regular publications, funds work on employment-based health care financing and labor market issues, and conducts research on private pension benefits. Since 1991, through a program administered by the United States Department of Labor's Bureau of International Labor Affairs, he has provided technical assistance in the reform of social insurance programs and the development of private pension systems to the governments of the Czech Republic, Slovakia, Romania, Bulgaria, Poland, and Hungary. He has a MPA from Columbia University and is a CFA.

Ronald D. Hurt is Vice President for Employee Communications and Client Relations at MetLife's Defined Contribution Center. With more than twenty years experience in employee and investment communications, Mr. Hurt has responsibility for all employee communications programs for MetLife's defined contribution clients, including enrollment materials and ongoing investment education. He is also responsible for overseeing all aspects of account management and ongoing relationships with existing clients for MetLife's 401(k) business. He is a graduate of Swarthmore College.

Edwin C. Hustead is Senior Vice President in charge of the Hay/Huggins Washington, DC office and governmental actuarial and benefits consulting. He is also the leader of the Hay Group Task Force on National Health Care Reform. Mr. Hustead has conducted a number of major governmental studies on pension and health policy for agencies including the Department of Labor, Health and Human Services, Defense and the Congressional Research Service. He is chair of the Academy of Actuaries Work Group on Medical Savings Accounts. He is a Fellow of the Society of Actuaries, a member of the American Academy of Actuaries, and an Enrolled Actuary under the Employee Retirement Income Security Act.

Richard A. Ippolito is Chief Economist at the Pension Benefit Guaranty Corporation. He has published numerous books, articles on the investment, tax, regulatory and labor market aspect of pensions, including work on the economics of pension insurance. Dr. Ippolito received the Ph.D. in economics from the University of Chicago.

Andrea L. Kusko is a Senior Economist at the Board of Governors of the Federal Reserve System. Her areas of interest include public finance and health economics. She holds a BA in economics from the University of Pennsylvania and a Ph.D. from Stanford University.

Richard G. Marcis is Assistant Vice President for Research and Deputy Chief Economist at the Investment Company Institute, where he is responsible for monitoring and analyzing economic, financial and regulatory developments in the investment company industry. Dr. Marcis has written on financial markets, monetary policy and financial institutions; he is currently president of the National Economists Club in Washington, DC. Dr. Marcis received the bachelor's degree from Wittenberg University and the Ph.D. in economics from the University of Kentucky.

Joseph M. Milano is a research assistant in the Economic Studies Program at the Brookings Institution. He has worked on issues relating to tax policy, pensions, and saving behavior. Mr. Milano received the bachelor's degree in economics from Duke University.

Olivia S. Mitchell is the International Foundation of Employee Benefit Plans Professor of Insurance and Risk Management, and Executive Director of the Pension Research Council, of the Wharton School at the University of Pennsylvania. Her research interests include the economics of retirement and benefits, social security and pensions, and public as well as private insurance. Dr. Mitchell has served on the Board of Directors for Alexander and Alexander Services Inc., the Board of the National Academy of Social Insurance, and the CSWEP Board for the American Economic Association. She is also a Research Associate at the National Bureau of Economic Research and serves on the Steering Committee for the University of Michigan's HRS/AHEAD projects, funded by the National Institute on Aging. Dr. Mitchell received the BS in economics from Harvard University and the Ph.D. in economics from the University of Wisconsin.

Brian T. Ortelere is a partner in the Philadelphia office of Pepper, Hamilton & Scheetz specializing in employee benefits litigation. He is currently researching a study on ERISA litigation practice. Mr. Ortelere earned the JD from the College of William and Mary and holds the bachelor's degree in political science from Muhlenberg College.

James M. Poterba is the Mitsui Professor of Economics at the Massachusetts Institute of Technology, Director of the Public Economics Research Program at the National Bureau of Economic Research, Associate Department Head for Economics at MIT, and a Fellow of the American Academy of Arts and Sciences and the Econometric Society. His research focuses on the economic analysis of taxation, government expenditure programs, and financial markets. Dr. Poterba received the BS in economics from Harvard University, and the Ph.D. in economics from Oxford University.

John D. Rea is Vice President of Research and Chief Economist at the Investment Company Institute, where he supervises economic research and analyzes regulatory policy issues affecting the investment company industry. Dr. Rea holds the bachelor's degree in economics from the University of Missouri at Columbia and the Ph.D. in economics from the University of Wisconsin at Madison.

Sylvester J. Schieber is Vice President of The Wyatt Company and the Director of the Research and Information Center in Washington, DC. He is also a Board member of the Pension Research Council. Dr. Schieber writes on public and private retirement policy and health policy issues, and develops ongoing survey programs focusing on these issues. He received the Ph.D. in economics from the University of Notre Dame.

John A. Turner is Deputy Director of the Office of Research and Economic Analysis at the Pension and Welfare Benefits Administration at the United States Department of Labor; he is also Adjunct Professor of Economics at George Washington University. Dr. Turner's publications include works on pensions, employer-provided health benefits, and social security policy. He received the Ph.D. in economics from the University of Chicago.

David W. Wilcox is a Senior Economist at the Federal Reserve Board in Washington, DC. His principal research interests are household spending and saving behavior, the economics of retirement, monetary policy, and the measurement of the cost of living. He received the BA in mathematics from Williams College, and the Ph.D. in economics from the Massachusetts Institute of Technology.

David L. Wray is president of the Profit Sharing/401(k) Council of America (PSCA), a national non-profit association of companies that sponsor profit-sharing and 401(k) plans. He is also executive director and secretary of the Profit Sharing/401(k) Education Foundation and president of the International Association for Financial Participation. Mr. Wray holds the bachelor's degree in political science from Creighton University and a master's degree in political science from the University of Colorado.

Index

The Pension Research Council

The Pension Research Council of the Wharton School at the University of Pennsylvania is an organization committed to generating debate on key policy issues affecting pensions and other employee benefits. The Council sponsors interdisciplinary research on the entire range of private and social retirement security and related benefit plans in the United States and around the world. It seeks to broaden understanding of these complex arrangements through basic research into their economic, social, legal, actuarial, and financial foundations. Members of the Advisory Board of the Council, appointed by the Dean of the Wharton School, are leaders in the employee benefits field, and they recognize the essential role of social security and other public sector income maintenance programs while sharing a desire to strengthen private sector approaches to economic security.

Executive Director

Olivia S. Mitchell, *International Foundation of Employee Benefit Plans Professor*, Department of Insurance and Risk Management, The Wharton School, University of Pennsylvania, Philadelphia.

Institutional Members

Actuarial Sciences Associates, Inc.
Buck Consultants, Inc.
Ford Motor Company
General Electric Company
Hay/Huggins Company, Inc.
Instituto Cultural de Seguridade Social
Investment Company Institute

John Hancock Mutual Life Insurance Company
J. P. Morgan Investment Management Inc.
KPMG Peat Marwick LLP
Loomis Sayles & Company, L.P.
Merck & Co., Inc.
Metropolitan Life Insurance Company
Morgan Stanley & Company
Mutual of America Life Insurance Company
New York Life Insurance Company
Price Waterhouse LLP
The Principal Financial Group
The Prudential Foundation
The Segal Company
TIAA-CREF
ULLICO Inc.
The Variable Annuity Life Insurance Company
Watson Wyatt Worldwide
William M. Mercer Companies, Inc.

Board

Vincent Amoroso, FSA, *Principal,* KPMG Peat Marwick, Washington, D.C.

David S. Blitzstein, *Director,* United Food & Commercial Workers International Union, Washington, D.C.

Marshall Blume, *Howard Butcher Professor of Finance and Director, Rodney L. White Center for Financial Research,* The Wharton School, Philadelphia

Zvi Bodie, *Professor of Finance,* Boston University, Boston

Michael S. Gordon, Esq., Law Offices of Michael S. Gordon, Washington, D.C.

P. Brett Hammond, *Director of Strategic Research,* TIAA-CREF, New York.

William Madden, *ALM Pension Consultant,* Towers Perrin, Chicago.

Judith F. Mazo, *Senior Vice President and Director of Research,* The Segal Company, Washington, D.C.

Alicia H. Munnell, *Peter F. Drucker Chair in Management Sciences,* School of Management, Boston College, Boston.

Robert J. Myers, FSA, *International Consultant on Social Security,* Silver Spring, Md.

Richard Prosten, *Director,* Washington Office, Amalgamated Life Insurance/Amalgamated Bank of New York, Washington, D.C.

Anna M. Rappaport, FSA, *Managing Director,* William M. Mercer, Inc., Chicago.

Jerry S. Rosenbloom, *Frederick H. Ecker Professor of Insurance and Risk Management,* The Wharton School, University of Pennsylvania, Philadelphia.

Sylvester J. Schieber, *Vice President and Director of Research and Information Center,* The Wyatt Company, Washington, D.C.

Richard B. Stanger, *National Director,* Employee Benefits Services, Price Waterhouse LLP, New York.

Marc M. Twinney, Jr., FSA, *Consultant,* Bloomfield Hills, Mich.

Michael Useem, *Professor of Management and Sociology,* The Wharton School, University of Pennsylvania, Philadelphia.

Jack L. VanDerhei, *Associate Professor of Risk and Insurance,* Temple University, Philadelphia

Paul H. Wenz, FSA, *Second Vice President and Actuary,* The Principal Financial Group, Des Moines, Iowa

Howard Young, FSA, *Consultant,* Livonia, Mich.

Stephen Zeldes, *Benjamin Rosen Professor of Economics and Finance,* Columbia University, New York.

More information about the Pension Research Council is available at http:prc.wharton.upenn.edu/prc/prc.html

Pension Research Council Publications

Demography and Retirement: The Twenty-First Century. Anna M. Rappaport and Sylvester J. Schieber, eds. 1993.

An Economic Appraisal of Pension Tax Policy in the United States. Richard A. Ippolito. 1991.

The Economics of Pension Insurance. Richard A. Ippolito. 1991.

Fundamentals of Private Pensions. Dan M. McGill, Kyle N. Brown, John J. Haley, and Sylvester J. Schieber. Seventh edition. 1996.

The Future of Pensions in the United States. Ray Schmitt, ed. 1993.

Inflation and Pensions. Susan M. Wachter. 1991.

Pension Mathematics with Numerical Illustrations. Howard E. Winklevoss. Second edition. 1993.

Pensions and the Economy: Sources, Uses, and Limitations of Data. Zvi Bodie and Alicia H. Munnell, eds. 1992.

Pensions, Economics and Public Policy. Richard A. Ippolito. 1991.

Positioning Pensions for the Twenty-First Century. Michael S. Gordon, Olivia S. Mitchell, and Mark M. Twinney, eds. 1997.

Providing Health Care Benefits in Retirement. Judith F. Mazo, Anna M. Rappaport, and Sylvester J. Schieber, eds. 1994.

Retirement Systems in Japan. Robert L. Clark. 1991.

Search for a National Retirement Income Policy. Jack L. VanDerhei, ed. 1987.

Securing Employer-Based Pensions: An International Perspective. Zvi Bodie, Olivia S. Mitchell, and John A. Turner. 1996.

Social Investing. Dan M. McGill, ed. 1984.

Social Security. Robert J. Myers. Fourth edition. 1993.